A HISTORY OF
LUTHERANISM

A HISTORY OF
LUTHERANISM

Eric W. Gritsch

Fortress Press

Minneapolis

Cover art: Engraving shows (left to right) Melanchthon, Luther, Pomeranus, and Crucigar in 1532 and was photographed by Charles Phelps Cushing. Color photo of contemporary congregation is copyright © 2002 Photodisc, Inc.

Cover design: Marti Naughton • Interior design: Beth Wright

PHOTO CREDITS: Photo of the Lutheran World Convention in Eisenach (p. 234) is courtesy of the archives of the Evangelical Lutheran Church in America. Used by permission. • Photo of Lutheran Church centennial in Tanzania (p. 245) by Kathy Kastilahn is reprinted from the December 1993 issue of *The Lutheran,* © 1993 Augsburg Fortress. • Photo of Dietrich Bonhoeffer (p. 222) is © Chr. Kaiser/Gütersloher Verlagshaus GmbH, Gütersloh. Used by permission. • Photo of Bishop Ludwig Müller (p. 224) is © Keystone Pressedienst, Hamburg, Germany. Used by permission. • Photo of Karl Barth (p. 229) is by Ben Martin, © Ben Martin/Time Pix; photo of Paul Tillich (p. 232) is by Alfred Eisenstaedt, © Time Pix; and photo of Martin Niemöller (p. 224) is by Dmitri Kessel, © Dmitri Kessel/Timepix. All are used by permission of Time Pix. • Photo of the ecumenical center (p. 235) is copyright © Peter Williams/WCC. Used by permission of the Lutheran World Federation. • Photos of the Jerusalem hospital (p. 234); the first International Congress for Luther Research (p. 239); the Strasbourg Institute (p. 238); the Batak delegates (p. 236); the Helsinki Eucharist 1963 (p. 233); Anders Nygren (p. 231); and Josiah Kibira (p. 245) are all copyright © Lutheran World Federation. Used by permission.

The publisher gratefully acknowledges Eric Lund's assistance in obtaining several other illustrations in this volume.

Library of Congress Cataloging-in-Publication Data

Gritsch, Eric W.
   A history of Lutheranism / Eric W. Gritsch.
      p. cm.
   Includes bibliographical references and indexes.
   ISBN 0-8006-3472-1 (pbk. : alk. paper)
     1. Lutheran Church—Doctrines—History. I. Title.
   BX8065.3 .G75 2002
   284.1'09—dc21

                                    2002019871

Manufactured in the U.S.A.

06	05	04	03	02	1	2	3	4	5	6	7	8	9	10

To the faculty of Gettysburg Lutheran Seminary
1961–1994

Contents

Illustrations   ix

Preface   xi

Abbreviations and Short Titles   xiii

World Lutheranism   xiv

Chapter 1: Birth of a Movement, 1517–1521   **1**

Conditions for Reform / 1
Luther's Struggle / 6
Theological Insights / 11
The Power of the Status Quo / 15
Blueprints for Reform / 21
Trial and Verdict / 26
Impasse / 31

Chapter 2: Growth and Consolidation, 1521–1555   **36**

Models of Renewed Christian Life / 36
Pitfalls and Enthusiasm / 41
The Augsburg Confession / 45
The Scandinavian Connection / 50
Beyond Germany and Scandinavia / 56
Neuralgic Issues / 60
A Fragile Peace / 65

Chapter 3: Confessional Identity, 1555–1580   **71**

A Catechetical Way / 71
The Melanchthon Factor / 76
Judged by Rome / 82
Intra-Lutheran Controversies / 86
Mediation / 92
A Formula of Concord / 95
The Church of the Lutheran Confessions / 100

Chapter 4: Orthodoxy, 1580–1675   **109**

The Territorial Imperative / 109
Presuppositions / 113
The Quest for Pure Doctrine / 118

Bible and Inspiration / 122
Polemics / 126
An Irenic Interlude / 131
The Dangers of Uniformity / 135

Chapter 5: Pietism, 1675–1817   141
A Pietist Manifesto / 141
The Halle Foundation / 146
Zinzendorf Piety / 151
Revival of the Parish / 156
Radicals / 161
Missionaries / 166
Link to the New World / 171

Chapter 6: Diversification, 1817–1918   179
A Confessional Awakening / 179
Inner Mission / 184
Toward Institutionalization in North America / 189
The Missouri Way / 194
European Theological Schools of Thought / 199
Beyond Europe and North America / 204
The Impact of the Great War / 211

Chapter 7: New Ventures, 1918–   217
Pioneering the Ecumenical Movement / 217
The Struggle with Tyranny / 222
Theological Trends / 228
The Lutheran World Federation / 233
Ecumenical Dialogues / 239
Global Constellations / 244
Confession and Culture / 250

Conclusion: Forward to Luther?   257

Chronology   261
Notes   271
Bibliography   312
Index   334

Illustrations

World Lutheranism   xiv

Elector Frederick of Saxony   9

Pope Leo X   11

The Castle Church at Wittenberg   13

John Tetzel   16

Philipp Melanchthon   18

Andreas Bodenstein (Carlstadt)   19

Emperor Charles V   27

Title page of the papal bull issued against Luther   28

The Wartburg (castle)   31

A manuscript page of Luther's translation of the New Testament   32

Thomas Müntzer   34

Katherine of Bora   38

Title page from Luther's Small Catechism   40

Public reading of the Augsburg Confession   46

Death of Luther (sketch)   65

Elector John Frederick of Saxony surrounded by the Wittenberg Reformers   66

Concentrations of Major Christian Groups in Central Europe, 1560   70

Luther and others serving communion   74

Ulrich Zwingli   79

Cardinal Bellarmine   85

Andreas Osiander   89

John Brenz   109

John Arndt   117

John Gerhard   118

Valentin Löscher   128

Philip Jacob Spener   142

August Hermann Francke   147

Nikolaus Ludwig of Zinzendorf   151

John Albrecht Bengel   159

Jerusalem Church, Tranquebar, India   167

Graduating class of the Theological Seminary of the Leipzig Mission,
    Tranquebar, India   168

The emigrants' farewell to their native land   171

Henry Melchior Muhlenberg   173

Gustavus Adolphus II, King of Sweden   177

Wilhelm Löhe   181

Nikolaj F. S. Grundtvig   182
Hans Nielsen Hauge   183
Carl Olof Rosenius   183
The deaconess house at Kaiserswerth   185
John H. Wichern   185
Frederick Bodelschwingh   186
Gertrude Reichardt, the first deaconess   186
William A. Passavant   188
Samuel S. Schmucker   189
Gettysburg Seminary   189
C. F. W. Walther   194
Søren Kierkegaard   203
German Christ Church, Jerusalem   209
Luther Monument, Washington, D.C.   214
Nathan Söderblom, Bishop of Sweden   217
Dietrich Bonhoeffer   222
Adolf Hitler shaking hands with German Christian Reichsleiter
    Christian Kinder   223
Bishop Müller with Nazi party officials on the steps of the
    Rathaus, Wittenberg, Germany   224
Martin Niemöller   224
Karl Barth   229
Anders Nygren   231
Paul Tillich   232
Celebrating the Eucharist during the 1963 Assembly of the
    Lutheran World Federation   233
First Lutheran World Convention, 1923   234
Sylvester Michelfelder designed the LWF flag, shown here at the
    Augusta Victoria Hospital in Jerusalem (1953).   234
The signing of the LWF charter at the first assembly in Lund, Sweden (1947). 235
The Ecumenical Centre in Geneva (opened 1964) houses the
    LWF, the WCC, and other organizations.   235
Participants from the Huria Kristen Batak Protestan at the Minneapolis
    Assembly, 1957   236
The Institute for Ecumenical Research   238
The first meeting of the International Congress on Luther Research
    (Denmark, 1956)   239
Bishop Josiah Kibira   245
Celebrating the centennial of the Lutheran church in northern Tanzania
    (October 1993)   245
The Luther seal   258

Preface

Lutheranism originated as a reform movement within the Roman Catholic Church in the sixteenth century. The name "Lutheran" was given the movement by its Roman Catholic opponents, specifically by the Dominican theologian John Eck (1486–1543). Luther himself rejected such a designation because he, as he put it, called for a return to what is truly "Christian" rather than creation of a new "party name."[1] The collection of authoritative Lutheran statements in *The Book of Concord* of 1580, known as "Lutheran Confessions," also avoids the designation "Lutheran." Instead, they speak of their concern for what is "evangelical" (from the Greek, *euangelion,* gospel or "good news") or of "churches of the Augsburg Confession," the principal founding document submitted to the Holy Roman Emperor Charles V at the Diet (assembly) of Augsburg in 1530. Sixteenth-century Lutheran theologians often spoke of an "evangelical-catholic church" *(ecclesia catholica evangelica).* The term "Lutheran churches" began to appear in the seventeenth century.[2]

This book offers a distilled history of the reform movement as it became shaped and institutionalized by what can be loosely described as *culture,* the changing ways of life since the days of Martin Luther. In this sense, I am providing a sequel to the book I authored with Robert W. Jenson that presented a historical-theological exposition of the Lutheran Confessions collected in the Book of Concord (BC).[3]

Up to now, no one has attempted (or perhaps dared) to write a history of global Lutheranism. It is a daunting task because of the vicissitudes of the history of Lutheranism on all the continents of the world. Nevertheless, I decided to make a first attempt because a generation of Lutheran seminarians, pastors, ecumenists, and curious minds in general have been looking for a comprehensive history in the face of numerous narratives covering specific periods or geographic locations of Lutheranism (for example, Lutheranism in North America). Others have tried to move closer to a history of global Lutheranism, but no one has tried to tell the story of worldwide Lutheranism.[4]

In the face of such work, I attempted to produce a history of Lutheranism that is neither too voluminous nor too brief, so that readers may get a sense of the historical flow of Lutheranism without being distracted by massive details or becoming impatient for more substance. Indeed, I hope that this first attempt might motivate others to improve my work in whatever way necessary, given the massive sources and complex hermeneutical decisions on how to deal with them.

I have learned much from many specialists and libraries at home and abroad on various aspects of the history of Lutheranism. To list all of them would take too much space, and to single out some of them would be unfair. All of them have helped me, like the parts of a jigsaw puzzle, to elaborate this history of Lutheranism consisting of numerous, fitting parts.

I am especially grateful to three colleagues for their reading of the manuscript and for their helpful suggestions for its improvement: Günther Gassmann, former director of the Commission on Faith and Order at the World Council of Churches, Geneva, Switzerland, and distinguished visiting professor at the Lutheran Theological Seminary, Gettysburg, Pennsylvania; Martin Schwarz Lausten, professor of church history at the University of Copenhagen, Denmark; and Todd W. Nichol, King Olav V professor of Scandinavian-American Studies at Saint Olaf College, Northfield, Minnesota, and professor of church history at Luther Seminary, Saint Paul, Minnesota.

The endnotes contain a minimum of sources and readings that show readers how I have used the historical evidence and its scholarly interpretation. Thus, the bibliography fits the economy of the narrative. The massive historical-theological German encyclopedia, *Theologische Realenzyklopädie* (TRE), provides information about almost any name, place, and topic, with extensive bibliographies. The *Historical Dictionary of Lutheranism* is a smaller yet very helpful English encyclopedia.[5] A collection of English publications is also available.[6] The *Encyclopedia of the Lutheran Church* provides information on a smaller, dated scale.[7] I encourage readers to turn to these encyclopedic sources for detailed information.

This book is dedicated to the institution that offered me the opportunity to educate students for the ministry at home and abroad, to do research and writing, and to engage colleagues in dialogue for thirty-three years.

On the eve of the Day of St. Martin, the day of Martin Luther's birth
November 10, 2001

Abbreviations and Short Titles

BC	*The Book of Concord: The Confessions of the Evangelical Lutheran Church.* Edited by R. Kolb and T. J. Wengert. Minneapolis: Fortress Press, 2000.
BS	Baur, Jörg. *Die Bekenntnisschriften der evangelisch-lutherischen Kirche.* 3d ed. Göttingen: Vandenhoeck & Ruprecht, 1930.
CH	*Church History.* Chicago, 1932–.
Documents	Lund, Eric, ed. *Documents from the History of Lutheranism, 1517–1750.* Minneapolis: Fortress Press, 2002.
DS	*Enchiridion Symbolorum.* Edited by H. Denzinger and A. Schönmetzer. 37th ed. Freiburg: Herder, 1991.
ET	English translation
LCW	Bachmann, E. Theodore, and Mercia Brenne Bachmann. *Lutheran Churches in the World: A Handbook.* Minneapolis: Augsburg, 1989.
LW	*Luther's Works.* Edited by Jaroslav Pelikan and Helmut Lehmann. 55 vols. Philadelphia: Fortress Press; St. Louis: Concordia, 1955–1986.
ODCC	*The Oxford Dictionary of the Christian Church.* Edited by E. A. Livingstone. 3d ed. Oxford: Oxford University Press, 1997.
OER	*The Oxford Encyclopedia of the Reformation.* Edited by Hans J. Hillerbrand. 4 vols. Oxford: Oxford University Press, 1996.
RGG	*Die Religion in Geschichte und Gegenwart: Handwörterbuch für Theologie und Religionswissenschaft.* 7 vols. 3d ed. Tübingen: Mohr, 1957–1965.
TRE	*Theologische Realenzyklopädie.* Edited by G. Krause and G. Müller. 31 vols. Berlin: de Gruyter, 1977–.
WA	*D. Martin Luthers Werke.* Kritische Gesamtausgabe [Schriften]. Weimar: Böhlau, 1883–.
WA.BR	Briefwechsel. Weimar: Böhlaus, 1930–1948.
WA.DB	Deutsche Bibel. Weimar: Böhlaus Nachfolger, 1906–1961.
WA.TR	Tischreden. Weimar: Böhlaus Nachfolger, 1912–1921.
ZKG	*Zeitschrift für Kirchengeschichte.* Stuttgart, 1877–.

World Lutheranism

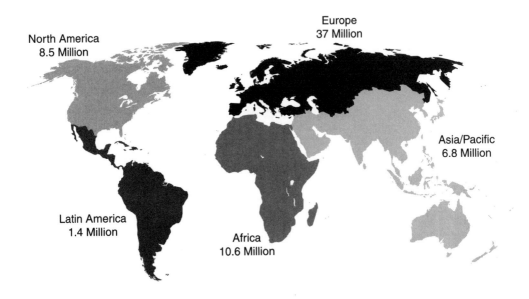

North America
8.5 Million

Europe
37 Million

Latin America
1.4 Million

Africa
10.6 Million

Asia/Pacific
6.8 Million

World Lutheran population: 64.3 million

Source: Lutheran World Federation (2001)

1

Birth of a Movement
1517–1521

Conditions for Reform

In 1054 c.e., after a millennium of unity, Christendom experienced a tragic schism between the Greek Christians in the East (later labeled "Eastern Orthodox") and the Latin Christians in the West (known as "Roman Catholics"). Half a millennium later, in 1517 c.e., Martin Luther's Ninety-five Theses against the abuse of Roman Catholic indulgences signaled a second schism, resulting in the formation of a variety of churches known as "Protestant." The time before Luther, often called "the late Middle Ages," was marked by a radical decline of the traditional values of a revered Christian civilization. With respect to the church in the West, led by the Roman hierarchy, sharp, realistic, sixteenth-century minds compared the origins of Christianity with the conditions of the church in their day and concluded that radical reforms were needed. Sensing their critique and using the traditional image of the church as a ship, one could make the judgment that, after a millennium and a half of sailing the dangerous waters of history, the institutional church had changed from an ark of costly discipleship to a ship of fools addicted to cheap grace. Such a historical verdict is justified if one compares the origins of Christianity with its condition as a church in the sixteenth century. Religion and politics had produced a way of life, a culture, guided by the praise of ruthless might in *The Prince* of Niccolo Machiavelli rather than by the devotion to selfless love in the teachings of Jesus.[1]

Emperors, kings, and princes had made sufficient compromises with popes, bishops, and the clergy to enjoy broad powers in a society shaped by hierarchy ranging from totalitarian privilege to enslavement of peasants, who only paid, prayed, and obeyed. Popes shared worldly power with princes. At age thirty-seven, Pope Innocent III was a master diplomat and political tyrant who excommunicated kings, transformed the Vatican into a world power, and promulgated new doctrines. Between 1309 and 1378, seven popes transferred their residences to Avignon, France, where they lived in great pomp and circumstance. Contemporary scholars nicknamed their loyalty to French kings as "the Babylonian captivity of the papacy" (analogous to the Babylonian exile of the people of Israel, 585–536 B.C.E.).[2] When the popular Italian mystic Catherine of Siena (1347–1380) advocated that the pope return to Rome, he did but without the dissolution of the office in Avignon. Two popes tried to rule the church from 1378 until 1414, excommunicating each other and even being threatened by a third pope elected by a council of bishops in Pisa, Italy.[3] Another council, held in Constance, Germany (1414–1418), finally succeeded in ending the schism by removing the Pisan pope, John XXIII,[4] and electing Martin V as the one and only pope.

But *conciliarists,* advocates of the equal authority of bishops meeting in a council, could not diminish the growing power of *curialists,* supporters of the authority of the papal curia, the senate of the pope. Pope Julius II enforced his rule at the head of a private army and symbolized his spiritual power by laying the cornerstone of the great St. Peter's Cathedral in Rome in 1506. Pope Alexander VI was a member of the infamous Borgia family; his illegitimate son, Caesar Borgia, became a cardinal before he was twenty years old, resigned, and turned into a corrupt prince. Frequently, money was the sole interest of ecclesiastical princes. Pope Innocent VIII sank so low in his quest for money that he pawned his headdress, the tiara, for a large sum.

The church tried to keep people in line through a theological ideology that depicted a wrathful God who had to be appeased by a rigorous penance manifested in obedience to the church, the mediator of salvation. Church members were encouraged to do good works to merit divine mercy and sacramental grace from cradle to grave (through the seven sacraments of baptism, eucharist, confirmation, marriage, confession, final unction, and, above all, ordination). Formal church teaching on salvation through the merits of Christ alone was watered down in practice to a pastoral climate of suspicion demanding a never-ending chain of penitential acts. Fear of punishment in hell or purgatory dominated and drove the faithful to enumerate their sins before the priest in private confessions.[5] People heard again and again the message that Christ's atonement for human sin became the treasure of the church to be brought forward, as it were, from the deposit Christ made at Golgotha to sinners by the priest who heard their individual confessions. But even priests had become the victims of spiritual transgression by lack of spiritual formation, indeed, malformation through the sins of the flesh, ranging from drunkenness to living with concubines.

In addition to internal deformations, medieval Christendom was threatened by the rise of Islam, founded by Mohammed in 622. Turkish armies had overcome Christian crusades to the Holy Land and moved as far as Vienna by 1529. They were finally forced to retreat to southern Europe, where they established enduring strongholds. Europe also became linked with the newly discovered lands across the oceans, such as the American continent claimed by Spain in 1492. The geographical discoveries confronted Europeans with new ways of thinking, trading, and living. Augsburg, Germany, became a dominating banking and trade center under the leadership of Jacob Fugger, who controlled the spice and cotton trade and, as an expert banker, managed much of the wealth of popes and emperors. At the same time, Johann Gutenberg revolutionized Eastern printing by printing from movable type, thus speeding the distribution of money and ideas.

There was opposition to the tyranny of church and state. Jan Hus, the priest and professor from Bohemia (now the Czech Republic), created a reform movement in Prague, teaching ideas he had learned from the English reformer John Wycliffe (c. 1325–1384). Wycliffe had attacked the abuses of the church in England, calling for a reform through committed, patriotic, secular princes. He pitted the authority of Scripture as the law of God against the institution of the church governed by the pope. Praising the Franciscan ideal of poverty, he called for the disendowment of the church's political power and for a return to apostolic poverty. He attracted a large following, especially among common folk, and was blamed for the Peasants' Revolt of 1381. Hus disseminated the ideas of Wycliffe, creating a large following in Prague among intellectuals, nobles, and common people. Because the publications of Wycliffe had been labeled heretical and then burned in 1409, Hus, too, was branded a heretic. He was ordered to defend his views at the Council of Constance in 1415, having been granted safe conduct. But on arrival he was jailed, tortured, and burned at the stake. Wycliffe was exhumed in 1428; his burned remains were thrown into the Swift River. But the Hussite movement survived imperial opposition, first in fierce underdog battles in Czechoslovakia, then as the pacifist group Unity of the Czech Brethren (known as the Moravian Brethren).[6]

The most radical call for the reform of the medieval church came from the Italian Dominican Jerome Savonarola (1452–1498), who tried to transform the city of Florence from a "city of vanities" to a place for a new millennium, the beginning of the second advent of Christ. Educated as a biblical scholar under the rule of the Medici popes, especially Alexander VI, Savonarola intensified his apocalyptic preaching during the last three years of his life. After he organized a public system of welfare for the sick and the poor, he predicted the divine punishment of Florence and its rulers when they opposed his program of reform. He was arrested, tortured, and executed as a heretical fanatic but praised later as a forerunner of Martin Luther's Reformation.[7]

A more sophisticated and peaceful cry for reform originated within an international movement of intellectuals who advocated a rebirth (French: *renaissance*) of pre-Christian art and a concentration on earthly life (humanism).[8] The Renaissance centered in Florence, Italy, and generated pioneering examples of writers, poets, and artists (such as the philosopher Marsilio Ficino and the powerful intellectual Leonardo da Vinci) whose influence was soon felt all over Europe. Christian humanism (best represented by the German humanist John Reuchlin and the Dutch Erasmus of Rotterdam) called for a critical investigation of historical sources, such as the Bible, the creeds, and the ancient church, favoring a return to the simpler Christian life of the first century. Hindsight attributed to humanism the reforming power linked to the work of Martin Luther (a celebrated saying of the sixteenth century: "Erasmus laid the egg and Luther hatched it").[9]

Members of religious orders and of the laity promoted an otherworldly mystical piety (such as the German Dominican John Eckhart and the Brethren of the Common Life, who called their attention to the inner life and manual labor a "new devotion" [devotio moderna]); they created communal centers in the Low Countries (now the Netherlands) and in Germany along the river Rhine. One of their finest disciples was Thomas à Kempis, who was praised as the author of the best-selling spiritual classic, Imitation of Christ.[10]

The demand for change and reform also affected the various schools of theology. Although the church had sanctioned Thomism, the massive, systematic arrangement of doctrines by Thomas Aquinas (c. 1225–1274), some theologians had spawned disciples holding a great variety of views. Others shied away from anything new. As one of Erasmus's satirical characters put it, "I heard a camel preaching at Louvain that we should have nothing to do with anything new."[11] The key issue was the relationship between reason and revelation, exemplified in the doctrine of transubstantiation, the attempt to explain the presence of Christ in the eucharist. The first and normative explanation was given at the Fourth Lateran Council in 1215. Accordingly, the substance of Christ (his resurrected reality) is in the bread and wine when the priest (male, adult, celibate, and ordained by a Roman bishop) speaks the words of institution (consecrates) over the elements of bread and wine ("This is my body"); the "accidents"—the external characteristics of bread and wine—however, are not changed.[12] Unless one accepts the dualistic Aristotelian distinction of "substance" and "accidents," no such explanation is possible. That is why non-Thomists called transubstantiation a mystery beyond the grasp of human reason. They were most powerfully represented in the school of nominalism, based on the theology of William of Ockham (c. 1280–1349).[13] The nominalists contended that conclusions are to be drawn on the basis of observation or experience and not on the basis of abstract logic. Logical conclusions regard only names (nomina) or concepts rather than what is real and true. No link exists, then, between reason and revelation, indeed between faith and reason. For God alone wills what can be known through the divine power of order over against absolute divine power. The incarnation of God in Christ as well as Christ's presence in the eucharist are grounded in the absolute power of God, not in the ordained power. Thus, transubstantiation is not a helpful doctrine and needs to be expressed by the faithful assertion of the real or bodily presence of Christ. Many humanists could agree with the nominalists, arguing that the truths of Christianity are authenticated in Scripture and tradition, that is, in a succession of communication through the ages.

Rome responded with strict measures of security rather than with a sense of toleration or indeed with an appreciation of Christian freedom. Pope Gregory IX (1227–1241) created an inquisition, controlled by the papacy, to detect and eradicate heresies. In 1478, the pope granted to Spanish kings the right to establish and to conduct the Inquisition. Inquisitors had power over all religious orders and, since 1531, even over bishops. The Inquisition became the basic instrument of identifying the enemies of the church, mainly heretics, Jews, and witches. But the cry for church reform from top to bottom was heard almost everywhere. A Lateran Council made a limp attempt to listen to the cry for reform in sessions from 1512 to 1517. With pomp and ceremony, pope and bishops deliberated a great variety of disturbing matters. But their decisions reflected little, if any, interest in basic reform: schism and heresy should be suppressed; Turks must be fought as enemies of Christendom; professors must preserve the truth about the immortality of the soul; Roman mobs must be prevented from sacking the homes of cardinals when a pope died; and other irrelevant matters.[14] It is one of the ironies of history that a single individual, Luther, made more compelling pronouncements than did a church council in his Ninety-five Theses on the greedy sale of indulgences (excuses from punishment for sin) in the same year when the Fifth Lateran Council ended its insignificant work.

It was on the eve of the Reformation, tied to Luther's name, that advocates of the Renaissance and of humanism talked about a thorough reform of church and society "in head and in members."[15] What they meant by *reformation* was determined by hindsight that viewed the period of the early formation of the church (also called ancient or primitive) as an ideal to be restored. It was viewed as the golden age, followed by a fall, just as Adam and Eve had fallen into sin by trying to be like God (Gen. 3:5). Critics of medieval Christendom charged that their culture also tried to be like God, with its tyrannical authority over body and soul. Ever since Constantine I (274–337), they contended, the church had become idolatrous in its fusion with the state, and its idolatry was disclosed in its search for power. They looked at the first apostles as models of the humble life mandated for Christians in their mission of forgiveness, love, and hope for an eternal life with God through Christ. The slogan of the humanists, "Back to the sources," was matched by the proclamation of itinerant preachers, "It is vanity to follow the desires of the flesh."[16] A steady stream of books, pamphlets, and cartoons rolled from the printing presses, calling for change.

Divine kingship, papal theocracy, and scholastic synthesis had had their day. Reformers like Luther rejected this unholy trinity and derived their rationale for reform from the literal meaning of the word *authority* (Latin: *auctoritas*): "origination." Thus, they did the bidding of the humanists: to return to Christian origins, to discover not just true humanity but also true divinity.

Luther's Struggle

Martin Luther was born and died in the small city of Eisleben (November 10, 1483, to February 18, 1546).[17] He was raised and educated by conservative parents, relatives, and tutors, destined by his father to become a lawyer. So young Martin was trained in the medieval liberal arts (three basic Latin disciplines of grammar, rhetoric, and dialectic; and four technical disciplines of astronomy, geometry, arithmetic, and music). After such education in private schools in Eisenach and Mansfeld, Luther transferred to the University of Erfurt in 1501. Living in a dormitory called *bursa*, he excelled in his studies, earning the nickname "philosopher"; he was also known as being cheerful at parties, where he often played the lute. He received the bachelor of arts degree in 1502 and a master of arts degree in 1505. Then he entered law school. Being a lawyer was the popular way to get part of the fortune of the rich and noble.

But after a few weeks of law school in Erfurt, the twenty-one-year-old Luther joined the Augustinian Hermites in the city. Why the radical change of vocation? Luther credited it to an encounter with lightning on July 2, 1505. While hiking from his parents' home in Mansfeld to Erfurt, he was thrown to the ground, and he cried out, "Help, St. Anna, I will become a monk!" She did, and he did. Anna, the mother of Mary, the mother of Jesus, was the most fashionable saint at that time. Later, in 1521, Luther told his disappointed father that "the agony of death and terrors from heaven" drove him into the monastery.[18] He pondered the decision for two weeks before he entered the monastery. Then he called his closest friends for a farewell gathering. They accompanied him to the monastery and with tears in their eyes, heard him say, "Today you see me the last time."[19]

Many young men and women joined religious orders for the same or similar reasons. Luther was a child of his age, sensitive to the inexplicable trials and tribulations besetting medieval society. Among them were plagues for which there was no medical help; magic and sorcery, concrete evidence of the devil's work; and the fear of a life after death subject to God's wrath. That is why Luther joined the "toughest" order, the strict order of the Augustinian Hermits. They had been fighting the devil and all his works since 1256, when they began as a begging order with stern rules for spiritual and academic formation. Each friar lived in a small cell with one window and no heat, cut off from communication with the world. He had to obey the strict dress code of the order: a long white robe covered with a black cowl and hood girded by a leather sash (underneath, a white shirt and white socks; coat and hat for traveling). Even during their short sleeping hours, the friars were not permitted to undress. Hourly prayers and daily masses in addition to academic work were intended to keep the friars constantly alert and prepared for a life of chastity, poverty, and obedience. The two simple meals a day were supposed to be endured, not enjoyed. In contrast to the world outside, friars were not to compete with themselves but develop an enduring character of humility.

Luther was determined to do his best. He studied hard, tried to mortify his flesh by fasting and praying, and was praised by friend and foe alike as an exemplary monk. When he missed doing all the required daily prayers, he asked the *abbot*, the administrator of the monastery, to have Saturday off to catch up with the other monks. One time, Luther prayed for three days without food or drink, ending up with a terrible headache. "As a consequence I could not close my eyes for five nights, lay sick unto death, and went out of my senses. . . . Thus our Lord God drew me, as if by force, from the torment of prayers."[20]

Given such living conditions and the lack of modern medicines, it is no wonder that young Luther underwent what researchers have dubbed "the monastic struggle."[21] Yet despite all the pressures, Luther continued the daily grind that the Augustinian order imposed on him. When he took the monastic vows in 1506, he was elated, for he had been promised the peace of mind and the state of grace due to a friar who dedicates his entire life to serving God and the church. He decided to become a priest to enhance even further his relationship with God. He quickly received the holy orders of subdeacon and deacon, and in 1507, he was ordained a priest. He recalled his fear of unworthiness when he celebrated his first mass. "When I stood there during the Mass and began the canon [the consecration through the words, "This is my body . . ."], I was so frightened that I would have fled if I had not been admonished by the prior."[22] Luther's father attended the mass and the festive dinner following it. But he reminded Luther that he had violated the Fourth Commandment ("Honor your father and your mother") by becoming a monk and priest. "But I was so sure of my own righteousness," Luther told his father later, "that in you I heard only a man, and boldly ignored you; though in my heart I could not ignore your word."[23]

But monastic discipline and priestly authority did not diminish Luther's fear of death and the judgment of God. The traumatic thunderstorm experience took on further spiritual dimensions even though Luther thought that commitment to strict Christian formation in the monastery would relieve, if not eliminate, his fear of divine punishment. Fellow friars and superiors who heard his frequent private confessions tried to assure him that the reduction of sins through a meritorious monastic life would call forth peace with God rather than keep doubts in his heart. After all, the church taught that personal penance and assistance from Mary and the saints assisted penitent sinners to experience divine forgiveness. Luther listened to such notions with real doubts of whether God had chosen him to be saved. The lack of inner peace convinced him that God might condemn rather than save him. Luther said later that he was grateful for having access to the Bible in the monastery, for this religious order more strongly recommended the study of the Bible than did others. He memorized whole portions of the Bible (available in the Latin translation of St. Jerome, c. 348–420) and used various existing methods of interpretation. "Sometimes one important statement occupied my thoughts for a whole day," Luther recalled later; and he reminded others that Bible study should always begin with prayer rather than the assumption that diligence and intelligence would facilitate a proper reading.[24]

Luther found this kind of approach to Bible study confirmed in the writings of the great church father Augustine rather than in the scholars of the Middle Ages. What Augustine had to say in *The Spirit and the Letter (De spiritu et litera)* decisively shaped Luther's early struggles with the Bible.[25]

Luther was such a good academician that his superiors, at the behest of the leader of the German Augustinian Hermits, Vicar-General John von Staupitz, sent him to the University of Wittenberg in the fall of 1508. He was to replace the Augustinian professor of moral philosophy and lecture on Aristotelian ethics. At the same time, he was to continue his studies for the last degrees before the doctorate: the biblical baccalaureate *(baccalaureus biblicus),* which would make him a specialist in biblical studies, and the master of sentences *(sententiarius),* which would entitle him to lecture on the standard and systematic exposition of Christian doctrines in the Middle Ages, *The Sentences of Peter Lombard* (c. 1100–1160). Wittenberg awarded him the first degree in the spring of 1509, and Erfurt granted him the second that fall.

The monastic order gave the twenty-six-year-old rising star an opportunity to leave the monastery for a lengthy period in 1510. Together with another friar, Luther was to travel to Rome to appeal the merger of two divergent chapters of the Augustinian Hermits in Germany, the Conventional and Reformed Augustinians. Whereas the Reformed—among them Erfurt—pressed for strict spiritual discipline and high academic standards, the Conventional wing favored less rigorous, indeed a lax, adherence to the Augustinian rule. Luther made it well known that he favored the Reformed position. With the approval of Vicar-General Staupitz, the three most obstinate convents—Erfurt, Nuremberg, and Kulmbach—decided to send Luther to Rome after he and his Erfurt teacher, John Nathin, had been unsuccessful in persuading the archbishop of Magdeburg to oppose the merger.

It took almost forty days to make the 850-mile journey from Saxony to Rome, and it was Luther's only trip abroad. The appeal failed; the head of the Augustinian order, General Aegidius of Viterbo, rejected the petition. But the journey, during the winter of 1510–1511, made a lasting impression on Luther. During his stay of four weeks, he experienced firsthand what many others had deplored: a confusing papal bureaucracy, general moral decay, and spiritual apathy. Despite such circumstances, Luther used the journey to alleviate his own spiritual struggle. After all, Rome was the capital of divine forgiveness, a place where one could get indulgences through a variety of activities, such as visiting the places of martyrs, making a general private confession, covering all of one's previous life, and making the prescribed pilgrimages to seven main churches. Luther did as much as he could to appease God. He visited the catacomb on the Via Appia where forty popes and seventy-six thousand martyrs were buried, because a devout visit yielded the forgiveness of all sins. Luther even climbed on his knees the Lateran palace steps, taken from the palace of Pontius Pilate in Jerusalem. For pilgrims were told that if they did so and prayed one Lord's Prayer at each step, they could release a soul from purgatory. Luther did the exercise in order to release his grandfather Heine but could not suppress his doubts, saying to himself, "Who knows whether this is true?"[26]

Much of what Luther had to say about Rome would be influenced by the sights and sounds he had experienced in that decaying capital of Christendom. After his

return, Luther agreed with Staupitz that the feud among the Augustinian Hermits should be settled by a compromise. But irreconcilable differences of opinion prevailed. Especially the Erfurters stubbornly clung to their independence.

Staupitz, who was concerned about Luther's future, transferred him to Wittenberg in 1511 and made him subprior at the monastery, with the responsibility of supervising academic studies there.

Wittenberg was a very small town with just under twenty-five hundred inhabitants. Its university had been founded by Elector Frederick of Saxony (later dubbed "the Wise"). Professors sent there complained that they had been called to teach "at the border of civilization." Frederick was best known for his collection of

Elector Frederick of Saxony

nineteen thousand relics that yielded more than 1.9 million days of indulgence when seen with devout eyes.

Luther lived with about forty other friars in the monastery. His struggle for peace with God increased. Because Vicar-General Staupitz spent the winter of 1511–1512 in Wittenberg, he tried to counsel his favorite friar. Luther seemed to be desperate, confessing that he still felt himself to be near death like during the thunderstorm six years earlier. He sounded like a seminarian or divinity school student who had done fine academic work but always failed his psychology tests, indicating an abnormal personal spirituality. Finally, Staupitz, like a wise Marine officer, gave Luther a direct order: "You must become a doctor and a preacher. This way you will be kept busy." Luther objected. "You will bring me to my death! I will never endure it for three months." But Staupitz had his way. "Don't you know that our Lord God has many great matters to attend to? For these he needs wise and clever people to advise him. If you should die, you will be received into his council in heaven because he too has need of some doctors."[27] Luther confessed later that his doctorate saved his life and provided the only legitimate foundation for his call to reform the church. "I would not exchange my doctor's degree for all the world's gold. . . . I entered into this work [of reform] publicly and by virtue of my office as teacher and preacher."[28] The academic vocation of research and teaching elevated Luther from the bondage of the medieval world into a freedom more powerful than expertise in law or the bloodline of nobility.

It would make Luther's father proud after all. Now Luther was given a handle, as it were, to deal with what he called his spiritual *Anfechtung*.[29]

When Luther struggled with the question of how to find a gracious God, Staupitz told him to view the sacrament of penance not as a means to appease God but as a spiritual exercise concentrating on God's love for sinful creatures expressed through the cross of Christ. Luther compared this notion of penance with biblical statements about penance, and he discovered no deviation. "Biblical words came leaping toward me from all sides," he told Staupitz, "clearly smiling and nodding assent to your statement."[30]

Luther was awarded the doctorate on October 9, 1512, and began teaching as professor of Holy Scripture *(lectura biblica)* in the fall of 1513. The award of the doctorate included an oath to be loyal to the Roman Catholic Church; a lecture with disputation; and a faculty banquet. Luther had become the successor of Staupitz, who had to relinquish teaching because of his increasing administrative duties.

Sometime during his early years as priest-professor in Wittenberg, Luther experienced a "conversion" or spiritual "breakthrough."[31] It is linked to Luther's work and teaching on Psalms (1513–1515), Romans (1515–1516), Galatians (1516–1517), and Hebrews (1517–1518).[32] He had become involved in an intensive search for the proper meaning of *righteousness*. Does it belong to God rather than to the human creature, thus being an "alien righteousness"? Or can righteousness be attained through human good works, an "active righteousness" meriting salvation? Luther rediscovered the ancient prophetic insight into the covenant between God and

Israel: one becomes righteous by trusting only in God's love for humankind. "The righteous live by their faith" (Hab. 2:4). One is righteous "by faith alone," by yielding to God, the only source of a never-ending relationship. Luther, therefore, rediscovered the God who, like a loving parent, loves the children without first asking whether or not they deserve it. He felt "born again" because he had focused his attention on what God did in Christ rather than on what he, Luther, could do for God. Luther described this experience with the Bible in a recollection penned when he was

sixty-two, in 1545.[33] It was a radical change from monastic anxiety over whether or not he would ever be able to appease God (active righteousness) to the conviction that he was loved by God without such appeasement (passive righteousness). Thus subsided Luther's rage "with a fierce and troubled conscience." Paul's Letter to the Romans (especially 1:17 and 3:28) had opened for Luther "the gate to paradise."

Pope Leo X

Luther now understood that faith alone is the bond that unites with the love of God in Christ. The church is the bride of Christ, who is the bridegroom, and the two shall become one. "This is a great mystery" (Eph. 5:32). Luther called this union the result of a "cheerful exchange and argument" *(fröhlicher Wechsel und Streit)* in his famous treatise "The Freedom of the Christian," 1520, dedicated to Pope Leo X. The "wedding ring of faith" makes Christ, the bridegroom, share the sins of the bride, and the bride, in turn, is given life and salvation. "This rich and divine bridegroom Christ marries this poor, wicked harlot, redeems her from all her evil, and adorns her with all his goodness."[34]

Theological Insights

A variety of factors influenced the young theologian: his increasing doubt about the spiritual value of Aristotelian methodology, even when modified or criticized by the modernist theology of William of Ockham and his nominalist disciples; his study of the church fathers, especially Augustine; his relaxation with Latin poetry and prose, especially Ovid, Virgil, and Plautus; his identification with German mystics such as John Tauler and the *Theologia Germanica* (German theology) that Luther edited with praise in 1516;[35] contact with other Augustinian friars whom he visited after 1515, when he was elected district vicar of the eleven monasteries in the Congregation of the Reformed Augustinians in central Germany; and above all, his intensive Bible study, especially Psalms and the Letters of Paul.

Luther later talked about his radically new insights through his work on biblical texts as a "tower experience" because of his study in the "tower room" *(Turmstube)* of the Wittenberg monastery: "The Holy Spirit unveiled the Scriptures for me in this tower." He experienced such inspiration in the part of the tower room called the "heated room," "the secret place of the monks," "the lavatory" *(cloaca).*[36]

Luther cautiously disclosed his views in lectures and disputations at the University of Wittenberg and in sermons at the monastery and in the town church where professors of theology were called to preach. In his sermons, he questioned the popular practice of granting an indulgence for any human effort of penance or satisfaction—from joining a crusade to giving money to the church. Both the doctrine and the use of indulgences had become complex and controversial.[37] Normative doctrine understood an indulgence to be a partial or total remission of punishment for sins that had already been forgiven; indulgences were part of payment or satisfaction. Thus, a penitent had to do a good deed, usually in the form of a cash payment. Fear of purgatory, the popular belief in the efficacy of prayers for the dead and the edifice complex (love for buildings) of church officials encouraged the sale of indulgences. Bishop Albrecht of Mainz used the sale of indulgences to finance his advancement to archbishop. Part of his large financial payments to lobby for the new title in Rome were used there to build St. Peter's Cathedral.

Luther used three occasions to expose the dangerous interrelation between doctrinal assertions and ecclesiastical practice, most evident in the symbiotic relationship between a greedy debit and credit system, based on printed money, and the popular indulgences. First, in the examination of one of his students for the degree of *sententiarius* in the fall of 1516, Luther used the disputation to argue that the grace of God, not the human will, determines the process of salvation from sin. Then, a year later, he contended in another such public disputation during the examination for a baccalaureate that Aristotelian methodology, the scholastic notion of free will (the human choice for or against salvation), and the reliance of theologians on philosophical speculation must be abandoned in favor of the biblical teaching that salvation from sin comes through Christ alone—by sheer grace and unconditional trust in his merits. Finally, he called for a public disputation on the power and efficacy of indulgences, in the now famous Ninety-five Theses of October 31, 1517.[38] The first thesis summed up Luther's fundamental insight: "1. When our Lord and Master Jesus Christ said, 'Repent' [Matt. 4:17], he willed the entire life of believers to be one of repentance."

Luther's focus on the financial stewardship of the church, related to the abuse sale of indulgences, created the reform movement linked to his name. Historical hindsight suggested that the age of the Reformation (next to Renaissance and Humanism) began in the year 1517.

Luther continued to expound his views, supported by the former head of the German Augustinian Hermits, Staupitz, who wanted to make certain that the new Wittenberg theology would get a hearing. So Luther was invited to present his theological insights at the plenary meeting of his order in Heidelberg in 1518. It was his farewell to Aristotle and his medieval scholastic disciples. Luther called his theology "a theology of the cross," grounded only in the revelation of divine grace through Christ and totally segregated from any human speculation about God without Christ or any effort to appease God through human merits. Referring to Paul's contrast between speculative wisdom and the folly of Christian proclamation, Luther insisted that God can be recognized only "through suffering and the cross." For this reason, true theology and recognition of God are possible only through the crucified Christ.[39]

The Castle Church at Wittenberg

Luther was not a systematic theologian who offered his views in the neat, orderly way one might expect of a German theologian. He was so intensively involved in the affairs of his sixteenth-century world that he had hardly any time to withdraw to the peace and quiet of a scholar's study. That is why Luther scholars have a hard time summarizing Luther's theological insights either by pursuing a single theme or by elaborating what appears to be the focus of extensive theological reflections. Nor did Luther perceive the task of theology to be that of offering a system of thought. Rather, he viewed the task of the theologian, particularly the biblical theologian, as being "practical," not "speculative." Theology is practical when it is related to the reality of life—with its struggles, suffering, joys, and frustrations—for realistically seen, life is overshadowed by one's continual desire to be in charge, to dominate, to be "like God" (Gen. 3:5). The way of the serpent always seems more attractive than the way of Christ; the sin of pride is stronger than love of neighbor. This conflict between God the creator and man or woman, the created, was for Luther the cause for all other conflicts in life. Why this is so is a mystery. Theologians could speculate about the mystery of original sin in various ways, but such speculations, Luther contended, are futile because they attempt to penetrate the "hidden God," the God who is not disclosed to the human mind. God is only disclosed, albeit not totally, in God's humanity, in Jesus Christ. "We have enough to learn about the humanity of Christ in whom the Father revealed himself. But we are fools who neglect the revealed word and the will of the Father in Christ and, instead, investigate mysteries which ought only to be worshipped. As a result many break their necks."[40]

Luther's own *Anfechtung* or anxiety helped him to understand why God is disclosed in the suffering humanity of Jesus rather than reached through human efforts. He remembered his monastic life, which never provided a consoling answer to the question, "When will you finally rejoice in having done enough so that you will get a gracious God?"[41] One must forgo such frustrating introspection, Luther realized, and concentrate on what God does from the outside. In this sense, theology "snatches us away from ourselves" and calls for concentration "on that which is outside ourselves, that is, the promise and truth of God which cannot deceive."[42]

Luther summed up this focus on the humanity of God in Christ and total trust in such a God with the biblical slogan "justified by faith apart from works prescribed by the law" (Rom. 3:28). Thus, he made a distinction between grace and law. God's grace is known through the communication that total trust in Jesus Christ mediates salvation from sin; this communication is gospel (*euangelion*, "good news"). God's law, once the gracious covenant relationship between God and the people of Israel, is a mandate that can no longer be fully obeyed because original sin violated the original covenant; Adam and Eve desired to be equal with God, violating the most important divine Commandment: "You shall have no other gods." The distinction between gospel and law, Luther asserted, is "the greatest skill in Christendom" because it keeps Christians alert to the enduring temptation of using the gospel as law and the law as gospel.[43] It is the difference between the language of "If . . . then" and "Because . . . therefore." The former imposes a condition; the latter does not. Luther learned from Paul and Augustine that the love of God in Christ is unconditional: it is a gift without any strings attached ("because you are my child, therefore I love you," not "if you do such and such, then I will love you"). That is why the law will cause despair when depicted as the way to be saved, for no one is able to do everything the law demands. But it will disclose the self-righteousness that is typical of the human condition. "Therefore the best use of the law is to be able to employ it to the point that it produces humility and a thirst for Christ."[44] Luther rediscovered that there is no way to argue for any self-justification before God. Nor is there a way to appease God with moral deeds that might extinguish guilt about sin. Neither syllogism nor moralism has a place in Christianity. Faith is simply more than just belief in certain rational truths about God. Faith means to be apprehended by God's word that Christ is the meaning of life. "Faith makes the person, the person does good works, good works neither make the faith nor the person."[45]

Faith, according to Luther, is the experience of being apprehended by the love of God through the story of God's incarnation in Christ. In this sense, Luther tied justification by faith to the dogma of the Trinity: the God who is revealed is the God who is in Christ, and Christ is the one who reconciles sinners with God, who, as Holy Spirit, endows them with faith. When theology is so grounded, it is essentially doxological. It is no longer analytical or explicatory but doxological—a praising, adoring summary of what God did in Christ. Luther's christocentric theological insights guard the mystery of the incarnation from rationalist explanations and moralistic interpretations, be they anchored in legitimate Greek metaphysical tradition or in honest attempts to please God by moral action. That is why Luther did not succeed in his attempt to produce a scholastic treatise on justification by faith; he ended up calling it a "rhapsody."[46]

Luther's harvest of biblical theology yielded theological insights into the most fundamental aspect of Christian thought: salvation from sin through faith in Christ (usually called *soteriology*). To Luther, sin is idolatry, the desire to be like God. This desire was the first or original sin, committed by the first humans and inherited by all the rest. The Bible talks about it as the evil life "east of the garden of Eden" (Gen. 3:25). Because there is no return to the West, to the paradise of the good life with God, only God can bridge the distance through law, which, when we obey it, creates a condition of survival but never a life without evil. The "diabolical" (Greek: *diaballein*, "to throw about, to confuse") remains; the devil still rules. Salvation from evil, relief from confusion, comes only through another bridge besides the law, through the gospel as the promise of new life as a gift, given "by grace alone" and received "by faith alone." Moreover, certainty of salvation comes through the divine word of promise from the outside, not through concentration on internal feelings about God. Such feelings always revive the old desire to be like God and to remain confused about reality with God. To Luther, the same God who is in charge of everything is also the God who justifies the ungodly as the incarnate God in Christ. He is the center of all soteriological thought. "Christ is the point at the center of a circle, with all eyes inside the circle focused on him. Whoever turns his eyes on him finds his proper place in the circle of which Christ is the center. . . . To seek God outside Jesus is the devil."[47]

Luther's theology has been called "a Copernican revolution" in the history of Christian thought. Just as astronomer Nicolaus Copernicus (1473–1543) shifted the attention from the earth to the sun, so Luther changed Christian thought from an anthropocentric stance to a theocentric one. But it is one of the ironies of history that Luther rejected Copernican cosmology as a threat to biblical authority. "I believe the Holy Scriptures, for Joshua commanded the sun to stand still and not the earth [Josh. 10:12]."[48]

The Power of the Status Quo

Luther quickly learned what it meant to oppose medieval ecclesiastical authority. The chief promulgator and defender of the indulgence traffic, John Tetzel, tried to malign Luther by publishing 106 theses, charging Luther with heresy. Tetzel had been commissioned by Archbishop Albrecht of Magdeburg and the Fugger bank

John Tetzel

in Augsburg to use the Dominican order to sell indulgences (using the effective slogan, "As soon as the coin in the coffer rings, the soul from purgatory springs"). The chief justice of the Roman curia, Auditor-General Bishop Jerome Ghinucci, requested the master of the sacred palace, Sylvester Mazzolini (known as Prierias, the name of his hometown), for an expert evaluation of Luther. He also declared Luther's teaching erroneous and heretical because Luther had questioned the church's unquestionable right to control faith and morals.[49] John Eck, a well-known professor of theology at the University of Ingolstadt in Bavaria, attempted to expose weaknesses in Luther's argumentation by publishing *Obelisks* (Greek: *obeliskos*, "little dagger"), stabbing, as it were, Luther with abusive names like liar, heretic, and rebel. Luther countered quickly in kind with *Asterisks* (Greek: *asterikos*, "little star"), charging that Eck was too ignorant to understand Luther's cause.[50] A real low point of relationships! Luther had tried to prevent the dissemination of the Ninety-five Theses, for he was afraid that they might be used to cause political strife between Elector Frederick and Bishop Albrecht.[51] He also published a lengthy explanation of the Ninety-five Theses even though his bishop, Jerome Schulze of Brandenburg, had forbidden the publication.[52]

Many students and younger theologians supported Luther's call for a return to biblical theology and to the teachings of the ancient church, especially the writings of Augustine. The Wittenberg faculty revised the curriculum, stressing the study of biblical Hebrew and Greek and of the historical sources discovered by the humanists. Students began to matriculate at Wittenberg University rather than at the older, better-known University of Leipzig. Luther felt supported and liberated from vocational anxiety, and for a while, he signed his letters "Friar Martin, the Eleutherius" (in Greek, *eleutherios*, "one who has been set free").[53]

What saved Luther from the full blast of Rome's fury was the powerful political status quo of Elector Frederick of Saxony.[54] As elector, he was courted by possible successors of Emperor Maximilian I, who was near death. He also was badly needed in supplying men and money to fight the threatening Turkish invasion from the south. Impressed by Luther, Frederick assigned his trusted counselor and court chaplain, George Spalatin, to be the intermediary between the Wittenberg professor and the Saxon court. Spalatin liked Luther and became a major supporter of his reform movement. He and the university faculty also persuaded Elector Frederick to insist that Rome deal with Luther on German soil.

After detailed negotiations, Luther met October 12–14, 1518, with the apostolic legate (official representative of the papacy) to the German diet in Augsburg, Cardinal Thomas de Vio (known as Cajetan). He was a Dominican expert on Thomism. Luther was quite apprehensive about the meeting because Cajetan represented the ecclesiastical power of the status quo. Accompanied by Staupitz and two counselors of the Saxon court, he presented his views in writing and declared his willingness to be examined by any Roman theological faculty such as that in Paris or Louvain. But the meeting only revealed substantial theological differences between Luther and the authorities of his church. The most important issue was papal authority. Should the pope have the power over the treasure of merits deposited by Christ to the church for the remission of sins of penitent believers? Luther denied this claim, and Cajetan could not convince him to recant his view.[55]

Rumors spread that Luther would be brought to Rome by force if necessary. So Luther decided to follow tradition by appealing to a general ecumenical council because the pope apparently failed to provide pastoral leadership and justice demanded by his office. The document "Appeal for an Ecumenical Council" was drafted by a lawyer, John Auler, and was solemnly read aloud by Luther on Sunday afternoon, November 28, 1518, in the Holy Spirit Chapel of the Wittenberg Town Church. This juridical act was modeled after other such appeals previously made by the University of Paris and other academic institutions on various issues.

Presenting a list of grievances, especially that of having been accused of heresy without proper hearings, the appeal called for an opportunity to address a council at a safe place and hear Luther or his attorney without threats and with a verdict based on proper evidence.[56] When Staupitz heard of Luther's appeal, he told him to expect little else than suffering persecution, because Rome seemed bent on trying him for heresy. "Leave Wittenberg while there is still time," the retired Staupitz wrote to Luther, "and come to me [in Salzburg, Austria] so that we may live and die together."[57] Luther was quite willing to leave Saxony to spare Elector Frederick and the university embarrassment and trouble. But he refused to recant unless proven wrong.

Meanwhile, Elector Frederick had arranged a meeting between one of his contacts in Rome, the German papal nuncio (ambassador) Karl von Miltitz, and Luther at the home of the court chaplain, Spalatin. Apparently, the elector wanted to create a number of meetings between Luther and representatives of the Roman status quo for the purpose of collecting evidence of Luther's nonheretical views; so again Saxon lawyers and other court officials accompanied Luther. Luther tried to convince the nuncio in a carefully written paper that his detractors had falsely accused him of heresy when, on the contrary, he had defended the honor of the Roman Catholic Church. Miltitz wanted Luther to admit that his teaching on indulgences was wrong. Finally, they reached a compromise. Luther promised to keep silent if his adversaries remained silent, and Luther's case was to be settled by arbitration, probably by the archbishop of Salzburg. Miltitz left Saxony convinced that he had avoided an impending religious schism. "We separated amicably," Luther wrote to a friend, "with a kiss (a Judas kiss!) and tears—I pretended that I did not know that they were crocodile tears."[58]

The death of Emperor Maximilian I in 1519 only increased Elector Frederick's influence in the case of Luther. The pope was eager to secure Frederick's vote for Francis I of France in the forthcoming election; he even went so far as to write a conciliatory personal letter to Luther in which he interpreted the controversy about indulgences as a quarrel between a learned Augustinian professor and a crude Dominican monk, and he tried to seduce Luther to come to Rome. "We desire to hear you personally, so that you may be able safely and freely to make before us, the vicar of Christ, that recantation which you feared to make before our legate [Cajetan]."[59] The letter had been sent to the Saxon court rather than to Luther himself in order to persuade Frederick to send Luther to Rome. Frederick withheld the letter from Luther, suspecting that he might become even more defiant in the face of the pope's seemingly friendly persuasion to recant. Luther was only aware of another attempt by Miltitz to stage a hearing in Germany, this time in Koblenz where Cajetan and Miltitz were visiting the archbishop of Trier. Luther declined Miltitz's written invitation, telling him in a letter that he had no time to go on another journey.

VIVENTIS·POTVIT·DVRERIVS·ORA·PHILIPPI
MENTEM·NON·POTVIT·PINGERE·DOCTA
MANVS

Philipp Melanchthon

Luther's request for an academic debate was granted in the summer of 1519. Duke George of Saxony, a staunch defender of Rome, asked the reluctant theological faculty of Leipzig University to support John Eck in his attempts to silence the new Wittenberg theology and Luther in particular. An increasing number of students had matriculated at Wittenberg. The nascent reform movement had set its hope on Luther and on the new Wittenberg faculty member, Philipp Melanchthon, who was the best Greek scholar in Germany and who had joined the faculty at age twenty-one in the fall of 1518.[60] There also was Dean Carlstadt (Andreas Bodenstein from Karlstadt), who had continued the literary debate with Eck while Luther was busy defending himself against attacks from Rome. When the Leipzig debate finally took place (June 27 to July 14, 1519) after lengthy negotiations between Wittenberg and Leipzig theologians and politicians, it was one of the great events of the century, full of pomp and circumstance.[61]

Carlstadt and Luther were accompanied by the president of Wittenberg University, Duke Barnim of Pomerania, and by Melanchthon, several other colleagues, and

about two hundred students, most of them armed. Eck's entourage was smaller, but Leipzig University provided him with an honor guard of officials and students. The famous choir of St. Thomas performed a mass that had been composed for the occasion.

The debate itself, held at Pleissenburg, Duke George's castle, gave Luther an opportunity to tackle the issue that eventually made him a heretic in the eyes of Rome: whether or not the papacy is the divinely instituted teaching authority for all Christians. In preparing for the debate, Luther had completed extensive historical research regarding the origins

Andreas Bodenstein (Carlstadt)

and growth of teaching authority in the first five centuries of church history. He had read of the development of doctrine through the actions of ecumenical councils, especially the Council of Nicea (325), which initiated the formulation of the trinitarian dogma in 325 CE. He discovered discrepancies between the claims of canon law and the conciliar evidence.[62]

Although the Leipzig debate was scheduled to deal only with the subject of indulgences in the context of the relationship between sin and grace, Eck made it clear that papal authority was the real issue. In a series of theses published as blueprints for the forthcoming debate, Eck had openly challenged Luther's thesis 22 of the "Explanations" of 1518: that the pope cannot remit penalties in purgatory that, according to canon law, should have been paid in this life.

Luther had supported this thesis with the statement that before Pope Sylvester V (314–335) Rome had no jurisdiction over other churches, especially not over the Greek churches, and that therefore the church could offer indulgences only to people living under the authority of Rome. Because he had been attacked first, Luther felt no obligation to abide by his agreement with Miltitz to be silent. So in February of 1519, he answered Eck by publishing his findings concerning papal primacy in the first five centuries and concluded the lengthy treatise with his own thesis 13 in response to Eck's challenge: "The very callous decrees of the Roman pontiffs which have appeared in the last four hundred years prove that the Roman Catholic Church is superior to all others. Against them stand the history of eleven hundred years, the text of divine Scripture, and the decree of the Council of Nicea, the most sacred of all councils."[63]

The issue of papal primacy, which Cajetan had tried to avoid at the hearing in Augsburg, had now become the central issue at Leipzig. After Eck and Carlstadt debated the question of sin and grace without any significant results, Eck and Luther engaged in the battle everyone had been expecting. Eck argued that Christ had made Peter and his successors vicars of his power (according to Matt. 16:18). Luther countered with the argument that such an interpretation restricted the lordship of Christ, who had promised, "I am with you always, to the end of the age" (Matt. 28:20). Luther made it quite clear that the real issue was the difference between the authority of Scripture and the authority of the Roman tradition, which interpreted Scripture in a particular way. The five-day debate on papal primacy culminated in a clash between Eck and Luther on the authority of ecumenical councils. Luther had acknowledged the authority of the Council of Nicea because it was not under the power of the Roman pontiff, and Eck now pressed for his opinion on the authority of the Council of Constance (1415), which had condemned Jan Hus of Prague for denying papal authority. When Luther stated his view that councils were only the creatures of the infallible word of God and could err, he needed to say no more. The church had never officially admitted that pope and councils could err in matters of faith and morals.

The appointed umpires of the debate, the universities of Paris and Erfurt, were unable to reach an official verdict immediately, even though many theologians on both faculties sided with Eck. On April 16, 1521, the University of Paris issued its verdict and condemned as heretical 104 statements of Luther. But the verdict was based in part on Luther's writings published after the Leipzig debate, and the Paris theologians did not directly address the issue of papal authority.[64] Erfurt refused to issue a verdict, on the grounds that Paris had not really done so and that Dominicans and Augustinians had been excluded from the list of eligible judges. However, several Erfurt theologians let it be known that they did not side with Luther. The universities of Cologne and Louvain also condemned a series of Luther's statements that, in their judgment, confused official teachings on sin and grace, on good works, on indulgences, and on other normative assertions including the primacy of Rome. The verdict was based on Luther's collected writings, which had been published in the fall of 1518 by the famous printer John Froben in Basel, Switzerland.[65] By this time, Luther no longer cared for the judgment of the universities. He called the Leipzig debate a "tragedy" and a "complete fiasco" because the participants displayed too much glory and hatred.[66]

Although Eck seemed to emerge as the winner of the Leipzig debate, Luther won more support than did Eck. The Froben collection of his works had three more editions by the spring of 1520 and was smuggled to England, the Netherlands, France, and Italy. Luther was called the "new Daniel," who would liberate the people of God from their bondage to scholastic theology.[67] Moreover, many scholars and theologians heeded his pleas for a fair debate based on evidence from historical sources, and Luther and his followers conducted lively literary feuds against adherents of the status quo after the Leipzig debate.

Blueprints for Reform

Luther's own literary production moved into high gear between the fall of 1519 and the spring of 1521. A secretary transcribed 116 sermons for publication, and Luther himself delivered sixteen treatises to the printers within six months of the Leipzig debate. He was also working on his interpretation of Psalms and finished his first lectures on Galatians.[68] Devotional discipline occupied Luther's mind for a while. His exposition of the Lord's Prayer in a personal prayer book and brief homilies on preparing to die, on repentance, on baptism, and on the ban became models of devotional life in the new Lutheran movement.[69]

He was also concerned with economic justice. A treatise on usury summarized Luther's concerns and was communicated from the pulpit in the fall of 1519 and in the spring of 1520. He basically agreed with the view of canon law that interest rates of 30 to 40 percent led to economic injustice and thus defended the papally approved rate of 4 to 6 percent for substantial transactions involving money or property.[70]

The debate over papal primacy continued. Augustine Alveld, a Franciscan monk from Leipzig, defended the papacy as a divine institution in two treatises, using Matthew 16:18 as the biblical foundation for his argumentation. He called Luther a "wolf among the sheep," a "madman," and a "heretic." Luther's old enemy, the Dominican Sylvester Prierias, joined Alveld in attacking Luther in a widely circulated pamphlet. Luther responded with a well-reasoned defense of his position that the papacy is a human rather than a divine institution.[71] Leipzig theologian Jerome Emser also joined the fray. Referring to his coat of arms, Luther published two treatises as an "answer to the hyperchristian, hyperspiritual and hyperlearned goat in Leipzig."[72]

Having bid farewell to Rome, Luther turned his attention to the budding reform movement that had become quite visible. German nationalists like the knight Ulrich von Hutten, anticlerical humanists associated with Erasmus of Rotterdam, and artists like Albrecht Dürer supported Luther's cause for a variety of reasons. Luther nurtured the movement with four seminal publications in 1520, supplying a "Lutheran" stance, a defiant witness against the status quo: (1) "Treatise on Good

Works," (2) "To the Christian Nobility of the German Nation Concerning the Reform of the Christian Estate," (3) "The Babylonian Captivity of the Church," and (4) "The Freedom of the Christian."[73]

"Treatise on Good Works"

This treatise was a response to basic concerns on the part of political friends, particularly at the court of Elector Frederick, such as the following. If one is justified by faith alone, why perform good works at all? Or why adhere to law and order when one is really not rewarded for doing good? Did not Luther's basic stance lead to the demise of the existing moral fabric of life in the world?

The substantial treatise, dedicated to Duke John, brother of Elector Frederick, was originally intended to be a sermon to the Wittenberg congregation. Its thesis is that good works are the natural consequences of a truly trusting relationship between the faithful and God, grounded in the atonement of Christ. The divine mandate to do good, summarized in the Decalogue, can only be fulfilled when Christ has become the driving force within the faithful. Consequently, faith is not a decision to try to do good or an assent to divine teachings, mediated by the church, but rather the source of all relationships of life on earth. All of these relationships find meaning only in the relationship between God and Christ, whose death redeemed a sinful world. "Faith, therefore, does not originate in works; neither do works create faith, but faith must spring up and flow from the blood and wounds and death of Christ."[74]

In this sense, doing good is always the consequence of trust in God, who wants believers to love others the way Jesus, a suffering servant, loved the world. This is the true meaning of the "first table" of the Decalogue, which commands that one should not have other gods but should honor the Father of Jesus Christ and should worship God through him. That is the way the new Adam and Eve fight the old Adam and Eve in the name of Christ: the temptation to be like God (Gen. 3:5) must be fought with self-mortification, making way for God's works.[75]

Luther admonished his readers to return to this basic understanding of the Decalogue, above all its First Commandment to let God be God. Only then would Christians be able to endure the earthly conflicts that will end only when Christ returns at the end of time. Because the Roman Catholic Church has abused the Decalogue, Luther contended, faith in the First Commandment and common sense in following the other nine must prevail. "We have to act as good children whose parents have lost their minds," Luther suggested in the context of his exposition of the Fourth Commandment (to honor one's father and mother).[76] One should know the difference between what is commanded for the maintenance of the basic values in life and what is not commanded, namely, "the building of churches, beautifying them, making pilgrimages and all those things of which so much is written in the ecclesiastical regulations."[77] Finally, one should know that original sin will never be eliminated by any commandment. "It may be checked, but it cannot be entirely uprooted except through death. It is for this reason death is both profitable and desirable."[78]

"To the Christian Nobility of the German Nation"

This address offered Luther's detailed analysis of the deformation of medieval Christendom. Officials at the Saxon court, Wittenberg intellectuals, and other influential Germans had requested the analysis. Luther cast himself into the role of court jester in the treatise, a traditional figure who would make painful political advice more palatable to powerful princes. Praising the newly elected emperor, Charles V, as a divine sign for "a time of grace," Luther began by calling for the demolition of three walls behind which the papacy had established its authority: the notion that there is a divinely instituted difference between clergy and laity, the claim that only the pope can interpret Scripture, and the assertion that only the pope can summon an ecumenical council and approve its actions. He then listed a great variety of ecclesiastical abuses that had contributed to the maceration of moral and political life. In this section, Luther was following the tradition of listing German "grievances" against Rome.[79] He ended by offering proposals for reform, including suggestions for the educational and economic renewal of Germany.

The most revolutionary portion of the treatise dealt with the relationship between baptism and Christian responsibility in the world. Luther called on the German nobles to assume leadership of the organized church as "emergency bishops" because the pope and the bishops had betrayed the gospel. The princes were qualified to do this on the basis of their baptism, which must shape reform. "For whoever has come out of the waters of baptism can boast that he is already a consecrated priest, bishop and pope although of course it is not seemly that just anybody should exercise such office . . . without the authority and consent of the community."[80] This view of a common ministry of all the baptized (later called the common priesthood of all believers) was Luther's weapon against the "three walls of the Romanists." Hindsight suggests that it was a radical, naive, indeed utopian notion. For secular princes were often as corrupt as the bishop princes, and they hardly ever ruled on the basis of communal consent. Here, Luther exposed the sins of the church without any critique of the state. He suggested that the emergency episcopate of princes should hold an ecumenical council to deal with abuses and institute reforms stressing the proper distinction between spiritual and temporal powers. But he criticized only the pope for confusing this distinction in his rule over the kingdom of Naples and Sicily. Luther concluded the treatise with a call for reform in Germany, conceding that he may have been "outspoken" and "considered impractical," yet like a good court jester he had a duty to speak up.[81]

"The Babylonian Captivity of the Church"

This was Luther's prelude to his most significant battle with the Roman Catholic Church, namely, regarding its sacramental system, which, according to Luther, had been carefully constructed to have tyrannical control over every member of the church. Luther asserted that, just as the people of Israel had been liberated from the tyranny of the Babylonian empire, so must European Christians be freed from the tyranny of the Roman Catholic Church and return to the Bible and the ancient tradition as the highest authority for Christian life on earth. Combining biblical scholarship with polemics, Luther dealt extensively with the true and false understanding of sacraments, particularly the Lord's Supper and baptism. The Lord's Supper, Luther contended, had been perverted by a particular concept of the ordained ministry that ascribes metaphysical powers to priests in the ritual of the mass and deprives the laity of full participation by withholding the cup and reserving it for priests. As a consequence, the priestly celebration of the mass and its elaborate ritual had become burdened with self-righteousness and nearly lost its pastoral significance for people in need of consolation. Common folk had been taught for centuries to view priests as superior people endowed at ordination with a special gift called "charism" (Greek: *charisma*, "gift of grace") and a special character described as indelible.

He lashed out specifically against the doctrines of transubstantiation and concomitance (promulgated in 1215 and 1415). The doctrine of transubstantiation was intended to safeguard the mystery of Christ's presence in the eucharistic bread and wine. Using the categories of Aristotle's philosophy, the church taught that when an episcopally ordained priest recites the canon of the mass (Christ's words at the Last Supper, "This is my body") the *substances* of bread and wine (their generic identity or essential being) become the true body and blood of Christ while their *accidents* (their properties, such as quantity and chemical composition) remain the same. This transubstantiation occurs when the priest performs the rite properly, when the priest correctly enacts the prescribed liturgy regardless of his faith or that of the recipient. Thus, the rite communicates the true body and blood of Christ "through the function itself" (Latin: *ex opere operato*) without regard to the feelings or convictions of priests and parishioners. In this sense, transubstantiation taught the objective efficacy of the sacrament (no human condition) and the subjective benefit (the desire to receive it). The doctrine of concomitance stated that the whole Christ is truly present in a single element or "species," be it bread or wine, and thus allowed for "communion in one kind," that is, offering only bread to laypeople. This doctrine was designed to safeguard the consecrated wine from being spilled or otherwise endangered by careless handling. The remaining bread was preserved in an ornamented locked box known as the tabernacle (Latin: *tabernaculum*, "tent," the holy place for Israelites during their exodus from Egypt). The "reserved host" was also shown in procession at the Feast of Corpus Christi on Thursday after Trinity Sunday since 1246.

Luther declared that these doctrines and rituals denigrated the mystery of the sacrament of Holy Communion. Moreover, they undermined the true meaning of baptism, because baptism enables every Christian to join a common priesthood to witness in the world. Baptism is the truly royal sacrament, Luther contended, through which the Holy Spirit is given, thus transforming sinful unbelievers into faithful servants of God. Every baptized member is a priest in this sense although some are and always will be called to the special ordained ministry of word and sacrament. But no one has a special status before God. To take special vows in order to please God or to create a special class of people smacks of self-righteousness and is unscriptural. If one uses Scripture as the norm, Luther argued, only two sacraments, namely, baptism and the Lord's Supper, have been given to the church. For only these two have been duly mandated by Jesus as "promises" of salvation with "signs" attached to them. Jesus mandated baptism in the words, "Go therefore and makes disciples of all nations, baptizing them" (Matt. 28:19) and promised that through the sign of water people will be saved (Mark 16:16). He also told his disciples, "Do this . . ." when he invited them to the supper before his death (1 Cor. 11:23-26), and he promised forgiveness of sins through the signs of bread and wine. Both sacraments are sufficient for Christian life: baptism initiates believers into a never-ending relationship with Christ, and the Lord's Supper sustains them during their pilgrimage on earth.[82]

"The Freedom of the Christian"

Luther wrote this devotional booklet as a goodwill offering and dedicated it to Pope Leo X. Luther had promised to make the gesture during the discussions with papal emissary Miltitz regarding ways of reconciling with Rome. But the booklet contains no compromises. Although not polemic in tone, it clearly presents Luther's celebration of the freedom of the gospel, God's liberating power in the face of tyranny and adversity. True Christian freedom, Luther argued, consists in complete trust in God, who in Christ has made Christians subject to none on the one hand and yet subject to all on the other. By faith and trust in God, Christians are freed from all earthly bondage, yet by love and sacrifice, they are bound to their neighbors in need.

Luther saw such freedom reflected in Paul's description of Christ, who freely emptied himself and took on himself the form of a servant in order to free others from sin, evil, and death (Phil. 2:5-11). Thus, Christian freedom is genuine discipleship as the faithful way of following Christ.

All four literary productions lay out a reform program that bids farewell to the medieval church as Luther knew it. The call for a common priesthood of all the baptized, the rejection of the sacramental system, and the relocation of ethics from meritorious obligation to free love for the neighbor in need were the substantial components of the ancient Christian tradition rooted in the Bible. Luther rediscovered them, using the tools of learning and research still available to him as a monk, priest, and university professor. But the church viewed his rediscoveries as dangerous to the faith and morals of contemporary Christians.

Trial and Verdict

While Luther was busy constructing the theological platform of the reform movement, Rome was busy trying Luther in absentia. In January 1520, the case against him was reopened in order to find evidence to support the charge of "suspicion of heresy." Unlike Miltitz, Eck provided a rather clear picture of Luther's views to the curia after the Leipzig debate. Accordingly, his judges no longer saw Luther as a bright young theologian who had difficulties with certain teachings of the church. At issue was the ecumenical question of the proper relationship between the word of God disclosed in Scripture and the authority of the church manifested in the pope and the general council of bishops.

Pope Leo X ordered a careful investigation of Luther's teachings, appointing Cardinals Pietro Accolti, an expert in canon law, and Cajetan to lead the investigation, with Eck and John Hispanus of the University of Rome serving as theological advisors. The papal commission met four times to consider the evidence against Luther, taken from treatises and sermons, not from Luther's biblical work, and using some of the judgments of the Cologne and Louvain faculties that had condemned some of Luther's teachings after the Leipzig debate. Finally, on June 15, 1520, the pope signed a *bull* (Latin: *bulla,* imprint of papal insignia on a document) threatening Luther with the ban unless he recanted certain views within sixty days. Titled *Exsurge Domine* (from Ps. 74:22, "Rise up, O God"), the bull listed forty-one assertions that the church declared erroneous. These were Luther's assertions regarding the very doctrines he had wanted to debate: indulgences, penance, the relation of sin and grace, the right of the laity to receive not only the bread but also the wine in the eucharist, good works, purgatory, and matters relating to papal teaching authority. The evidence was not systematically arranged, without topics or themes; it simply listed statements of Luther.[83] "A wild boar in the vineyard of the Lord" was the bull's appellation for Luther, whose followers were threatened with the same fate; he was not to be protected by anyone, and his writings were to be burned if he did not recant within sixty days.

Officials of the curia in Rome and Pope Leo himself wrote letters to Elector Frederick urging him not to become involved in Luther's heretical cause and to deliver

him to Rome. Frederick, on the other hand, assured Rome that he would adhere to the original agreement to have Luther tried in Germany; he did so as an obedient son of the church. At the same time, he was also hoping to win the support of Emperor Charles V for a fair trial of his famous professor. To this end, the Saxon court asked Luther to state his case to the emperor, which he did in a short letter dated August 30, 1520. Luther stressed that he had become a reformer against his will, that he had nothing but the truth of the gospel on his mind in the face of "superstitious traditions," and that he should be given a fair chance to debate his views. "I ask for only one thing," Luther concluded, "that neither truth nor falsehood be condemned without being heard and defeated. Your Most Serene Majesty owes this to Christ, who has power over so many kingdoms."[84] The emperor did not respond.

Emperor Charles V

John Eck, who had helped draft the bull, was charged with its dissemination in Germany in September 1520. But people in various cities and towns tore down the posted bull as soon as it was put up. When Luther read a copy of it, he told Spalatin that he felt liberated by the cause of reform and that the pope had been revealed as the Antichrist.[85] He knew that the die was cast. Having just completed the non-polemical treatise "The Freedom of the Christian" for Pope Leo X, Luther now penned an angry attack on the "execrable bull of the Antichrist." With regard to his excommunication, Luther denied being worthy of it, and he then excommunicated "blasphemous Rome," leaving it to Christ which excommunication would be valid in the end. On November 17, 1520, Luther once more published a formal appeal for a general council, calling on secular authorities to force Rome to call one.[86] He accompanied the appeal by a defense of all the articles Rome had condemned.

There was news that all over Germany Roman Catholic authorities were encouraging the burning of Luther's writings. His friends, led by Melanchthon and John Agricola (a former student now on the faculty), instigated a counteraction. On December 10, 1520, three months after Luther's deadline to recant, they posted a notice at the Wittenberg Town Church announcing a public burning of books on canon law and scholastic theology. The book burning took place at the Elster Gate, leading to the "yard of oppression" (Schindanger), the traditional place for public punishment. Luther himself threw a copy of the bull Exsurge Domine into the bonfire after others had thrown in editions of canon law, handbooks on confession, writings by Luther's enemies, and some theological books. Students celebrated a mock funeral of canon law.

Luther felt that justice had been done in the face of the injustices leveled against him. In a public account titled "Why the Books of the Pope and His Disciples Were Burned," he listed thirty erroneous claims of papal power as evidence that the papacy represented the Antichrist rather than being a guardian of Scripture and biblical tradition. The papacy never used Scripture or reason to refute opponents; it never submitted cases to a court of justice, Luther complained. Rome simply claimed to be above Scripture, judgment, and any authority but its own.[87]

Given Luther's theological and political position as well as his defiant refusal to recant, Rome had no choice but to follow through with the threat to ban the Wittenberg professor. His friends and many of his foes had already interpreted Rome's first bull as a kind of ban. But on January 3, 1521, Pope Leo X ordered Luther banned in the bull, *Decet Romanum Pontificem* ("It is fitting for the Roman Pontiff"). The bull presented these reasons for banning Luther: he had refused to recant, and he encouraged others to follow his example; therefore, he and they must suffer punishment. All ecclesiastical authorities were put under obligation to enforce the ban. Archbishop Albrecht of Mainz was appointed the official inquisitor, and he could, if necessary, ask Emperor Charles V for help against the new heresy.[88]

Despite Rome's fury, Elector Frederick had his way. Because the Diet of Worms was scheduled for the winter of 1520–1521, Frederick conducted a series of careful negotiations with imperial counselors and with the emperor himself, even arranging a hearing of Luther before Emperor Charles V. The papal legate to the diet, Jerome Aleander,

Bulla contra erroes Martini Lutheri z sequacium.

Title page of the papal bull issued against Luther

and other papal emissaries and delegates tried hard to avoid a hearing for Luther and pressed for a simple condemnation. That was the least Rome expected the diet to do after the church had banned Luther. But Aleander was quickly made aware of the anti–Roman Catholic sentiments that existed in Germany. In a secret diplomatic pouch, he sent word to Cardinal Medici in Rome that "nine-tenths [of Germans] raise the war-cry 'Luther' while the watchword of the other tenth who are indifferent to Luther is 'death to the Roman Curia.'" He also mentioned the daily appearance of Lutheran writings, and he expressed the fear that he might be stoned in public if he ventured to walk the streets.[89]

Luther received a written request from the emperor in March 1521 to appear at the diet. The emperor addressed him as "honorable, dear and pious Sir," using the appropriate language of the day. He promised safe conduct, and he told Luther to appear within twenty-one days. Luther was burdened by anxiety (*Anfechtung*, his favorite German word for it) during the journey to Worms and his stay there, despite the good company of another Augustinian friar, John Petzenheimer; his good friend, Nicholas von Amsdorf (a former student and instructor on the faculty); and three other companions, among them the lawyer Justus Jonas from Erfurt. Though well-wishers triumphantly received him wherever he stopped along the road during the two weeks of the journey (April 2–16), Luther's fortitude was severely tested. He described his anxiety to Spalatin but told him that he was determined to "enter Worms in spite of all the gates of hell."[90]

Luther stayed at the Johannite Inn together with officials of the Saxon court. He did not feel well in his stomach when he appeared before Emperor Charles V and the diet on April 17 at 4:00 P.M. But he had listened to a confession of a sick Saxon official in the morning and had celebrated the eucharist with him. He wore his monastic habit, looking gaunt when he met the diet at the episcopal residence next to the cathedral. The emperor had appointed John von der Eck, an official at the court of the archbishop of Trier, to be imperial orator (to speak for the emperor). Von der Eck asked Luther in Latin and in German to answer two questions: Did he confirm the authorship of books published under his name? Did he hold to their content, or was he ready to recant? Before Luther could answer, Jerome Schurf, Elector Frederick's lawyer, requested the reading aloud of the titles that legate Aleander had brought to the hearing. Then Luther answered softly, first in German and then in Latin, that he had authored the books, in addition to others not there. With regard to the second question, Luther requested one day to deliberate before responding because, he said, it would not be wise in matters of faith and salvation to confess something that had not been thoroughly thought through. Usually, such an interruption of a hearing on heresy would not be granted. The emperor, trying to please Elector Frederick, granted Luther's request. But he admonished Luther, through his orator, to be penitent and aware of his errors and to return the next day at the same time to give an oral, not a written, response.

On the next day, Luther's voice was once more clear, and he spoke with fervor, again in German and in Latin. He asked for forgiveness in case his behavior did not fully correspond with the noble etiquette required at such occasions, but he was only a lowly monk who did not know better. Then Luther separated his writings into three kinds: those that tried to teach good Christian piety, something that even his opponents acknowledged; those written against defenders of the papacy, who had devastated the body and soul of Christendom; and those written against specific persons who had attacked him under the cover of Roman Catholic tyranny. But Luther declared all his writings enhanced rather than threatened Christian unity because conflict is part and parcel of the ministry of the word of God. Finally, Luther insisted that his cause not be identified with political ambitions in Germany.

The imperial orator reminded Luther that his teachings appeared to be in line with previously condemned heretics and that he had been ordered to give a clear answer, not to debate issues. Thus pressed to give a simple answer, Luther, heavily perspiring because of the heat in the room (after 6:00 P.M. with torches for light), responded in German with the now famous words: "Unless I am convinced by the testimony of Scripture or by clear reason (for I do not trust either the pope or councils alone since it is well known that they have often erred and contradicted themselves), I am bound by the Scriptures I have quoted. And as long as my conscience is captive to the word of God, I cannot and will not recant anything because it is neither safe nor right to go against conscience. God help me. Amen."[91] Luther's words adjourned the diet for a day. Members of the imperial entourage led him from the room; his friends and a large crowd accompanied him to his quarters in the inn, where Luther raised his arms like a victorious knight at a joust and shouted, "I made it through, I made it through" (Ich bin hindurch). During the recess, the emperor pledged all his efforts to preserve the unity of Christendom.

Luther impressed the diet with his commitment to the word of God and his readiness to be led by Scripture and reason. So a number of delegates asked the emperor to let them make a final attempt to persuade Luther. An imperial commission was created composed of two electoral princes, the archbishop of Trier and Duke Joachim of Brandenburg; two princes, George of Saxony and the margrave of Baden (represented by Chancellor Vehus), who led the negotiations; two bishops, Jerome Schulze of Brandenburg (Luther's superior) and the bishop of Augsburg; two representatives of the cities, Dr. Hans Bock from Strasbourg and the well-known humanist Dr. Conrad Peutinger from Augsburg; and Grandmaster Dietrich von Cleen of the Knights of the Teutonic Order, who strongly supported Luther. When Luther met with the commission on April 24, 1521, they asked him to consider a compromise that would not violate his conscience but could prevent further difficulties with pope and emperor.

Luther in turn expressed deep appreciation for the meeting but insisted that any compromise must be judged by Scripture.

The archbishop of Trier proposed a theological discussion and arranged a meeting between Luther, Nicholas von Amsdorf, and Saxon court official Jerome Schurf on the one hand, and the imperial orator John von der Eck and the theologian John Cochläus on the other. But the lengthy meeting, at times only between Luther and Cochläus, failed to achieve any compromise. Finally, the archbishop of Trier met with Luther alone but without any positive results. On April 25, 1521, the imperial orator John von der Eck and another delegate told Luther that the emperor would have to move against him and that he had twenty-one days to return to Wittenberg. He was not to preach or write along the way so as to preserve unrest among the people. Luther promised to abide and left Worms the next day, still under safe conduct and surrounded by curious crowds.

On May 26, 1521, the Edict of Worms declared Luther guilty of high treason and called on everyone to assist in his capture. It applied the traditional negative language against a heretic: Luther spread innumerable varieties of wickedness collected in a stinking pool, and he was a demon in monk's garb. Anyone caught aiding and abetting him was to be arrested and tried for the same crime of high treason.[92]

Impasse

Before Luther left Worms, someone in Elector Frederick's entourage alerted him to the elector's arrangements for hiding him safely until it had become clear what kind of verdict the Edict of Worms had in store for him. "I would have preferred to suffer death at the hands of the tyrants . . . but I must not disregard the counsel of good people," Luther wrote to his artist friend in Wittenberg, Lucas Cranach.[93] When Luther and his imperial protectors reached Hesse on April 29, he dismissed the safe-conduct team, saying that he would be quite safe from then on. He also asked the imperial herald who headed the team to deliver a letter to the emperor. In the letter, Luther once again summarized his conviction that the word of God should be free in the church. He closed the letter with the humble petition to be heard in the church on the basis of Scripture. "With my whole heart I desire, of course, that Your Sacred Majesty, the whole empire, and the most noble German nation may be preserved in God's grace as happy people."[94] The emperor never received the letter.

Luther was invited to preach twice during his journey home, in Hersfeld on May 2 and in Eisenach on May 3. Then he continued his journey with only two companions, the friar Petzenheimer and the faculty colleague Amsdorf, who knew of the arranged kidnapping of Luther. On May 4, horsemen forced the three from the carriage and took Luther to the Wartburg castle in the Thuringian forest.

Friar Petzenheimer was allowed to escape, and Amsdorf went to Wittenberg. So Luther, isolated at Wartburg, had gone underground, so to speak. He grew a beard and posed as

The Wartburg (castle)

"Knight George." Besides the elector, only a few trusted friends knew that he was alive and at Wartburg, his home for almost a year, his "island of Patmos" (Rev. 1:9) in the "land of the birds." Plagued by various *Anfechtungen,* among them insomnia and constipation, Luther soon returned to the monastic habit of praying and working. Melanchthon and other friends in Wittenberg and at the Saxon court kept in touch with him through letters and messengers, so various literary pieces found their way to printers in Wittenberg. Some of these pieces were published before Luther's return from exile in the spring of 1522, thus keeping people guessing whether or not they were published posthumously. The lonely exile at Wartburg frequently felt besieged by the devil, but the story that he once threw an inkwell at him was created by Luther hagiographers and tourist guides.[95]

But the time of solitude provided an opportunity for a variety of reflections that Luther immediately wrote down. Always at work with the Bible, he wrote the "Magnificat," an exposition of Luke 1:46-55 and dedicated the work to Elector Frederick's nephew, John Frederick. This liter-ary piece was followed by a series of other works, among them a collection of sermons for the Christian year that would become favorite reading material in Lutheran households. But Luther's greatest achievement in exile was the translation of the New Testament into German, known as the "September Bible" of 1522.[96] He translated the Old Testament in 1534. The Luther Bible of 1546 represents the final edition. Luther was guided in his gigantic effort of translating by the way in which common folk speak in the mar-ketplace, "to look at the way in which they use their mouth."[97] Luther focused on the German spoken at the Saxon court as well as on the dialects prevalent along trade routes and rivers, such as the Meissen German spoken along the river Main. He used the Hebrew text of the Bible, edited by the humanist John Reuchlin and his school; and he used the Greek New Testament edited by Erasmus in 1516.

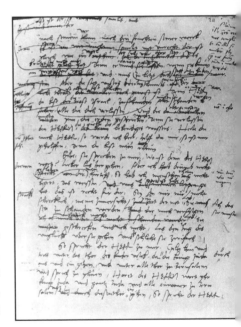

A manuscript page of Luther's translation of the New Testament

Luther also settled the indulgences controversy with Albrecht of Mainz, who had become a cardinal in 1518. When he heard that the cardinal announced another campaign to sell indulgences to visitors to his collection of relics in Mainz, Luther advised the cardinal to stop the abuse; he would attack him publicly if he did not do so. The cardinal apologized within a few weeks. Although condemned and concealed, the reformer now seemed to have more power than a cardinal![98]

In a treatise on monastic vows, Luther offered his final conclusions on celibacy and religious orders, aware that some monks in Wittenberg had left the monastery and gotten married. He dedicated the treatise to his father. Luther distinguished between true and false vows, contending that a good vow is linked to a good vocation, like farming, and is not necessary to attain salvation. Only people over sixty should become monks or nuns, Luther suggested, so as to avoid the pitfall of a troubled conscience in the light of the freedom of the gospel.[99]

When Luther heard there was confusion and unrest in Wittenberg, he paid a secret visit there between December 4 and 10, 1521. Students and monks called for various reforms, but life in the city was normal. Luther had a good time with his friends, even having himself painted as Knight George by Lucas Cranach, but he avoided public appearances.

Luther's most significant reflections at Wartburg were on biblical authority and "justification by faith"; they appeared in his lengthy reply to the Louvain theologian Jacobus Latomus. Luther told him that theologians must take seriously the power of sin after baptism. That is why God instituted "law"—the Decalogue and secular government. It is the function of law to reveal sin (Rom. 3:20). But God in Christ defeats sin for those who believe in his mercy—good news, "gospel." In Scripture and in theology, law and gospel must be properly distinguished as the "two testaments" of God through which God deals with sin. The first testament, the law, reveals the corruption of human nature, the evil humans inflict on themselves when they do what they want, and it discloses divine punishment, the evil God inflicts on creatures because they disobey God. The second testament, the gospel, also does two things. It gives righteousness, faith in Christ, who died for human sin (Rom. 3:28). Such faith enables believers to do good works for their neighbors, thus avoiding self-righteousness. Righteousness is accompanied by grace, the goodwill and mercy of God for those who believe in Christ. Such grace enables believers to fight remaining sin and to look at God as the merciful Father of Jesus Christ. Thus, life is a struggle between sin and grace.[100]

Luther had told Latomus that the distinction between law and gospel was the best possible methodological (hermeneutical) principle of theological reflection. This distinction led Luther to the assertion that a Christian is "simultaneously righteous" by faith in the gospel and "sinful" by the law *(simul justus et peccator)*. Thus, Luther tried to express what Paul had argued in Rom. 4:7, when quoting Ps. 32:1, that there is a difference between being accounted righteous by God and still being aware of sin.[101]

When more disturbances occurred in Wittenberg, Luther sent a treatise on "insurrection and rebellion" to Spalatin. In it, he opposed any rebellion against the

state, especially any in Luther's name. For the only
proper "insurrection" is headed by Christ through
the preaching of the gospel, which signals the end of
time.[102] But they did not heed Luther's warning.
Dean Carlstadt introduced radical changes in public
worship: the chalice for laypeople, no ecclesiastical
vestments, clerical marriage, and the removal of
clergy defending the status quo. Melanchthon hesitated to undertake anything without Luther's consent, and Elector Frederick favored careful reflection
and education rather than immediate action. But
radical students and outside agitators continued to
call for a radical reform foreshadowing the end of
the world and the imminent return of Christ, who
would institute the reign of God. The most radical of
these "prophets" was Thomas Müntzer, who eventually joined the peasant rebellion and was executed in
1525.[103]

Thomas Müntzer

When negotiation for law and order seemed to fail, Luther decided to return to
Wittenberg, disobeying the order of Elector Frederick to stay. Still in his disguise as
Knight George, with beard and sword, Luther preached a series of sermons on the
first eight Sundays in March of 1522. Instructing the Wittenbergers on the difference
between essentials and nonessentials, such as worship and fasting, he called for commitment to Christ by faith and diversity in Christian life, stressing a difference
between unity and uniformity. The church might keep much of a tradition for the
sake of advancing the word of God (such as Christian art, various languages in worship, or even monastic vows) as long as it did not totally identify tradition with word
and sacrament. If the Wittenbergers fell for all kinds of proposed changes, they were
playing a dangerous game that would destroy true reform through the word of God
and kill mutual Christian love.[104]

Luther's opponents viewed the Wittenberg disturbances as the logical sequence
of his refusal to recant at the Diet of Worms. Duke George of Saxony asked the imperial court in Nuremberg to issue a mandate against the Wittenberg reforms. On January 20, 1522, a mandate was indeed sent to Elector Frederick, prohibiting any
change in public worship and also forbidding monks to renounce their vows. Elector Frederick, however, politely refused to allow any interference in the internal
affairs of electoral Saxony.[105] But Luther and his supporters had begun to institute
changes without any opposition, using careful teaching and preaching. Because the
marriage of priests and obedience to political government had become issues for

many minds, Luther preached about both and finally published his views in treatises. Regarding marriage, Luther advocated a change of view from sacrament to "worldly undertaking": marriage is grounded in the order of God for heterosexual partnership and the propagation of humankind; when marriage cannot function because of "bodily or natural deficiencies," such as adultery or refusal to do one's conjugal duty, it should be dissolved. Regarding obedience to political authority, Luther offered the basic features of a theory of two realms, the realm of God and the realm of the world. Because Christians belong to the realm of God through the gospel and the realm of the world through the law, they have to discern the difference between the two realms in each situation they face. Luther advised to practice passive resistance in the face of oppression by tyrants. Christian princes, on the other hand, should be devoted to their subjects and be just.[106]

Although Wittenberg was peaceful and became a model of Christian reform, the rest of Germany experienced an impasse regarding the enforcement of the Edict of Worms. Both the newly elected pope, Hadrian VI (1522–1523), and Emperor Charles V tried to enforce the edict. But the German Diet of Nuremberg rejected their efforts in favor of calling for an ecumenical council to deal with matters of reform. Church and state could not agree how to deal with the Lutheran reform movement, which had attracted many German princes who were reluctant to execute the orders of Rome.

Now the reform movement showed what a renewed Roman Catholic Church could be according to the microcosmic model of Wittenberg: a community with a proper distinction of church and state; an assembly of believers where all the baptized would be assisting ministers in matters of worship and Christian life; and an ecumenical pilgrim church consisting of "strangers and foreigners on earth" seeking "the city of God" (Heb. 11:13, 16).

2

Growth and Consolidation
1521–1555

Models of Renewed Christian Life

After 1522, Luther presided like a bishop over a fast-moving reform movement. He was protected by powerful princes, surrounded by loyal friends, and constantly giving counsel and advice. His four closest friends helped him shape the movement that bore his name. Philipp Melanchthon had become a widely respected linguist in Greek and Hebrew; John Bugenhagen, pastor at the Wittenberg Town Church, was able to console Luther as his confessor in private confession; Justus Jonas translated many of Luther's writings from Latin into German; and Nicholas von Amsdorf was a staunch supporter whom Luther installed Bishop of Naumburg in 1541.[1] Spalatin and others helped spread the movement through diplomacy. Some noblemen used Lutheranism to advance their own cause. Francis of Sickingen, supported by some other German knights and by the humanist Ulrich von Hutten, fought for independence from Rome and the empire; they were defeated in 1523 and died shortly thereafter. Luther, who had corresponded with both, refused to lend his support to the knights' uprising, associating the attempt with Satan.[2]

While princes deliberated about the enforcement of the Edict of Worms, Luther worked with the Saxon court to reform Wittenberg and the surrounding countryside. How should ecclesiastical authority be exercised when there is a common priesthood of all the baptized? Luther began to answer this question by addressing first the issue of personal piety. In 1522, he published the "Personal Prayer Book," offering a brief, pragmatic exposition of the medieval catechism consisting of the Decalogue ("what to do"), the Creed ("what to believe") and the Lord's Prayer ("how to pray"). It quickly became a best-seller.[3] At the same time, he dealt with the problem of poverty manifested in widespread begging. The political authorities created a "common chest" in Wittenberg, with funds to help the poor. Again, Luther was quite pragmatic and realistic, advising patient, careful, and just implementation. "The world must remain the world," he concluded, "and Satan its prince. I have done what I can, and what I am duty bound to do."[4]

Next, Luther dealt with the question of how pastors should be called. Reaffirming the common priesthood of all the baptized, he ascribed to the local congregation the power held only by bishops in the Roman Catholic Church. Because bishops had abused their calling, Luther contended, the congregation of the baptized might call certain of its members into the ministry of word and sacrament. But such advice was for the emergency situation created by medieval abuse. Luther's basic view of the ministry included the order of bishops as long as they were decent and not viewed as divinely ordained.[5]

Finally, Luther turned to the reform of public worship, to be approved by Elector Frederick and the Wittenberg town council. His proposals called for the abolition of daily full masses in favor of a liturgy consisting of Scripture lessons, sermons, prayers, and hymns, and reserving the full mass for Sundays. Luther sought a middle way between radicals and defenders of the status quo. He therefore advocated, instead of the "rattling and prattling" of priests, aesthetic simplicity. "We can spare everything but the word," he told the Wittenbergers. "Again, we profit by nothing as much as by the word." The Mass should not be abrogated, but it should nevertheless be cleansed of "everything that smacks of sacrifice"; all propitiatory words and gestures should be abolished in favor of giving thanks to God for the sacrifice of Jesus Christ. All else in the Mass is secondary and is to be arranged according to the best of tradition and the needs of the people. Luther himself composed and arranged thirty-six hymns, among them the one that celebrates the justification of the ungodly through Christ, "Dear Christians, Let Us Now Rejoice."[6]

In addition, Luther published a liturgy of baptism with participation of parents and godparents as baptized "common priests," with all the features acquired through centuries of liturgical traditions: exorcism of evil in Latin, anointing with holy oil, spraying of salt, a white baptismal garment, and a burning candle given to godparents—all this in order to show the glory of holy baptism! When people objected to many of these odd-looking medieval features, Luther revised the "booklet on baptism" (1523) in 1526.[7]

Many people who supported Luther's cause were confused about the power of the common priesthood of all baptized believers. Wittenbergers had seen Dean Carlstadt renounce his academic titles and become a country pastor, ostensibly to devote himself to what he called "the simple life" (usually referring to first-century Christians), propelled by the inspiration of the Holy Spirit rather than by human wisdom. Although Luther had declared that congregations could elect their own pastors, political rulers, including Elector Frederick, claimed to have legal rights to install "evangelical" pastors. Luther sensed an urgent need for education as a consequence of baptism, which initiated every believer into a ministry in the world, be it the vocation to preach the word and administer the sacraments or to make shoes. So Luther began to speak out in favor of education. His programmatic ideas are contained in the treatise addressed "To the Councilmen of All Cities in Germany that They Establish and Maintain Christian Schools." Many monastic schools had been closed. Consequently, Luther pleaded for public schools because congregations as well as parents appeared to be too unconcerned about the education of the young. Moreover, about a third of the population seemed to be illiterate. Luther insisted that education was an investment in the future. History and classical languages, especially Latin and Greek, should be taught because Germany needed young people who had learned to use their reason wisely. "We have been German beasts too long. Let us for once make use of our reason that God may perceive our thankfulness for the divine benefits and other nations see that we too are human beings." He also recommended that public libraries be established to encourage citizens to become civilized and to learn more about the world. "No effort or expense should be spared to provide good libraries or book repositories, especially in the larger cities which can well afford it." According to Luther, the renewal of the church catholic also called for a renewal of the mind. All the children of God, young and old, were called to be faithful witnesses of Christ wherever they may be.[8]

Luther became a personal model of renewed Christian life when he married the apostate Cistercian nun Katherine of Bora in 1525 in the midst of the political unrest caused by his condemnation. He was forty-two; she was twenty six. A year earlier, he had given up the monastic habit and wore civilian clothes resembling a patrician, the higher class of citizens; Elector Frederick had given him the fabric for it, and a tailor had made the clothes. Luther still lived in his monastery, where he had free room and board as the Augustinian professor at Wittenberg University. He had met "Katie," as he called her, and eight other apostate nuns during the Easter season of 1523. He tried to help them survive and to find husbands for them. He succeeded in arranging marriages for the eight nuns, but Katherine resisted all his attempts to match her with someone else.

Luther initially rejected any notion of getting married himself. Because the Edict of Worms had made him subject to the death penalty, he had no wish to expose a spouse and children to his own danger. "I daily expect death and punishment due to a heretic," he told Spalatin, who had heard rumors about a wedding.[9] But conversations with his parents, the biblical ideal of

Katherine of Bora

marriage, the death of Elector Frederick on May 5, 1525, and the consequent reminder that life seems short when surrounded by death finally convinced Luther. Following tradition, he and Katherine exchanged vows in a private ceremony in the monastery on June 13, 1525. Five of Luther's friends witnessed the ceremony, among them Justus Jonas and Lucas Cranach, with whose family Katherine had resided. Melanchthon was not present because he had difficulties with Luther's controversial action, but he supported the marriage later. The public wedding took place June 27 and included a festive procession to the Wittenberg Town Church and a banquet for a small number of people, including Luther's parents. Elector John, the successor and brother of Frederick, presented the couple with the monastery as a parsonage and a hundred gulden for the new household.[10] Katherine became treasurer and manager of the family, many guests, a garden, farm animals such as chickens and pigs, and a dog named Tölpel (lout). A year after the wedding, Luther fell deeply in love with Katherine, his "rib." He liked the surprise of "seeing a pair of pigtails lying beside him which he had not seen there before."[11] Eventually, six children were born: Hans in 1526, Elizabeth in 1527, Magdalena in 1529, Martin in 1531, Paul in 1533, and Margaretha in 1534. The Luthers also raised six or more other orphans, children of relatives. In addition, they frequently boarded students and entertained numerous guests.[12]

Luther continued to strengthen, organize, and broaden what had become known as the Reformation. It was supported by princes who established the "Lutheran" military League of Torgau in response to a Catholic military alliance in Dessau. This tense situation prompted the Diet of Speyer in 1526 to make another compromise concerning the enforcement of the Edict of Worms: each territorial prince had the right to treat the matter in such manner as he thought "is responsible towards God and His Imperial Majesty."[13] This compromise was interpreted as a license to fuse religion and territorial politics. Electoral Saxony used the compromise to strengthen Lutheranism in its territory. Luther and Melanchthon, with the help of the town council of Wittenberg and the electoral court, moved to link reform of public worship with educational reforms. They devised a plan of "visitations" in order to discern what needed to be done in the Saxon countryside. Teams of four "visitors" toured the territory, two of them to examine the economic situation and the other two to evaluate parish life. Melanchthon composed a guidebook, "Instructions," based on Luther's suggestions; Luther wrote its preface. The guidebook appeared early in 1528 after the first visitation resulted in suggestions for improvements. Luther was convinced that this effort to reform Saxony was similar to the cooperation of church and state at the Council of Nicea (325 CE), which had established orthodoxy under Emperor Constantine.

Each visitation team had the duty to investigate eighteen matters: doctrine (the difference between Roman Catholic and Lutheran assertions), Decalogue, prayer life, morality ("tribulation"), baptism, the Lord's Supper, penance, private confession, satisfaction for sin, human order in the church, marriage, free will, Christian freedom, the Turks (a significant issue for Christian foreign policy), worship, the ban (excommunication), the office of bishop (called superintendent), and schools. The team's main concern was the competence of pastors.[14]

Title page from Luther's Small Catechism

Under the impact of the first visitation that he helped to conduct, Luther immediately detected the need for catechetical instruction. Consequently, he composed a German or Large Catechism, using the materials from catechetical sermons he had preached during Lent of 1528. This catechism consisted of a preface and five parts: Decalogue, Creed, Lord's Prayer, Baptism and Lord's Supper, concluding with "A Brief Exhortation to Confession." A Small Catechism in the form of posters that could easily be attached to walls appeared together with the Large Catechism. It was illustrated with woodcuts and was designed so it could be easily memorized. The catechism used a question-and-answer method to initiate the young into Christian life after baptism. An appendix included morning, evening, and table prayers. Luther admonished readers in the preface to the Large Catechism to be formed by daily catechetics "until they have proved by experience and are certain that they have taught the devil to death."[15]

Worship and education were to Luther the twin pillars of Christian life. That is why he urged everyone, especially pastors, to use the liturgy of word and sacrament, together with the catechism, as the bridge from false security and vanity to proper conflict with the world's evil. Some hindsight suggests that Luther may not have been successful in creating models of renewed Christian life in his home territory of Saxony and elsewhere.[16] But it is difficult to show statistically whether Luther and his programs transformed the old, apathetic believers into creative instruments of Christian witness. Luther advocated a Christian formation by parents and princes, providing models for worship and education. "His pedagogical theory is fundamentally collaborative and reinforcing," with the emphasis on voluntary education at home, enforced in church and school.[17] Wittenberg, to be sure, did become a model of renewed Christian life because the small town could be more easily reformed than the villages in the Saxon countryside. But political authorities on all levels began to favor Lutheranism rather than Catholicism, with its reluctance to rid society of the abuses it had created.

Lutheranism must have been an increasing threat to Catholicism, because the Diet of Speyer in 1529 repealed the decision on religion at the Diet of Speyer in 1526: not conscience should dictate the policies of territorial princes but practical compromise. If decisions in favor of Lutheranism could not be reversed, the commission declared, at least no further innovations should be permitted; a general church council of bishops, chaired by the pope, should then decide what else needed to be done. Six powerful princes, led by Elector John of Saxony, and fourteen imperial cities objected but were not heard. So the group filed an official "Protestation" on April 25, 1529, stating their obedience to the emperor as long as he and the diet did not violate obedience to God according to the apostolic witness (Acts 5:29). The diet dissolved without settling the issue of the religious schism in Germany, and the signatories of the "Protestation" became known as "Protestants."[18]

Pitfalls and Enthusiasm

Luther's reform movement encountered problems from within, pitfalls that snared and confused good minds. Luther labeled such minds "swarmers" (Schwärmer), enthusiasts or fanatics whom he compared to wild, swarming bees, and he became very allergic to them. He sensed a satanic connection between them and the "papists." The prototype of all enthusiasts, according to Luther, was Thomas Müntzer, who founded a "covenant of the elect" in 1523 to be the nucleus for a large-scale rebellion against the feudalism of princes. Müntzer linked his cause with rebellious peasants who thought that Luther's proclamation of Christian freedom meant liberation from the slavery of feudal landlords. In Müntzer's eyes, Luther was "the soft-living flesh of Wittenberg" hiding behind biblical rhetoric and the power of the German princes.[19]

Luther opposed the rebellion as an illegitimate mob action that must be crushed. So encouraged, an army led by the Catholic George of Saxony and the Protestant Philip of Hesse killed several thousand peasants in a so-called battle at Frankenhausen in May 1525, losing only a few men on their side. Catholics and Protestants were on the same side because they agreed that the rebellion rejected the divinely ordained political order of princes. Müntzer was captured, tortured, and beheaded. Luther praised these actions as obedience to the word of God because the gospel should never be identified with the cause of violent rebellion. "Anyone who is killed fighting on the side of the rulers may be a true martyr in the eyes of God. . . . Anyone who perishes on the peasants' side is an eternal firebrand in hell." Such a judgment later prompted German Communist and Socialist propaganda to condemn Luther as the enemy of the revolution that ended medieval feudalism in Europe.[20]

Another "enthusiast" was the former dean of the University of Wittenberg, Andreas Bodenstein of Carlstadt, known as Carlstadt. Luther initially accused him of inciting rebellion but blasted him in a literary feud as a heretic who denied the presence of Christ in the Lord's Supper. Carlstadt had claimed that the word *this* in the sentence "this is my body" (1 Cor. 11:23-26) referred to Jesus himself, his own body, rather than to bread and wine. According to Carlstadt, Jesus pointed to himself when he said, "This is my body," an interpretation without precedent or antecedent. Carlstadt went to a small village, Orlamünde, to create his own model congregation. But Elector Frederick, urged by Luther, had banned him from Saxony in 1524; Carlstadt finally became a professor of Old Testament in Basel, Switzerland, where he died in 1541.[21]

But the year 1525 was dominated by a controversy that Luther regarded as the most significant encounter in his life: his literary debate with Europe's most famous philosopher, Erasmus of Rotterdam, on the question of whether or not the human creature has the freedom to accept or refuse divine grace. Erasmus had initially supported Luther's efforts to reform the church but had become fearful of the divisions thus created within Christendom. In the elegantly argued "Diatribe," he pleaded for a compromise between two extreme positions that had already arisen in Western theology during the fifth-century debate between the North African bishop Augustine and the British monk Pelagius, one that he saw as an issue between Rome and Luther: the view of a deterministic God who predestines creatures whether they like it or not and the view of the human creature, who, even in the face of God's power to save or condemn, is endowed with the image of God and thus has free choice.

According to Erasmus, neither the abuse of indulgences, which encourages common folk to try to earn salvation through financial good works, nor Luther's radical denial of human cooperation with the will of God for salvation, which tempts people to become amoral, reflected the true intent of Scripture and Christian tradition. There is clear evidence even in Scripture, Erasmus asserted, that the human creature has the freedom to accept or refuse divine grace. Otherwise, it would truly be nonsense to assert both the justice and the mercy of God. God is neither a tyrant requiring the sacrifice of human intellect and freedom nor a creator ruled by the whims of human creatures. Erasmus viewed God as the wise creator who wants creatures to exercise the basic freedom given to them when they were created "in the image of God" (Gen. 1:27).

Luther's response was vehement and elaborate, unequivocally asserting "the bondage of the will."[22] Attempting to refute the Erasmian argument point by point, Luther attacked a "theology of observation," with the theologian Erasmus observing God from a neutral corner. In contrast, Luther defended a "theology of the word," with the theologian already drawn into the struggle between God's "good news" in Christ and Satan's "bad news" in the temptation to become God (Gen. 3:5). Luther saw no neutral ground between the gospel and Satan, between God's revelation in Christ and the mysterious opposition to it by hardened hearts like that of Pharaoh

(Exod. 7:13). The Christian theologian must concentrate on what God has disclosed rather than on what is mysteriously hidden. Luther expressed the most important aspect of his theological method, which is the hallmark of the way Lutherans learn to talk about God.

> We have to argue one way about God or the will of God as preached, revealed, offered and worshipped, and in another way about God as God is not preached, not revealed, not offered, not worshipped. To the extent, therefore, that God hides and wills to be unknown to us, it is no business of ours. . . . God must therefore be left to God in divine majesty, for in this regard we have nothing to do with God. But we have something to do with God insofar as God is clothed and set forth in the divine word, through which he offers himself to us.[23]

Luther had to test such God-talk in his controversy with the Swiss theologian Ulrich Zwingli, the reformer of Zurich. Zwingli had adopted and elaborated the interpretation of the Dutch humanist Cornelius Hoen, who had argued that the Lord's Supper is basically a memorial at which "spiritual" and not "material" eating and drinking takes place. Therefore, the words of Jesus, "This is my body," mean "This *signifies* my body," and the celebration of the Lord's Supper is an affirmation of personal faith and commitment to Christ rather than an event of Christ's "bodily presence" as taught by Roman theologians and Luther.

The controversy began in the fall of 1525 with literary skirmishes between Zwingli supporters, especially Basel reformer John Oecolampadius and Strasbourg reformer Martin Bucer, and Luther supporters like Pastor John Bugenhagen and the Schwäbisch Hall reformer John Brenz. Luther had no choice but to get involved. He opposed Zwingli's distinction between "spiritual" and "material" as an Aristotelian misinterpretation of the dogma of the Trinity, which affirms the equality of Christ's two natures. Furthermore, he could not concede that God as "body" must be limited to realities determined by Greek logic or physics (a body cannot be simultaneously at two locations). Christ can be "seated at the right hand of the Father" and also be in bread and wine. God's "ubiquity" is unlimited, and because God promised in the gospel to be present in the Lord's Supper, that promise is a better source of what is true and real than the speculations of a Greek mind. On the other hand, Luther insisted, if God is truly incarnate, then Christ can be everywhere because he is also God, who breaks through all modes of human existence. Thus, Luther contended that Zwingli neither trusted the gospel nor reasoned well.[24]

The controversy with Zwingli discloses Luther's unconditional commitment to God's incarnation in Christ communicated through the "audible word" of speech and the "visible word" of sacraments.[25] When the Protestant prince Philip of Hesse insisted on a colloquy between Zwinglians and Lutherans in Marburg in 1529, Luther reluctantly agreed to attend with a delegation. Luther and his Wittenberg colleagues prepared themselves for the meeting in Marburg by drawing up a consensus statement known as the "Schwabach Articles"; they met the Zurich delegation at Marburg castle from October 2 to 3, 1529. They agreed on all articles of faith except on the one dealing with the Lord's Supper. Luther left, convinced that no theological concessions should be made for the sake of political alliances, because such alliances tend to diminish rather than further the gospel.[26]

When Luther heard that some Protestant groups rejected the practice of infant baptism in favor of an adult "believers' baptism" after a personal confession of faith, he linked them to all the other enthusiasts and fanatics he had encountered. Because Thomas Müntzer had been the first in Luther's encounters with them, he associated them with the "spirit" of the Saxon radical. Dissenters from Zwingli's movement in Zurich advocated only adult baptism, calling themselves the Swiss Brethren, but they were nicknamed Anabaptists (Greek: *anabaptizein*, "to baptize again"). They soon were persecuted everywhere because imperial law had condemned the practice of baptizing twice as a heresy since the time of Justinian I (527–565).[27] Luther agreed with this law, contending that the church must follow Christ's command to baptize (Matt. 28:19) rather than wait until individuals make a commitment to Christ. The command to baptize is therefore more important than an adult's confession of faith. Moreover, because individual faith is not as reliable as corporate faith, Luther declared, one would have to baptize all the time; besides, if infant baptism "were not right, it would follow that for more than a thousand years there was no baptism or any Christendom, which is impossible."[28]

For the most part, Luther relied on rumors about Anabaptist behavior, and so he did not investigate what the Swiss Brethren and their disciples really taught. Consequently, he never realized that most Anabaptists were pacifists committed to suffering persecution without resistance, in imitation of the attitude of first-century Christians toward the Roman government.[29] However, the outside assessment of Anabaptist enthusiasts was apparently confirmed in 1534 when a small Dutch group of fanatic Anabaptists succeeded in persuading the authorities of Münster, Westphalia, to transform the town into what they considered the political realization of the reign of God on earth. They abolished Sunday worship in favor of "love feasts"; they instituted polygamy, in accordance with Old Testament practice; and they executed in the marketplace all citizens who resisted them. Popular accounts of the Münster events linked them to Thomas Müntzer, mindful of the similarity in names and the proximity of events (Müntzer's death of 1525); Luther simply linked "Münster" with "Müntzer." A number of princes formed an army, besieged Münster, and massacred the Anabaptists in 1535. Their leaders were caged on the church tower and left to rot. Luther and other theologians approved of the death penalty for heretics who were seditious but called for banishment of those who were not.[30]

Luther wanted to assure friend and foe that he was neither a schismatic nor a heretic, but a reformer concerned with the health of Christendom. He made his case with a treatise regarding the defense of Christendom against the enemy in the south, the Turks. But he separated himself from any notion of a religious crusade against the Muslim threat. According to Luther, a war against the Turks was to be a defensive "just war" begun and ended in repentance. He added that it is best to fight against the Turks only in the name of the emperor in order to avoid unnecessary battles and bloodshed. But he chided the German princes for using their power to harass Lutheranism instead of doing their work as guardians of peace and justice. "What devil commands you to deal so vehemently with spiritual things concerning God and matters of conscience which are not committed to you, and to be so lax and slothful in things that God has committed to you?"[31]

Luther tried to steer a middle course between a "left wing of the Reformation," consisting of radicals like Müntzer, the Münster Anabaptists, the Zwinglians or "sacramentarians"; and a "right wing" consisting of the truly faithful still on the side of the "papists." In this sense, he tried to avoid the pitfalls that can so easily beset any reform movement.[32]

The Augsburg Confession

Emperor Charles V finally agreed to give the Lutheran party a hearing at the Diet of Augsburg in 1530. He sounded conciliatory when he summoned the participants to a hearing at the diet, "considering with love and kindness the opinions and views of everybody."[33] Luther consented to have Melanchthon write the Augsburg Confession. He was advised to stay at the Coburg castle north of Augsburg because, as a condemned heretic, he could not be part of the proceedings. "I know nothing to improve or change in [the work of Melanchthon]," he told Elector John. "Nor would this be appropriate since I cannot step so softly and quietly."[34] Melanchthon had begun to summarize "Lutheran theology" in a brief exposition of 1521, *Loci Communes rerum theologicarum* (Basic theological themes).[35] No other mind was considered better than Melanchthon to draft a Lutheran confession for a hostile audience. So Melanchthon went to work on the Augsburg Confession in Latin and in German, drawing on such previously drafted statements as the Schwabach Articles of 1529, and incorporating the advice of a Lutheran conclave in Torgau. He wanted the diet to know that the Lutheran movement had removed ecclesiastical abuses in electoral Saxony and elsewhere; that Lutherans advocated a conservative, ecumenical stance; and that they were committed to continuing reform, with a willingness to compromise. The result of Melanchthon's work was a masterfully written confession signed by seven German princes and two city councils, with John of Saxony, the brother and successor of Frederick the Wise (1525–1532), heading the list. It is the Lutheran Magna Carta, as it were, drafted by a lay theologian totally committed to the reform of the church.[36] In the afternoon of June 25, 1530, the electoral chancellor George Brück read the Augsburg Confession to the emperor and to the diet.

Part I of the Confession presents "Articles of Faith and Doctrine" as evidence of an ecumenical consensus needed for the work of reform. Part II presents "Disputed Articles, Listing the Abuses that Have Been Corrected." The preface clearly states a threefold Lutheran intention: (1) to present articles of faith that have been communicated on the basis of Holy Scripture and have been taught "in our lands, principalities, dominions, cities and territories" (BC 32:8); (2) Lutherans "shall not have failed in anything that can or may serve the cause of Christian unity, as far as God and conscience allow" (BC 32:13); and (3) Lutherans are ready "to participate in such a general, free, Christian council" of the church as requested by German diets (BC 34:21). Each article is introduced

Public reading of the Augsburg Confession

with phrases like "It is taught among us" or "Our churches teach" without any mentioning of "Lutheran."

Articles 1 to 3 affirm the dogma of the Trinity, showing the Lutheran agreement with the theological foundation of the ancient church. God is triune as Father, Son, and Holy Spirit (BC 36, I); there is "original sin" (BC 36–37, II); and the Son of God atones for it and all other sins, using the Holy Spirit to sustain believers until he comes again (BC 38, III). These three articles want to make it clear that the "chief article of faith" of the Lutheran reform movement, the justification of the ungodly through the love of God in Christ, is an integral part of the activity of the triune God and not just a subjective struggle for faith (as Luther's opponents assumed).[37] Articles 4 to 6 describe the way in which God's love is communicated: "out of grace, for Christ's sake, through faith" (BC 38–40, IV:1–2); through the ministry of word and sacraments as the means through which the Holy Spirit is given, "who produces faith where and when he wills, in those who hear the gospel" (BC 40, V:2–3); and resulting in a "new obedience" that makes faith "yield good fruit and good works" (BC 40, VI:1–2). Article 5 alerts the clergy to concentrate on gospel communication and not on numerical success (an antiburnout codicil, as it were), because preachers are tempted to worry more about the numbers they convert than about creative means to preach the gospel).

Articles 7 to 15 deal with the church. It must be united but not uniform, and it will last forever as the assembly of believers who know that "it is enough" to have word and the sacrament; "it is not necessary . . . that uniform ceremonies, instituted by human beings, be observed everywhere" (BC 42, VII:2–4). "Human traditions" enhance unity but do not guarantee it. Everything else in the church is negotiable for the sake of its mission in the world. But Melanchthon was a realist. He knew that the church is a mixed body, consisting of true believers and "hypocrites, and even public sinners" (BC 42, VIII:1). Membership in the church begins with baptism. The ecumenical tradition of infant baptism is affirmed, perhaps because infant baptism shows that no one can be righteous before God by merits; how could an infant have accumulated merits? The Lord's Supper is the second sacrament disclosing Christ as "truly present" in contradistinction with the view of a "spiritual [invisible] presence" held by the Swiss reformers Ulrich Zwingli and John Calvin (BC 44, X:1). Private confession and public repentance are the means by which sins committed after baptism are forgiven (BC 44, XI–XII). The mystery of sacraments is not to be explained but to be used to "awaken and strengthen our faith" (BC 46, XIII:2). The ministry of word and sacraments needs to be regulated through ordination and calling. All this should be done "to maintain peace and good order in the church" (BC 48, XV:1–2).

Article 16 teaches that Christians may serve in political offices because God created them for the sake of good order. "But if a command of the political authority cannot be followed without sin, one must obey God rather than any human beings (Acts 5[:29])" (BC 50, XVI:7). Article 17 asserts the second advent of Christ, who will save the faithful and condemn the ungodly. Articles 18 to 20 clarify the relationship between the gift of faith and the obligation to do good works. Human creatures have free will to make decisions in the world, but they have no such free will to choose their salvation from sin. "This happens through the Holy Spirit, who is given through the Word of God" (BC 50, XVIII:3). There is the mystery of the power of sin that is neither willed by God nor created by human creatures. Melanchthon affirms the traditional view of the devil as the cause of sin. Moral deeds are done as the fruit of faith, which is always the gift of the Holy Spirit through word and sacraments rather than a merit that earns salvation. Article 20 is the longest one in the Augsburg Confession because the issue of "good works" was in the center of Luther's struggle with Rome. Its thesis is summarized in the assertion that "because the Holy Spirit is given through faith, the heart is also moved to do good works" (BC 56, XX:28–29, 31).

Article 21 expresses the Lutheran view of saints. They are faithful members of the church who should be remembered after their death as examples of strong faith for those still living who need models in their own calling (BC 58, XXI). Part I of the Augsburg Confession concludes with the reminder that its teaching "is clearly grounded in Holy Scripture and is, moreover, neither against nor contrary to [the teaching] of the universal Christian church—or even the Roman church—so far as can be observed in the writings of the Fathers [of the ancient church in the West]" (BC 58).

The articles of Part II cover a wide range: offering the eucharistic cup to the laity, the marriage of priests, retaining the worship form of the Mass, private confession, fasting, monastic vows, and bishops (BC 60–105). The conclusion again reminded readers that among Lutherans "nothing in doctrine or ceremonies has been accepted that would contradict either Holy Scripture or the universal Christian church" (BC 104:5).

Emperor Charles V called for an immediate critical response to the Augsburg Confession. So John Eck, Luther's old enemy, and some twenty-six theologians drafted a "Caesarian" rather than a Roman *Confutation*.[38] It was a conciliatory response, conceding abuses and leaving room for more dialogue while asserting traditional Catholic doctrine regarding the controverted teachings on justification, sin, grace, and ecclesiastical authority. A committee of fourteen (two princes, two jurists, and three theologians from each side) conducted an amiable dialogue on each article of the Augsburg Confession. The leaders of the committee, John Eck and Melanchthon, registered substantial agreement on many issues except the problems of merit and moral satisfaction. Indeed, the Catholic team praised the Lutheran view of the eucharist, focusing on the presence of the entire Christ.[39] But the negotiators were pressed from both sides not to make too many concessions. Moreover, the diet once again called for the enforcement of the Edict of Worms of 1521 that had condemned Luther. "We will never again get as close together as we did at Augsburg," he was heard to say in 1530.[40]

Melanchthon was frustrated and composed a defense, the Apology of the Augsburg Confession, published in 1531 with the Augsburg Confession. Its first draft was submitted to the emperor in Augsburg on September 22, 1530, but he refused to accept it. So Melanchthon decided to respond to the *Confutation* in a detailed, scholarly fashion focusing on Luther's central article of faith, justification, the longest portion of the Apology. The rest of the Apology offers an intensive critique of Catholic medieval theology as disclosed in the *Confutation*.[41]

Luther was told by Saxon jurists that the Lutheran territories would have to engage in armed resistance against the imperial forces if attacked. In a treatise of 1531, titled "Warning to His Dear German People," Luther cautiously justified his support of armed resistance to the emperor. "I want to make a distinction between sedition and other acts and to deprive the bloodhounds of the pretext of boasting that they are warring against rebellious people."[42] He only reluctantly accepted the alliance of the reform movement with political territorial power, but his loyalty to what he considered to be divinely instituted government proved to be stronger than his obedience to the church that ordained him. Commenting on the Diet of Augsburg, he compared himself to Jan (or John) Hus, whose work continued beyond his death. "St. John Huss prophesied of me when he wrote from his prison in Bohemia, 'They will roast a goose now (for 'Huss' means 'a goose'), but after a hundred years they will hear a swan sing, and him they will endure.'"[43]

Luther was right. The powerful Lutheran territories, led by those who signed the Augsburg Confession, once again prevented emperor and pope from successfully implementing or enforcing the Edict of Worms. They expanded the League of Torgau into the military League of Smalcald in 1531, with members who totally supported Luther's cause: the successors to Elector Frederick, his brother John (1525–1532) and his nephew John Frederick (1532–1547). Afraid of losing the much-needed support of the German princes for the struggle against the Turkish threat from the south, Emperor Charles V agreed to a truce between Protestant and Catholic territories in Nuremberg in 1532. The agreement stated that any legal and military actions between Catholic and Lutheran territories should be avoided until pope and emperor convened a free, general council to deal with the schism.[44] Thus, the Lutheran movement was, for the first time, officially tolerated and could enjoy a place in the political sun of the Holy Roman Empire.

The Augsburg Confession of 1530 had become the doctrinal rationale for a political movement consisting of Lutheran territories aligned in the Smalcald League of 1531. Would Catholics have agreed to tolerate Lutherans for doctrinal reasons? Probably not. Politics captured religion on both sides. The Nuremberg truce of 1532 enabled the Lutheran reform movement to establish a number of territorial churches adhering to the Augsburg Confession and protected by the Smalcald League. Luther, Melanchthon, and the Wittenberg faculty could return to teaching and research. Melanchthon drafted new statutes for the university in 1533, focusing on festive public debates in connection with the awarding of doctoral degrees. In 1536, Elector John Frederick provided a generous endowment to be used for four academic disputations each academic year, with a committee of twelve professors, chaired by Luther, arranging these disputations. The University of Wittenberg had become one of the finest academic institutions in Germany. Luther himself wrote the material for disputations on the key issues of justification by faith and anthropology.[45]

Even Rome seemed impressed by the success of the reform movement. When the papal emissary Pietro Vergerio traveled to Germany to test the political waters for a general council on the religious issues, he made a formal visit to Wittenberg and discussed the matter with Luther, who again insisted on a "free, not a papal council."[46] Shortly thereafter, the Strasbourg reformer Martin Bucer urged a meeting with the Wittenberg reformers to work toward a compromise between Zwingli's and Luther's

diverging views on the Lord's Supper. At a meeting in Wittenberg in 1536, both parties developed a consensus on the controverted matter, declaring in a formal statement, *The Wittenberg Concord,* that Christ is "truly and essentially present,
distributed and received" in the eucharist.[47] Although a united Protestant front
against Rome now seemed assured, *The Wittenberg Concord* did not last long.
Zwinglians in Zurich and elsewhere immediately criticized the agreement; by the
early 1540s, the eucharistic controversy flared again. Melanchthon composed
another draft of the Augsburg Confession, known as the "Altered Augsburg Confession" (Latin: *variata*), trying to win support for another, more "liberal" view of the
Lord's Supper (article 10).[48]

When Pope Paul III scheduled a papal council for 1537 in Mantua, Italy, the
Smalcald League met in the same year in Smalcald and invited Luther to attend.
Members of the league wanted to know what to do at the council, if invited, or, in
case of war, what to die for. Luther was pessimistic because he, still a heretic, could
not attend the council. But he went to the meeting of the league, despite severe pain
from kidney and gallstone attacks, to make sure that nothing would be compro-
mised through diplomacy. He penned a theological testament, later known as the
Smalcald Articles of 1537. Reaffirming the teaching of the Augsburg Confession,
though in a different, quite emotional style, Luther centered the articles in the doctrine of justification as the "first and chief article" on which the church stands and
falls.[49] Plagued by pain and fear of death, he left Smalcald before the end of the meeting, leaving Melanchthon in charge of the theological discussions. But the fast journey in a carriage on rough roads seemed to relieve Luther from a terminal attack by
stones in his kidney and gallbladder; he arrived in Wittenberg almost cured.

Forty-three theologians and churchmen joined Luther in signing the Smalcald
Articles. Melanchthon added a conciliatory reservation to his signature, affirming a
papacy by human, not divine, right. But realizing how idealistic such an expectation
would have to be, given historical reality, he drafted a Latin "Treatise on the Power
and Primacy of the Pope," which the league endorsed as a supplement to the Augsburg Confession and printed in German in 1541.[50] Now he seemed to agree with
Luther that there could not be any reconciliation regarding the papacy. True Christians, he declared, could no longer be under the pope, who had become the
"Antichrist."[51] The optimistic author of the Augsburg Confession, labeled "soft-
stepper" by Luther (German: *Leisetreter*), had finally put his foot down hard!

The Scandinavian Connection

The Lutheran reform movement spread quickly to the north, establishing the first
strongholds in the duchies of Schleswig and Holstein through Lutheran preachers

since 1522. Its growth in Scandinavia was conditioned by specific political circumstances grounded in the royal Union of Kalmar, which united Denmark, Sweden, and Norway from 1397 to 1523. Complex power struggles determined subsequent Scandinavian history, exemplified by "the bloodbath of Stockholm" where Christian II of Denmark tried to end a Swedish rebellion by executing eighty-two nobles in 1520. But the rebellion still succeeded in establishing an independent Sweden in 1523. Norway was under the dominion of Denmark, but it had its own national council and royal governor until 1536, when it became a province of Denmark. Denmark continued to rule Norway until 1814, when Sweden gained Norway, which was granted independence in 1905. Finland was part of Sweden until 1809, then was annexed by Russia, and finally became independent in 1917. Iceland belonged to Denmark until 1944, when an Icelandic referendum favored independence.

King Christian II of Denmark (1513–1523) contacted Wittenberg in 1520, requesting Saxon clergy for help in developing a humanistic academic curriculum. Student Martin Reinhart and his teacher, the dean of Wittenberg University, Andreas Carlstadt, spent some time in Copenhagen in 1521. The king's eldest grandson, Christian III (1534–1559), established some sixty Lutheran parishes around Haderslev in the duchy of Schleswig; his father, King Frederick I (1523–1533), did not interfere. Two German theologians from Wittenberg, Eberhard Weidensee and John Wendt, helped lead the movement, thus creating the first Lutheran territorial church in Scandinavia in 1528.[52] It was modeled after Wittenberg; the ministers had to pledge loyalty to the duke, and they were supervised by a "superintendent." Humanism, mixed with Erasmian calls for church reform, paved the way for a greater influence of the Lutheran movement. A Carmelite provincial, Paul Helie (c. 1480–1534), taught a biblical humanism at the University of Copenhagen but without converting to Lutheranism. A council of nobles met twice in Odense (1526 and 1527) and declared Denmark free from the pope; King Frederick I did not oppose the decision because he believed that each person should decide how to stand before God. But he desired a national church under his rule, a goal realized by Christian III, who defeated the Catholic opposition in a civil war (1534–1536). A council of nobles supported the king and approved the nationalization of monasteries and episcopal revenues including tithes. Bishops were removed from their office, and a Lutheran national church was formed in 1537. The king appointed Luther's pastor in Wittenberg, John Bugenhagen, to be the leader of the ecclesiastical reorganization for two years (1537–1539). Following tradition, he crowned the king and queen, and he installed seven new Lutheran bishops who, however, were no longer in the "apostolic tradition" because Bugenhagen himself was not ordained as a bishop, and bishops were no longer members of the national council. Other bishops were elected by the clergy but had to be approved by the king, who was de facto the supreme head of the church. Moreover, the king claimed authority over the medieval practice of the bishop's tithe, which included the exemption of the nobility from the tithing. Catholic priests continued their ministry as Lutherans. Education in general, and university education in particular, was still considered the task of the church, with supervision by bishops and the king's pastor. The University of Copenhagen was modeled after the University of Wittenberg.

Danish Lutheran doctrine and theology were first shaped by the Copenhagen Confession (Latin: *Confessio Hafniensis*) of 1530, which disclosed more humanistic than strictly Lutheran, Wittenberg ideas.[53] But after 1536, doctrine and theology were aligned with "Wittenberg theology" because Christian III was a committed Lutheran who, however, did not allow doctrinal controversies. He corresponded with Luther and other Wittenberg reformers and promoted Danish theologians who were trained in Wittenberg, especially Peder Palladius, the first Lutheran bishop of Zeeland, who had graduated from Wittenberg and decisively shaped Lutheranism in Denmark. Hans Tausen, who also studied at Wittenberg University, helped draft the first Lutheran church ordinance of 1537 and became bishop of Ribe in Jutland.[54] The Augsburg Confession of 1530 was adopted as a normative summary of Lutheran doctrine in Denmark. The first Danish Bible appeared in 1550, based upon the Wittenberg Bible of 1545. A Danish New Testament had appeared already in 1524.

Lutheranism was introduced in Sweden by Olavus Petri, the "Martin Luther of Sweden," who had studied in Wittenberg during the turbulent years leading to the Nine-five Theses of 1517. He was assisted in his work for reform by his younger brother, Laurentius, who had also studied in Wittenberg. The new, first king of Sweden, Gustavus Vasa (1523–1560), who had led his people to victory against Denmark in 1523, favored reform. After some political unrest caused by the king's stern rule and by Rome's opposition to a Lutheran archbishop of Uppsala, a diet of nobles in 1527 at Västeras agreed with the king to create a Lutheran national church. Its structure and teaching reflected the Wittenberg reform in Germany. Olavus Petri and his supporters published a Swedish New Testament, a manual for the clergy, and a Swedish Mass, imitating much of the Wittenberg reform in Germany. The king pressured the Catholic bishop of Västeras, Petrus Magni, to install three other bishops in 1528 but without papal approval. He then installed Laurentius Petri as archbishop of Uppsala and the other Swedish bishops. "Thus it was that the historic episcopate was maintained by accident in the Lutheran church of Sweden."[55] But the Petri brothers were not eager to align the church with German confessional Lutheranism, stressing educational and gradual nurture away from Rome. A Swedish Bible was published in 1541, and its use in every parish influenced religious education.

Power struggles within the royal family interfered with the reform movement. King Erik XIV (1560–1568) involved Sweden in a war against Denmark, Poland, and

Lübeck (1563–1570); he also favored Calvinism. He was overthrown by his younger brother, who, as John III (1568–1593), favored a high church liturgical stance and even was converted to Roman Catholicism through Jesuits. His political behavior, however, was a bit odd: he told Pope Gregory XIII that he would make his conversion public only under the condition that Rome would allow Swedish clergy to marry, celebrate Mass in Swedish, and change Holy Communion by offering the chalice to communicants. When the pope refused, John III denied that he had converted and expelled the Jesuits from Sweden. Rome remained silent because the successor of John III was his son, who had been raised Catholic in Poland and crowned its king as Sigismund III Vasa (1587–1632). But before he could take the Swedish crown, he was outmaneuvered by the younger brother of John III, Charles, who convened a church assembly in 1593 in Uppsala. Fearing a Counter-Reformation by Rome, the assembly strongly reaffirmed the work of Olavus Petri and his supporters, required everyone, including the king, to subscribe to the Augsburg Confession, and declared that all future kings had to be Lutheran. Sigismund III Vasa tried to invade his native Sweden in 1598 but was repulsed. Charles continued to rule Sweden and was crowned as Charles IX (1604–1611). Sweden had become entirely Lutheran.

Norway experienced the Reformation as a province of Denmark.[56] Its largest city, Bergen, saw some activity of Lutheran preaching in 1526, imported from the Hanseatic region of Germany; a friar named Antonius advocated Lutheran teachings in Bergen. In 1537, Christian III of Denmark decreed a transition from Catholicism to Lutheranism. The Catholic archbishop of Trondheim, Olav, left the country; other bishops were dismissed. Their ecclesiastical property and monasteries were nationalized. But the Danish royal court did not move fast toward Lutheranism. Priests were not removed from office until new bishops were nominated. In the meantime, the Danish administrator of Bergen, tenant in chief Eske Bille, was asked to administer the diocese of Bergen. A royal Danish church ordinance of 1537–1539 required that all bishops and clergy swear an oath of allegiance to the king. During his stay in Copenhagen, Wittenberg pastor John Bugenhagen installed the first Lutheran bishop in Norway, Geble Pedersson, in 1537, and in 1539, Oslo and Hamar were merged into a single diocese. By 1541, there were Lutheran bishops in all four dioceses (Bergen, Trondheim, Stavanger, and Oslo), among them one Dane (Hans Rev in Oslo).

The reform movement in Norway was neither strong nor strictly Lutheran. Future bishops and clergy studied a theology that was close to humanism and Calvinism. "The only religious booklet written during the Reformation period" was published in 1572 by Jens Skielderup, bishop of Bergen, against Catholicism: *A Christian Instruction from the Holy Writ about the Considerations a Christian Should Take on Idolatry*.[57] During his tenure (1557–1582) and that of his successor, Anders

Foss (1583–1607), the new church in Norway was administered like the Danish Lutheran church. But educational and economic reforms, rather than Lutheran doctrine, marked early Norwegian Lutheranism, which became institutionalized as a national church in 1607 through the adoption of a church ordinance. The ordinance was drafted by the bishops of Oslo, Bergen, Trondheim, and Stavanger; it was revised by the Danish court with assistance from the faculty of Copenhagen University; and it was approved by the Danish king, Christian IV, as an extension of the Danish ordinance of 1537. But Norwegian bishops and clergy did not follow the letter of the new church law in their views of doctrine, liturgy, and pastoral practice. Although most of the Catholic priests in Norway became Lutheran and served parishes in the new church, they did not eagerly adopt Lutheran views (exemplified by the reminder in the ordinance that not only bread but also wine should be distributed in Holy Communion). Although Luther's Small Catechism and the Augsburg Confession were eventually widely used in shaping popular Lutheran Christianity, the Book of Concord was not accepted in Norway and Denmark.

The Lutheran reform movement in Finland was tied to the king of Sweden, Gustavus Vasa, who broke away from Rome in 1523. But because the Finns spoke an unusual language (Finno-Ugric, unrelated to any other European language except Hungarian) written communication of new ideas was intimately tied to the work of Michael Agricola (1510–1557), who, like Luther, refined existing vernacular language patterns into a common Finnish language. Thus, he virtually created Finnish literature by devising his own orthography. As the child of Swedish-speaking farmers, he became acquainted with new ideas springing from humanism and the German Reformation. At age eighteen, he was employed as a secretary at the Cathedral of Turku, headed by the Catholic bishop Martin Skytte, an Erasmian humanist sympathetic to Luther's movement. He motivated Agricola to study in Wittenberg (1536–1539), graduating with a master's degree. Compelling recommendations from Luther and Melanchthon made him the headmaster of the best school in Finland, the cathedral school at Turku. All his successors studied in Wittenberg, thus assuring an enduring connection with the intellectual center of German Lutheranism.

Agricola's literary production created a rich Lutheran theological soil in Finland and enhanced Finnish literature. He was the author of the first book in Finnish, the *ABC-Book* of 1541, containing the alphabet, numerals, and a catechism based on Luther's Small Catechism. A massive prayer book followed in 1544, offering more than six hundred prayers, including some from Luther, Melanchthon, and Erasmus. Agricola's most ambitious publication was the Finnish New Testament of 1548, translated from the Greek text of Erasmus; the Catholic text known as the Vulgate (Latin: *vulgata,* meaning "common"); Luther's Bible; and the Swedish Bible of 1541.

Because the Swedish court refused to finance the translation of the entire Bible into Finnish, only selections from the Old Testament appeared in Finnish, notably Psalms and selected prophets; a Finnish Bible was published in 1642. Agricola also provided a Finnish church manual and Mass, translated from the Swedish works of Olavus Petri.

The Swedish king appointed Agricola bishop of Turku but diminished episcopal power by creating another diocese in the east, Wiborg. Although Agricola did not agree with the division, he was satisfied with the appointment of one of Luther's students, Paavali Juusten, as bishop of Wiborg. Both bishops were committed to gradual, not radical, change, without much polemics against Catholicism. When the Lutheran church of Sweden affirmed the Augsburg Confession in 1593 as a norm for faith and life, Finnish Lutherans had to follow suit, but they did so in the spirit of Agricola who viewed Lutheranism as a broad, cultural movement marked by a common creed and vernacular worship.[58]

Iceland was decreed Lutheran by the Danish church ordinance of 1537. Earlier, German merchants from Hamburg had conducted Lutheran worship services in the diocese of Skalholt, and two young assistants of the bishop, Gizur Einarsson and Oddur Gottskalksson, had become converts. They assembled other young men to study Lutheran teachings, without telling their blind old bishop. Gottskalksson worked on a translation of the New Testament, published in 1540 in Denmark; it is "the oldest known book printed in Icelandic."[59]

But the introduction of a new church through foreign legislation, the Danish church ordinance, met so much resistance that the king decided to send an army to Iceland in 1541. The appointment of Einarsson as bishop of Skalholt (1542–1548) improved the political situation, but not for long. Now, a Catholic majority voted against Lutheranism, headed by a powerful prince-bishop, Jon Arason, who was beheaded in 1550 after an unsuccessful military attempt to restore Catholicism. Since then, Lutheranism remained unopposed. The new Lutheran bishop of Holar, Gudbrandur Thorlaksson, printed a number of books, notably an Icelandic Bible in 1584 and a hymnal, which strengthened the Lutheran church in Iceland.

Scandinavian Lutheranism, like German Lutheranism, was established by political fiat embodied in kings rather than territorial princes. There was no single, powerful reformer who, like Luther, was an accomplished theologian or a potential martyr. Laurentius and Olavus Petri in Sweden and Michael Agricola in Finland stand out as leaders who shaped nationalized Lutheranism. In Denmark, Norway, and Iceland, Lutheranism is marked by a clear line of doctrine and practice from the beginning; the birth of Lutheranism in Sweden is linked to political turmoil until 1597, when a confessional national church emerged. The German Lutheran Confessions did not become the force that shaped Scandinavian Lutheranism, even though in Sweden they would eventually have more influence than in the other northern European countries.

Beyond Germany and Scandinavia

Luther's reform movement was like strong-flowing water, expanding from its spring in Wittenberg in various directions. Watering much of Germany and virtually all of Scandinavia, creating a new religious landscape, the movement spread in many rivulets through the rest of Europe in the first half of the sixteenth century. In this fashion, it established itself in the Baltic (Lithuania, Latvia, Estonia), in the east (Poland, Czechoslovakia, Hungary, Romania), and even penetrated in some measure the Catholic south and west (Austria, Italy, France, Spain).

In the Baltic, the Lutheran movement was influenced by the Teutonic Order, a German community of knights, originally dedicated to treat victims of the Crusades in a hospital in Jerusalem in 1190. In 1198, Pope Innocent III established them as an order of knights who would be sent to pacify troubled areas in Christendom through commerce, diplomacy, and if necessary, military action. In 1226, a Polish duke invited them to settle in Western Poland and convert the native Prussians. The order succeeded and began to establish its own culture in urban centers such as Danzig and Königsberg. Eventually, their increasing power and expansion had to be stopped by Poland, whose king defeated them and assigned them the territory of East Prussia, but under the dominion of Poland. Under Grandmaster Margrave Albrecht of Brandenburg (1490–1568), Lutheranism was introduced in the territory in 1523. Afterward, Albrecht visited Luther and Melanchthon in Wittenberg and was advised to dissolve the order and create an independent state.[60] He did so in 1525 with the approval of the Polish king, and in 1526, he married Dorothy, the daughter of Lutheran King Frederick I of Denmark. The two Catholic bishops of the region converted to Lutheranism and ordered all Catholics to do the same. The new Prussian dukedom embraced Lutheranism without any difficulties, using Luther's writings, his liturgy, and Wittenberg church polity to transform the reform movement into a church in 1525. Grand Master Albrecht appointed a German Lutheran refugee, Paul Speratus, as bishop of Pomerania (1530–1551). Speratus had become acquainted with Luther in 1523 and translated some of his writings into German; he worked with others on the first Prussian hymnbook of 1527. The University of Königsberg became known as the Wittenberg of the East, and confessional Lutheran doctrine prevailed.

Lutheran ideas appeared first in Riga, now Latvia (then part of Livonia) in 1521.[61] A disciple of the humanist Erasmus and an assistant to the school principal John Bugenhagen in Treptow, Pomerania, Andreas Knopcken had contacted Melanchthon in Wittenberg and began teaching Lutheran ideas as a chaplain at St. Peter's Church. After he defended his stance in a public disputation of 1522, he was joined by another convert from Rostock, Germany, Sylvester Tegetmeyer, who was called to be pastor of St. Jacob's Church. City officials supported the two leaders of the reform movement, encouraged by a brief correspondence between the influential city clerk John Lohmüller and Luther between 1523 and 1525. Thus, Lutheranism in Latvia was quickly established as a decisive force in the region's history.

In Estonia (part of Livonia), Lutheran teachings began to appear in 1523, disclosed in sermons preached at the three major churches in Reval (now the capital, Tallinn).[62] A diet of three cities (Riga, Reval, and Dorpat) formed an alliance against the archbishop of Riga. Citizens in Reval clashed with monks in 1524, and the Dominicans were driven from the city in 1525. Some peasants in villages revolted against their landlords, who used the political unrest to seize Catholic lands. By 1535, the new reform movement was well consolidated, based on a new order of worship imported from Riga and on an increasing number of books printed in Estonian. Most schools taught a Lutheran catechism based on Luther's. The Livonian Diet of Wolmar (now Valmiera) of 1554 proclaimed religious freedom, allowing a Catholic minority to prevail in the countryside and in some monasteries, with bishops in Reval and Dorpat. After various encounters with its strong neighbors (Denmark, Sweden, and Poland), Estonia became part of Sweden in 1629. Ever since, confessional Lutheranism dominated in the region, which continued to be burdened by aggressive political neighbors.

In the duchy of Lithuania, Lutheranism appeared after 1530, advocated by members of the nobility, the townspeople, and the clergy.[63] They had mixed motives for religious change. Some disliked Catholicism, with its medieval rules for living, its tax-exempt wealth, and its primitive educational system (without secondary schools and universities). Others desired ecclesiastical independence from Catholic Poland and enjoyed the new spirit emanating from Germany through various publications and curricula at universities, especially Wittenberg. But supporters of Lutheranism were not yet tolerated and had to migrate to the open-minded duchy of Prussia. There, Albrecht of Brandenburg sponsored the printing of the first Lithuanian Lutheran catechism in 1547: *The Simple Words of the Catechism*. Its author, the Lithuanian pastor Martin Mosviolius also worked with colleagues, publishing hymnbooks and other materials, and thus created the first Lithuanian literature. Johan Bretke translated the entire Bible in 1591. But Lutherans did not constitute a majority in Lithuania. Reformed (Calvinist) groups developed their own programs, and the Catholic Counter-Reformation, sponsored by Poland and led by the Jesuit order, took its toll. Some Lutheran congregations survived. The large town of Kaunas even signed the Augsburg Confession in 1550. *Boyars* (members of the Russian

aristocracy) and other nobles agreed in the Warsaw Confederation of 1573 to tolerate various confessions in Lithuania and in Poland, a measure that endured until
1840. Common folk, however, did not enjoy the privilege of tolerance. The com-
plexities of politics, geography, and language did not permit a smooth expansion
and consolidation of Lutheranism in the Baltic. Worship and catechetical instruction, rather than confessional theology, were the means of propagation and formation of Lutheran ideas. Moreover, Baltic Lutherans could rely only on the assistance
of the Teutonic Order in Prussia and the Lutheran churches in Scandinavia, especially in Sweden. And yet the Lutheran reform movement created a common language in the midst of a multilingual culture and became a forceful agent of change.

In Poland, Luther's call for reform was heard early: people in Gdansk (Danzig)
read the Ninety-five Theses in 1518, one year after Luther posted them in Wittenberg.[64] Although King Sigismund I (1506–1548) immediately prohibited the import
of Luther's ideas, the city government of Gdansk legislated the end of Catholicism.
The furious king responded by executing fifteen members of the city government.
But Luther's ideas still circulated at the University of Krakow. Although Erasmian
humanism found strong disciples in Poland, exemplified in the Calvinist theologian
Jan Laski (1499–1560), it had hardly any connection with Lutherans in German-
speaking settlements. Only in Ciezsyn, a town near the Czech border (southwest
from Kraków) did Lutherans survive since 1523, when they held the first worship
service of the Reformation in Poland. Protestant members of the Diet of Piotrikow
in 1562–1563 established the Consensus Sendomiriensis of 1570, which united
Lutherans with other non-Catholics. Later, Lutherans constituted a church based on
the Augsburg Confession. In the kingdom of Bohemia and the margraviate of
Moravia (later combined as Czechoslovakia), the Lutheran reform movement found
immediate enthusiastic support because of a well-established anti-Catholic Hussite
stronghold in Prague and among dispersed Hussites throughout the Czech territory.[65] Germans in Bohemia, who lived close to the Saxon border, knew of Luther,
"the Saxon Huss," since 1520. But when the brother of Emperor Charles V, Archduke
Ferdinand of Austria, became king of Bohemia in 1526, he prohibited any anti-
Catholic activities, and he continued to do so as Emperor Ferdinand I (1556–1564).
The Hussites, known as Bohemian Brethren, were banned but survived in Moravia
and Germany. The son of Ferdinand I, Emperor Maximilian II (1564–1576), was
more tolerant and accepted the Bohemian Confession (confessio Bohemica) of 1575,
a common confession of Czech Protestants (mainly Bohemian Brethren and Lutherans) that was basically compatible with the Augsburg Confession.

Moravia was also controlled by Archduke Ferdinand because he simultaneously
became king of Bohemia and margrave of Moravia in 1526. As in Bohemia, the
Lutheran reform movement found immediate support by Moravian Hussites. They

were led by Jan Roh, who had supported Luther since 1520 and then paid Luther several visits together with other Hussite clergy.

Another supporter of Lutheranism was Paul Speratus, who had come to Moravia as a refugee until he could settle in Prussia under the protection of the Lutheran Teutonic Order. Despite some doctrinal differences, such as Hussite clerical celibacy and the meaning of sacraments, the "Moravian (Bohemian) Brethren" were accepted by Luther as "true Christians."[66] But the Brethren were soon influenced by Zwinglian and Calvinist views, and Anabaptist refugees spread their ideas in Moravia. A Lutheran minority survived and continued good relations with the Brethren.

In Hungary, Lutheranism became first known through traveling merchants.[67] Luther's Ninety-five Theses were read from a pulpit in Lubica (near Kezmarok), and his tracts appeared elsewhere. Hungarian students matriculated in Wittenberg beginning in 1522. One of them, Matyas Devai, was called "the Hungarian Luther." Supporters of Luther's cause could also be found at the court of Buda. Because Lutherans had connections with Germany, "the German heresy," as officials called it, was soon opposed by bishops and noblemen. The Hungarian Diet of 1523 tried to enforce the 1521 German Diet of Worms by designating Lutherans as heretics and enemies of the Virgin Mary. This action had been advocated and strongly supported by the Hapsburg king of Hungary, Ferdinand I; the papal legate to Hungary, Cardinal Lorenzo Campeggio; and the archbishop of Esztergom, Cardinal Laszlo Szalkai, who sent a commission to various cities to confiscate Lutheran publications. The Turkish victory at Mohacs in 1526 created a good climate for Lutherans, who began to establish a great number of schools. Even the viceroy of King Ferdinand I, Alexius Thurzo, became a Lutheran. But most Lutheran intellectuals were humanists who were not much concerned about doctrine; they wanted practical reforms based on Scripture and common sense. Thus, the humanist Janos Sylvester translated the New Testament in 1541, and a colleague, Michael Sztarai, founded many congregations that did not hold strictly Lutheran views (for example, on the Lord's Supper), even though a Hungarian edition of Luther's Small Catechism was used in schools after 1550. Synods did subscribe to the Augsburg Confession but often combined its views with Reformed (Calvinist) ideas.

The Lutheran reform movement also reached the German settlement in Transylvania (German: *Siebenbürgen*), now Romania. Saxon Germans had settled there since 1140, developing profitable farms and building fortified churches to protect the land from the Turks. Turkish rulers liked to divide their conquered territories, allowing a native ruler to govern Transylvania. Thus, quick contact was made between Saxony and Transylvania when Luther made a name for himself. Already in 1520, his ideas became known among the Saxons in Romania, contributing to a rapid growth of the reform movement. Such growth was also politically encouraged by conflicts between Ferdinand I of Hapsburg and Hungary as well by a tradition of local control. Consequently, local leaders in the cities, led by Kronstadt and Hermannstadt, introduced Lutheranism in the churches and schools. After 1543, there was an organized Lutheran church in Transylvania called the Church of God of the Saxon Nation, which subscribed to the Augsburg Confession since 1572.[68]

Even in the staunchly Catholic Hapsburg lands, such as Austria, Lutheranism spread quickly in the first half of the sixteenth century.[69] Fifteen of Luther's writings were published in Vienna between 1519 and 1522. The German reformer Paul Speratus preached Lutheran sermons on monastic vows, marriage, and baptism at St. Stephen's Church in Vienna in 1522 while fleeing from authorities who called for his excommunication. Lutheran ideas quickly spread to Carinthia in the southeast by 1526. Peasant uprisings in Tyrol at that time caused a wave of persecution of Lutherans. When King Ferdinand I issued a mandate against Lutheranism a year later, threatening confiscation of property and death, the reform movement slowed down. But individual noblemen in various regions of Austria continued to support reforms; sons went on the traditional grand tours to study in Wittenberg and other reform-minded universities. Political problems after the Turkish siege of Vienna in 1529 and the tolerant attitude of Emperor Maximilian II (1527–1576) prevented any Catholic Counter-Reformation until the end of the sixteenth century. Lutheranism, however, survived in the form of the Evangelical Church of the Augsburg Confession (since 1781). Although Lutheranism spread to Italy, France, and Spain, it could not find enduring roots in the arch-Catholic soil of the home of the papacy and its most loyal Hispanic ally, or it was absorbed by French Calvinism. Far to the west, Anglicanism had its way in England.

Neuralgic Issues

The establishment of Lutheran territories, marked by loyalty to the Augsburg Confession, banished any hope for avoiding a religious schism that would weaken papal and imperial power in Europe. Luther had become the leader of a successful reform movement. Pope Paul III and Emperor Charles V had been unable to silence him through ban and edict. The Wittenberg professor even stated the conditions for a general council of the church in a lengthy treatise in 1539. First, he called for a distinction between the first four councils that had formulated the dogma of the Trinity: Nicea (325), Constantinople (381), Ephesus (431), and Chalcedon (451). Luther then defined other councils as assemblies of representatives of the church charged with keeping order in the church, just like a "consistory, a royal court, a supreme court, or the like, in which the judges, after hearing the parties, pronounce sentence."[70] Finally, he described the church as the gathering of Christians known to the world by seven characteristics: the proclamation of the word of God, baptism, Lord's Supper, the power of penance and forgiveness, the office of the ministry, worship, and suffering. Luther also expressed the feeling that he might have reached the end of his busy work. "For one person I have done enough," he told his dinner guests. "All that is left is to sink into my grave. I am done for, except for tweaking the pope's nose a little now and then."[71]

Emperor Charles V hoped to avoid the religious schism by quiet negotiations. A Catholic delegation of theologians led by Luther's old enemy John Eck and a Protestant team under the leadership of Melanchthon held several meetings in 1540 and 1541, and they reached some doctrinal agreements at Regensburg. But Rome refused to endorse these results, and Luther rejected their widely publicized consensus on the doctrine of justification as an attempt to "glue together" what really needed to be kept apart, unless Rome were willing to recant its treason against the gospel.[72] Wittenberg and Rome remained at odds.

An incident unfortunate for the Protestants allowed Charles V to gain the upper hand in his political struggle with the Protestant princes led by the head of the Smalcald League, Philip of Hesse. The unhappily married Philip had entered a bigamous marriage in 1540 with a young lady at his court after intensive negotiations with lawyers and theologians, including Luther. Even though bigamy was against the law and could invoke the death penalty, Luther himself favored bigamy over divorce, as he had earlier advised regarding the divorce of Henry VIII of England, citing examples from the Old Testament.[73] Thus, when Philip of Hesse asked for advice on the matter, Luther and Melanchthon advised him in a special memorandum that bigamy was acceptable to God as a "Turkish marriage" (because Turks allowed marriage to more than one woman), but Philip should keep the second marriage a secret because the advice was given under the seal of confession. However, Philip's sister somehow got wind of the whole affair, and the story of the bigamy quickly spread. Informed of Philip's violation of the seal of confession, Luther felt betrayed. But he used his medieval training in casuistry as a confessor and advised the prince to deny the existence of a second marriage. His rationale for such advice was the rule of protecting the absolute secrecy of an oral confession to a priest. Consequently, Luther told Philip to tell a "lie of expediency" (German: *Nutzlüge*) rather than divulge the content of a private confession. But Philip refused to lie about the affair.

Philip's behavior caused an uproar in Germany, particularly among the members of the Smalcald League. To avoid severe punishment by law, Philip was forced to bargain with the emperor, renouncing his opposition to him. With its most powerful leader neutralized, the Smalcald League was doomed to be defeated in the Smalcald War of 1546 and 1547. Philip, who nevertheless fought in the war, was captured and became the emperor's prisoner for five years; he died in 1567. Lutherans had to set-tle for a compromising peace.

Luther vented his frustration about politicians in a polemical treatise against one of the worst enemies of Lutheranism, Duke Henry of Braunschweig/Wolfenbüttel, who had called Elector John Frederick Luther's "Hanswurst" (a German carnival fig-ure of a fool who carries a leather sausage around his neck and wears a clown cos-tume).[74] Luther employed his entire arsenal of abusive language and satirical wit to expound the distinctions between the true church of the gospel and the false church of Rome. He addressed the duke as "Hanswurst Harry"; then accused the Roman Catholic Church of being the "devil's whore"; and called Duke Henry, Cardinal Albrecht of Mainz, and the pope the evil pillars of a false church, persecuting those who try to be faithful to Christ, Elector John Frederick and Luther himself.

Duke Henry did not fare well in his controversy with Luther. Bad political moves, scandalous affairs with women, and tyrannical behavior ruined his reputation as a defender of orthodox religion. In 1542, he fled to France; after Luther's death, he returned, somewhat chastened, to his territory.

Luther was convinced that there was an intimate relationship between the tur-moils within his reform movement and the end of the world. "I think the last day is not far off," he commented at table. "My reason is that a last great effort is now being made to advance the gospel. It is like a candle: just before it burns out it makes a last great spurt, as if it would continue to burn for a long time, and then it goes out."[75] He drafted a will in 1542, making minimal legal arrangements for bequeathing his worldly possessions to Katherine, even though it was illegal to designate a woman as an heir. But he reminded the world that he was a public figure "known both in heaven and on earth, as well as in hell, having respect or authority enough that one can trust or believe more than any notary."[76] It was such gallows humor that helped Luther to go the final mile.

The Black Cloister, the Luther family's home, had become a place of suffering at this time. Katherine had been seriously ill in 1540, and thirteen-year-old Magdalena died after a painful illness in 1542. Luther grieved long and hard; all the Wittenberg-ers came to the funeral. But Luther's frustrations grew worse. When he heard rumors of Jews trying to convert some Christians, he vented his frustrations against the Jews in the most controversial treatise of his life, "On the Jews and Their Lies" (1543). Although he had first opposed any Christian anti-Semitism, he now adhered to it, claiming that God had deserted the Jews because they did not accept Christ as their Messiah.

This claim, however, violates Luther's theological rule that one should never speculate about the will of the hidden God; one should only communicate God's love, not divine wrath. As he put it once with typical humorous brevity when a student asked where God was before the creation of the world: "God was making hell for those who are inquisitive."[77] In other words, one must be limited to speak only of the revealed God, best known in Christ, not of the hidden God whose incomprehensible ways would drive one to despair. But in regard to the Jews, Luther claimed to know the hidden will of God, namely, that God had forsaken them for fifteen hundred years: they had no land, no temple, and no God. "For it is impossible that God would leave his people, if they were truly his people, without comfort and prophecy so long."[78] Jews, therefore, must be persecuted, Luther concluded, and in some ways anticipating the wholesale persecution later realized by Adolf Hitler, he succumbed to the fiercest form of medieval anti-Semitism: synagogues and schools should be burned; Jewish literature should be confiscated; Jews should not be given safe-conduct on highways; they should have no money; and they should be made to work in camps. "If God were to give me no other Messiah than such as the Jews wish and hope for, I would much, much rather be a sow than a human being."[79] Luther advised all authorities in church and state to execute his anti-Semitic program even though Jews had already been driven from most of Germany and Europe several years earlier. It is hard to believe that a biblical scholar like Luther would make such a tragic error in the light of what his favorite New Testament author, Paul, said regarding the conversion of Israel: the Jews, his own people, remain the people of God despite "a hardening"; their conversion to Christ has been reserved for the end time; and this is the "mystery" Christians must accept as the "unsearchable" and "inscrutable" ways of God (Rom. 11:25-35).

Jews, Turks, the pope, *Schwärmerei* ("sacramentarians," "fanatics," "enthusiasts") pestilence, disease, even deteriorating moral life among Wittenberg students—all of these *Anfechtungen* were indeed potent clues in Luther's mind that the world was approaching the end. "I am fed up with the world," he told Katherine during the winter of 1542–1543, "and it is fed up with me. . . . I thank you, dear God, that you do allow me to stay in your little flock that suffers persecution for the sake of your Word."[80] But in 1544, Luther engaged in one more battle against his old enemies, the "sacramentarians" and the pope. A Silesian theologian, Caspar Schwenckfeld, taught the view that only the divine nature of Christ is present in the Lord's Supper. Luther drafted anew his position that Christ is truly present in the eucharist, in both human and divine natures; he vowed to die with this view.[81]

When Luther received the news that Pope Paul III had finally announced that the long overdue general council would be convened in 1545 in Trent, Italy, he decided to deliver a final blast against the papacy's political ambitions. The result was the treatise "Against the Roman Papacy, an Institution of the Devil." It raised one more time the most neuralgic issue debated since Leipzig in 1519: whether the papacy is of divine or human origin. By now, Luther had nothing good to say about "the Most

Hellish Father," the pope. Employing abusive and violent language, Luther denied that the pope is the successor of Christ, proclaiming that he is not above Scripture and tradition and that he can be judged or even deposed. "If I should die meanwhile, may God grant that someone else make it a thousand times worse, for this devilish popery is the last misfortune on earth."[82]

Luther now felt that his work was finished. Others could carry on. He returned to his lectures on Genesis and finally finished the gigantic project of ten years in 1545. To cheer him up, Prince Philip of Hesse sent him an Italian pamphlet in German translation about Luther's death! An anonymous author had recorded "a terrible sign" of God, the death of the Wittenberg heretic. The author described how Christ handed the body over to the devil in a noisy and awful ceremony; only "a sulfurous smell" remained near the empty tomb where Luther had been laid. Luther printed a comment, saying that he had enjoyed the news about his death, but he hoped that his final prayer would make his enemies in Rome recant their sins.[83]

Luther anticipated his own death with a clear head and with the certainty that he had been faithful to the word of God. His last days have been meticulously recorded by the friends who accompanied him on his final journey to his birthplace, Eisleben, in 1546.[84] Luther had been asked to help settle a family feud between the two counts of Mansfeld over the proper division of rights, privileges, and responsibilities in their domain. The feud was settled amicably. Luther was not feeling well during the cold winter journey nor while he stayed in his native town. He was accompanied by his three sons (Hans, age nineteen; Martin, fourteen; and Paul, thirteen), his secretary Aurifaber, and his friend Justus Jonas. He preached several times, the last time on February 15, 1545. But he had become weak and frail, often unable to walk because of an open sore on his leg and virtual blindness in one eye. A physician tended him as best he could, but an angina attack increased the pain he was already suffering from stomach disorder, stones, insomnia, and headaches. Shortly after midnight, on February 18, 1545, Luther was awake with chest pains; he cited biblical passages about God's love in Christ (John 3:16) and the Lord who saves from death (Ps. 68:20), and he recalled old Simeon, who had seen the baby Jesus before he died (Luke 2:29). Finally, he repeated three times, "Into your hand I commit my spirit" (Ps. 31:5). Jonas and Coelius asked him, "Reverend Father, do you want to die in the name of your Lord, Jesus Christ and for the teaching you have preached in his name?" Luther answered clearly, "Yes." He then fell asleep and died at about 3:00 A.M. It was a death without the traditional final rites of Catholicism celebrated by a priest. Luther's death was a testimony to his reform movement. His final writing was a note ruminating about the difficult task of understanding. It takes time and experience, he wrote, to understand ancient literature about farming and politics, indeed Scripture with its prophets, Christ, and the apostles. "We are beggars. That is true."[85] Luther's elaborate funeral ended with his interment directly in front of the pulpit of

Death of Luther (sketch)

the Castle Church in Wittenberg. (Melanchthon was interred in 1560 directly in front of the lectern.)

Luther is a formidable figure in the Christian tradition. He has been a saintly hero in Lutheran biographies and a devilish villain in Catholic polemics until the development of a more balanced Luther research starting in 1883, when the reformer's works appeared in the Weimar edition, resulting also in his virtual rehabilitation by Rome after the Second Vatican Council (1965). An International Congress for Luther Research has tried since 1956 to exercise the best possible hindsight.[86] But Luther will always remain a neuralgic figure, causing acute pain radiating along the course of the nerves in one or another Christian body, indeed in the universal body of Christ, the whole church on earth. He himself saw the symbol of his reform movement of the church catholic embodied in the signet ring that Elector John Frederick gave him in 1530. The seal became known as "the Luther rose": a blue ground on which is a white rose within a circle; a red glowing heart in the rose, with a black cross embedded in it. The cross symbolizes faith, which makes the heart glow; the rose signifies peace and joy; the blue ground indicates hope; and the golden circle depicts eternity. All are consequences of the Christ-event, which was the focus of Luther's life and work.[87]

Melanchthon's commemorative address at the funeral of Luther on February 22, 1546, signaled the beginning of Lutheranism: a reform movement led by Luther, whose ministry linked him to the long succession of biblical patriarchs, prophets, apostles, and essential teachers of the church; marked by an enduring fidelity to the gospel in word and sacrament, based on Scripture rather than rebellious opinions; and anchored in the doctrine of justification. In this sense, Melanchthon understood the ecumenical significance of Lutheranism, whose founder pointed away from himself to the enduring challenge for all Christians to rediscover the Christian origins in Christ and to embody him in faithful discipleship.[88]

A Fragile Peace

Luther died in the midst of political developments that threatened the survival of his reform movement. Pope Paul III had admonished Emperor Charles V in 1544 that his gradual toleration of Lutheran territories violated church (or canon) law. At the same time, Rome offered the emperor 12,500 mercenaries and generous financial support for a war against the Lutheran Smalcald League. Having gained military superiority, the emperor placed the Lutheran territories of electoral Saxony and Hesse under imperial ban; and he transferred the electoral title of the banned Elector John Frederick to the duke of the other part of Saxony, Maurice. But Maurice engaged in a diplomacy of brinkmanship. As husband of the daughter of the bigamous Philip of Hesse, Maurice was allied with the Lutheran cause. But in his greed for political power as elector of Saxony, he also supported the emperor. When the emperor declared war against the Smalcald League in 1546, Maurice fought on his side, thus contributing to the defeat of the league in Saxony, in the battle of Mühlberg in 1547. A year later, he was solemnly sworn in as the new elector of Saxony. His father-in-law, Philip of Hesse, and the deposed elector, John Frederick, were imprisoned by the emperor.

Elector John Frederick of Saxony surrounded by the Wittenberg Reformers

Playing the role of a benevolent victor, Emperor Charles V drafted an interim declaration at the Diet of Augsburg in 1548, mandating that all the estates of the empire "can live and dwell together piously and peacefully" until the general council at Trent had dealt with the religious issues.[89] The document, known as the Augsburg Interim, was based on negotiations about doctrines between Catholic and Lutheran theologians. But concessions to Lutherans were limited to the marriage of clergy and the distribution of both eucharistic elements (Catholics had withheld the cup). But most of the imperial estates did not agree with one or the other items of the Interim. England, France, and even Archduke Ferdinand of Austria, the brother of Charles V, opposed it. Moreover, Lutheran theologians were divided over the question of Luther's doctrinal legacy. Melanchthon led a more liberal, ecumenical group of Lutherans but was opposed by conservatives who rejected any concessions to Catholics. To complicate matters, the new elector of Saxony, Maurice, continued his political brinkmanship by turning it into turncoat diplomacy: while besieging the center of Lutheran resistance to the empire, the city of Magdeburg, he negotiated a secret alliance with France, promising King Henry II the strategic region of Toul, Metz, and Verdun as a reward for the military defeat of the emperor. At the same time, Maurice arranged his underground support of the German Protestant territorial princes led by Elector John of Brandenburg. Another version of the Interim, drafted at the end of 1548 for the Diet of Leipzig, also failed to gain support among the estates in the empire. Thus, Lutheranism was destined to survive by political power plays rather than by doctrinal agreement. Emperor Charles V was forced into a war against France through the treacherous politics of Elector Maurice. He lost the war and was forced to negotiate the Treaty of Passau in 1552. The treaty humiliated the emperor. His own brother, Ferdinand, helped negotiate it, claiming it was necessary for the sake of unity against a new threat by the Turks in the south; a majority of imperial estates agreed to secularize all church property; and the Interim was revoked. Maurice of Saxony had made all this possible, thereby gaining a powerful place in the constellation of European political power; he died in 1553. It is one of the ironies of history that the survival and formal recognition of Lutheranism depended on this most controversial politician of the Reformation. The Peace of Augsburg in 1555 accepted the religious schism and created the conditions for the future of Lutheranism. But it was a fragile peace because it consisted of an unhealthy mixture of politics and religion. The peace treaty was worked out by diplomats and lawyers, headed by the brother of the emperor, Archduke Ferdinand of Austria, and the son of the emperor, Philip II of Spain.[90] Both became the heirs of Emperor Charles V, who withdrew from the public eye and abdicated in 1556, dying in seclusion in a Spanish monastery two years later.

The most important decision of the treaty was the recognition of Lutheran and Catholic territorial rulers as heads of church and state. "Where there is one ruler there should be one religion" (later labeled "the right to reform," Latin: *ius reformandi*, and defined in the slogan, "Whoever rules the region determines its religion," *cuius regio, eius religio*). Other communions, such as Zwinglians, Calvinists, and Anabaptists (Mennonites, Hutterites), were not legally recognized. But they were not persecuted except in Burgundy, France, part of the patrimonial dominion of the emperor where the heresy laws remained in force. The traditional medieval ecclesiastical princes (bishops and abbots with secular power) could no longer exercise religious control; only lay princes could. In this sense, Luther's call in 1520 for lay princes to become emergency bishops was realized, and the emergency became an enduring tradition. Lutheran territories now were defined as estates (electors, princes, dukes, and counts) adhering to the Augsburg Confession.

A special provision was made for ecclesiastical rulers who desired to turn Lutheran, such as bishops and abbots. The provision was called "ecclesiastical reservation." It determined that these rulers would lose their offices and authority if they adhered to the Augsburg Confession. Thus, quick conversions of Catholic bishops and abbots to Lutheranism were averted, a legislative favor to Catholics without any Lutheran opposition. Another exception to the main decision of the treaty, the right of rulers to decide the religion of their subjects, was made with regard to Lutheran knights and towns. They could adhere to the Augsburg Confession even though they were subjects of ecclesiastical rulers. The right of religious freedom, limited to Catholicism and Lutheranism, was not extended to the subjects of the imperial estates. If Lutherans lived in the region of a Catholic prince, they had to leave. They only had the right to sell their property and to emigrate. The same stipulation, of course, applied to Catholics. Imperial free cities (those not ruled by a territorial prince) were allowed to accept both Catholic and Lutheran believers after 1555.

The Peace of Augsburg intended to settle the question of religion only provisionally, until the general council of Trent would make a final decision. In the meantime, rulers were expected to achieve reasonable compromises in the spirit of Christian love and peace. If this were not the case, the peace was to be "eternal." But territorial princes liked the power given to them through the treaty, cherishing the title that would become popular, "supreme bishop" *(summus episcopus)*. Consequently, the peace lasted until political and religious tensions led to another war, the Thirty Years' War (1618–1648).

Lutheranism spread in north and east Germany; Catholicism remained entrenched in the south and the west. "The Reformation," as the age of sixteenth-century reform became known, ended in 1555 with a compromise between Lutheran and Catholic territories. The territorial imperative, well known in the world of animals, had its way in the world of human politics. But humans create a complex bureaucracy when a territory is ruled by uniformity in all phases of life. An ecclesiastical hierarchy quickly developed parallel to a secular one; both were controlled by the territorial ruler. He quickly appointed officials in the church headed by a superintendent (formerly bishop) who chaired a consistory (in Wittenberg) or a church council (in Württemberg). There was no freedom of conscience, as Luther had advocated at Worms in 1521. Territorial uniformity only permitted one set of doctrines, one form of public worship, and a specific morality created by the officials of church and state. The territorial prince had veto power in all phases of life in his territory. Lutheran territories tended to be more absolutist, indeed autocratic, than Catholic ones, perhaps because Catholic rulers also belonged to a worldwide church with more room for deliberations, despite the strong arm of Rome. Moreover, Lutheran princes became rich landowners through the secularization of ecclesiastical property whereas Catholic rulers had to live with well-endowed prince-bishops.

Luther's call for a more democratic church through a "common priesthood of all the baptized" was not heeded by Lutheran rulers, who used their power as emergency bishops to keep the medieval class distinctions. Thus, the laity was only empowered in its noble ranks while peasants and burghers were kept in their medieval chains. On the other hand, Lutheran territories had a married clergy called to educate the common folk and nurture public worship with lay participation (especially by singing hymns). Lutheran theology also dominated at the universities in Lutheran lands, and the arts and sciences had more freedom in Lutheranism than in Catholicism. Luther's efforts to provide a common German language through his translation of the Bible helped create German literature; choral music graced Lutheran worship; and artists like Lucas Cranach (1472–1553) and Hans Holbein (1497–1543) opened German culture to the finer things of life.

The Peace of Augsburg put Lutheranism on the map of Europe. Most numerous in Germany and Scandinavia, the adherents to the Augsburg Confession could be found even in the remote region of Russia, known as Moscovia or Muscovy, where young Czar Ivan IV (1553–1584) showed curiosity about Lutheran writings imported from Denmark. The marriage of his niece to his Danish vassal, Duke Magnus of Oesel, increased the traffic of Lutheran ideas in Russia, resulting in the establishment of a small German Lutheran church in Moscow. Eventually, Russian Orthodox bishops would complain about "Martin the German" who ruined the West, just as Mohammed had ruined the East.[91]

The Peace of Augsburg established territorial regions of Lutheranism based on the notion that territorial rulers can enforce political uniformity rooted either in the Roman Catholic Church or in the Augsburg Confession. To this extent, Lutheranism was still tied to the medieval concept of "Christendom," that is, the fusion of church and state. The Church of England followed a similar path when it made Anglicanism a servant of the English crown through the political "settlement" by Elizabeth I shortly after the Peace of Augsburg in 1559. Only Calvinism (also labeled the "Reformed" communion) continued to grow under different circumstances, extending in confessional variations from Geneva to Western Europe until the Peace of Westphalia of 1648 acknowledged Calvinists as equal with Lutherans, Anglicans, and Catholics.

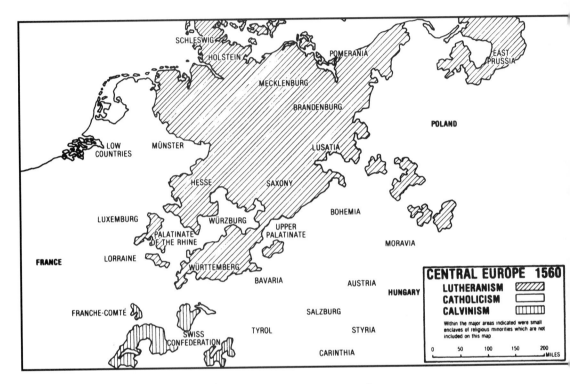

Concentrations of Major Christian Groups in Central Europe, 1560

3

Confessional Identity
1555–1580

A Catechetical Way

German Lutheran territories adhered to the Augsburg Confession as a summary of Lutheran teaching and used Luther's catechisms (Greek: *katechein,* "to instruct orally") as the means to instruct children and adults. Because Luther had advocated a spiritual equality between clergy and laity based on baptism, he made the ordained and nonordained partners in Christian formation through worship and education. Accordingly, participants in worship need to understand and become part of the Sunday liturgy, and they need to experience their station in life as a divine calling to make faith active in love. Thus, there is an intimate link between the Sunday celebration of God's love in Christ and the Monday obligation of love of neighbor.[1] Worship through word and sacrament is the inhaling of divine power, as it were, and making a living in the world is the exhaling. Enduring instruction, grounded in catechetics, is necessary for proper public worship (liturgy) and Christian behavior in the world (ethics). That is why education became the principal way of establishing Lutheran confessional identity, ranging from sophisticated research of the ancient church to picture posters for children on Christian essentials. This identity was firmly linked to the best of the Christian tradition, which needs reform or expansion, be it by new language or by including neglected components (as Luther did when he added the sacraments of baptism and Holy Communion to the ancient catechism on the Creed and Lord's Prayer to which Augustine (354–430) had added the Decalogue.[2]

If Scripture is the "touch stone" by which all Christian teaching is to be judged, then the catechism is the whetstone that sharpens minds and shapes hearts in the church.[3] Luther's catechisms became the blueprints for a theological vision of existence under God, who—as creator, redeemer, and Holy Spirit—pursues, recruits, and employs human creatures as witnesses to unrivaled divine majesty and unconditional love.[4]

The Decalogue

The Decalogue discloses "what God wishes us to do and not to do." The First Commandment summarizes God's demands: "You shall have no other gods." That is a matter of faith, trust, and confidence. "To have God . . . does not mean to grasp him with our fingers, or to put him into a purse, or to shut him up in a box. Rather, you lay hold of God when your heart grasps him and clings to him. To cling to God with all our heart is nothing else than to entrust ourselves to God completely." That is the foundation of Christian life on earth. But this foundation is continually undermined by the temptation to be like God (Gen. 3:5), "to wrest heaven from God." The attempt to play God is the only real original sin; it is idolatry. That is why the First Commandment leads to the fulfillment of the other Commandments. "If the heart is right with God and we keep this commandment, all the rest will follow on their own." Those who trust God as their real source of life will act in any situation in a way that lets God be God and helps the neighbor in need. They can now concentrate fully on the needs of others in the world without the notion that their moral deeds earn merits before God. The First Commandment, therefore, is the rationale for a responsible "situation ethic" that is no longer governed by casuistic divine mandates but rather by a basic stance—a freedom from self-righteousness and bondage to a faith active in love and justice. One must let the First Commandment "run through all the commandments, like the clasp or the hoop of a wreath that binds the end to the beginning and holds everything together."[5] Neither the keeping of the Sabbath nor any other mandate in the Old Testament Decalogue is "necessary for salvation." The Commandments provide equity and justice in a world of sin, death, and evil. But salvation is given through faith alone in the God who died in Christ for a world that has forfeited all rights to be with God. That is why human power does not have to be used anymore to please God, to earn God's favor. Rather, all human efforts are to be used for the task of living with others in a balanced and just relationship grounded in the gospel of God's unconditional love.

The Creed

The Creed discloses "all that we must expect and receive from God." The first article (God) reveals the divine gifts of creation, which God also daily guards against evil and misfortune. Human creatures are stewards of God's creation; we need "to learn at first, both about what we have and receive from God and about what we owe him in return." The second article (Christ) shows how God takes care of rebellious creatures. Luther offers a definition of the chief article of faith for all Christians, justification by faith, without mentioning the phrase: "I believe that Jesus Christ . . . is my Lord. He has redeemed me, a lost and condemned human being . . . not with gold or silver but with his holy, precious blood and with his innocent suffering and death . . .

in order that I may belong to him, live under him in his kingdom and serve him in eternal righteousness." The third article (Holy Spirit) shows that the Holy Spirit "sanctifies," makes holy, through the communication of the gospel, the good news that Christ has made such holiness possible. It is embodied in a clearly visible church in which every member is linked with every other member in the world. "The Holy Spirit has called me through the gospel, enlightened me with his gifts, made me holy and kept me in the true faith, just as he calls, gathers, enlightens and makes holy the whole Christian church on earth and keeps it with Jesus Christ in the one common true faith." Moreover, the church is like a group of pilgrims wandering toward the final, holy place with God. Thus, members of the church "are only halfway pure and holy" and need to grow daily in their sanctification through the work of the Holy Spirit, "granting us daily forgiveness until we attain to that life where there will be no more forgiveness."[6]

The Lord's Prayer

The Lord's Prayer teaches "how we are to pray." Prayer is part of the rhythm of Christian life, the "drum" that asks God to preserve the faith. It is an instrument of survival in a dangerous world filled with unreliable, tempting relationships. That is why one must pray all the time. "Otherwise, if you attempt to help yourself by your own thoughts and resources, you will only make the matter worse and give the devil a wider opening."[7]

Baptism

Baptism is the sacramental embodying of God's love for sinners in the world. It is God's "visible word" of promise for salvation.[8] Baptism is commanded by Jesus; it mediates the Holy Spirit; and it provides power to survive evil and death.[9] Lutheranism shares the ancient view that sacraments are efficacious, even without faith in them, and beneficial when faith clings to them.[10] That is why infants are to be baptized, "washed" by God, who precedes everything and everybody, being there before one is even conscious of a divine presence. So baptism is God's way of meeting human creatures, just as a desert host washes the tired guest who survived the dangers of the desert. So God seals God's love in the water of baptism for those who have to face the desert of life. Besides, God has commanded baptism. "How dare we think that God's word and ordinance should be wrong and invalid because we use it wrongly? I myself, and all who are baptized, must say before God: 'I come here in my faith, and in the faith of others, nevertheless I cannot build on the fact that I believe and many people are praying for me. Instead, I build on this, that it is your word and command.'" Baptism is the wedge God drives between human sin and divine love; it is a daily experience of struggle. "It signifies that the old creature in us with all sins and evil desires is to be drowned and die through daily contrition and repentance, and on the other hand that daily a new person is to come forth and rise up to live before God in righteousness and purity forever." In the face of sin, evil, and death, Luther gives the order, "Back to the future," that is, return to baptism as the first step forward, toward true change: penance. "Therefore let all Christians regard their baptism as the daily garment that they are to wear all the time."[11]

The Lord's Supper

Christ encounters each Christian in the eucharistic meal of bread and wine. The words "for you" and "for the forgiveness of sins" during the meal "are the essential thing in the sacrament." Like baptism, the Lord's Supper is efficacious "even though a scoundrel receives or administers the sacrament . . . For it is not founded on human holiness but on the word of God." In addition, this meal sustains those who are baptized and, like human food, should be consumed very often, as a "daily food." That is why "people who abstain and absent themselves from the sacrament over a long period of time are not to be considered Christians." Luther counsels absentees to read the Bible and to look at the world and their neighbors in order to experience the reality of sinful human existence. Such a reality check should make them run to the nearest eucharistic celebration![12] Because the Lord's Supper, like baptism, establishes an inexplicable, undeserved encounter with divine love

Luther and others serving communion

in Christ, his "true body and blood . . . under the bread and wine," it should also be offered to children "because they must all help us to believe, to love, to pray, and to fight against the devil."[13] Here, Luther echoed the saying of Jesus: "unless you change and become like children, you will never enter the kingdom of heaven" (Matt. 18:3). Thus, the Lord's Supper is a divine mystery that is to be celebrated rather than explained. That is why Lutheranism, like Eastern Orthodoxy, remains open to the practice of infant communion.[14]

Lutheran education is Christian formation for survival in the world. Thus, the focus is on struggle, expressed in the rhythm of penance and forgiveness. That is why Lutheran catechisms cherish the practice of public and private confession, especially the latter, because it, like the Lord's Supper, provides an intimate, personal encounter with God. The daily Christian temptation to abandon obedience to God in favor of ego power is best confronted in the practice of private confession, an ancient pastoral custom refined to the point of abuse in the medieval church. But proper "auricular" confession has two significant components: "when I lament my sin and desire comfort and restoration for my soul" and "when God absolves me of my sins through the Word placed in the lips of another person." The two components must be carefully distinguished, but in such a way as to stress the word of absolution rather than the value of listing sins. "We should set little value on our work but exalt and magnify God's word. . . . The word or absolution . . . is what you should concentrate on, magnifying and cherishing it as a great and wonderful treasure to be accepted with all praise and gratitude." To go through life without the experience of confession and absolution handicaps people. "Therefore, when I exhort you to go to confession, I am doing nothing but exhorting you to be a Christian."[15]

The catechetical way established a Lutheran confessional identity that is characterized by three enduring aspects. First, the catechisms are a testimony to what can be called the "rabbinical" way of the Christian life. The emphasis on learning and teaching for life reflects the classic rabbinical combination of preaching and teaching, adopted by the ancient church as *kerygma* (proclamation) and *didache* (teaching). Consequently, catechetics is not an added specialty of the ministry, be it ordained or not ordained, but rather the most essential part of the ministry to which Jesus commissioned his disciples. That is why the Lutheran reform movement insisted on solid theological education as a prerequisite to ordination and created the office of the pastor-theologian whose vocation was the discernment of how to communicate the gospel in the midst of other "good news" or confusing religious activities. In this sense, the ordained are the ones who create, maintain, and use their theological education as the whetstone of baptism: to prevent the baptized body of Christ, the church, from getting dull and apathetic. Thus, there is a truly learned clergy, ordained for life, equipping the laity to be effective witnesses in their various vocations. The catechisms are designed to keep the vigil for the freedom of the gospel in a world tempted by idolatry, beginning with a confusion of divine and human power. Solid, continuing theological education, grounded in a catechism, is like a good snowplow: it clears the road so that destinations can be reached.

Second, the catechisms are intimately linked to worship. There is a liturgy of the mind, as it were, related to the liturgy of word and sacrament. Christians, as children of God, are first initiated into the church, as the family of God, by preschool activities such as immersion in baptism, sharing the Lord's Supper, hearing stories about God, and other means suited to the elementary level of human growth. Christian learning begins with initiation into worship, with all its ritual and symbolism. In this sense, Christian pedagogy differs from what is called natural pedagogy: Christian nurture is not based on the development of ego-potential—the completion of something good that is inherent in human nature and is brought out by education (Latin: *educare*, "to lead out"). Rather, Christian nurture or formation occurs through intimate contact with the symbolic, ritual, and sacramental culture of the church, in the never-ending relationship of the baptized with the visible and audible words, that is, the eucharistic meal and the story of the gospel.

Third and finally, the catechisms are designed to prevent ecclesiastical triumphalism, the flaunting of Christendom as an institution of divine privilege, ranging from chancel prancing to doctrinal infallibility. Good catechetics keeps people aware of the limitation of life in the mean, the time between Christ's first and second advent, between baptism and death. Luther instilled in his reform movement a sagacity for any kind of works-righteousness, be it individual pride before God or ecclesiastical institutional arrogance before the world.

> Let all Christians drill themselves in the Catechism daily, and constantly put it into practice, guarding themselves with the greatest care and diligence against the poisonous infection of such security and vanity. Let them constantly read and teach, learn and meditate and ponder. Let them never stop until they have proved by experience and are certain that they have taught the devil to death and have become more learned than God himself and all his saints. If they show such diligence, then I promise them—and their experience will bear me out—that they will gain much fruit and God will make excellent people of them. Then in due time they will make the noble confession that the longer they work with the catechism, the less they know of it, and the more they have to learn. Only then, hungry and thirsty, will they for the first time truly taste what now they cannot bear to smell because they are so bloated and surfeited. To this end may God grant his grace! Amen.[16]

The Melanchthon Factor

The chief architect of Lutheran confessional identity is Philipp Melanchthon (1497–1560), who had joined the new theological faculty in Wittenberg in 1518, enriching nascent Lutheran ideas with the gifts of humanistic scholarship. As professor of Greek, he began studying theology with Luther and became convinced for life that God accepts sinners by grace alone for the sake of Christ; all attempts to appease God by human efforts must be rejected. This basic theological position is the centerpiece in Melanchthon's *Loci Communes* (Common places), the first Lutheran theological handbook, published in 1521. Three later writings became part of the normative Lutheran Confessions, edited in the Book of Concord of 1580: the Augsburg Confession (1530), the Apology [defense] of the Augsburg Confession (1531), and Treatise on the Power and Primacy of the Pope (1537).

Melanchthon clarified and refined Luther's basic insight that sinners are justified before God by grace through faith, without the works prescribed by the law (Rom. 3:28). Both agreed that the good news about God's grace must be distinguished from the law in such a way that the law is used only for witness in the world (for example, in the pursuit of justice); sinners cannot be justified before God by the law.[17] But Melanchthon systematized Luther's view of the law by distinguishing between three uses or functions: as "civil law," it creates justice in the face of chaos created by sin and evil; as "theological law," it leads to repentance and to the gospel in the face of human failures to remove sin and evil; and in its "third use," the law provides instruction for believers regarding their witness in the world. Melanchthon, therefore, advocated teaching the ethics of Aristotle as a means to establish moral justice without using such morality to appease God.

Between 1527 and 1538, Melanchthon produced a Christian philosophical ethic, followed by a work on physics in 1549 and an anthropology in 1553.[18] He wanted to teach about human beings and inanimate objects, drawing as much as possible on ancient, pre-Christian science and philosophy. At the same time, he pressed hard for a pragmatic linkage of confessional identity with ecumenical initiatives because Lutheranism was a reform movement within the Roman Catholic Church rather than a root for another church. The restoration of Christian unity was the most significant item on Melanchthon's agenda. He advocated such unity in the curriculum of Wittenberg University as a star member of the theological faculty and as president from 1523 to 1524. He contended for educational and ecclesiastical reforms in his travel to other universities, such as Tübingen, Leipzig, and Jena; and he tried to initiate ecclesiastical reforms in various German territories and, with the assistance of others, in Prussia, Denmark, and Transylvania.

Melanchthon's Apology of the Augsburg Confession (1531) clearly illustrates how its author worked for Christian unity in the midst of bitter controversies. "In these controversies I have always made it a point to adhere as closely as possible to traditional doctrinal formulas in order to promote the attainment of concord." Explicating articles 1 to 3 on God, sin, and Christ, Melanchthon contended that the Lutheran movement "said nothing new" in the debate on original sin, or anything "that is alien to Scripture or to the church catholic . . . but cleansed and brought into light the most important statements in the Scriptures and the Fathers that had been obscured by the sophistic quarreling of recent theologians." Article 4 on justification is the first Lutheran monograph on the topic. Here, Melanchthon presents the pastoral power of being right with God by faith in Christ alone. "Terrors of conscience" are only consoled by total reliance on what God did: "by faith itself we are regarded as righteous for Christ's sake, that is, we are acceptable to God. And because 'to be justified' means that out of unrighteous people righteous people are made or regenerated, it also means that they are pronounced or regarded as righteous. . . . We reject the notion of merit."[19]

Justification is not just the beginning of a process of regeneration, as medieval Roman Catholic theology taught, but the decisive action of God to redeem sinners without merit. "Christ does not stop being our mediator after we are reborn. They err who imagine that he has merited only a first infusion of grace and that afterward we please God and merit eternal life by our fulfillment of the law. Christ remains the mediator." This is Melanchthon's pastoral answer to those who were terrified by God's wrath, which, as they were told in private and public confession, must be appeased by good works. He made a subtle but clear distinction between faith and merit. "We concede that works are truly meritorious, but not for the forgiveness of sins or justification. Works are meritorious for other bodily and spiritual rewards, which are bestowed in this life and in the life to come . . . according to that passage in Paul [1 Cor. 3:8], 'Each will receive wages according to the labor of each.'" To live in this distinction is often a severe struggle because faith has its existence in penitence and must grow stronger despite many temptations. What counts is the conviction "that God has accepted us on account of Christ by faith."[20]

Articles 7 and 8 (articles 5 and 6 on ministry and new obedience needed no defense) on the church again contend, "We have not said anything new here." The church is not "some Platonic republic" consisting of sinless people. On the contrary, "the ungodly" are in the church and even hold offices in it. But the church must have true unity in faith even though human traditions may differ. Melanchthon contended that Lutherans were loyal Catholics. "With a very grateful spirit we cherish the useful and ancient ordinances, especially when they contain a discipline by which it is profitable to educate and teach common folk and ignorant." The issue is not whether Scripture alone guides the church, but whether specific traditions, such as the Roman papacy, should have divine authority. "The question is whether or not the observances of human traditions are religious worship necessary for righteousness before God. This is the point at issue in this controversy. Once it has been decided, it will be possible to decide whether for the true unity of the church it is necessary to have similar human traditions everywhere."[21]

Articles 9 to 13 defend the Lutheran view of sacraments and their proper use (baptism, confession, Lord's Supper). In contrast to Luther, Melanchthon lists three genuine sacraments: "baptism, the Lord's Supper and absolution (the sacrament of repentance). For these rites have the commandment of God and the promise of grace, which is the essence of the New Testament." Melanchthon defended the unity of word and sacrament against radical, left-wing reformers like Ulrich Zwingli (1484–1531) or Thomas Müntzer (1490–1525), who affirmed only the authority of the word. "For just as the Word enters through the ear in order to strike the heart, so also the rite enters through the eye in order to move the heart. The word and the rite have the same effect." He then expressed his high regard for the ordained ministry:

Ulrich Zwingli

ordination to the office of word and sacrament could be called a sacrament because it is commanded by God and has the sign of the laying on of hands.[22]

Article 14 on church order again stresses Christian unity, speaking of "our greatest desire to retain the order of the church and the various ranks in the church—even though they were established by human authority." Article 15 views human traditions as ways to witness the gospel in the world. Lutherans "gladly keep the ancient traditions set up in the church because they are useful and promote tranquillity, and we interpret them in the best possible way, by excluding the opinion that they justify." Public worship is done more faithfully in Lutheran churches than in Catholic ones: "We keep the ancient canons better than our opponents." Above all, true pastoral care must make a proper distinction between liberty and traditionalism, be it the tradition of fasting or other forms of spiritual formation. "Liberty in these matters should be exercised moderately, so that the inexperienced may not take offense, and on account of abuse of liberty, become more hostile to the true teaching of the gospel."[23]

Article 18 (articles 16 on political order and 17 on Christ's return needed no defense) on free will distinguishes between "civil" and "spiritual" righteousness, "which is ascribed to the operation of the Holy Spirit in the regenerate." One is free to make decisions regarding life in this world but not regarding one's salvation; that is a matter of the Holy Spirit. Article 20 (article 19 on the cause of sin needed no defense) accuses medieval theologians of affirming "good works" as means of salvation. "Therefore, the blasphemy of attributing the honor of Christ to our works must not be tolerated. These theologians have lost all sense of shame if they dare to smuggle such thinking into the church."[24]

Article 21 on saints makes a clear distinction between "invocation" (the request of the living for help from the dead) and "veneration" (honoring the dead for what they accomplished when they were alive). Deceased saints, Melanchthon declared, should be venerated by giving thanks for what they did; they should be viewed as examples who can strengthen the faith of the living; and they should be imitated as models in their various callings on earth.[25] Lutherans affirm "only this much, that Scripture does not teach us to call upon the saints or to ask the saints for their help." "There is also one mediator between God and humankind, Christ Jesus" (1 Tim. 2:5). "They apply the merits of the saints to others in the same way as the merits of Christ (thereby transferring to the saints' merits the honor that properly belongs to Christ."[26] In article 22 on the Lord's Supper under both kinds (bread and wine), Melanchthon reminded Catholics that Lutherans continued a long tradition, still kept by the Greek Orthodox Church, when they offered bread and wine in the eucharist.[27] Article 23 on the marriage of priests also appeals to Scripture and tradition in its defense of such marriage. Marriage is "truly a divine ordinance" based on the command of Gen. 1:28; celibacy is "a special gift" that "is voluntary rather than obligatory," according to the tradition defended by the great church father of the West, Ambrose (340–397); and priests are more faithful married than celibate because marriage keeps them pure.[28]

In article 24 on the Mass, Melanchthon points to its weekly celebration among Lutherans who, like the ancient church fathers (again represented by Ambrose), call the Mass a "sacrifice of praise" and "consolation for the conscience." He reminded his opponents that masses for the dead were prayers for them rather than "the transfer, *ex opere operato*, of the Lord's Supper to the dead. . . . If they [the church fathers] were to come back to life now and were to see how their sayings are being used as pretexts to support the most notorious falsehoods that the opponents teach about *ex opere operato*, they would express themselves far differently."[29]

Article 27 (25 on confession and 26 on the distinction of foods are not defended) on monastic vows contends that such vows became entangled with notions of Christian perfection, and the history of monasticism discloses only the danger of a selfish morality claiming divine merit. That is why Lutherans are opposed to such vows, contending that "Christian perfection" ought to be part of every calling in life, "that is, growth in the fear of God, in faith, in the love of neighbor and in similar spiritual virtues."[30]

Finally, Article 28 on ecclesiastical power again affirms "the old division of episcopal power into "the power of order," that is, "the ministry of word and sacraments" and "the power of jurisdiction," namely, "the authority to excommunicate those who are guilty of public offenses or to absolve them if they are repentant and ask for absolution." Bishops must be subject to the word of God, which allows them to create traditions, "but they must not be required acts of worship but a means for preserving order in the church for the sake of peace."[31]

Melanchthon's ecumenical platform conceded too much to Catholics, according to conservative Lutherans who called themselves Gnesio-Lutherans (Greek: *gnesios*, "authentic"). So the Melanchthon party, known as Philippists (from his first name, Philipp), soon became embroiled in controversy, being accused of making unnecessary concessions to Catholics and Calvinists, thus earning the nickname Crypto-Calvinists (Greek: *kryptos*, "secret"). But Melanchthon clearly understood Luther's cause as a call to rid the church of abuses and to reaffirm unity, not uniformity, in the gospel. But it took some time to appreciate this legacy of Melanchthon.[32] As the acknowledged leader of Lutheranism after Luther's death, he had a stronger sagacity than Luther for the danger of allowing territorial rulers to become "emergency bishops." That is why he lobbied to retain the traditional but reformed episcopal constitution of the church, which would preserve the proper distinction between church and state. He had persuaded Luther and the Wittenberg faculty to see this matter his way. Consequently, they presented an official "opinion" to Elector John Frederick of Saxony in 1545.

> To keep order in the church, one must have bishops, a degree higher than priests, and they must have a designated authority. One must have a number of them to ordain, to instruct ordinands, to make visitations, to serve on tribunals, to advise, to write, to represent, and to staff synods and councils, just as Athanasius, Basil, Ambrose and Augustine had to do all these things in order to preserve correct doctrine in their own and in other churches. If the existing form of episcopacy were torn apart, barbarism and desolation without end would result, for temporal power and princes are burdened with other matters, and only a few respect the church or reflect on its teachings.[33]

Although the historic episcopate, in a reformed sense, was quite acceptable to Melanchthon as the best way to strengthen the ministry of the gospel in a sinful world, the papacy of the Western church was not. It belonged to the dangerous abuses together with a domineering cult of the saints, the adoration of the eucharistic host at the Feast of Corpus Christi, and the tyrannical use of the sacrament of penance that destroyed the liberty of conscience. Prevailing Catholic abuses and controversies between Lutheran factions on doctrine and life prevented Melanchthon from achieving his goal of creating a clear, commonly accepted doctrine that would make Lutheranism the ecumenical movement it was to be, according to Luther, who rejected any notion of founding a church. This goal may have been unrealistic because doctrine and life are also linked to human emotions and the power of symbols. That is why Melanchthon has to be seen more as the father of the Lutheran orthodoxy that dominated Lutheranism for almost a century after his death.

But Melanchthon needs to be remembered as the reformer who related the world of humanism to the Lutheran movement and to the Reformation in general. He united the revival of the Greco-Roman world with the renewal of Christendom, specifically the historical-critical view of sources with the interpretation of the Bible. This union of the intellectual legacy of Western antiquity with ancient Christianity became most visible in Melanchthon's educational reform, especially in the universities; he deserves the honorable title of "teacher of Germany" (*praeceptor*

Germaniae).[34] As such, he saved Lutheranism from an anti-intellectual spiritualism (represented by radical, left-wing reformers) and from a rationalist supernaturalism (represented by the Catholic adherents to medieval philosophy). At the same time, he singled out the best of the two worlds so that reason and revelation, knowledge and faith, philosophy and theology could provide an attractive platform for a creative Christian witness in the world.

Judged by Rome

The Council of Trent (in northern Italy, 1545–1563, with interruptions) disclosed Rome's judgment on Lutheranism. Ever since Luther's systematic attack on abuses and his call for reform in 1520, there had been many demands for a council led by Rome to deal with the growing schism between the reformers and their church. Only when Emperor Charles V called for a council, after the condemnation of Luther at Worms in 1521, did Rome begin to plan one. A quarter century later, Pope Paul III finally agreed to convene a council, aware that the division within Western Christendom had become a reality. What had been originally viewed as a council governed by honest dialogue for Christian unity now became a court ready to render a verdict of guilty on Lutherans and other reformers in absentia. Although some Protestant delegates had been sent to Trent late in 1552 under pressure from the emperor, their conditions for participation were immediately rejected by the council fathers; Protestants had demanded that the pope must accept councils as the highest authority in the church, and the debate on all decrees already approved must be reopened.[35]

Though seemingly uniform in its formal decisions, the council was marked by lack of cooperation among bishops, bewilderment regarding the division in the church, and haste on the part of Rome to get the conciliar job done. The first phase (1545–1547) began with thirty-one Italian bishops who eventually were joined by non-Italian delegates. The newly founded Jesuit order, established in 1540 as the Society of Jesus, led by its general, Ignatius of Loyola (1491–1556), dominated the proceedings with what would become known as the trademarks of the order: absolute obedience to the pope, rigorous spiritual and academic discipline, and dedication to the Catholic cause among non-Catholics. The council sessions of the first phase dealt with the key differences between Lutheranism and Catholicism, the authority of the Bible, and the doctrine of justification by faith.

With respect to the authority of the Bible, the council reaffirmed the authority of the apostolic traditions embedded in the Holy Scriptures. Accordingly, the Bible is the sufficient source of revelation that cannot be surpassed but only interpreted. But this interpretation is only valid when it is done by the ecclesiastical tradition represented by the general council of bishops chaired by the pope. Here, the Council of Trent secured the parallel authorities of Scripture, anchored in the apostolic legacy, and tradition, embodied in the apostolic succession of bishops. This succession was viewed as the implication of the promise of Jesus that Peter, "the rock," would be the foundation on which Jesus would build his church (Matt. 16:18). Accordingly, Peter and his successors, seen as presiding bishops in Rome, would constitute the teaching authority in the church (Latin: *magisterium*). It is truly exercised when the council of bishops, assembled and chaired by the bishop of Rome, the pope, decrees specific articles of faith by extending apostolic assertions recorded in Scripture to their full meaning for the sake of shepherding the faithful. Thus, for example, the biblical assertion of Christ's birth by the Virgin Mary can be extended to the notion of Mary's own virgin birth through her immaculate conception in the womb of her mother, Anna, a dogma defined on December 8, 1854, by Pope Pius IX.[36] According to Catholic teaching, this is not a new truth besides biblical truth but a theological extension through a dogma illuminating the traditional truth of Mary's virgin birth. The dogma of Mary's assumption into heaven, defined by Pope Pius XII on November 1, 1950, was like a logical sequence to the dogma of Mary's immaculate conception,[37] but it had even greater significance because it was promulgated as infallible by a pope who could invoke papal infallibility since Vatican I in 1870. In terms of the council's decree: as the "supreme teacher of all Christians," he has the authority "in matters of faith and morals" to issue an infallible dogma even without the consent of the church.[38]

With respect to the doctrine of justification by faith, the council endured a long debate on the relationship between divine grace and human nature. In this debate, the general of the Augustinian Hermits (Luther's monastic order), Jerome Seripando, prevailed in stressing grace over nature, echoing the conviction of Augustine that humankind is helplessly entangled in sin and can only be saved by the grace of God. Consequently, the council taught that human sin can only be overcome through the merits of Christ rather than by any human effort and that these merits are mediated through the sacrament of baptism. But the council fathers made a distinction between *original sin* (the sin of Adam and Eve) and *concupiscence* (the continual desire to sin). The council taught that baptism remits only original sin and its punishment, not the sins of concupiscence. This theological assertion was based on Augustine to show that Luther's view was not Augustinian. For Luther taught that all of sin, regardless of such distinctions as original sin and concupiscence, is forgiven only by faith alone in Christ alone. Justification is not one action by God in Christ, but the first step in a process or journey that gradually returns sinners to the divine family; the family began with Adam and is redeemed through Christ, the second Adam. Justification, then, is a conversion process.[39] Christ and the church guide this process through sacramental grace, promising eternal life as a reward or merit. The council did not want to be silent about merit. But instead of linking it to human effort, as much of medieval theology had done, it viewed merit in the context of divine promise and grace. The final formulation of the relationship between divine grace and human merit connects both in a hairline fashion. On the one hand, "the good deeds of one justified are gifts of God"; on the other hand, they are divine gifts in such a way that they are also "the good merits of that same justified person." In short, the justified person, by the good deeds that he or she does, through the grace of God and the merit of Jesus Christ (of whom he is a living member), truly merits an increase of grace, eternal life, and the attainment of that eternal life (if indeed he die in grace), as well as an increase in glory.[40]

Such subtle phrasing of the problematic issue of the cooperation of divine grace and human will tried to save the old medieval doctrine of free will: human beings have been created by God to make a decision to accept the grace of God. Catholic interpreters of Trent insist that, although the "process" of justification always begins with God, there is the need for human cooperation. *Cooperation* here means that the sinner does not reject grace. "To be justified is to be turned freely by God's grace from sin to divine friendship. This process of being turned involves a human turning and thus cooperation."[41] Trent stressed faith in the process of salvation, but not faith alone, as Lutherans would have liked to hear. Moreover, Trent hammered out its doctrine of justification with the help of the old scholastic categories of cause and effect: The final cause is eternal life; the efficient cause is the Holy Spirit, who cleanses the justified; and the final effect is the satisfaction of Jesus, made for sinful creatures to God.

Though stressing the primacy of faith in the process, the council's insistence on human cooperation prevented any agreement with Lutheranism. When all was said and done by Trent on justification, Lutherans rejected its formulations point by point.[42] Trent, on the other hand, labeled "justification by faith alone" as an erroneous teaching.[43] The remaining sessions of the council reaffirmed old teachings, such as the understanding of sacraments, and strengthened discipline by removing many abuses of power on the part of clergy and bishops. Accordingly, seminaries were instituted in order to guarantee a uniform academic and spiritual formation for future leaders in the church. In addition, the council created strict rules for the well-being of the church as an institution: specific norms for the appointment of cardinals and bishops, annual assemblies of the diocese, and annual visitations of the diocese by the bishop.

An official papal bull by Pius IV in 1564 sanctioned the decisions of the council as the formal rejection of Protestantism. In addition, Rome summarized the dogmas of Trent in the "Profession of the Tridentine Faith," to which all clergy had to swear allegiance; it was simultaneously an oath of obedience to the pope. This action was followed by five other components that were to secure and to enforce the decrees of Trent: (1) the Index of Prohibited Books, a constantly updated bibliography disclosing anti-Catholic, mostly Protestant, teachings (no longer in effect today); (2) the Roman Catechism, to be used by the clergy to propagate the teachings of Trent; (3) the Roman Breviary to be used by clergy for their spiritual discipline (especially daily prayer); (4) the Roman Missal, to coordinate worship through the various celebrations of the Mass; (5) a new edition of the Latin Bible, the Vulgate, which was to represent the final edition of the Latin Bible.

What became known as Tridentinism was created through the Jesuit theologian, bishop, cardinal, and saint, Robert Bellarmine (1542–1621), who spent much of his

life studying and refuting Luther, John Calvin, and other Protestant theologians. His polemical views were taught at the Roman College and summarized in his massive work titled *Controversies.* Its three volumes appeared in twenty editions beginning in 1593 and represented the most popular summation of Catholic teachings according to Trent. As cardinal, Bellarmine spent more than a decade in Rome to create five so-called *Congregations* (papal administrative departments) that were to supervise dogma and discipline. The most important of these was the one on faith, better known as the Holy Office of Inquisition.[44] Bellarmine represented the sophisticated, indeed fair-minded voice of the so-called Counter-Reformation, which, dominated by Jesuits, engaged in a systematic refutation of Protestantism through theological education and political power.

Cardinal Bellarmine

The streamlined teachings of the Council of Trent created an ideologically charged Catholicism intent on closing the door to any dialogue between Rome and Lutheranism or Protestantism. Though not explicitly named, Luther was condemned because he did not integrate his totally Christocentric faith based on Scripture with the Catholic tradition defined by what Rome called its apostolic tradition. At the same time, the rejection of the chief Lutheran article of faith, justification by faith alone, opened the door to a restructuring of Catholic faith and ecclesiastical structure firmly controlled by Rome. In this sense, the opposition to the Protestant Reformation, once labeled Counter-Reformation, has also been called the Catholic Reformation because the Council of Trent removed many abuses and reorganized Catholicism. This reorganization had a strong pastoral component, calling for a clergy dedicated to serve and to lead parishes as vibrant witnesses of Christ and his successor, the pope in Rome. Clergy were to be faithful in the administration of sacraments, especially the Mass and confession; bishops were to ensure pastoral care in the parishes through parish records and visitations; and old abuses were to be abolished, such as superstition, magic, and witchcraft. To this extent, the post-Tridentine age was for Catholics a vast program of "social regimentation" and a period of severe testing for Lutherans.[45]

Intra-Lutheran Controversies

The Council of Trent removed any hope harbored by Philipp Melanchthon and the Philippists for any further constructive dialogue for unity. Opponents of Melanchthon, the Gnesio-Lutherans, felt that the time had come to establish a clear, anti-Catholic Lutheran identity. This quest for a systemic, dogmatic definition of Lutheranism engulfed German Lutheran theologians and their political supporters in theological controversies that debilitated the body of Lutheranism and marked it with ugly and enduring scars. The basic issue was the interpretation of the Augsburg Confession of 1530. Six controversies struggled with this issue. Four disputes dealt with the proper meaning of *justification by faith*. One tried to clarify Lutheran relations to Catholicism (what is essential and what is nonessential, adiaphorist); another dealt with relations to the Reformed or Calvinist tradition (because of the issue of how to interpret the Lord's Supper).

The Antinomian Controversy

This controversy wrestled with the question of whether or not Old Testament law should have authority over those who live under the New Testament promise. If one is justified by the gospel, is there still need for any law? How are law and gospel to be properly related? As early as 1527, John Agricola, one of Luther's disciples in Eisleben, had questioned Melanchthon's Roman view of penance as contrition (fear of punishment), confession (of sins), and satisfaction (doing good works). Not fear of the law and punishment lead to repentance, Agricola contended, but faith in the promise of the gospel. Luther managed to reconcile the opposing views for a while at a meeting at Torgau, calling the controversy a war of words. Faith in general knows the God who threatens punishment of sin, Luther declared, but only faith in justification before God through Christ forgives sin; thus, both fear and love move sinners to penance (as Luther repeatedly said in the Small Catechism).

But Agricola was not satisfied with Luther's compromise. After joining the Wittenberg faculty in 1536, he was accused of Antinomianism by colleagues who heard him deny the law (Greek: *nomos*). Indeed, Agricola preached and taught that true penance must focus on loyalty to the promise in baptism and not on fear of violation of divine law. The only law to be feared is the mandate of Jesus in Luke 24:47

that "repentance and forgiveness of sins must be proclaimed in his name to all nations." Consequently, only the gospel, not the law, leads to faith and penance.[46] Such an assertion so infuriated Luther that he executed, as it were, Agricola in absentia in an academic disputation: he prohibited the publication of his views but published them anonymously in 1537 with a refutation in a public disputation at the university and without Agricola's presence! When Luther's fury ceased, Agricola's wife, Elsa, managed to reconcile her husband with Luther, as did Melanchthon in the next two years.

In 1539, Agricola persuaded Luther to clarify his views on law and gospel in the treatise *Against the Antinomians.* In the treatise, Luther stressed the need for a proper distinction of law and gospel in the face of the tension between faith and idolatry: the law moves frightened sinners to faith in Christ, a faith that must be sustained by spiritual discipline against the work of the devil. Luther viewed Antinomians as idealists and dangerous *Schwärmer*, exemplified by Thomas Müntzer, who misled lawless peasants to revolt in the name of the gospel, envisaging a sinless society on earth; but the gospel needs the law because sin still plagues believers. When Agricola persisted in his teaching that the word *law* need not be used in theology, he was dismissed from the Wittenberg faculty in 1540, moved to Berlin, and continued to support Lutheranism there. He even published a retraction of his views, became a superintendent (or bishop), and continued his veneration of Luther.[47] But the controversy was revived again after Luther's death in 1546 by the Gnesio-Lutherans, led by Matthias Flacius, the most ardent disciples of Luther. They charged that Melanchthon and his disciples, the Philippists, propagated a confusion of law and gospel by teaching that the gospel alone creates true penance. The Gnesio-Lutherans viewed this stance as a shift from the pastoral language of Luther, who understood the gospel as consolation for troubled consciences. Moreover, Melanchthon had also linked the gospel with the law as moral precepts, ranging from natural law to the Decalogue. All this seemed to be too rationalistic and moralistic to the Gnesio-Lutherans.

The Synergist Controversy

This controversy struggled with the question of the cooperation between the human will and divine grace. Does justification by faith alone allow such cooperation? Or is salvation a matter of divine election, indeed predestination? The Augsburg Confession taught that there is "some measure of free will . . . to live an externally honorable life and to choose among the things reason comprehends." But salvation from sin "happens through the Holy Spirit, who is given through the Word of God."[48] But the Gnesio-Lutherans heard some Philippists say that the human will can "work together" (Greek: *synergein*) with divine grace to accomplish salvation. Flacius, therefore, accused some theologians of teaching *synergism*, a cooperation between penitent sinners and the Holy Spirit; he identified such teaching with Catholicism.

By 1556, the Gnesio-Lutherans exposed two Lutheran synergists at Leipzig, the superintendent John Pfeffinger and the leading theologian from Jena, Viktorin Strigel. Pfeffinger had published a treatise in 1555, titled *Five Questions Concerning the Freedom of the Will*, which tried to convey the notion that the human will had some role in accepting divine grace; otherwise, each person would be like a wooden block in the reception of divine grace, without any responsibility at all.[49] He was attacked by the Gnesio-Lutheran Nicholas von Amsdorf, who alleged that Pfeffinger made salvation dependent on free human assent. Flacius and Amsdorf then persuaded Elector John Frederick of Saxony to issue the *Book of Confutation*, refuting synergist errors; all pastors in the territory were to renounce them. Strigel refused to renounce and was imprisoned, then kept under house arrest. In a colloquy in Weimar in 1560, he and Flacius debated the issue. Flacius argued that *conversion* meant a passive reception of faith based on repentance. Strigel maintained that it was a lifelong process in which the human will played an active role. He compared the human will to the payment of a rich and poor man, stressing that even the poor man can pay although it may be only a penny. The word of God is always attached to the human will, Strigel contended, but regenerates the will and moves it to a response. But Flacius insisted that the human will is like a dead block of wood in the act of conversion; indeed, there is nothing but sin in the substance of human nature. To say that there is nothing good in human nature after the fall (Genesis 3) seemed to be heretical even to the friends of Flacius. So Elector John Frederick changed his mind and exiled Flacius from the territory! Strigel got scared and escaped from Leipzig, eventually residing in the Reformed (Calvinist) territory of the Palatinate, part of west Germany.

The Majoristic Controversy

Named after George Major (1502–1574), this controversy focused on the relationship between good works and salvation. What is the place of good works when one is justified by faith alone? Are they necessary for salvation? Major, a theologian from Wittenberg and supporter of Melanchthon, had tried to clarify the teaching of the Augsburg Confession "that good works should and must be done"[50] by using the phrase in 1551 "good works are necessary for salvation." He was immediately attacked by the Gnesio-Lutherans—Nicholas of Amsdorf, Matthias Flacius, and others. They defended the confessional position of doing good works, "not that a person relies on them to earn grace, but for God's sake and to God's praise."[51] Major, in turn, declared that he did not teach that good works merit salvation. *Good works*, he wrote, refer to everything done by Christians anchored in trust in the gospel; and *salvation* means all of Christian life, not just the event of becoming a Christian.[52] Justus Menius, the Philippist from Erfurt, tried to support Major by contending that "the new obedience is necessary for salvation."[53] Infuriated, Nicholas of Amsdorf replied with the provocative phrase "good works are harmful for salvation."[54] The Gnesio-Lutherans lobbied successfully for a synod in Eisenach in 1556. It demanded subscription to theses that obscured the terminology of the emotionally charged controversy: Although good works are necessary for salvation, the synod declared, human sin prevents using good works and the law for salvation. Philippists saw in the statement a denial of good works, which now seemed to be only hypothetically, but not actually, necessary. Some attending theologians even contended that good works are not necessary for salvation because Jesus upheld the law as a way of salvation and viewed good works as spontaneous fruits of the Holy Spirit.

A few years later, the controversy gained strength again when the Gnesio-Lutheran Andreas Musculus, a student and brother-in-law of Nicholas of Amsdorf, and the Philippist Abdias Praetorius locked theological horns in Frankfurt an der Oder. Musculus bitterly argued that good works come from faith alone rather than from the threat of the law; and Praetorius countered with the view that good works are part of the law, that is, its "third use" (besides leading to justice and penance; BC 587). By 1563, Praetorius withdrew to Wittenberg, but the controversy flared up again in Brandenburg, involving Gnesio-Lutheran and Philippist factions of the clergy. George Major returned to his work as a scholar and theologian in Wittenberg, editing some volumes of Luther's works and interpreting the Pauline Letters. Though quite influenced by Luther and Melanchthon, he seemed unable to hand on their legacy without obscuring it through unnecessary infighting.

The Osiandrian Controversy

Andreas Osiander (c. 1496–1552), principal Lutheran pastor in Nuremberg and first professor at the theological faculty in Königsberg, Prussia, initiated a controversy on justification by faith when he defined it as the indwelling (German: *Einwohnung*) of Christ in the believer. He intended to preserve a holistic view of justification: God reckons faith in Christ as righteousness and then regenerates, as Melanchthon had taught (to be "regarded righteous" and "made righteous" through faith conceived by the Word[55]). But most Lutheran theologians stressed the first part, forensic justification, and tended to neglect the second part, effective justification; they tried to stay away from any Catholic metaphysical view of infused grace. Osiander drew the wrath of Gnesio-Lutherans and Philippists in the final two years of his life when he spoke

Andreas Osiander

only of the effective justification that occurs when Christ, the living word, enters the heart of believers and makes them righteous.

After Osiander's death, the controversy continued, led by the Gnesio-Lutheran Flacius, who published sixteen treatises against him. Duke Albrecht of Prussia (also known as Albrecht of Brandenburg and as Grandmaster of the Teutonic Order), who initially had supported Osiander, asked theologians for a formal opinion on his professor and discovered that almost all Lutheran theologians rejected Osiandrianism, with the exception of the Württemberg theologians, led by John Brenz, who lobbied for a compromise without any success. The controversy turned ugly when a lone defender of Osiander, the court preacher of Duke Albert of Prussia, Jon Funck, was tried and beheaded in 1566. The quest for pure doctrine had become polluted by fanaticism.[56]

The Adiaphorist Controversy

This controversy arose after the defeat of Lutheran forces by Emperor Charles V in 1547. A year later, the victorious emperor assembled the territorial princes in Augsburg to negotiate a transitional agreement regarding religious unity until a general council of the church would produce a final solution, as promised by Rome. The key document, outlining a transitional arrangement, became known as the Augsburg Interim of 1548 and was adopted by a majority of princes. Its twenty-six articles called for a return to Catholic teachings and ceremonies, with some care for Lutheran concerns: *justification by faith* was defined as renewing divine love enabling believers to do good works without anticipating divine rewards; priests were allowed to marry; and Holy Communion was offered in both kinds.[57] But few territories implemented the interim agreement. Moreover, Rome, France, England, and other political authorities opposed the Augsburg Interim as a symbol of dominating Hapsburg power. Even Elector Maurice of Saxony, who had previously sided with the emperor, now disagreed with him and encouraged Lutheran theologians to work for a better theological compromise. Melanchthon and his supporters drafted a carefully worded statement, insisting on the Lutheran understanding of justification by faith and of the Mass, but accepting Catholic tradition, such as the bishop's power to ordain and liturgical ceremonies. The statement, adopted by the Saxon estates at an assembly in Leipzig in 1548, became known as the Leipzig Interim. Elector Maurice of Saxony and Duke Joachim II of Brandenburg adopted it as the basis for religious life in their territories. Melanchthon had used the strategy of making a difference between essentials (Greek: *adiaphora*) and nonessentials: the Lutheran view of justification by faith and of the Mass were essential for salvation; Catholic ceremonies and structure were not.

The Gnesio-Lutheran Flacius and his younger disciples in Wittenberg immediately opposed Melanchthon's compromise, contending that the agreement restored the power of the pope, the "Antichrist," and sacrificed the Christian freedom for which Lutherans had died in battle. The concept of adiaphora could not be used, argued the opponents, because in times of persecution, nonessentials are essential as faithful witnesses of the gospel.

Both sides used pastoral concerns in defense of their position. Gnesio-Lutherans thought that parishioners would be offended by adopting customs that had been abused, ranging from making the sign of the cross to prayers at shrines. Philippists thought that Lutheran theological sophistication might tolerate again Catholic customs in order to avoid the enforcement of every Catholic doctrine and structure, as had been done by military force in some territories. The controversy raged until 1552, when the Treaty of Passau prepared the way for the Peace of Augsburg in 1555, which left the matter of religion in the hands of territorial princes, be they Lutheran or Catholic. Nevertheless, the question of adiaphorist freedom (what can and cannot be accepted as essential for salvation) prevailed and remains an enduring challenge for Lutheran theology and practice.

The Crypto-Calvinist Controversy

This controversy dealt with the Augsburg Confession's language of Christ's true or real presence in the Lord's Supper.[58] How is *real* to be interpreted? Luther and the Gnesio-Lutherans refused to go beyond the literal meaning, agreeing with the reformer's position that there is "oral eating and drinking" in the eucharist; "it does not rest on human belief or unbelief but on the word and ordinance of God," Christ present "in and under" the bread and wine."[59] The Reformed (Calvinist) interpretation of Christ's eucharistic presence was anchored in John Calvin's view that the real presence of Christ (in contrast to unreal or deceptive) means that Christ is spiritually present in bread and wine but remains bodily in heaven, because a body cannot be in two locations at the same time. Calvin here agreed with the Aristotelian view of the distinction between soul and body, or physical and nonphysical entities. The sacramental entities or elements become instruments of the Holy Spirit, who facilitates Christ's eucharistic presence by bridging heaven and earth. Thus, Christ remains "seated at the right hand of God" (as the Apostles' Creed puts it) but also becomes present in the eucharistic bread and wine. Believers communicate with the resurrected Christ through prayer, proclamation, and other means, but the communication by faith is sealed, as it were, in the eucharist, which, like other events in the church, is a celebration of thanksgiving for God's love.[60] In short, Luther bequeathed to Lutheranism the notion that God can be present in Christ according to the divine will. Such ubiquity may be specific, as in word and sacrament, or general, as in creation. Calvin accepted only one way of God's ubiquity, namely, through the Holy Spirit, who empowers word, sacrament, and creation for divine purposes.

Mediation

Melanchthon tried to find a middle way between these two positions, hoping for a united Protestant (German-Swiss) front against Catholics. He already had softened the language of the Augsburg Confession in an altered version of 1540, known as *Variata*. Its article on the eucharist tried to be conciliatory to the Swiss reformers, especially Calvin. It stated that Christ is present "with" the bread and wine, omitting Luther's "in and under." But such language was linked to the problematic medieval view of consubstantiation (*con* is derived from the Latin *cum* ["with"]); Reformed theologians used the term to characterize the Lutheran position. Luther never used the term, and Lutheran theologians rejected it.[61] The Hamburg Lutheran pastor Joachim Westphal attacked the position of Calvin in 1565, accusing him of degrading the sacrament of the altar, as Zwingli had done before. After the Peace of Augsburg in 1555, Gnesio-Lutherans began to target Melanchthon as a dangerous compromiser, indeed, a betrayer of Lutheranism.

They staged a colloquy in Worms in 1557, demanding a recantation of the Philippist error regarding the Lord's Supper. In addition, they persuaded Elector John Frederick of Saxony to subscribe to a book of *Confutation* listing the Philippist errors. They also denounced the results of conferences in Frankfurt (1558) and Naumburg (1561) because they were supported by Elector Frederick III of the Palatinate, who had formally joined the Reformed tradition and had made it the religion of his territory; he claimed that Melanchthon's *Variata* of 1540 and the Reformed Heidelberg Catechism of 1563 agreed on the matter of the Lord's Supper.

The rapid rise of Calvinism and the Philippist attempt to find a way to unite with the Reformed tradition drove the Gnesio-Lutherans to even greater isolation. When both sides met for a last attempt to compromise in Altenberg in 1568 and 1569, they could not even agree any longer on the crucial topics of justification and good works. But the Wittenberg theologians remained convinced that Melanchthon was the faithful guardian of Luther's legacy. So they published six of his works, together with the three ancient ecumenical creeds (Nicene, Apostolic, and Athanasian) and titled the edition *Complete Summary of the Right, True Christian Doctrine of the Holy Evangelists*. The other part of Saxony, Albertine Saxony (separated from electoral Saxony), formally adopted this summation as the religious norm of the land. Both sides continued to publish polemical literature. But the Philippists never grew tired of praising Melanchthon as the architect of Lutheran unity, comparing him and Luther to the prophetic fraternity of the biblical Elijah and Elisha. Trying to stem the tide of Calvinism, Gnesio-Lutherans often succeeded in persuading territorial rulers to legislate against Reformed doctrine rather than overcoming it with theological arguments. The territory of Württemberg required all clergy to subscribe to Luther's view of ubiquity: that the whole Christ, with his physical and spiritual natures, is present in heaven and in the eucharist. Because most Philippists simply affirmed a generic eucharistic presence of Christ, as it were (based on Melanchthon's *Variata*, that Christ is present "with" bread and wine), they became subject to legal prosecution. Two of them, Albert Hardenberg in Bremen and Zacharius Ursinus in Breslau, were removed from office. They were now labeled crypto-Calvinists (Greek: *krypto*, "secret"), charged with promoting Calvinist sacramental theology. Ursinus did just that when he moved to the Palatinate and helped establish Calvinism there in 1561.

Melanchthon, who had tried to be as irenic as possible, died in the midst of all this factionalism in 1560, dismayed about "the madness of theologians" *(rabies theologorum)*.[62] He was buried under the lectern of the Castle Church in Wittenberg, next to Luther, who rested under the pulpit. Hindsight would see them always close together. In electoral Saxony, Calvinism was strictly forbidden, and the disciples of Melanchthon in Wittenberg, consisting of his son-in-law, Caspar Peucer, a professor of medicine, and theologian Christopher Pezel, tried to steer a middle course between Lutheran and Calvinist eucharistic doctrine. When the crypto-Calvinist theologian Viktorin Strigel announced a lecture in Leipzig, moderate Philippists locked him out of the lecture room! But radical Philippists continued their efforts to unite in some way with Calvinism in order to have more Protestant clout in Europe. They even had a secret correspondence with Calvin's successor in Geneva, Theodore Beza. That was too much for those Lutheran theologians who were committed to Luther's view that the eucharist mediates the real presence of Christ as a mystery without rational explanation.

Still, Philippists persisted in their drive toward unity with Calvinism. But at a colloquy in Dresden, Philippists drafted a consensus stating that there is a sacramental union between Christ and the eucharistic elements through the words of institution ("This is my body"). Such language avoided the notion of a union of two natures, which raised the question whether Christ's human body is fully shared with his divine body (as the Gnesio-Lutherans claimed); if so, his human body would be everywhere, even in "stone and wood." Rather, Christ's body and blood were truly "with" and "under" the bread and wine. The drafters of this consensus claimed that their position was in harmony with Luther's and Melanchthon's teaching as well as with the doctrine of the ancient church. But the Gnesio-Lutherans still viewed Philippists as crypto-Calvinists. Elector August of Saxony (1553–1586) agreed with them and had several Philippists, including Caspar Peucer, arrested in 1574. He spent twelve years in prison; some of the others died in jail. This ugly side of the controversy prompted many leaders of church and state to call for negotiations resulting in Lutheran unity even though it had to be done without some consensus with Calvinism. Electoral Saxony ended the controversy by declaring the Dresden

Consensus and Luther's catechisms as normative teachings. Such legislation was accompanied by the interpretation that Luther and Melanchthon had always been united in the essentials of Christian teaching; differences were attributed to their personalities and different historical contexts. But substantial differences remained among Lutherans. In Albertine Saxony, Philippists prevailed before and after 1574. The most visible Gnesio-Lutheran mind, Bishop John Wigand of Magdeburg, kept writing against them.

So far, mediation had failed to create Lutheran unity. One churchman finally succeeded in creating a theological foundation for unity: Jacob Andreae of Württemberg, who was the provost of the University of Tübingen (1561–1590). He traveled through the countryside in electoral Saxony and assisted Duke Julius of Braunschweig-Wolfenbüttel in introducing Lutheranism in his territory after 1568. Andreae also worked with two other churchmen who were eager to support the cause of unity: Martin Chemnitz, the superintendent of Braunschweig (1567–1584), a sophisticated supporter of Melanchthon, and Nicholas Selnecker, a Philippist theologian who was the superintendent and pastor of the famous St. Thomas Church in Leipzig (1568–1586).

Andreae used a brief theological summary as a formula for unity, consisting of five articles on justification, good works, free will, adiaphora, and the Lord's Supper. But a meeting of the various factions did not produce the desired unity. So Andreae switched from teaching to preaching, publishing his work as *Six Sermons on the Division among Theologians of the Augsburg Confession* in 1573. He affirmed both Gnesio-Lutheran and Philippist positions on the most sensitive issues; he abandoned radical views, such as the Flacian teaching that all of human nature is sinful or the Philippist notion of a cooperation between grace and human works (synergism). But leaders of Lutheranism in northern Germany, especially David Cytraeus of Rostock and Joachim Westphal of Hamburg, did not like the form of sermons as a platform for unity negotiations. They and some Württemberg theologians persuaded Andreae to change his work into a document of theses and antitheses, titled *Swabian Concord* (1574). Then the northern theologians, led by Chemnitz and Cytraeus, reworked the document into the *Swabian-Saxon Concord* (1575). Finally, Andreae used the influence of Duke Ulrich of Württemberg, Count George Ernst of Henneberg, and Margrave Karl of Baden to bring their theologians into the team of unity theologians, resulting in the *Maulbrunn Formula* (1576).

Help also came from Elector August, who had wanted to unite Lutherans in Luther's homeland. He asked Andreae and Selnecker to join other theologians in drafting a formula of concord. This effort was also supported by two other powerful territorial princes, Elector John George of Brandenburg and Julius of Braunschweig-Wolfenbüttel. A team of six of the unity theologians finally met at Torgau (from

May 28 to June 7, 1576): Andreae, Selnecker, Chemnitz, Cytraeus, Andreas Muscu-lus, and Christopher Körner. They composed a text for circulation in all of Germany. Their Torgau text was revised in Bergen, near Magdeburg, in 1577. The *Bergen Book* constituted a longer version of a formula of concord, known as the Solid Declara-tion, and Andreae summarized the *Torgau Book* in a draft called "Epitome." Both constituted the Formula of Concord of 1577. It united almost all Lutherans in Ger-many, be they Gnesio-Lutherans or Philippists, thus creatively combining the thought of Luther and Melanchthon; this last was well represented by Chemnitz and Cytraeus, who used his methodological framework in the drafting of this enduring concord.[63]

Three electoral princes, twenty dukes, twenty-four barons, thirty-eight imperial cities, and approximately eight thousand theologians subscribed to the formula. It intended to be, according to its subtitle, "A Thorough, Clear, Correct and Final Rep-etition and Explanation of Certain Articles of the Augsburg Confession on Which Controversy Has Arisen for a Time among Certain Theologians Adhering to This Confession, Resolved and Settled according to the Direction of God's Word and the Summary Formulation of Our Christian Teaching."[64]

A Formula of Concord

The Formula of Concord (FC) contains twelve articles, elaborated as "Solid Declara-tion" and summarized in an "Epitome." It begins with a statement on the Bible as the arbiter in controversies: "the binding summary, basis, rule and guiding principle, how All Teaching Is to be Judged in Accord with God's Word and How the Errors That Have Arisen Are to Be Explained and Decided in Christian Fashion."[65]

The Bible, then, has authority in its "prophetic and apostolic writings of the Old and New Testaments," not in every detail.[66] The drafters of the FC make it quite clear that they are not fundamentalists who believe in the literal inspiration of Holy Scrip-ture. Rather, they establish a hierarchy of authority, as it were, consisting of Holy Scripture and the ancient Christian tradition summarized in the three ecumenical creeds (Apostles', Nicene, and Athanasian). According to FC, Lutheran doctrine is grounded in this hierarchy of authority and is summarized in the various formula-tions known as Lutheran Confessions: the Augsburg Confession (1530), the Apology of the Augsburg Confession (1531), the Smalcald Articles (1537), and Luther's Large and Small Catechisms (1529).[67] These confessions represent "the summary and model of the teaching that Dr. Luther of blessed memory had thoroughly set forth in his writings," which are expositions of the word of God, "the only guiding principle and rule of all teaching."[68] The drafters of FC even set forth rules of theological engagement in case more controversies should arise. "We have come to fundamental,

clear agreement that we must steadfastly maintain the distinction between unnecessary, useless quarrels and disputes that are necessary. The former should not be
permitted to confuse the church since they tear down rather than edify. The latter,
when they occur, concern the articles of faith or the chief parts of Christian teaching; to preserve the truth, false teaching, which is contrary to these articles, must be
repudiated."[69]

Articles 1 (original sin) and 2 (free will or human powers) address the issues of
the synergist controversy. Using sophisticated Aristotelian terminology, FC distinguishes between substance (Latin: *substantia*) and accident *(accidens)*, between
"either a self-subsistent essence or something contingent to such an essence." Viewed
from this perspective, "original sin is not a substance but an accident."[70] FC thus
agrees with the core of the Christian tradition that there is something good left in
human nature even though its disposition is evil since Adam and Eve disobeyed God
(Genesis 3). Following such great teachers as Augustine and Luther, FC declares that
"original sin is not the nature itself but an accidens (that is, a contingent lack and
defect in nature)."[71]

Consequently, the human creature is "substantially" good, but "accidentally" sinful. Moreover, God is not the creator of sin; reason cannot fathom its true nature;
Satan is to be blamed for this evil disposition, which is transmitted by conception
and birth to all of humankind.[72] Regarding free will and human powers, FC teaches
that conversion, regeneration, or any other spiritual experience is initiated by God.
Any salvation from sin cannot be ascribed "to the human powers of the natural free
will—neither totally, halfway, somewhat, nor in the slightest and smallest bit—but
rather . . . to divine activity and to the Holy Spirit alone."[73] But such a stance does not
mean that one cannot turn to God to receive forgiveness of sin. "It is not God's will
that any are damned but that all turn to him and be saved."[74]

Article 3 (righteousness of faith before God) addresses the issues in the Osiandrian controversy on "righteousness of faith before God." How does the justification
of the sinner happen? "Faith does not make people righteous because it is such a
good work or such a good virtue, but because it lays hold of and accepts the merit of
Christ in the promise of the holy gospel." If one speaks of the indwelling of divine
righteousness in the human heart, as Osiander taught, one must view the indwelling
as the work of the Holy Spirit "which is the result of the righteousness of faith which
precedes it . . . the acceptance of poor sinners by grace, only because of Christ's obedience and merit." Thus, there is first "forensic righteousness," that is, God's justification of sinners on account of their faith in Christ; and then there is the effect of
justification, the sanctification of the heart through the work of the Holy Spirit. God
always works first outwardly through word and sacrament and then inwardly
through the gifts of the Holy Spirit.[75]

Article 4 (good works) addresses the issues in the Majorist controversy anchored in the question whether good works are necessary for salvation (because faith alone might do). Here, FC affirms the holistic view of faith, taught by Paul and Luther, offering a very quotable definition of faith. "Faith is a living, daring confidence in God's grace, so sure and certain that the believer would stake life itself on it a thousand times. This knowledge of and confidence in God's grace makes people glad and bold and happy in dealing with God and with all creatures."[76]

Articles 5 (law and gospel) and 6 (third use of the law) address the issues in the Antinomian controversy. Article 5 calls for a proper distinction of the preaching of repentance (law) and of forgiveness (gospel). The proper function of the law is "reproving sin and teaching good works." The proper function of the gospel is to communicate that "through him [Christ] alone we are restored to God's grace, obtain the forgiveness of sins through faith . . . and are saved eternally." One must avoid any confusion between law and gospel.[77]

Article 6 tries to clarify the use of God's law. It serves "(1) to maintain external discipline and respectability against dissolute, disobedient people [justice] and (2) to bring such people to a recognition of their sins [repentance]. (3) It is also used when those who have been born anew through God's Spirit, converted to the Lord, and had the veil of Moses removed for them, live and walk in the law [Christian formation]." The "third use of the law" is based on the realistic insight that believers need some kind of "spiritual formation" or discipline "so that they do not fall back on their own holiness and piety and under the appearance of God's Spirit establish their own service to God on the basis of their own choice, without God's Word or command." Article 6 views the third use of the law as a wedge against the enduring power of sin. "For the old creature, like a stubborn, recalcitrant donkey, is still a part of them, and it needs to be forced into obedience to Christ . . . until the sinful flesh is completely stripped away and people are perfectly renewed in the resurrection."[78]

Articles 7 (Lord's Supper), 8 (person of Christ), and 9 (Christ's descent into hell) address the issues in the crypto-Calvinist controversy. Article 7 stresses the "real presence" of Christ in the eucharist over against any limitations regarding what is real: Christ is present "under," "with," and "in" the bread and wine; and there is a "spiritual eating" by faith and an "oral eating" by mouth. The "words of institution" ("This my body," 1 Cor. 11:24-25) and the distribution of bread and wine are the instruments of Christ's real presence. "For wherever what Christ instituted is observed and his words are spoken over the bread and cup and wherever the consecrated bread and cup are distributed, Christ himself exercises his power through the spoken words, which are still his Word, by virtue of the power of the first institution. He wills that his Word be repeated." The article also draws attention away from the "holy elements" (consecrated bread and wine) to "holy time" in order to avoid the problem of "the reservation of the host" (the preservation of leftover bread in a container at the altar, the tabernacle). What is holy in the eucharistic "use" or "action" is "the entire external, visible administration of the Supper: the consecration, or words of institution, and the distribution and reception or oral partaking of the consecrated bread and wine, Christ's body and blood." The holy time of the Lord's Supper could be somewhat extended to bring consecrated bread and wine to the sick or other disabled people. But when the holy time ends, bread and wine would return to their nonconsecrated state. FC 7 also makes the helpful distinction between the efficacy and benefit of the Lord's Supper: the "words of institution" make the sacrament, not faith; but faith enjoys its benefit, the relationship with the living Christ and the forgiveness of sins.[79]

Article 8 defines the real presence of Christ in the Lord's Supper as the full presence of both natures of Christ, the human and the divine. Zwinglians, Calvinists, and some Philippists (crypto-Calvinists) had taught that only the divine nature is present in the eucharist because the human, physical nature of Christ cannot be in two places at the same time, at the right hand of God in heaven (as the ancient creeds declared) and in the consecrated bread and wine. FC 8 defends the presence of both natures in the eucharist, referring to the ancient doctrine of the equality of the two natures, the "communication of properties" (Latin: *communicatio idiomatum*), as defined by the Fourth Ecumenical Council of Chalcedon in 451: "Christ is truly God and truly man . . . acknowledged in two natures without confusion, without change, without division, without separation."[80] Accordingly, a division of the two natures of Christ, or giving priority to his divine nature, violated the tradition of the ancient creeds that Lutherans cherish; here, sacramentology becomes a matter of Christology. For whatever is said about the resurrected Christ must be said about his eucharistic presence. "Therefore, there is and remains in Christ only one single divine omnipotence, power, majesty and glory. They are the characteristics only of the divine nature; they shine forth, reveal and show themselves fully, but spontaneously, in, with and through the exalted assumed human nature in Christ."[81] Lutherans thus asserted "the majesty of the human nature" (Latin: *genus majestaticum*) against the teaching of the Reformed (Calvinist) tradition, the *extra Calvinisticum*: "that it is impossible for Christ, because of the characteristics of the human nature, to be in more than one place at the same time—much less to be bodily present in all places."[82]

Article 9 affirms the teaching of the ancient creeds regarding Christ's descent into hell. What is said here about this teaching was meant to apply to Christology as a whole (including Christ's real presence in the Lord's Supper). "We should not bother ourselves with lofty, sophisticated ideas about how this [descent into hell] occurred. . . . We can only hold to the Word. Thus, we retain the heart of this article and derive comfort from it, so that 'neither hell nor the devil can capture us' and all who believe in Christ."[83]

Article 10 addresses the issue in the adiaphorist controversy. FC 10 affirms that every Christian community has the right to have a variety of customs or rites "according to circumstance in an orderly and appropriate manner, without frivolity or offense, as seems most useful, beneficial and best for good order, Christian discipline, evangelical decorum and the building up of the church." But at a "time when confession is necessary" (Latin: *in statu confessionis*), that is, persecution, adiaphora become essentials again. If, for example, I am gagged and bound by adversaries and can move only one finger, I can make the sign of the cross as my only witness to Christ. Under normal conditions, I do not have to make the sign of the cross; it is a matter of indifference. But Christian freedom is often used to open the door to idolatry. "Human commands will ultimately increase and will be regarded as service to God equal to that which God has commanded; even worse, they will be given precedence over what he has commanded." FC 10 calls for a critical interpretation of the place of the church in the world in order to keep the church free from any deification of human power often masked in such areas as polity, doctrine, and ethics.[84]

Article 11 (eternal foreknowledge and divine election) addresses issues in a brief controversy between Lutherans and Calvinists in Strasbourg and Lower Saxony in 1563.[85] John Calvin and his successor, Theodore Beza, had taught "that God does not want all people to repent and believe the Gospel."[86] This teaching became known as divine "double predestination," that is, that God elects some human creatures to be damned and others to be saved. FC 11 sides with Luther, who taught that there is a difference between the hidden God, who does things one will never understand, and the revealed God, who loves human creatures through Jesus Christ. "We should concern ourselves with this revealed will of God, follow it, and devote our attention to it because the Holy Spirit bestows grace, power and ability through the Word, through which he calls us. We should therefore not attempt to fathom the abyss of God's hidden foreknowledge."[87]

Article 12 (factions that never accepted the Augsburg Confession) lists radical groups within the Reformation, especially "Anabaptists," "Schwenckfelders" (named after Kaspar von Schwenckfeld [1489–1561], who rejected externals as means of salvation, such as bread and wine in the eucharist) and "new anti-Trinitarians" or Unitarians (who reject the dogma of the Trinity).[88]

FC concludes with the declaration that all its articles conform to the word of God, the ancient ecumenical creeds, the Augsburg Confession and its Apology, as well as to Luther's Smalcald Articles and his two catechisms.[89] The following outline shows the relationship of articles in FC to the Augsburg Confession:

FC 1 (original sin) and 2 (free will): synergistic controversy; Augsburg Confession 2, 18, 19.

FC 3 righteousness: Osiandrian controversy; Augsburg Confession 4

FC 5 (law and gospel) and 6 (third use of the law): Antinomian controversy; Augsburg Confession 6

FC 7 (Lord's Supper) and 8 (person of Christ): crypto-Calvinist controversy; Augsburg Confession 10

FC 9 (Christ's descent into hell): controversy with Calvinists; Augsburg Confession 17

FC 10 (adiaphora): adiaphorist controversy; Augsburg Confession 15

FC 11 (divine election): controversy with Calvinists

FC 12 (factions and sects that never accepted Augsburg Confession).

The Church of the Lutheran Confessions

Exactly fifty years after the submission of the Augsburg Confession, on June 25, 1580, Lutherans published their formal teachings in the Book of Concord (later subtitled "The Confessions of the Evangelical Lutheran Church"). An extensive "catalogue of testimonies" from the Bible and the history of the church appeared in an appendix. It lists many ancient sources of doctrine, focusing on the Trinity and demonstrating the ecumenical and territorial character of nascent Lutheranism, as the original title indicates.

> Concordia
> Christian, Recapitulated, Unanimous Confession of the Teaching and Faith by the Undersigned Electors, Princes and Estates of the Augsburg Confession and by Their Theologians, [Whose Names Are Subscribed at the End of the Book]. With an Appended Declaration—Well Grounded in the Word of God as the Only Guiding Principle—of Several Articles about Which Controversy and Strife Occurred after Dr. Martin Luther's Blessed Death. Prepared for Publication with the Unanimous Agreement and Order of the Aforementioned Electors, Princes and Estates for the Instruction and Admonition of Their Lands, Churches, Schools and Descendants.[90]

The preface stresses the same intention. "We are minded not to manufacture anything new through this work of concord nor to depart in either substance or expression to the smallest degree from the divine truth, acknowledged and professed at one time by our blessed predecessors and us. . . . On the contrary, by the grace of the Holy Spirit we intend to persist and remain unanimously in this truth and to regulate all religious controversies and their explanations according to it."[91]

BC then begins with the text of the three ancient ecumenical creeds (the "Three Chief Symbols"). Lutheranism now had a canon, a norm and plumb line to discern what was edifying and abusive in the church. Its quick spread in Germany and Scandinavia was accompanied by the removal of abuses in the church. Lutherans agreed with the ancient wisdom that abuse should not eliminate proper use. Consequently, Scandinavian territories, together with many German principalities, kept such traditions as the historic episcopate (without any apostolic succession linked to Rome), the liturgy of the Mass (without any essential difference between how priests and baptized laity participate), and private confession (without any notions of merit). Lutherans wanted to be reformed Catholics who lived in harmony with Scripture and tradition as faithful witnesses of Christ in the world. Although the Peace of Augsburg in 1555 prescribed a territorial settlement of religious issues ("whoever rules the region determines its religion"), Lutherans tried to make the best of it by remaining committed to Christian unity, even though it seemed to become an increasingly elusive goal. For the BC understood Lutheranism as a reform movement within the church catholic, indeed within sixteenth-century Catholicism. At stake was the retrieval of the ancient Christian convictions for all of Christendom, and Lutheranism became the inevitable historical constellation for such a retrieval, even though it became an organized church when medieval Christendom refused reform.

Here follows a list of ten basic theological convictions that establish the identity of the church of the Lutheran Confessions in the sixteenth century. They reflect the way in which "a pure declaration of the truth might be transmitted to posterity."[92]

Affirming God's Loving Condescension as the Only Way to Salvation

God, the creator of the world, joins humanity in Jesus Christ in order to save disobedient sinners from eternal destruction. Consequently, God hides divine majesty in human weakness and is exposed to human violence in the suffering and death of Jesus. But in the resurrection of Jesus, God becomes the victor who overcomes the enslaving power of evil and death in the world. The gift of faith through the Holy Spirit, offered in the humanity of the word and the corporeality of the sacraments, becomes the means of survival until the day when believers will see God face to face.

This focus on condescension and corporeality, embodied in Christ, was a way to lift up the basic motif of the biblical message that the salvific encounter between God and human creatures is possible only through the initiative of God rather than any human endeavor, by faith alone in Christ alone through grace alone. At the same time, Lutheran God-talk, theology, stresses the earthly, temporal, and external ways in which God initiates and completes the work of salvation. Thus, Lutheranism rejects theological convictions that are grounded in an exclusively internal, mystical piety without external word and sacrament; such convictions were propagated by radical reformers in the sixteenth century, the *Schwärmer*, and subsequently by philosophical minds advocating a nonsacramental spirituality, pietists of various stripes. At the same time, Lutheranism rejects a theology of divine-human cooperation grounded in metaphysical speculation; such convictions were popular in sixteenth-century Catholicism and later, though in more moderate ways.

The church of the Lutheran Confessions viewed such faith in the condescending God as a guardian against any ecclesiastical triumphalism or selfish charismatic piety. For the divine treasure of salvation comes on earthen vessels rather than in the glory of an institution or the pride of believers claiming purity of spirit. Neither the power of historical events nor of political deeds in the world disclose the salvific power of God; it is manifested in the cruciform discipleship of believers, who anticipate glory only at the end of time.

The Gospel of Divine Justification in Christ as the Norm of Ecclesiastical Proclamation and as the Basis of Christian Life

God created humankind for communion with God and to participate in the divine work in the world. True humanity exists only when human creatures affirm this communion, making it the ground of their being and acting in the world. But they have abandoned communion with God through disobedience, self-deification, and idolatry; they have become sinners but still remain God's creatures.

God, however, willed a new beginning of the old relationship with human creatures, by grace alone in the life, death, and resurrection of Jesus. Thus, God provides a new life of forgiveness, free from the power of sin and filled with the hope of a never-ending relationship. Believers are destined to be Christ's disciples in the world, to praise God through worship as the inhaling of faith and through love of neighbor as the exhaling of faith. The gospel is the message about this gracious, loving action of God in Christ, and the whole activity of the church is centered and measured by this divine initiative.

Justification by faith in Christ is the legitimate biblically grounded alternative to the medieval theology and practice that viewed institutional rituals and obligations as necessary means for salvation. The church of the Lutheran Confessions, however, views all Christian thought, word, and action as means for propagating God's love of the world, that is, as missionary adiaphora rather than as essentials. Only God's revelation in Christ is essential for salvation; everything else serves to communicate this revelation. This focus on justifying faith without any expectation of merit serves as a guardian against the prevailing tendency to create an asocial Christian individualism or a utopian view of society as the kingdom of God in progress toward perfection. Lutheranism itself has succumbed at times to such tendencies and has to do a continual theological reality check in order to remain faithful to its confessional heritage. Such a reality check includes dialogue with other Christians because the call for faithful witness of God's gracious love is inextricably linked to Christian unity.

The Distinction of Law and Gospel as the Means to Safeguard the Message of Divine Grace

The word of God in the Bible addresses humankind as a demanding and judging word, as law, and as a liberating and renewing word, as gospel. This distinction safeguards the character of divine graciousness from any legalism, which perverts the graciously given divine righteousness into a meritoriously achieved human righteousness. Sinful human creatures innately favor this perversion and need the mirror of the law to see themselves as helpless creatures who need sheer grace to change their attitude, that is, do penance, and cling to the gospel, which promises forgiveness of sin through faith in Christ's victory over sin.

Thus, the law calls for justice and penance, driving sinful human creatures to the gospel as the true means of a joyful life with God in this world and in the one to come. If only the law were proclaimed, an unreal sense of haughtiness would rule the human heart, bound to end in despair about human paralysis in the face of evil. If only the gospel were proclaimed, divine grace would become cheap, a pious rhetoric without realistic involvement in the life of the world or a childish longing for utopia. That is why law and gospel must be properly distinguished; otherwise there would be a hopeless confusion about divine and human reality, a diabolic life (Greek: *diaballein*, "to throw about, to confuse").

The church of the Lutheran Confessions uses the distinction of law and gospel as the most significant component of the theological reality check that, like a compass, shows the proper direction to salvation. The law provides minimal justice to prevent total chaos in the world and creates a longing for a better life than one filled with sin, evil, and death; in this sense the law leads to a vision of change, to penance as the lens of faith through which one can see the better life promised by the gospel. But neither the law alone nor the gospel alone provides the much needed Christian realism. They should not be separated or united, but distinguished as a means to interpret the dialectic of earthly life, be it the daily grind of leisure and work or the scary struggle for survival. The law-gospel distinction safeguards against a gospel romanticism that tends to negate the daily grind against evil in the world, and it alerts believers not to make Christianity dependent solely on the fulfillment of ethical demands. Christians need law and gospel as guideposts on their way through the wilderness of the world to the city of God beyond it. Thus, law and gospel compel believers to faithful and careful action in the interim between Christ's first and second coming, the meantime when there is no glory without the cross.

The Prominence of Word and Sacrament as Necessary Means of Salvation through Which Christ Creates and Maintains His Church

Christ is truly present when the gospel is proclaimed, believers are initiated into the church through baptism, and Holy Communion is celebrated. In this manner, Christ grants reconciliation and gathers his community. This happens primarily in worship when the gathered congregation hears the word and receives the gifts of salvation. Here, God is honored and intercession for the world is made. Then follows the witness and service in the world.

Ordination into the service of words and sacrament is a divinely instituted office in the church, and it is Christ himself who works through this office. But there is freedom with regard to the way this office is established and organized, just as there is freedom with regard to church order and liturgical practice. It is not an arbitrary freedom but a freedom for responsible witness guided by the mandate for Christian unity. Word and sacrament are the most decisive marks of the unity of the church, which is a creation of God. Lutheranism reduced the marks of the medieval church to word and sacrament because they are firmly attested in the Bible and serve as a safeguard against regarding various other traditions, institutions, and practices as necessary for salvation. But word and sacrament do not exclude other ways of God's reconciling work in the world, such as ordination, confession, and institutional order even though Lutherans have frequently focused on some of these ways more than on others. But the church of the Lutheran Confessions views the prominence of word and sacrament as the only essential condition for Christian unity.

The Emphasis on the Priesthood of All the Baptized as an Indication that All Christians Are Equal before God and Have an Apostolic Obligation for Mission

To be *apostolic* means to be part of the Christian mission in the world mandated by Christ. All baptized members of the church are in the apostolic succession for witness in the world. The ordained office of the ministry is neither derived from the priesthood of all the baptized nor unrelated to it. Both are parallel to each other, and the priesthood of all the baptized has the duty and obligation to set up the ordained ministry and care for it.

This emphasis on lay ministry rejects the notion of an essential, qualitative, and spiritual difference between laity and clergy as the medieval church taught.

Lutheranism at times tends to create a "church of pastors" (in German, *Pastorenkirche*) and then needs to rediscover the ministry of the laity. In this sense, the church of the Lutheran Confessions represents an ecumenical bridge between churches subscribing to a spiritually elitist notion of ordination (the indelible character of the priesthood) or to the secular model of the pastor as professional (the congregation delegates its exclusive authority to a chosen leader). Lutheranism affirms the biblically attested view of the church as the people of God who are responsible for an orderly succession and execution of mission by the partnership of clergy and laity. The divinely instituted ordained office of the ministry may be functionally and hierarchically organized for the sake of an effective witness in the world in the freedom of the gospel.

The Affirmation of the World as the Creation of God, Who Guides the Earth to Divine Glory

God's inscrutable love creates life, which humankind ought to see as a host of embodied blessings. Day and night, food and weather, friendship and family, scientific discovery, and all the other varieties of human existence on earth ought to instill a deep sense of gratitude for all the gifts God provides. Yet the sin of ecological abuse often appears to be far greater than the need to offer thanks and praise to the Creator. Nevertheless, God does not withdraw from the earth but affirms its divine origin through the incarnation in Christ, who will bring the final victory over all sins. That is why the earth is to be shared in a partnership of human friendship and love; believers know that they cannot rule the world for their own advantage.

The church of the Lutheran Confessions rejects the medieval ideal of a piety that sees Christian perfection as an otherworldly, ascetic ideal calling for flight from the world. The renunciation of marriage and earthly vocations by Christian perfectionists is a questionable way to exorcise sin. For the human creature, not nature, needs a regeneration through word and sacrament in order to fulfill the divine mandate to cooperate with God in the affairs of the world, in the family, in economics, and in government. God charges humankind with the stewardship of creation; flight from the world (asceticism) and Christian attempts to purify it (puritanism) miss the mark of true Christian discipleship. The church of the Lutheran Confessions welcomes and supports worldly progress through science and technology as long as they do not lead to a destructive exploitation of nature.

Here, Lutherans affirm the penultimate character of all human endeavors in the light of the biblical message that this world will not be perfect until God transforms it.

The Designation of Worldly Christian Responsibility as Obedient Cooperation with God's Work in the World

God enlists human creatures in maintaining law and order in the world as a sign of divine love. Faith in the gospel liberates Christians for the call to work in the world without seeking their own advantage. They can now use their reason, works of love, even suffering, as ways to cooperate with God. But they must also know that such good works do not lead to their salvation from sin nor to a progressive Christian improvement of the world, an earthly reign of God, as it were. The church of the Lutheran Confessions teaches that the church is the partner of God in maintaining worldly order without, however, legitimizing it, as the medieval church tried to do. The church must be a watchdog in the world, called to discern whether churchly and worldly order supports or neglects the divine intention for maintaining a good creation.

The church of the Lutheran Confessions originated in a world when spirituality ruled over secularity in medieval Christendom. The rediscovery of Christian freedom, anchored in God's unconditional love for the world in Christ, opened up a new view of the world as the arena of divine work. This rediscovery became the basis for the Lutheran doctrine of two realms or kingdoms, according to which God works in both realms, the spiritual and the worldly. Although Lutheranism has, at times, misinterpreted this doctrine (viewing the church as subordinated to the state), a correct use of it calls for full involvement in the world without any notion of perfection. For a proper distinction, not separation, of the two realms enables Christians to work for justice, peace, and love, and at the same time to create a critical sense for the enduring temptation to injustice, violence, and tyranny.

Lutheran ethics, therefore, oppose a passive stance toward the world, affirming only a status quo; it tries to prevent the use of secular ideologies or the claim to use otherworldly tendencies as Christian, and it views each situation in the world from the position of the relationship between faith and social responsibility.

The Use of the Bible as Norm for Proclamation and Teaching in the Church with Simultaneous Attention to the Distinction, not Separation, between Gospel and Holy Scripture

The Bible is the norm of churchly proclamation and teaching because it attests to the gospel of Jesus Christ. The biblical literature as such is not the living gospel of Jesus Christ; it is disclosed as a message of salvation by the Holy Spirit, who creates faith as the means to receive the biblical message as the gospel. Thus, the gospel is the center of Holy Scripture. The interpretation of the Bible must be based on this center. The living word of proclamation transmits the gospel as the promise of salvation, and the proclamation must be derived from Holy Scripture in order to create faith through the Holy Spirit.

This view of scriptural authority rejects any notion of a biblical fundamentalism often disguised in the formula "Scripture alone" (in Latin, *sola scriptura*) and undergirded by the notion of a literal inspiration. Lutheranism also rejects the medieval custom of establishing biblical truth through a general council of bishops as the instruments of the Holy Spirit. At the same time, the church of the Lutheran Confessions frequently struggles with the question of the relationship between Scripture and Christian tradition because of the difficult distinction between text and context, analogous to the difficulty of distinguishing the gospel from what is not gospel in Holy Scripture. But a Christ-centered view of the Bible endures as the most cherished treasure of the church of the Lutheran Confessions.

Commitment to a Confession of the Church as the Means to Preserve a True Proclamation of the Gospel and Church Unity

Believing is inextricably linked to confessing or bearing witness. Such witness is not exhausted in an actual living confession but is also expressed in formulations and doctrines handed on from generation to generation. The church accepts them as binding norms and as means to preserve the church in space and time. The Lutheran

Confessions serve as such a binding norm centered in the Augsburg Confession and Luther's two catechisms. But they stand in a hierarchy of authority beginning with the gospel, followed by Holy Scripture and the ecumenical creeds.

Intensive Theological Efforts to Provide a Faithful and True Proclamation of the Gospel Here and Now

Lutheranism stresses both the historical tradition and living communication of salvation in Christ. The canon of Holy Scripture, church confessions, and the office of the ministry are the essential presuppositions and means of living communication in specific historical contexts. But the sources and methods of communication are not in themselves identical with the gospel and cannot guarantee its power. Lutherans reject any form of fundamentalism, be it biblical, doctrinal, or related to polity. They have learned, in the painful struggle with ecclesiastical triumphalism, that the freedom and power of the gospel are linked to a continual theological effort to distinguish between divine truth and human tradition. This effort involves a faithful, yet critical, exposure to Scripture and the church's tradition, accompanied by a critical study of contemporary culture. Moreover, there must be an encounter with other churches through dialogue seeking Christian unity and a listening to the spiritual and theological insights of the other churches. All such efforts are grounded in the conviction that Christ will preserve his church in the truth of the gospel.

Lutheran theology has put much emphasis on the proper distinction between gospel, Scripture, and tradition. At times, intra-Lutheran controversies have been part of the effort to clarify this distinction. In addition, Lutheran theological efforts to assure a faithful proclamation of the gospel also created a burden of diversity with a tendency toward the abstract. But in its best and brightest moments, Lutheran theology has achieved a good balance between theological reflection and ecclesiastical practice.

The Lutheran Confessions assembled in BC are decisive signposts in the history of Christian doctrine for they summarize the struggle for renewal in the sixteenth century, known as the Reformation. They are the evidence for confessional identity in the sixteenth century. But as documents in time, they are subject to human error and in need of correction on the basis of later ecumenical insights.

Luther's spiritual redirection, triggered by his intensive search for a merciful God behind the walls of monastic seclusion, was like an open fire rather than a cool stream. His dynamic experience cannot easily be transformed into cool, ecclesiastical doctrine; his faith will always be an enigma to theological and psychological architects of the church as a wise institution (in Latin, *ecclesia sapiens*). But Luther bequeathed to the church a theology of the cross focused on Christ as the source of transformation from earthly to eternal life. Being Lutheran means to focus on the cross of Christ in the heart. *Heart* is the biblical word for what makes humans tick, who they really are, and what they rely on. "For wherever your treasure is, there your heart will be also" (Matt. 6:21). The cross of Christ exorcises human life from the illusion of total individualism, from the sin of playing God. That is why the liturgy of baptism declares, "You have been marked by the cross of Christ forever."[93] It is a constant reminder that the time between birth and death reflects the interim, the meantime, between Christ's first and second advent. Lutherans call this reminder "preaching the law." It is the admonition to people in the world that they must be exorcised from the illusion of playing God and face the reality of life in obedience to God. The church, then, is the gathering of those who embody the ancient, apostolic sense of being a Christian who is like a "stranger" and "foreigner" in the world seeking a heavenly country (Heb. 11:13-16). Thus, Lutheran confessional identity means to experience the status of resident alien. This status offers a peculiar freedom and responsibility as well as a doxological sense of life in the face of the joyful future promised by the gospel.

In their own time, the Lutheran Confessions may have been viewed as diplomatic summaries by schismatic theologians. In hindsight, however, they are documentary evidence of a decisive historical constellation marked by a revolutionary conflict between the salvific word of God and the sinful arrogance of human power. This conflict was the source of the Lutheran reform movement, which attempted nothing more than a purification of Roman Catholicism according to a faithful interpretation of the Bible and the early Christian tradition. But European super-power politics rather than faithful reform would determine the immediate future with little regard for the ardent Lutheran desire to re-establish Christian unity.

4

Orthodoxy
1580–1675

The Territorial Imperative

The Peace of Augsburg in 1555 created Lutheran and Roman Catholic territorial churches under the authority of princes who functioned as heads of their churches (Latin: *summi episcopi,* "supreme bishops"). Lutheran churches were viewed as orthodox when they subscribed to the Lutheran Confessions in the Book of Concord of 1580; Catholic churches were guided by the norms of the Council of Trent (1545–1563). Lutheran orthodoxy was anchored in a university theology that tried to streamline all of Christian thought and life and to provide a single system for the sake of political and ecclesiastical uniformity. Its centers were universities whose graduates would become the pastors and teachers of "pure doctrine." Virtually all Lutheran territories in Germany and Scandinavia embraced the age of orthodoxy: electoral and ducal Saxony, Hesse, Württemberg, Brandenburg-Prussia, Braunschweig-Lüneburg, Pomerania, Strasbourg; Denmark, Norway, Sweden, Finland; and the Baltic states.[1]

John Brenz (1499–1570), the leading churchman of Württemberg, created a Lutheran model of a territorialism that united civil and spiritual powers; he also led

the reorganization of the University of Tübingen. The model is developed in the document titled the Great Church Order of 1559. It advocates a highly centralized territorial ecclesiastical polity with the territorial prince as the highest authority. The prince was to be assisted by a consistory (in German, *Kirchenrat*) of theologians and laymen working with the prince. Together they controlled the traditional church life, such as the calling of pastors, doctrine, worship, and financial management. A synod, made up of members of the consistory, had the special power to make church law and to excommunicate recalcitrant sinners. Superintendents (or bishops) controlled local clergy and congregations; their reports became the basis for the legislative work

John Brenz

of the consistory. This general system of a territorial fusion of church and state lasted in Germany until 1918–1919, when secular democratic principles won the day.

The territorial imperative can also be traced to philosophical ideas of the relationship between church and state, beginning with Marsilius of Padua's work *Defender of Peace* (*Defensor pacis*, 1324). He argued that, for the sake of good order, church and state should be controlled by rulers who derive their authority from the whole community rather than from a noble bloodline or the succession of popes. Thus, the church would no longer be an independent, indeed conflicting, polity entity, but part of a society of law and order headed by just leaders. Excommunication, therefore, was to be exercised by local congregations rather than by the church at large. Such a view became popular later among humanists, who also influenced the reformers of the sixteenth century.

The most notable defender of territorialism was Thomas Lüber (1524–1583), better known by his Latin name of Erastus, a physician and follower of Swiss reformer Ulrich Zwingli in Zurich and since 1558 professor in Heidelberg; he was also the personal physician of the Palatinate prince, Frederick III. Erastianism soon became the designation for a political system that viewed the territorial ruler as the highest Christian magistrate, mirroring the Old Testament pattern of the kings of Israel. Erastus thus opposed a Protestant theocracy as well as a Roman Catholic papalism that grants the highest spiritual authority to the church, be it in Geneva under a Calvinist-Puritan regime (first introduced by John Calvin in 1555) or in Rome under the pope. Instead, Erastianism called for a fair exercise of power by the territorial prince as the highest Christian magistrate. He would be assisted by an ecclesiastical court in the enforcement of laws through excommunication; and he was to seek advice from the clergy in matters of doctrine. Thus, Erastus advocated a political uniformity in territories but without tyranny. The basic elements of Erastianism stressed civil control over the church (rejecting its right to excommunicate) and the establishment and maintenance of a territorial religion as the basis for spiritual peace and political order.[2] These ideas became especially popular after the end of the Thirty Years' War (1648), especially in England, where the Enlightenment philosopher Thomas Hobbes (1588–1679) became the most ardent Erastian, though without Erastus's reverence for the church.

Not every Lutheran territorial ruler remained loyal to Lutheranism. In the Palatinate, Frederick III (1559–1576) adopted the Reformed (Calvinist) Heidelberg Catechism in 1563, influenced by theologians, an openness toward Western Calvinist Protestantism, and the immigration of Reformed Dutch refugees who escaped from Catholic Spanish domination in the Netherlands. Under the rule of Ludwig VI (1576–1583), Calvinism became again the enforced religion of the land. But many Lutheran nobles refused to change. The Thirty Years' War prevented civil unrest.

Elector Frederick V (1610–1623) turned to foreign policy as the leader of the Protestant Union against the Catholics. But the Protestants were defeated in the first phase of the war. The Reformed party prevailed, and the Palatinate was incorporated into neighboring territories by 1803.

Another exception was Brandenburg-Prussia, where Lutherans and Calvinists had occasional, polemic encounters with each other. When Elector John Sigismund turned Calvinist in 1613, he was resisted by the Lutheran constituency. It was the first time that the ruler of a territory was unable to impose his religion on his people; he remained a Calvinist but tolerated Lutheran subjects. Thus, the provisions of the Peace of Augsburg of 1555 seemed violated, because the people of the territory did not obey their ruler in matters of faith. The matter was finally settled when the Peace of Westphalia in 1648 granted religious equality between Lutheranism and Calvinism. After 1648, many Calvinists immigrated to Prussia from Western Europe.

In Denmark, orthodoxy was enforced by King Frederick II (1559–1588) through strict legislation, including censorship and rejection of foreign doctrines. This was exemplified by the dismissal of the most influential theologian at the University of Copenhagen, Niels Hemmingsen (1513–1600), who was accused of teaching a non-Lutheran, crypto-Calvinist doctrine of the Lord's Supper. This action by King Frederick II was governed by fear of foreign influence; he also refused to accept the German Formula of Concord of 1580. The state clearly dominated the church. The Danish king nominated bishops without advice from a consistory of the church (as was the custom in Germany), and an absolutistic view of political authority was endorsed by the church: the king is God's representative on earth, and even though the church has spiritual authority in matters of salvation, it is not an independent corporation with an independent canon law.[3]

Swedish Lutheranism avoided the intra-Lutheran controversies in Germany by steering a middle course between orthodoxy and a more liberal stance influenced by a foreign policy aiming at good relations with the house of Hapsburg and Poland. But Swedish kings always rejected Calvinism; they adopted the German Formula of Concord in 1663. The Swedish Lutheran folk church became accustomed to viewing monarchs as absolute rulers, like the ancient kings of Israel in the Old Testament. After 1719, the parliament, not the king, exercised the highest territorial power. Norway was annexed to Denmark and accepted the absolutist authority of the Danish kings in 1661. Although the Danish clergy tried to advocate its independence, Norwegian laws, drafted in Copenhagen, preserved the status quo. Clergy had to swear allegiance to the Danish king. Rumors about witchcraft only increased uniformity in religion, and orthodox Lutheranism created strong sentiments of penance and stressed pure doctrine. By 1645, clergy would perform weddings only if couples had a thorough knowledge of Luther's Small Catechism. Bible study and new hymns shaped Norwegian orthodoxy and edified the laity. Pastor Petter Dass (1647–1707) was the most influential poet of Lutheran orthodoxy; much of his work was based on the catechisms and was influenced by folk songs. Deviation from orthodoxy was not tolerated. The theologian Niels Svendsen (1606–1658) in Christiania was accused of being a *Schwärmer* (enthusiast) because of his mystical and apocalyptic teachings. After a verdict in court, he fled to Holland.

Finland, under the rule of Sweden, also experienced absolutist territorial power. Only Lutherans were acknowledged as citizens. Strong bishops, most of them from Sweden, enforced religious uniformity. The state university in Turku, founded in 1640, was staffed with a Swedish faculty. Schools taught orthodox doctrines; hearings at home by clergy tested orthodox teaching and praxis; and only persons who could read and participated in Holy Communion would be permitted to marry.

The Peace of Westphalia at the end of the Thirty Years' War in 1648 tempered territorial absolutism.[4] It affirmed the 1555 Peace of Augsburg, which had granted territorial rulers absolute authority in religious matters. Now, their authority was also extended to the Reformed (Calvinist) churches, which, like the Lutheran churches of the Augsburg Confession, had to be ruled by a Reformed prince in order to be tolerated. But the stipulations of the peace treaty also permitted, for the first time, other religious groups to stay in a territory not ruled by a prince of their religion. They could exercise their religion in private, without any official sanction but without the threat of exile or persecution, provided they obeyed territorial laws. Pacifistic groups, such as the Mennonites (rooted in the Swiss Anabaptist group called the Brethren [of Zurich]) were not tolerated. Moreover, imperial territories (the emperor's patrimonial dominions) were excused from the treaty's provisions so that in those lands inherited by the emperor, the stipulations of 1555 prevailed: under Catholic rulers, only Catholics were tolerated. Swedish diplomats succeeded in pushing through two exceptions: in Silesia, Lower Austria, and Hungary non-Roman Catholics could also exercise their religion in private.

Pope Innocent X issued an official protest against the Peace of Westphalia because of its compromise in the establishment of territorial religion. The peace weakened the Catholic superpowers, Hapsburg and Spain, and granted statehood to Protestant Switzerland and Holland. Various deviations from the Peace of Augsburg in 1555 opened the door to a secular view of the world and thus to what historians have dubbed modern times.

Lutheran orthodoxy justified the territorial imperative with its doctrine of two kingdoms (realms or regiments) that is usually traced to Augustine (354–430) and Luther. Luther stressed the proper distinction of the two divinely instituted realms, the realm of the world, governed by secular authority, and the realm of the Christian community, anchored in the gospel.[5] Christians belong to both realms; unbelievers belong only to the world. Neither authority, be it the secular government or the church, is to dominate the other. Because Luther experienced the domination of the church over secular government, he called on the German princes to become emergency bishops in order to avoid ecclesiastical tyranny.

Lutheran orthodoxy experienced both the positive and negative sides of such a call after Luther's death. Had he still been alive after the Peace of Augsburg, he certainly would have objected to any notion of enforcing religious uniformity by law for the sake of territorial peace and order. Luther taught that Christians must renounce any use of force in matters of faith, but they must permit the use of force for the sake of law and order. For Christians must always acknowledge the inevitable and powerful source of sin, anchored in the violation of the First Commandment to let God be God and not try to be "like God" (Gen. 3:5). Only when equity and justice are established is it possible to begin to obey the golden rule of the people of God, to love the neighbor as one loves oneself (Matt. 19:19). Looking at the world, Luther viewed the two realms as connected with three estates: the church, economics, and government. Here, he adopted parts of the medieval catechetical tradition that, in turn, was shaped by the moral philosophy of Aristotle. Government was to contain evil; economics was to manage nature as part of God's creation; and the church was to propagate the gospel. Measured by Luther's view of government, absolutist territorial power exceeded its God-given function when it enforced the propagation of the gospel in specific ways as orthodox (Roman Catholic, Lutheran, and so on).[6]

Philipp Melanchthon affirmed Luther's doctrine of two kingdoms but anchored the estate of government in natural law. Thus, he assigned more power to political rulers than Luther did. For they were not only agents of justice against human evil but also preservers of God's creation. Christians are to occupy various political offices, provided they do not confuse the divinely given distinction between political law and spiritual gospel. "Temporal power does not protect the soul, but with the sword and physical penalties it protects body and goods from the power of others."[7] Although Melanchthon advocated a greater power in the exercise of government, he, like Luther, never leaned toward an absolutist view that made the territorial ruler a supreme bishop. But the territorial imperative during the age of Lutheran orthodoxy tended to become the leitmotif, as it were, in the political sound of music, sidestepping, indeed ignoring, the careful distinction of church and state in the Lutheran Confessions, known as the doctrine of the two kingdoms.

Presuppositions

Lutheran orthodoxy lifted Luther from his historical context and viewed him as a prophet of indisputable divine truth. Theologians and churchmen wanted to preserve "the pure, infallible and unalterable Word of God" that Luther had rediscovered.[8] It became fashionable to portray him with an open Bible and lit candle, symbols of the true and Lutheran morality. Coins appeared in Germany with the inscription, "The word of God and Luther's thought will never come to naught." The Reformation was seen as a supernatural act of God, who had founded the Lutheran Church as an example of unadulterated preaching of the divine word and the proper administration of sacraments. Luther became an object of faith rather than a subject of historical research.[9] The theological faculty of Wittenberg University defended and perpetuated this hagiographic image of Luther. Other faculties joined in what was to become a massive attempt to develop a systematic theology designed to demonstrate the scientific truth of Lutheranism and the excellence of its ethos as the foundation of a Christian culture.

The scientific demonstration of theology begins with a concentration on the text of the Bible. It is read intensively by the theologian, with the assistance of philological methods in order to secure the original meaning of texts. Then, the meaning of individual biblical texts is summarized in "places" (Latin: *loci*), offering the reader a systematic survey of the meaning of the Bible for the sake of personal and communal spiritual and ethical discipline. Here, Melanchthon's brief systematic theology, the *Loci Communes* (1521), serves as a model. Thus, the interpretation of the Bible, *exegesis,* becomes the chief enterprise of Lutheran theology, resulting in *loci theologici* as the foundation of personal spiritual certainty. Some orthodox theologians recalled Luther's reference to three sources of theological work: "prayer" *(meditatio),* "eloquence" *(oratio),* and "temptation" *(tentatio).* It is a process leading to certainty.

Based on such certainty, systematic theology creates dogmatic insights that disclose the truth of God's existence, the power of divine reconciliation, and the errors within Christendom (2 Tim. 3:16). Properly executed, theology provides a scientific foundation for a life of "godliness" (*Gottseligkeit, pietas*). *Scientific* here means a logical arrangement of insights, grounded in the certainty about the truth of the Bible as the foundation for Christian survival in a world of sin, evil, and death.

Full-fledged orthodox theology combines its biblical foundation with reflection on the Lutheran Confessions as the most attractive way of summarizing the truth of the Bible. This is a move away from Melanchthon's humanistically oriented way of doing theology relying heavily on language and rhetoric. At the same time, Melanchthon's use of the notion of natural law is emphasized as an "ability of the soul" (Latin: *habitus*), echoing medieval Aristotelian anthropology. In this sense, the theologian becomes "a scholar of God" (*Gottesgelehrter),* enlightened by the Holy Spirit. Thus, there is a shift from an objective, scientific theology based on the biblical text to a subjective one, stressing the experience of salvation. The goal is the experience of salvation rather than the certainty of salvation in the Bible. This emphasis on the conversion of the mind, as it were, makes theology practical. It points to the goal of human existence under God rather than only to the certainty of God's existence as the redeemer of human sin in Christ.

The rebirth of Aristotelianism in the seventeenth century made it possible for Lutheran theologians to establish and secure Christian truths with philosophical ideas ranging from definitions of being (ontology) to logical assumptions of the afterlife (metaphysics). Although Luther's rejection of Aristotle as a helpmate of theology was not forgotten, Aristotle was cautiously used by the major minds of Lutheran orthodoxy. "Aristotelian philosophy is to be preferred above all others," declared the exemplary theologian John Gerhard, "because of its fuller way to do philosophy, and also because of opponents whom theology has to face; for most of them use Aristotelian philosophy."[10] The fuller use of philosophy referred to the teaching of ethics. It was a secular discipline for Luther, who taught Aristotelian ethics because good works have to be done for the sake of the neighbor in need rather than as means to redeem sins. Such redemption happened through faith in the merits of Christ and not through any human efforts. Consequently, Lutheran orthodox theologians used great caution regarding metaphysics.

Aristotle taught a logical connection between ontology and metaphysics: ontology (and anthropology) are viewed in a pyramidal structure, leading from sense perception at the bottom to the prime mover at the top; then the structure extends into a reversed pyramid depicting what is behind nature (Greek: *meta physis*). Orthodox theologians accepted this logical connection between worldly and otherworldly truths. But they traced the otherworldly truths to the divine revelation in the Bible, which was not logically connected to worldly truths. The basic otherworldly (metaphysical) truth is the revelation of God, the Christ who will in the end create a new world without sin, evil, and death. Worldly (physical) truth is the knowledge of God, the creator whose laws of nature sustain the physical world. It is known through reason whereas its redemption through Christ is known only through revelation. God, the Holy Spirit, provides the link between reason and revelation. In this sense, the dogma of the Trinity links both realms, the realm of the organic structure and value of the world and the realm of God. Both realms are not logically connected, as Aristotle taught, but theologically asserted within the framework of the Bible and the dogma of the Trinity. Some orthodox Lutheran theologians tried to present Christology in some metaphysical form related to Aristotelianism. But these attempts have not yet been well researched.[11]

Orthodoxy wanted to preserve the purity of Christian thought in a systemic way reflecting the age of the baroque (in Italian, *barocco*, referring to "quaint" or "grotesque"; in Spanish, *barroco*, an irregularly shaped pearl) with its concern for elaborate manners and taste. Thus, the typical product of such a focus, a systematic theology, began with extensive "prolegomena" (Latin: *prolegere*, "saying before"). Such an argument usually deals first with an elaboration of the quest for theology as scientific knowledge based on the Bible. Here, the decisions of the Catholic Council of Trent are targeted, especially its emphasis on the intimate link between Scripture and tradition. According to Lutheran orthodox theologians, Trent viewed Scripture as an unclear and ambiguous source of Christian truth, in need of interpretation by the allegedly inspired tradition of church councils (sessions of bishops chaired by the pope). But Scripture is clear and unambiguous, orthodoxy taught, because it is the word of God, which is, rather than reflects, divine revelation; as such it is "inspired by God" (2 Tim. 3:16). That is why the Bible is the unquestionable authority for Christian thought and life. Its inspiration makes it sufficient, efficacious, and inerrant. Some theologians taught a strict biblical fundamentalism, viewing the biblical canon as literally inspired. Other theologians regarded the interpretation of the Bible by the church fathers of the first five centuries as part of the inspired biblical truth, assuming an inspired ecclesiastical consensus (evidenced, for example, in the dogma of the Trinity).

The prolegomena led to the systematic elaboration of the doctrines of God, of Christ (Christology), of salvation (soteriology), of the church (ecclesiology), of the end of time (eschatology), and of moral theology (ethics). Here, orthodoxy used presuppositions that Luther denied, such as a general knowledge of God through nature, reason, and analogy. There is no longer a radical difference between the hidden and revealed God. Rather, there is a dialectical, indeed logical, connection in the work of God as creating (Father), redeeming (Son), and sustaining (Holy Spirit). This connection became the foundation for the most favored concept in Lutheran orthodoxy, the notion of an "order of salvation" (in Latin, *ordo salutis*). It integrated all the treated doctrines into a system propelled by the question of how God works in the process of salvation from sin. Accordingly, there is a logical sequence of salvation evident in seven steps: vocation, illumination, conversion, regeneration, justification, sanctification, and renovation—all evidence of the gradual work of grace by the trinitarian God. In this sense, divine salvation and human nature are "mystically united" *(unio mystica)*. Besides the order of salvation, there are the means of salvation, Word and sacraments. They are accompanied by penance, faith, temptation, prayer, and good works.

The notion of order was extended to the doctrine of the church but no longer as order of salvation. Here, church and society are viewed as mutual helpmates, based on the experience of the Reformation, a territorial Lutheranism combining church and state. Orthodox theologians rejected the Roman Catholic view of a salvific church order. They spoke of an ecclesiastical hierarchy of bishops, clergy, and councils in terms of a secular arrangement of the work of the church.

This work was usually seen in an order of activity encompassing preaching (homiletics), teaching (catechetics), and counseling (pastoral theology). Historical hindsight must also presuppose the age of baroque. It identified an intensification of the work of Renaissance art from a harmony of forms to much livelier shapes, to a thrilling immediacy, and to a differentiated diversity. All these and other components were united in the work of the Dutch painter Rembrandt (1606–1669), in the British poet John Milton (1608–1649), and in the architect of St. Paul's Cathedral in London, Christopher Wren (1633–1723). Music soared to new heights in the compositions of the German Lutheran musician Johann Sebastian Bach (1685–1750). Theaters and operas became popular. The end of the devastating Thirty Years' War (1648) seemed to create a hunger for order as well as for vivid expressions of human life and thought.

Most influential for liturgical and spiritual nurture were new hymns that shaped popular piety. The Lutheran poet and hymn writer Paul Gerhardt (1607–1676) became the most influential source of orthodox piety. He wrote more than a hundred German hymns, assisted by the musician John Crüger. Some minds turned mystical, such as the physician John Scheffler, who used the pen name Angelus Silesius (1624–1677) and converted from Lutheranism to Catholicism. He was influenced by the classic mystic Jacob Böhme (1575–1624), a meditating shoemaker who combined theological, astrological, and philosophical speculations in his writings about direct access to God. A mystical German society, the Rosicrucians, linked Christianity with Arabic thought and exhibited their views in an emblem showing a rose with a cross in its center, symbolizing the death and resurrection of Christ. The Württemberg churchman John Valentin Andreae (grandson of Jacob Andreae, a coauthor of the Formula of Concord in 1577), advocated reconciliation between these various groups, but with little success.

It was the Lutheran pastor and devotional writer John Arndt (1555–1621) who attracted people to a renewal of Christian life with the help of mystical insights. His works, *Four Books of True Christianity* (1605–1609), became best-sellers in the age of orthodoxy, though Lutheran orthodox theologians opposed any flirting with mysticism, Catholicism, and the Reformed (Calvinist) tradition. They strove for pure doctrine defended with polemics. Consequently, seventeenth-century Lutheranism was dominated by a spirituality enforced through preaching, teaching, and even territorial laws. Attendance at worship, especially Holy Communion, was based on examinations of orthodoxy as taught by the

John Arndt

institutional church and its approved theologians. Princes and pastors were united in the attempt to purify the morality of a decadent continent through a uniform theology and piety. Freedom of conscience and religious tolerance were presuppositions of a not distant future.

The Quest for Pure Doctrine

Graduates of Tübingen University are credited as the founders of orthodoxy in Wittenberg, led by Aegidius Hunnius (1530–1603), Polykarp Leyser (1552–1610), and Leonhart Hutter (1563–1616), who had also studied in Strasbourg. They, together with others, had the strong support of Elector Frederick William of Saxony, who desired to preserve Wittenberg University as "the chair of Luther" (*cathedra Lutheri*). They also aimed to continue the work of Martin Chemnitz, an architect of the Formula of Concord, dubbed as "the second Martin" and remembered in the age of orthodox by the dictum: "If Martin [Chemnitz] had not been, Martin [Luther] would hardly have remained."[12]

Hutter tried to be the most orthodox theologian by dislodging the enduring summary of Lutheran theology, Melanchthon's *Loci,* and replacing it with his own *Compendium* in 1610.[13] The work deals with thirty-four topics and is catechetically organized in terms of questions and answers. Each topic is biblically grounded and explicated according to the formulations of the Augsburg Confession and the Formula of Concord. Hutter cites as his literary partners Luther, Melanchthon, Chemnitz, and Hunnius. He praises Melanchthon as an academician but views him as too liberal because of his rapprochement with Calvinism, the target of Hutter's polemics. His *Compendium* became the standard work of theology; he propagated his views as president of Wittenberg University, as inspector of schools in electoral Saxony, and as member of the powerful consistory, which, like a department for religion and morals, oversaw public life in the territory for the sake of uniformity.

The second generation of orthodox theologians in Wittenberg was led by John Andreas Quenstedt (1617–1688), who published an exemplary theological, confessional system in the work *Didactic, Polemical, or Systematic Theology* (1685). It tried to show how orthodox Lutheran thought represents an analytical coherent system based on the Bible.[14] The chief voice of orthodoxy in Jena, intimately linked to the Wittenberg theology, was John Gerhard (1582–1637). He was an admirer of the

John Gerhard

popular writer John Arndt, who had ministered to him when he was seriously ill at age fifteen. As president and dean of Wittenberg University, Gerhard had great influence in Germany. His work is best summarized in nine volumes, titled *Loci theologici* (Theological loci, 1610–1622).[15] It is the magnum opus of Lutheran orthodoxy, contending on every page that pure doctrine is derived from biblical revelation and explicates the unconditional authority of Jesus Christ. Moreover, Gerhard also added a Christian ethics showing how doctrine is to be "used" (in Latin, *de usu*).

But Jena also was the home of a more moderate orthodoxy represented by John Musäus (1613–1681). He linked the pure doctrine of Christ with a natural theology that tolerated philosophical metaphysical insights. Accordingly, God's work of redemption can be perceived in creation and not exclusively in Christ.[16]

German Lutheran orthodoxy in the West was defended at the universities of Marburg and Giessen. The chief theologian was Balthasar Mentzer (1565–1627), who separated the concept of pure doctrine from Calvinism, a threat in the region. He exhibited great analytical skills, showing that pure doctrine in the Bible and the Lutheran Confessions are the results of accepted logical operations. He summarized the results of his work in a widely read publication, *Theologisches Handbüchlein* (Little Theological Handbook) in 1620.[17]

The University of Strasbourg, then on German soil, was dominated by a group known as the "Johannine triad": John Schmidt (1594–1658), John Dorsche (1597–1658), and John Dannhauer (1603–1666). Dannhauer was the most significant voice of the three. As director of the seminary and president of the consistory (*Kirchenkonvent*), he had great influence in combating Catholicism, Calvinism, and nonorthodox Lutheranism. His view of pure doctrine could not be combined with any ecumenical efforts to unite Catholics and Protestants. It is summarized in his dogmatics, *Hodosophia christiana sive theologia positiva* (Christian wisdom or positive theology, 1649). It is a portrayal of how fallen human creatures regain heaven in twelve ways, described in such images as pilgrim (earthly life), candlestick (the church as light in the world), and hindrances (sin, temptation). More than fifty other Latin books make Dannhauer one of the most prolific orthodox theologians.

Lutheran orthodoxy at the old University of Leipzig was best represented by John Hülsemann (1602–1661), whose textbook, *Breviarium theologiae* (A short summary of theology, 1641), was in wide use. He used his power as pastor of St. Nicolai Church and as bishop to propagate pure doctrine as a series of fundamental articles based on the Bible and the Lutheran Confessions.

In the north, the quest for pure doctrine was pursued at the University of Rostock and in Copenhagen, Denmark. John Quistorp Sr. (1584–1648) and his son John (1624–1669) advocated a strict spiritual discipline in tracts and sermons, stressing Bible study, rejection of polemics, and simple church services. They were supported by the theologian, pastor, and superintendent Henry Müller (1631–1675), who viewed pure doctrine more as a style of life than an academic enterprise. This trend toward piety is signaled in German rather than Latin publications, such as *Himmlischer Liebeskuss* (Heavenly kiss of love, 1659) and the hymnal *Geistliche Seelenmusik* (Spiritual music of the soul, 1659). In Copenhagen, Hans Resen (1561–1638) defended Lutheranism as "the holy faith" (in the tract *De sancta fide*, 1614), and as bishop in Zeeland, established Lutheran orthodoxy. But its best exponent was Resen's disciple, Jesper Brochmand, whose major work, *Universae theologiae systema* (A system of universal theology, 1633) made him the Danish John Gerhard, well known beyond the borders of Denmark.[18] His colleague, Cort Aslaksson (1564–1624), a Norwegian, defended the Formula of Concord but also had broad interests ranging from astronomy to physics.[19]

The very embodiment of Lutheran orthodoxy was Abraham Calov (1612–1686), raised, trained, and active in Königsberg, Prussia, and Wittenberg. He had his greatest influence as the superintendent of the Saxon churches and as "distinguished professor" *(professor primarius)*. He possessed all the qualities of a churchman of his time: an encyclopedic memory, an indefatigable industry, linguistic skills, effective administration, and an inflexible zeal for what he thought was pure doctrine as the deposit of divine truth. Immodest enough to call himself "a vigorous athlete of Christ" *(strenuus Christi athleta)*, he combined all of these qualities in a style of teaching that attracted hordes of students. Some territorial rulers prohibited their young men from studying in Wittenberg while Calov was there. More than five hundred students would crowd into one of his lectures. His literary output was amazing: twenty-eight books devoted to a single controversy and series of oversized volumes on every phase of biblical and theological imagination. Best known were a gigantic commentary on the whole Bible, *Biblia illustrata* (The illustrated Bible, 1672–1676), and twelve volumes under the title *Systema locorum theologicorum* (A system of theological loci, 1655–1677). It was later summarized for speedier reading as a handbook titled *Apodixis articulorum fidei* (Presentation of articles of faith), offering nonpolemical theological theses supported by biblical exegesis. Praised by friends and degraded by foes, Calov remained persistent in his personal and professional life. He always seemed to have the last word, and he remained the head of a family that survived five wives and thirteen children! He advocated most stubbornly the identity of faith and pure doctrine. According to his theological ideology, mind and heart always asserted the same truth. Calov is credited with the introduction of the term *ontology*, the doctrine of being (in Greek, *onta*, "the real").[20]

At the end of the age of orthodoxy, pure doctrine became heavily mixed with pastoral concerns. The pastor David Hollaz (1648–1713) personified this emphasis; he also was the final popular mind of Lutheran orthodoxy. Never a teaching theologian, but always a pastor and finally bishop of Jakobshagen, Pomerania (East Prussia), he summarized his views in a dogmatic work titled *Examen theologicum acroamaticum* (Theological examination to be heard, 1707).[21] The work is a masterpiece of arrangement and precision in fifteen hundred pages. Its pedagogy is exhibited in questions that are answered in the form of theses, antitheses, exegetical proofs from the Bible, and pastoral observations. Much of the arrangement of topics is borrowed from John Quenstedt's systematic theology. The love for biblical passages abounds throughout the book. It was edited eight times in the six decades following its publication. Historical hindsight encounters Hollaz as the rear entrance to the many quests for pure doctrine since the publication of the Book of Concord in 1580.

Hollaz's concerns were nurtured and advocated by his son, David, the oldest of thirteen children, and his grandson, also named David, who became a Pietist under the influence of the Moravian Brethren of Herrnhut, Saxony, under the tutelage of Count Nicholas of Zinzendorf (1700–1760).

Lutheran orthodox theologians tried to defend the doctrinal consensus achieved in the Formula of Concord of 1577. First, they tried to define pure doctrine through the method of loci, used by the first Lutheran systematic theologian, Melanchthon. This method joins together individual points of doctrine, showing how they are internally related through cause and effect (the step from before, a priori, to after, posteriori). Good works, for example, are caused by unconditional faith in Christ rather than by a desire to please God. Thus all loci are posteriori to the a priori of the chief article, justification by faith, based on Scripture.

The second method of defining pure doctrine was analytical, exemplified first in the work of John Gerhard. In this case, pure doctrine was the logical depiction of the event of salvation through Christ according to specific points of view, such as the goal and means of salvation. In this sense, resurrection (goal) and faith (means) are the individual parts that explain the whole (salvation in Christ), for analysis is the way of explaining the whole through its individual parts.

The analytical method of defining pure doctrine tended to include philosophical reflections bordering on metaphysics and natural theology, a close link between faith and natural human powers. This tendency in turn tended to weaken the chief enterprise of Lutheran orthodoxy, namely, to create a doctrine of Holy Scripture as the basis of pure doctrine. For if Scripture reveals salvation by Christ alone, through grace and faith, philosophical reflections about the relationship between Christ and believers seem quite inappropriate. Yet the notion of an "order of salvation" (*ordo salutis*) in many works of Lutheran orthodoxy seems to define pure doctrine as more inclusive than it might be on strictly biblical grounds.

The quest for pure doctrine created gigantic tomes of systematic theology, a listing of fundamental articles of faith based on the Bible and the Lutheran Confessions, philosophical reflection, lengthy preaching, the composition of stirring hymns, and the writing of devotional literature. Pure doctrine was the guardian against new doctrines, identified with Calvinism, Catholicism, atheism, and other threats to Lutheran uniformity. At the beginning of the age of orthodoxy, the Leipzig theologian and hymn writer Nikolaus Selnecker (1530–1592) expressed the plight of orthodoxy, a clinging to Christ despite all temptations of the human mind.

> And ever is there something new
> Devised to change Thy doctrines true;
> Lord Jesus! As Thou still dost reign,
> These vain, presumptuous minds restrain.
> And as the cause and glory, Lord,
> Are Thine, not ours, do Thou afford
> Us help and strength and constancy,
> And keep us ever true to Thee.[22]

Bible and Inspiration

Lutheran orthodoxy generally taught that the Bible is the word of God. Its chief theologian, John Gerhard, put it quite succinctly: "Holy Scripture is the Word of God, reduced to writing according to His [sic] will by the evangelists and apostles, revealing perfectly and clearly the teaching of God's nature and will, in order that man [sic] might be instructed from it to life everlasting."[23] Accordingly, God is the author of the Bible, using inspiration as the means to produce it as a solid witness for the church. Orthodox theologians, therefore, liked to speak of a primary author of Scripture, God, and of secondary authors, the biblical writers.

The notion of the inspiration of the Bible is rooted in Hellenistic (Greek) Jewish thought. Jewish thinkers liked to talk of biblical books as the result of mania and ecstasy. Ancient Christian writers adopted this stance, comparing the Holy Spirit to a flutist who is heard by the biblical authors. The influential Irenaeus (about 130–200) even spoke of a "dictation" based on verbal inspiration. Frequently, a distinction was made between verbal inspiration (word for word) and "plenary" inspiration (as a whole). But the general notion of biblical inspiration was preserved.[24] Martin Luther, however, clearly distinguished between Scripture and the word of God. The former may include various interesting noninspired books, such as the Letter of James, whereas the latter always is the "live (preached) voice" (viva vox) of God revealing "justification by faith." That is why the church ought to be a "mouth-house" rather than a "pen-house."[25] In contrast to Luther, orthodoxy insisted on the literal inspiration of the Bible. The Holy Spirit dictated to the biblical authors what they had to write. "There is no word of Scripture, not even a jot, that does not occur by divine inspiration."[26]

Proof for such literal inspiration was found in the Bible itself. The classical passage is 2 Tim. 3:16: "All scripture is inspired by God and is useful for teaching, reproof, for correction and for training in righteousness." If one asserts that "all" Scripture is inspired, one must conclude that every word is inspired. Another proof text is 2 Peter 1:21: "No prophecy ever came by human will, but men and women moved by the Holy Spirit spoke from God." Abraham Calov interpreted this to mean that the prophecy included words, not just thoughts; the biblical authors were urged by the Holy Spirit to write down what they thought. Their pen made them "secretaries" (Latin: *amanuenses*) of God.[27] Many other biblical passages were cited to show that the content of the Bible cannot be separated from words. Consequently, all texts are literally inspired.

Orthodox systematic theologians defended the logical sequence of inspiration, Scripture and word of God with the Aristotelian distinction of first and second causes. God, as the first cause, speaks, and the divine word is the effect of such speaking. It is written down by the appointed secretaries of the Holy Spirit, the biblical authors. Thus, the first cause, the word of God, effects the second cause, the written word. In this sense, the biblical authors are secondary authors. "The Holy Spirit wrote and spoke with the prophets and apostles in one and the same action but in a different sense, He [*sic*] as the first cause and they as the instrumental cause."[28]

According to orthodoxy, the biblical authors were neither in a state of ecstasy, as Hellenistic Judaism taught, nor without emotions like robots. Rather, they were ordinary beings who wrote with emotions and had enlightened minds. God made them willing writers of the divine texts. "They wrote voluntarily, willingly and knowingly."[29] But God accommodated the divine word to the individual style and grammatical rules of the individual biblical writers. As "secretaries of the Holy Spirit," they did not take dictation like some secular secretaries do, just writing down words without understanding their meaning; they knew what they were writing. Here, orthodox theologians again employed the Aristotelian distinction between matter and form (or essence and nature): the biblical writers used their various literary forms to express the matter of the divine word they had heard through dictation. This distinction was also used to differentiate between revelation and inspiration. Scripture is the form of the matter that is revealed. That is why orthodox systems do not have a locus on revelation. For what is revealed in Scripture is revelation itself. Outside of Scripture, there is no divine revelation of human salvation even though there is a divine disclosure in the order of nature as divine creation. Inspiration and revelation are synonymous "when divine mysteries are revealed by inspiration and inspired by revelation in the same writing."[30]

Orthodox theologians viewed divine verbal inspiration as the only reason that the Bible has its exclusive authority, "by Scripture alone" (Latin: *sola scriptura*). "Because the author of Scripture is God, by whose direct inspiration the prophets, evangelists and apostles wrote, it also possesses divine authority."[31] This authority cannot be questioned, reduced, or weakened by arguments of human reason. According to orthodoxy, any doubt, indeed rejection, of the sole authority of the Bible, is idolatry. On the other hand, theologians argued that the innate human "habit of destruction" *(habitus destructivus)* always insists on its own exclusive authority. That is why every Christian must accept the authority of Scripture "by faith alone" *(sola fides)*. Faith is the only possible response to God, who is beyond all human reason. Indeed, one must crucify and sacrifice the intellect for the sake of total commitment to the authority of the Bible. For belief in its exclusive authority means to believe what human reason considers impossible and absurd. "If our mind and intellect are to be taken captive in obedience to faith, then it is necessary for us to believe even if we cannot assent with our mind, nay, even if we are persuaded in our mind that what we believe is false."[32]

In this sense, orthodoxy distinguished between faith as divine certainty and human reason. But it also used human reason to show that the inspired Bible is the only true source of faith. The orthodox systematic defense of the Bible as the inspired inerrant word of God focused on the notions of authenticity, sufficiency, and efficacy. In regard to authenticity, orthodox systematic theologians faced a serious problem because of questions concerning biblical texts. How pure are they? Some theologians argued that even the Hebrew vowel signs in the text of the Old Testament were inspired and thus reliable. Others conceded that a text without the vowel signs was inspired, whereas the signs themselves were added by readers.[33] Even defenders of Lutheran orthodoxy admitted that the controversy over the age of vowel points "is one of the sterile chapters in the history of Christian thought."[34] Thus, the authenticity of the Bible as the word of God could be based only on the assumption of inspired texts without much regard to its variations in grammar and language.

Sufficiency meant that the canonical Bible contains everything one must believe to be saved and everything one must do to live a life pleasing to God. Accordingly, sufficiency is limited to God's revelation in Christ; other theological truths are kept from human knowledge by God. In that sense, the sufficiency of Scripture is exclusive: only Scripture can be used to establish what Christians ought to believe and do. The classic proof text is 2 Tim. 3:15-16 (the inspired Scripture teaches, reproves, corrects, and trains in righteousness). The Bible clearly teaches what is necessary for salvation, and its readers should not ask for more. The "what" is clear; the "how" and "why" are not. Here, orthodox theologians link authenticity with sufficiency. The authenticity of Scripture is given in the text, which creates the faith sufficient for salvation. As John Quenstedt put it: "I read in Scripture that clearly God is one and yet three persons. . . . Now if a person is not content with this but in an officious manner searches into the how and why of it, he [she] has no reason to espouse the obscurity of Scripture but every reason to condemn his [her] own effrontery. Faith does not rest on proofs from reason but on divine testimony."[35]

Orthodox theologians link the notion of efficacy to the power of the word of God. Scripture, the word of God, must be proclaimed as good news (gospel) for sinful human creatures. But not all of Scripture is good news. Much of it is law rather than gospel. For the power of the word of God as law also confronts and reveals sin and sinners. Its basic function is to drive sinners to Christ. "Although the law formally and directly knows nothing and teaches nothing about Christ, still by accusing, convicting and terrifying, it indirectly constrains the sinner to seek comfort and help in Christ the redeemer."[36] Thus the efficacy of Scripture converts sinners to a new life with Christ. God is the author of both the written and proclaimed word of God. Christ is the content, and the Holy Spirit makes the word of God powerful in the world. Here, orthodoxy echoes Luther, who, in contrast to Reformation radicals, the *Schwärmer,* always links word and spirit.

The arguments for authenticity, sufficiency, and efficacy were designed by orthodox theologians to prove that Scripture was true as the source of salvation. Or the reverse argument: that Scripture is true because it is inspired and thus inerrant. Because the Holy Spirit transmits biblical truth, Scripture must be true; the Holy Spirit is the spirit of truth. It directed the "hands and pens [of] the holy writers. . . . It cannot deceive or be deceived, neither can He [it] err or have a lapse of memory."[37] Indeed, Holy Scripture is infallible (a term attributed to the papacy since Vatican I [1870] under certain conditions). Any notion of errors in Scripture "vitiates the authenticity and authority of Scripture, and by such an opinion the certainty and assurance of faith are destroyed. . . . Unless we are made *infallibly* certain of the source of our faith . . . how can there be any assurance of salvation?"[38]

This doctrine of inerrancy tried to eliminate two kinds of errors generally assumed or discovered by readers: (1) that Scripture contradicts itself in the sense that one section does not harmonize with another and (2) that Scripture does not correspond to the data of the external world (history, geography, astronomy). For example: Matt. 27:9-10 quotes Zech. 11:12-13 as a quote from Jeremiah. Erasmus (1569–1536), the famous humanist, believed that the evangelist suffered from a loss of memory. But John Gerhard and other orthodox theologians deny the explanation, claiming that Christ conflated two prophets in the quotation or that Hebrew tradition confused the two. According to Hollaz, "nothing is said in the text about Jeremiah's writing. And so what Jeremiah said, his disciple Zechariah wrote."[39] A flippant explanation! But there are biblical passages that seem to be contradictory even to orthodox minds. "We grant that there are sometimes apparent contradictions found in Scripture, sayings that appear on the face of it to be contrary and contradictory."[40]

Orthodoxy also grants that the Bible is not a textbook for natural science. But it contains the truth about salvation, and this truth cannot be proven in any way from human experience. So one should live with some of the exegetical difficulties rather than question the truth of the Bible. If, for example, the moon is described as a great light (Gen. 1:14), it is done to take into account human observation. Thus, God created the moon as it actually is but took into account the human view of it.[41] When it comes to the difference between the Ptolemaic theory of the universe (earth-centered) and the Copernican one (sun-centered), Abraham Calov defended the former, certain that the Bible made it true. The theories of the astronomers of the previous generation, Nicolaus Copernicus (1473–1543) and John Kepler (1571–1630), "appeared more reliable to the reasonings in the physical sciences and mathematics."[42] But the orthodox Norwegian theologian Cort Aslaksson insisted that the Copernican theory was quite biblical in the sense that the cosmology of the first three chapters of Genesis speaks of *phenomena* (appearances) behind which can be scientific astronomical facts.[43] Thus, he tried to find harmony between the theory of the Danish astronomer Tycho Brahe (1546–1601), who favored the Copernican over the Ptolemaic view, but in the sense that all the planets, except the earth, rotate around the sun, but the sun revolves around the earth. This compromise seemed to unite biblical and sixteenth-century cosmologies.

Be it the Bible and science, or textual difficulties in the Bible, orthodox theologians tried hard to harmonize the biblical worldview with the views of their contemporaries. Accordingly, they developed peculiar hermeneutical principles: Scripture, at times, describes future events as having already happened; worldly words are used to speak of eternal matters; a mystical sense must be preferred to scientific data in interpreting specific passages; chronological discrepancies, numbering, and so on, must be ascribed to the diverse circumstances in which various authors lived; certain events, though true, are arranged by authors according to their style and preferences.[44]

Lutheran orthodoxy made the gigantic effort of reconciling all biblical texts with what they regarded as the true substance of the Bible, the promise of salvation through Christ by the law (leading to repentance) and the gospel (leading to eternal life). Inspiration was the motor driving the effort but with too much unnecessary exhaust.

Polemics

Sharp argumentation against other positions, quick identification of an enemy, and controversy in general belong to the fabric of Lutheran orthodoxy. Polemics also was the order of the day during the Reformation and post-Reformation periods. The most influential Roman Catholic theologian, Robert Bellarmine, titled his principal work *Controversies* (1583), and its many editions guided anti-Protestant polemics in the seventeenth century. Lutheran polemics against the Council of Trent was guided by Martin Chemnitz's massive work, *Examination of the Council of Trent* (1573). Lutherans also fought with the Reformed (Calvinists) over principal differences, best illustrated in mutual polemics regarding the eucharist. The Lutheran defender of orthodoxy, John Quenstedt, offered each locus of his massive systematic theology with a didactic and polemical section. The result was a series of antitheses to every article of faith, often providing more heat than light.

In the early days of orthodoxy, polemics centered on the use of philosophy in theology. For Luther had little good to say about any marriage between philosophy and theology granting its employment only in ethics. The revival of Aristotelianism and the endurance of humanism at German universities forced theologians to evaluate the role of philosophy. Daniel Hoffmann and Cornelius Martini spent much effort on this problem at the University of Helmstedt. Martini, a disciple of Melanchthon, was a humanist in favor of bringing metaphysics back into the curriculum. Hoffmann, a radical follower of Luther, condemned the teaching of metaphysics, indeed rejected the teaching of philosophy as ungodly.[45]

The controversy spread beyond Helmstedt but was stopped by the influential Jena theologian John Gerhard. Siding with Luther, Gerhard differentiated between various uses of philosophy. Whereas Aristotelian metaphysics is useless for theology, theologians must use rhetoric and logic as long as they claim to transmit rational knowledge. But there is a basic difference between "knowable things" (*cognoscibilia*) through human reason and theology, which deals with things grasped by faith. Thus one can assert with Luther that the statement "God is human" (in Jesus Christ) is true in philosophy but false in theology.[46] Moreover, "although in nature a thing is not true, in God it can be and is true."[47] God and faith cannot be subjected to the rules of philosophy. But theology must use categories of communication, like logic and rhetoric. Thus, there is some positive relationship between the two. One must also consider that Gerhard no longer encountered the medieval bond between theology and philosophy, as did Luther.

Abraham Calov went one step further in Wittenberg by contending that there need no longer be a conflict between philosophy and Lutheran orthodoxy. He stated his position in theses grounded in the basic assumption that all truth is located in God. Thus, there cannot be a "double truth," one in faith and the other in nature. Natural knowledge, communicated in philosophy, and faith, grounded in the Bible, are gifts of God.[48] Consequently, theologians can use philosophical arguments and scholastic terminology to systematize and defend biblical truth. But they should not harmonize divine revelation with philosophy as did medieval scholastic theologians.

Thus, philosophy is not the handmaid of theology, demonstrating the truth of revelation, but rather the rational fist, defending biblical truth and engaging its enemies in a duel of polemics.

This antiphilosophical position gained strength and held sway in the later period of Lutheran orthodoxy. It was especially cherished by Valentin Löscher (1673–1749),

Valentin Löscher

a Wittenberg theologian who had become the leader of Lutheranism in Dresden. He was the first to call the Lutheran chief article of faith "the article on which the church stands and falls" *(articulus stantis et cadentis ecclesiae).*[49] His antiphilosophical stance is argued in a 1708 work with the illuminating title, *Praenotiones theologiae contra naturalistarum et fanaticorum omne genus atheos, deistas, indifferentistas antiscripturiarios* (Preconceptions of theology against naturalism and fanatics of every kind: Atheists, deists, indifferentialists, anti-Scripturalists, etc.). He targeted especially the philosophical system of the British philosopher John Locke (1632–1704), who contended that all knowledge comes through sense perception, experience, and reflection, which ought to be the foundation for just living, facilitated through a government defined as a rational contract between the governor and the governed. Löscher, however, argued that all knowledge comes through God in basic, universal notions that, according to Rom. 2:15, are innate natural laws. To have such biblical proof was sufficient for him to reject Locke and the philosophy of the Enlightenment.

The core of orthodox polemics was directed against the Catholic doctrine of tradition as asserted by the Council of Trent. This doctrine declared, in essence, that the interpretation of the Bible must be sanctioned by an ecclesiastical council of bishops, chaired by the pope. For the best, authentic, and authoritative meaning of Scripture through the guidance of the Holy Spirit is confined to the Roman Catholic tradition because it was sanctioned by Christ when he chose Peter as the head of the church (Matt. 16:18). Orthodox Lutherans viewed this definition of tradition as a way to establish two sources of divine revelation, Scripture and tradition. They insisted on the principle of "Scripture alone" *(sola scriptura)* because the Bible was already sufficiently inspired by the Holy Spirit in its text, which in itself is without error. Thus, neither a pope nor a council of bishops have authority over Scripture by being the only interpreters who can define its authentic meaning. There is room for unwritten, nonbiblical tradition, Lutheran orthodox theologians conceded. But such traditions, like the veneration of saints or the enumeration of sins in private confession, cannot be placed beside Scripture as necessary worship; they are certainly not infallible as the Roman Catholic Church implies.

Catholics defended their way of combining Scripture and tradition as a rational way to clarify the meaning of the Bible. It sometimes needs a rational extension in order to reveal its full meaning. For example: Scripture asserts the virgin birth of Jesus, and in order to disclose the full meaning of *virgin birth,* one can assume that Mary also was born of a virgin (through immaculate conception) and remained a virgin (perpetual virginity), even though there are no biblical texts supporting such assumptions. Catholics defended the two assumptions, which attained the status of official church doctrines, as legitimate rational extensions of Scripture. Lutheran orthodox theologians saw in the Catholic employment of human reason the dangerous, sinful trend to dominate over Scripture and divine revelation. If reason is employed beyond an intelligent application of the principle "Scripture alone," it is abused. For human reason is corrupted by sin and, when used naively, always militates against the things of God (Rom. 8:7). The Bible attests that even those who are born again ridicule and deride the divine promises. John Dannhauer cited Sarah as an example because she laughed at God's promise that she would have a son in her old age (Gen. 21:6-7).[50]

The principal enemy of the Lutheran doctrine of verbal inspiration was Robert Bellarmine, who listed six reasons why Scripture needs the church to become clear: (1) many passages appear to be contrary to each other; (2) Scripture contains ambiguous words and statements; (3) it contains incomplete statements or thoughts (*anacolutha,* "inconsistencies"); (4) it contains preposterous statements (for example, Gen. 10:32 lists different nations, whereas Genesis 11 speaks of the whole earth speaking one language); (5) there are many Hebraisms; and (6) there is much figurative speech (allegories, metaphors, and so on). Lutherans insisted that Scripture was clear and that Rome simply wanted to keep the laity from reading Scripture. This is the real heresy of Rome, because it sets itself above God and thus proves itself to be the Antichrist.[51] Orthodoxy believed that Scripture interprets itself. Contradictions and other textual problems can be explained.

According to Michael Walther, who produced a popular harmony of the Bible in Nuremberg in 1696: (1) there is ignorance of the original languages; (2) language can be equivocative (allowing double meaning); (3) the context is often neglected; (4) readers can be confused about locations, occasions, or modes of speaking; (5) there are diverse statements that cannot be contradictory; (6) there is abuse of reason; and (7) there is lack of prayer.[52]

When desperate, some Lutheran theologians, like John Dannhauer, used a "doctrine of condescension." It states that God adjusted the Bible to the speech and style of uneducated people, "as when it calls Joseph the father of Christ because this was what was thought by common people, or when it says that stars fall from heaven because uninformed people think comets are stars."[53]

Opponents raised questions about the relationship between condescension as accommodation and error. The Socinians raised such questions and thus also became a target of Lutheran orthodox polemics. They derived their name from Fausto Sozzini (1539–1604), an Italian radical reformer who rejected the dogma of the Trinity and the doctrine of the incarnation (that God was incarnate in Jesus). He gathered and united a group of Unitarians in Poland, the Polish Brethren, who summarized their beliefs in the Rakow Catechism of 1605.[54] Orthodox Lutherans attacked the Socinians because they taught that Scripture was full of errors and thus was not a reliable source even for major Christian doctrines such as the incarnation. Moreover, they rejected the cosmology of the Bible as unscientific in the light of modern advances in astronomy and critical analysis of ancient historical texts. Sozzini, for example, used the new norms of textual criticism to establish the four Gospels as evidence of firsthand witnesses. Orthodox Lutherans charged that this Socinian approach to Scripture was rationalist exegesis rather than a faithful reading. Abraham Calov argued that one must distinguish between empirical evidence and biblical teaching. The former should not be used to judge the latter because the Bible is not subject to modern empirical norms.[55]

Lutheran orthodox insistence that the Bible was not subject to human rational analysis, based on historical-critical insights, was also strongly opposed by Reformed (Calvinist) theologians. They entered the fray of polemics with the charge that the notion of biblical inerrancy deified the Bible. The Lutheran side replied that the divine power of the word of God belongs to Scripture only "by virtue of communication," that is, the divine word is recognized in the words of Scripture.[56] But such hairline distinction between the content and communication of the Bible only increased the Reformed opposition. Moreover, differences regarding the understanding of Holy Communion had already divided Lutherans and Calvinists, who refused to speak of any real presence of Christ in the eucharist, favoring a spiritual union between the faith of the participants and their Lord.

Lutheran orthodox polemics is part of the work of theology that must make clear distinctions of what is true and false. Luther usually fired polemical broadsides against his foes. His seventeenth-century progeny integrated polemics into their arrangement of biblically based loci, thus creating what they called a didactic-polemical theology. The didactic part consisted of a systematic arrangement of biblical materials supporting each dogmatic locus. The polemical portion dealt with issues of terminology, interpretation, and historical development. The result was a system (systema), first produced by Abraham Calov in 1650. It was the task of polemics to establish antitheses to what was affirmed as true as well as to clarify the Lutheran position so that it could not be misunderstood. Such clarification was undergirded by the construction of a biblical basis as the "seat of doctrine" (sedes *doctrinae*). Most dogmaticians did not use invectives, offering their polemics within the confines of what they thought was cool reasoning. Consequently, they made polemics an integral part of doing theology in a third way, after studying Scripture and summarizing such study in theological loci. John Gerhard added two more ways: homiletics (the art of preaching) and the study of the history of doctrine (church fathers, especially Luther). Polemics, then, confronts contrary opinions with the biblical loci that become the weapons, as it were, in doing battle with opponents. Thus, the issue always was the right and wrong interpretation of the Bible as a guide for Christian life. Theologians like John Gerhard also viewed opposing views and polemics as "crowns of temptations" *(coronae temptationis)*, which the Holy Spirit uses, like the crown of thorns of Jesus, to mold and make theologians by afflictions.

An Irenic Interlude

Tired of polemics, some theologians searched for higher ground. Why should Protestants, largely Lutherans and the Reformed (Calvinists), not unite against the erroneous Catholics, Socinians, and other unorthodox radicals? The Reformed theologian Franciscus Junius (1545–1602), teaching in Heidelberg and Leiden, Holland, tried to make peace with Lutheran orthodoxy by proposing two essential dogmatic loci as the foundation for unity: the acceptance of the authority of Scripture and the centrality of Christ's redemptive death. Both groups should no longer quarrel about the interpretation of the Lord's Supper but celebrate it as a unifying mystery.[57]

But a meeting between the Lutherans and the Reformed in Leipzig in 1631 did not produce the desired unity even though the theological divisions were reduced during the first half of the Thirty Years' War, which pushed Protestants toward defeat. Moreover, the victorious Catholic, Emperor Ferdinand II (1619–1637), also demanded the restitution of the religious settlement of the 1555 Peace of Augsburg, which tolerated only the adherents to the Augsburg Confession, the Lutherans, and not the Reformed. In the face of such a threat, the Lutheran theologian George Calixt (1586–1656), professor of controversial theology at the University of Helmstedt, proposed a consensus among Protestants based on what he viewed as "the consensus of the ancient [Christian] times" *(consensus antiquitas)*. This consensus became known as "the consensus of the first five [Christian] centuries" *(consensus quinquesaecularis)*, a formula coined in 1648 by the Strasbourg theologian John Dorsche, who had opposed Calixt but also searched for a compromise.[58]

The notion of a peaceful theological compromise goes back to the efforts of humanists in the sixteenth century, especially Erasmus of Rotterdam, who used their historical research to unify divided, but not totally separated, religious parties. An example of such an irenic compromise is the Polish Consensus of Sendomir (consensus Sendomiriensis) of 1570, uniting Lutherans, the Reformed, and the Bohemian Brethren (descendants of the late medieval antipapal Hussites). This consensus became a model for later ones and is reflected in the irenic proposal of Calixt.[59] He developed his view of an ancient Christian consensus in his introduction to a new edition of Augustine's work, *Christian Instruction (De doctrina christiana)* in 1629. If Lutherans and the Reformed (Calvinists) would agree to accept the common teaching of the church fathers and church councils of the first five centuries, Calixt contended, they should adopt this ancient consensus as the basis for their own particular confessions. Consequently, Lutherans should regard the Book of Concord (1577) as evidence that Lutheranism is based on the consensus of teachings in the first five Christian centuries. Other Lutheran orthodox theologians, such as John Gerhard, also spoke of such a consensus. But Calixt proposed to use such a consensus as a norm next to the Bible, a proposal that caused an uproar among the conservative theologians who viewed the literally inspired Bible as the only norm for any consensus in the Christian church.

Initially, Calixt had pleased some Lutheran orthodox minds by arguing that Lutheranism preserved and honored the ancient Christian tradition of the first five centuries better than Rome did. He tried to show how the Roman Catholic Church had promulgated innovations, such as the celibacy of priests, indulgences, and the notion of purgatory; these teachings violated the ancient tradition. On the other hand, the Helmstedt professor also told his territorial prince, Duke August of Braunschweig, that Catholics and Lutherans should tolerate each other as "true Christians" as long as they rejected the abuses introduced after the first five centuries.[60] Indeed, he pleaded with all German Catholic universities to renew the dialogue between Protestants and Catholics after the Peace of Augsburg in 1555. Such dialogue, he contended, would be the best countermeasure to the increasing devastation of Germany by the religious war, later known as the Thirty Years' War. He published his ecumenical appeal as an appendix to a volume on moral theology in 1634.[61] The work itself was meant to be a refutation of one of Calixt's former students, Barthold Neuhaus, who had converted to Catholicism and, as an eager convert, attacked Calixt's notion of an ancient consensus as well as his moral theology.

Calixt made it clear that his ecumenical proposal advocated unity with the mother church of Lutheranism, the Roman Catholic Church, not just unity among Protestants. He called attention to a Catholic theologian in Cologne, Joris Cassander (1513–1566), who had advised Emperors Ferdinand I and Maximilian II as well as the French court to support such efforts toward unity.[62] Cassander also spoke of ancient Christian doctrines as the basis for such unity. But when the archbishop of Mainz asked to examine his views in a public disputation led by the Jesuit theologian Vitus Erbermann, they were viewed as too liberal, and Rome officially condemned them. Calixt once again summarized his ecumenical proposal in a lengthy treatise against Erbermann in 1646. But the Cologne theologian refused to discuss the matter further, contending that Calixt's proposal was arbitrary; moreover, any ecumenical proposal should presuppose obedience to the pope as a necessary condition for Christian unity.

Calixt, however, kept advocating his irenic views. An informal meeting with the anti-Jesuit Catholic theologian Valerian Magni, sponsored in 1651 by the landgrave of Hesse-Rheinfels in Frankfurt, raised new hope for progress. Calixt discussed papal infallibility with Magni in several treatises. But his proposal for unity had lost much publicity and became a topic in sermons and in polite conversations. He made a final attempt to put his views on the agenda of the Diet of Regensburg (1653–1654), again without any success.

Lutheran orthodox theologians rejected Calixt's proposal because it diminished the role and authority of the Lutheran Confessions. Calixt himself felt that Christian unity would be sufficiently secured by a consensus on the Apostles' Creed, which always constitutes the first part of the Book of Concord. Thus, the quarrel between Calixt and Lutheran orthodoxy was linked to the fundamental question of whether or not the Lutheran Confessions were indispensable in the quest for Christian unity. His opponents argued that they were indispensable because they taught justification by faith, the centerpiece of Christian teaching that was not explicitly affirmed in the Apostles' Creed. But Calixt found effective protection and support in his political superior, Duke August the Younger (1635–1666), who loved solid research and hated ideological quarrels about Christian affirmations. When Calixt was accused of being a covert Catholic (crypto-papist), he asked Duke August to put him on trial. The accusing theologian, Statius Buscher, fled from the territory and died soon thereafter. Such use of secular force in a theological conflict was immediately condemned by Lutheran orthodox theologians, who, however, would not have shied away from such political intervention if their own cause needed political support.

The ruling nobility tried to end the controversy through public colloquia. The Catholic Polish king, Wladislaus IV, and the Reformed duke of Prussia called for a colloquium in Thorn in 1645. Calixt welcomed such a move, hoping to unite Lutherans with the Reformed and to pacify Catholics. He collected pertinent documents, including his own reform proposal, the consensus on the first five Christian centuries, and hoped to be sent to Thorn as the representative of the city of Danzig. But the conservative Lutheran theologian Abraham Calov lobbied successfully against such representation. The Prussian duke wanted Calixt to join a Lutheran delegation headed by conservative theologians from Königsberg.

But Calov again prevailed, and Calixt was excluded from the colloquium. Calov and other Lutheran theologians accused Calixt of teaching *syncretism* (a fusion of different beliefs and practices originally taught in ancient Greece on the island of Crete), which Christians viewed as pagan. Lutheran orthodoxy used the term to describe the position of the Reformed (Calvinist) party because it tried to explain the Lord's Supper in various rationalist ways.

The syncretist controversy was intimately related to the attempts of Prussian rulers to create territorial religious uniformity by uniting Lutherans and the Reformed (Calvinists). The orthodox Lutheran theological faculty at the university in the Prussian capital of Königsberg persuaded various other faculties and politicians to subscribe to a judgment (censura) in 1648 against Calixt and his disciples in Helmstedt. In addition, the Saxon Elector John George I requested that the theological faculties of the universities of Wittenberg, Leipzig, and Jena join in condemning the theological faculty of Helmstedt. They did so by agreeing to publish an admonition (admonitio) written by the orthodox theologian John Hülsemann, and this decision made Calixt lose his otherwise good temper. In an open letter, he called those who accused him of deserting Lutheran orthodoxy "arch-rogues" who defamed him without convincing evidence; he even used colloquial German for his invective in an otherwise elegant Latin response. Moreover, he and his colleagues rejected any intervention of the electoral Saxon court in the "arrangement of holy things" (directorium in sacris) as a violation of the proper distinction between the secular and spiritual realms. They were supported by Chancellor John Schwarzkopff, Calixt's son-in-law, in their home territory of Braunschweig.

After the end of the terrible Thirty Years' War, the syncretist controversy affected all of German Lutheranism. Innumerable polemical tracts were published, with the Wittenberg theologian Abraham Calov as the archenemy of Calixt. After 1651, Calixt withdrew from the controversy and returned to scholarly pursuits without, however, abandoning his consensus as a proposal for Christian unity. When he died in 1656, his son, Frederick Ulrich Calixt (1622–1701), was called to the same chair at the University of Helmstedt.

The syncretist controversy was driven by the Prussian politics of religious uniformity trying to attain a united Protestant (Lutheran-Calvinist) front against Roman Catholicism. At stake was the understanding of Lutheranism. Was it to be an ecclesiastical institution based on a confessional absolutism summarized in the Book of Concord and especially the Formula of Concord? Or could Lutheranism remain a confessional reform movement within the church catholic as its initiators, especially Luther, viewed it? Calixt saw the answer to the question in what he believed was a consensus that transcended both questions: an agreement by all parties, including Catholics, that the teachings of the ancient church in the first five hundred years should become the basis for unity. In this sense, Calixt honored and valued the appendix to the Book of Concord, the Catalogue of Testimonies, which cites ancient traditional texts on the Trinity as the basis for the Lutheran Confessions. The Lutheran confessors wanted to put the Trinitarian language of justification by faith again into the center of their assertions and to speak "as the ancient church and its fathers and councils did."[63]

Calixt was unable to persuade his opponents to view his irenic proposal as the best way to Christian unity, or at least unity between Lutherans and the Reformed. Abraham Calov and his ultraconservative colleagues in Wittenberg and elsewhere saw only an intrusion of heresy in Calixt's proposal; they wanted to condemn him. They even tried to develop their own consensus in 1655, showing the difference between true Lutheranism and Calixt's heterodox assertions. But German Lutherans seemed to have had enough of controversy in the midst of the devastation of the Thirty Years' War.

Irenic meetings continued. Frederick William of Prussia (1640–1688) arranged a colloquy in Berlin in 1662–1663 without success. Frustrated, he issued a mandate prohibiting polemics in pulpits. Many Lutheran pastors disobeyed the mandate and were dismissed from their office, among them the famous hymn writer Paul Gerhardt. Other attempts toward peace between Lutherans and Calvinists were made in Hesse, arranged by Landgrave William VI, the brother-in-law of the Prussian ruler Frederick William. At a colloquy in Kassel in 1661, Lutheran Calixtinians and conservative Calvinists met but failed to reach a consensus.

But the notion of an irenic theology prevailed as a means to transcend polemical positions in favor of unity in essentials. This kind of theology paved the way for greater tolerance and freedom of conscience in matters of religion. Calixt pushed Lutheranism in that direction.

The Dangers of Uniformity

Lutheran orthodoxy fused the confessional Lutheran commitment to Christian unity with total uniformity in teaching, dogmatic uniformity. Article 7 of the Augsburg Confession had made it clear that "it is enough [satis est] for the true unity of the church to agree concerning the teaching of the gospel and the administration of the sacraments. It is not necessary that human traditions . . . be alike everywhere."[64] Accordingly, a distinction must be made between the authority of essentials and nonessentials. Essential is the communication of the gospel, circumscribed with the Lutheran catchword "justification by faith alone." This communication consists of the "audible word" (oral communication) and the "visible word" (liturgical, sacramental communication).[65] Article 7 calls for unity in gospel communication with great diversity in "ceremonies," that is, ritual, language, holy times and places. The gospel always is communicated in a historical context. This means that the arrangement for audible and visible communication through word and sacraments is the responsibility of human creativity: liturgical settings, hierarchical structures, legal mandates, and dogmatic statements will legitimately vary from time to time and from place to place. Some churches may keep the old tradition of the Mass to communicate the gospel; others may adopt other ritual features to do so. The unity of the church is not broken by liturgical variations of gospel communication, by a hierarchy of offices led by bishops, by a specific set of dogmatic statements. The decisive ecumenical point is a mutual recognition of true gospel communication, most visible in preaching and Holy Communion. The main Lutheran ecumenical goal is "fellowship in holy things" *(communio in sacris)*, not uniformity in ecclesiastical structure, liturgical settings, and dogmatic statements. The Lutheran Confessions know of no "infallible" ecclesiastical office or dogma except the "word of God," which can only be communicated, but not guaranteed, by "human tradition."[66] The unity of the church, therefore, is neither an inward, invisible, mystical one nor a uniformity in polity, dogma, and liturgy. Rather, it is a unity in the communication of word and sacraments. Such unity is necessary for the church and must be recovered whenever it is lost.

Lutheran orthodoxy inherited and was part of the schism of the church manifested in the sixteenth-century Reformation movements within the Roman Catholic Church, which, in turn, separated from the Greek Orthodox Church in 1054. Though claiming to be loyal to the Lutheran Confessions, Lutheran orthodox theologians did not seek unity in the "communion of holy things," as article 7 assumes, but in a uniformity of systematic thought, the dogma of the infallibility of the Bible. The Lutheran Confessions do not require uniformity but speak of two conditions for unity, expressed in the phrase "it is enough": the teaching of the gospel and the administration of the sacraments. The teaching of the gospel is to be done "according to a pure understanding."[67] Accordingly, any church or Christian community must engage in the theological enterprise of finding ways, together with other churches, to teach the gospel in every new situation without damaging the gospel. There must be discernment whether the gospel is taught by a community or whether something else is taught, pretending to be the gospel. Such discernment is done through theological reflection, indeed dogmatic assertions that produce and protect a pure understanding of the gospel. Article 7 demands that Lutherans listen to others when they teach the gospel, in order to discern whether they actually hear the gospel said outside of Lutheranism. The Lutheran Confessions also seek unity in the administration of the sacraments "in conformity with the divine word."[68] This means that there is to be no uniformity of teaching about the sacraments; rather, it is a mandate to seek unity in their celebration, in their performance. The "divine word" mandates the way in which sacraments are to be celebrated, namely, to do what Jesus commanded: to baptize disciples (Matt. 28:19) and to celebrate Holy Communion with the words he used (1 Cor. 11:23-26). Article 7 demands that Lutherans discern whether other communions celebrate the Lord's Supper the way it was instituted. If they do, there is "communion in holy things."

The same also applies to baptism, which, however, is more uniformly celebrated than the Lord's Supper. The ecumenical stipulation of article 7 ("It is enough") preserves a legitimate unity in diversity and rejects total uniformity, as demanded by Lutheran orthodoxy. It is the Lutheran sticking point designed to avoid the pitfalls of uniformity. Bluntly stated, when other communions discern the proper use of word and sacraments among Lutherans, they cannot demand other conditions for unity. Indeed, confessional Lutheranism must view any tendency by another communion to make further demands as evidence that the gospel is not communicated rightly in such a communion. But once the proper communication of the gospel in word and sacraments exists, then other arrangements for effective mission can be made, be they liturgical, juridical, hierarchical, or other ways to enhance the mandate to faithful witness in the world. Such arrangements are not unimportant but are a matter of free historical responsibility for the gospel. In this sense, article 7 calls on Lutherans and others to help believers to get together in the word and the sacraments as the only condition for unity.

The Lutheran Confessions have labeled what "is not necessary" (article 7) as "adiaphora." Ancient philosophy and medieval theology defined an *adiaphoron* as something neither commanded nor prohibited by divine law. Laws never cover all human possibilities of moral action. Lutheranism understood Christian life to be grounded in the word of God defined by the gospel. Consequently, such a life is governed by the law and the gospel, the law disclosing moral imperfection (sin) and the gospel promising salvation by faith alone. Lutheran adiaphorist controversies have shown how freedom in adiaphora can be easily misunderstood. Some contended that nothing is necessary to be done for salvation, but such a position would make all human action adiaphora. Others argued that faith alone is necessary for salvation, but this stance would make faith necessary for salvation (resulting in the message, "Only believe, anything else, especially what you do, does not matter"). But faith is a gift mediated through word and sacrament; it is not a condition for salvation, which is God's free act of love for sinful humankind. When all is said and done about adiaphora, the question remains: What is necessary to be done about the church's mission in the world? The confessional Lutheran answer is: whatever is necessary at a given place and time to do the best possible gospel communication through the common ministry of the baptized and the special ministry of the ordained. The caveat of article 5 applies here: the communication of the gospel through word and sacrament does not guarantee faith; it is a gift of the Holy Spirit, who "effects faith

138

where and when it pleases God in those who hear the gospel."[69] The Lutheran Confessions use Scripture and tradition to define Christian liberty and to avoid legalism.
Article 7 cites the apostle Paul in its rejection of uniformity regarding "rites, or ceremonies."[70] But the use of Scripture in particular created problems, indicated by the
fact that the Lutheran Confessions reject the Third Commandment ("Remember
the Sabbath day, keep it holy") as a law that must be observed; the Sunday is both a
"holy day" and a "holiday."[71] The traditional Lutheran use of Scripture is not a con-
sistent literal one, as Lutheran orthodoxy demanded, but is guided by the question,
integral to Scripture, whether any aspect of ecclesiastical practice and Christian life
is part of the biblical mandate to communicate the gospel in the world. Consequently, the biblical commands to proclaim, baptize, and celebrate the Lord's Supper
must be strictly obeyed because they establish the norms of Christian life, the fundamental forms of the gospel. Thus, there is no other way to celebrate the Lord's
Supper than the way prescribed in the biblical texts. Adiaphora, then, is everything
else about which the church can and must make judgments concerning the best use
of nonessentials for the communication of the gospel. Because such judgments have
to be made in the midst of history's ambiguities, they are always subject to debate
and reform.

Formal teaching (dogma), public worship (liturgy), and ecclesiastical structure
(polity) usually become the pitfalls of adiaphora. Lutheran orthodoxy advocated
church unity through a uniformity of dogmatic assertions, such as the authority of
Scripture based on the doctrine of verbal inspiration. A more enduring pitfall is
liturgy. Orthodox and other Lutherans often assume that liturgy need only communicate the minimum of word and sacraments through sermon, baptism, and Holy
Communion. The popular rationale is the flat judgment, "It does not matter" what
else happens in liturgical celebrations, such as symbols, vestments, body language,
music, and so on. But liturgy unites the audible word and the visible word. Like the
sermon, it must also be creatively done and cared for as gospel communication. The
Lutheran Confessions, however, also clearly stipulate that some liturgical questions
are never nonessential and adiaphorist. The Formula of Concord insists that the
"use" or "action" in the Lord's Supper "does not refer primarily to faith, or the oral
partaking, but to the entire external, visible administration of the Supper, as Christ
established the administration of the Supper: the consecration, or words of Institution, and the distribution and reception or oral partaking of the consecrated bread
and wine, Christ's body and blood."[72] How the celebration is to be done is an exegetical question based on the text describing the action of the ancient church. Besides
the words of institution, it involves giving thanks, deciding about the quality of
bread and wine and the way the liturgical action is done best by the whole assembly,
as well as other arrangements. The question of polity is also a painful adiaphorist

issue. The Lutheran Confessions simply assume a reformed medieval structure, such as bishops elected from the clergy, or synodical structures borrowed from the Reformed (Calvinist) tradition.

In the final analysis, Lutheranism asserts that nothing must be done to be right with God. God makes things right by grace alone, by faith alone, in Christ alone. Thus, the church is free to do its mission in the world as best as it can be done. God could always become impatient with the weakness of the church's witness and convert everyone at once. But God seems to have an infinite, loving patience with the church and creates ever new opportunities for human imagination, creativity, and faithfulness. Christ embodied the way of such divine love and patience. Total trust in him alone makes people right with God. The Lutheran assertion of Christian freedom is an immediate consequence of the doctrine of justification by faith. But it is a freedom achieved in human communication, just as the gospel becomes audible and visible in communication as word and sacrament. There is a diversity in this freedom manifested in mutual conversation, general interaction, and even debate. The Lutheran revival of the concept of adiaphora created the necessary space to sort out what is necessary for Christian unity. It is a unity in diversity rather than uniformity. Unity in essentials is the only realistic goal for the church as long as there is life in earthly space and time. Uniformity is unrealistic, indeed dangerous, because it reduces space and freezes time. Lutheranism views limited space and frozen time as an unhealthy climate creating a frozen people of God.

Lutheran orthodoxy had little, if any, room for adiaphora. Christian thought and life were viewed as a systemic order of salvation depicting the way God deals with creation. Critics have said that in this regard Lutheran orthodoxy had much in common with Roman Catholic uniformity anchored in the Council of Trent, even though Catholicism was the target of orthodox polemics. Yet both rely on notions of being, order, and salvation disclosing uniformity rather than unity in diversity.[73] Catholicism moved toward the infallibility of the pope while orthodoxy made the Bible into a paper pope. In a time of almost total collapse of all known values at the end of the Thirty Years' War, all mainline Christians longed for order and security. Protestants canonized Scripture as an inerrant source of divine truth; Catholics canonized the Western, Roman tradition of the church as the guarantee for the gospel. But Lutheran orthodoxy tolerated some diversity in its uniform culture. Johann Sebastian Bach (1685–1750) composed various forms of music steeped in the art of the baroque as well as in Luther's piety. Hymns and chorales graced Lutheran worship services next to long, boring sermons. Remnants of medieval mysticism can be found in religious literature, which often was used by both Protestants and Catholics. Lutheran orthodox theologians even adopted the notion of a "mystical union" *(unio mystica),* the transformation of the self through purification resulting in a fusion of human and divine substance. The doctrine of mystical union had been an integral part of Eastern Greek Orthodoxy and often found a place in Western theological systems. David Hollaz liked to speak of such a union in terms of the analogy of bride and bridegroom, according to Eph. 5:32. Here, union with Christ is compared to the union between a young husband and wife, symbolizing the relationship between Christ and the church. Both relationships are a "mystery." Hollaz even called the preacher the "bride father" (*Brautführer*) who leads the wedding procession.[74] He and other orthodox theologians ranked the mystical union as one of the last stages in the order of salvation, beginning with creation and ending with a final consummation when human and divine substances merge. But the Lutheran Confessions condemn this view as a violation of the doctrine of justification by faith, declaring "that not God himself but only the gifts of God dwell in believers."[75] Again, the drive for uniformity tempted theologians to go that far astray from the center. The greatest pitfall of Lutheran orthodoxy was its drive for a uniform relationship between thought and life, illustrated and mandated by the Bible. The Bible was no longer a collection of books in which the story of God's people was told in the context of ancient cultures and theological diversity. It was now the book of divinely inspired truth, used to edify the people in a political territory. Although almost exclusively marked by a religion of the mind, with traces of a religion of the heart, Lutheran orthodoxy had become an enforced custom by 1700, without much of a healthy spiritual life. Moreover, church attendance was largely enforced by law; attendance at the Lord's Supper was mandatory; and a religious individualism prevailed. But the tyranny of the territorial church, headed by a prince-bishop, had to give way to reform.

5

Pietism

1675–1817

A Pietist Manifesto

The new reform movement was a "second Reformation," as it were, since its pioneers understood themselves to be faithful disciples of Luther. Consisting of clergy and laity, it rejected orthodox uniformity within Lutheranism. The new reform program was to stress "a religion of the heart" over against "a religion of the mind." Advocates for reform called for a piety that was not a legally enforced adherence to dogma, liturgy, and polity but a true commitment of the heart to the word of God. Frustrated by the required uniformity of piety, some Lutheran minds tried to restore what they believed to be the ideals of the ancient Christian church: simplicity, total commitment to Christ, and the call to faithful witness in the world. Other critics of Lutheran orthodoxy tried to revive the mystical tradition of the Middle Ages, stressing the inner life with God as true edification. "The Pietistic strife for piety is related to Lutheran Orthodoxy as medieval mysticism was related to medieval scholasticism."[1] A few Lutheran orthodox theologians had become quite aware of the danger of dead orthodoxy, a rationalist stance without a healthy piety. John Gerhard created a "school of piety" *(schola pietatis)* in 1622 as an attempt to combine rational dogma with emotional piety. Orthodoxy did produce literature for edification, meditation, and prayer. But the move from mind to heart was reserved for another generation. It may have been the consequence of frustration of "the third generation after the Reformation," trying to make their own again what had become a distant self-evident experience.[2]

Hindsight suggests that the work of John Arndt (1555–1621) created the fertile soil for a general reform of Lutheran piety. He did so through the publication of *True Christianity* in 1610, the most popular and most influential book of the century and beyond it. Its four books in two parts deal in speculative, mystical ways with the restitution of the human image of God, focusing on the soul and nature.[3] Arndt wanted to show how the salvation in Christ becomes a way of sanctification through the three stages of purification, illumination, and unification of the soul with God.

Believers in Christ are to make their own what their faith promised: to be, that is, to be not only right with God (justified) through faith in Christ but to be also united with God in mystical stages, beginning with self-denial and ending with "the sweet taste of grace" in union with God. Prayer is in the center of Arndt's system as the edifying activity leading the soul to God. At stake is true piety, because "Christ has many servants but few disciples."[4]

Arndt's influence on Lutheranism did create some controversies because he was not orthodox enough for those who insisted on a strict adherence to the Bible (biblicism) and to the Lutheran Confessions (confessionalism). But his call for a prayerful piety evident in a style of life prevailed, strengthened by a stream of popular treatises, catechetical writings, and published sermons.[5]

Some of Arndt's disciples pursued his speculative ideas concerning the final union of the soul with God. These left-wing followers, such as Christian Hoburg (1607–1675), no longer represented traditional Lutheranism but concentrated on mystical descriptions of spiritual rebirth or the end of the world. Hoburg even combined ideas of Arndt with the so-called heretical musings of Caspar Schwenckfeld (1489–1561), who talked about a mystical eating of the flesh of Christ and abandoned Luther's reforms.[6] Hoburg summarized his peculiar teachings in a study whose title translates as *Arndtian Practice, That Is, the Sighing of the Heart about the Four Books of True Christianity of John Arndt,* published in Amsterdam in 1642.[7] Philip Jacob Spener (1635–1705), however, became the disciple who preserved Arndt's strong concern for a revival of spiritual life.

Spener was born and raised in Alsace. In his boyhood, he had read Arndt as an advocate of true penance and an effective prayer life. Life in the age of Lutheran orthodoxy and intensive studies in theology at the universities of Strasbourg and Basel made him aware of the need for a biblically based reform of Lutheran piety. He trained himself in the biblical languages of Hebrew and Greek; he traveled to Geneva where he was tutored by the French Reformed Pietist Jean de Labadie (1610–1674), whose popular treatise, *The Christian Practice of Prayer and Meditation,* he translated into German in 1667.[8] After the completion of doctoral studies in Strasbourg (with a dissertation on Rev. 9:13 and 21, without any sensational conclusions), Spener accepted a call to become the dean *(Senior)* of the Lutheran Ministerium in Frankfurt am Main in 1666. He tried to exercise his leadership by supporting orthodox laws compelling attendance of Sunday worship and catechetical instruction. But he was soon convinced that legal force would never instill the kind of piety that Arndt had advocated. In a ser-

Philip Jacob Spener

mon on July 18, 1669, Spener criticized the "pharisaical righteousness" of Lutheran orthodoxy and its lack of what Luther had called "true, living faith." Soon thereafter, Spener began a correspondence with like-minded pastors. The group deplored the lack of good piety among the clergy, concluding that the principal cause for the lack was the separation of academic training from spiritual formation in the training of clergy. Beginning in 1670, a small group of men met twice a week in Spener's study at his official residence. Spener said later that four or five men had expressed their desire to reflect on the bad state of church and society, indeed to find ways for mutual edification and friendship. They also complained about the degeneration of church and society after the Thirty Years' War (1618–1648). The group became known as the "collegium of piety" *(collegium pietatis)*. It was the spore of the Pietist movement.

Spener's group quickly expanded. Craftsmen, domestic workers, and women joined the small group of clergy and intellectuals, but women were not permitted to speak and had to listen to the discussions from an adjacent room. The group read and discussed religious books and edifying literature. Debates or talk about people not present were prohibited. The meetings opened and closed with hymn and prayer. By 1680, more than a hundred persons attended Spener's Pietist meetings. From 1674, the nickname Pietist was used to describe the disciples of Spener. A Leipzig professor of rhetoric, Joachim Feller, composed a brief poem in 1689 that quickly became popular in German Lutheranism: "The name 'Pietists' has become notorious everywhere. What is a Pietist? He who on God's word in his study feeds and then, accordingly, also a holy life leads."[9]

Frankfurt Pietists maintained contact with the disciples of Labadie in Geneva, whose collegia concentrated on Bible study, using 1 Corinthians 14 as a model. Spener shared this return to the ideals and ideas of the first Christian communities. He summarized his own ideas for a reform of Lutheran piety in a preface to John Arndt's popular collection of sermons on the biblical Gospels, published in 1616. This preface was published in 1675 as a book titled *Pia Desideria* (Pious desires, or heartfelt desire for a God-pleasing improvement of the true evangelical church).[10] The *Pia Desideria* read like a political manifesto. Part I offers a diagnosis of the degeneration of the church; Part II follows with a prognosis; Part III advocates a reform program consisting of six components; it is the center of the Pietist manifesto.

Part I analyses the decadent state of the church by distinguishing between teaching and life. Though Lutheran dogma claims to be pure, Spener contends, all of church life is decayed. The culprit is territorial government, whose disease has affected the two other estates, the clergy and the secular common folk in the congregations. The territorial princes have failed to exercise their political duty of being "stewards and wet-nurses of the church," according to Is. 49:23 ("Kings shall be your foster fathers and queens your nursing mothers"). As appointed "supreme bishops" *(summi episcopoi),* they practice an "irresponsible caesaropapism,"[11] acting like the medieval popes, who claimed superiority over church and state. The clergy has degenerated into a class of ambitious, career-oriented professionals who create dogma and defend it without living a life that shows illumination through the Holy Spirit. They no longer are "imitators of Christ" (1 Cor. 1:1). Theologians permit medieval scholastic theology to return through the back door after Luther had driven it out through the front door. Lutheran theology has become "an apparatus of showy human erudition"[12] without any inner power. The secular common folk in the congregations lack love of neighbor; moreover, they are subject to alcoholism, selfish competition, and financial greed that leads to "the subjection and bleeding of the poor."[13] In short, the general degeneration of life in the church creates a scandal that prevents the conversion of Jews and papists; it offends "pious minds."

Part II speaks of hope for the future through reform based on biblical promises: the conversion of the Jews (Rom. 11:25-26),[14] the fall of papal Rome (Revelation 18 and 19), and the restoration of the whole church to "a much more blessed and glorious state than that in which it is now," similar to the situation of the first century. Such hope for the future, Spener argues, should inspire Christians to do anything necessary for reform. Part III offers a reform program, the nitty-gritty, as it were, consisting of six steps.

1. A Richer Presence of the Word of God. Congregations should come to know the Bible beyond the reading of texts in public worship. Private Bible reading needs to be encouraged. The illiterate should come to public Bible studies. There should be assemblies "held in the manner in which Paul describes them in 1 Corinthians 14:26-40 [orderly use of spiritual gifts]."[15] Accordingly, pastors should invite their congregations to "exercises"[16] in addition to public worship so that people have a chance to share their various spiritual, biblical insights. (Such sessions were later called conventicles.)

2. A Revival of the Common Priesthood of All Believers. Spener called it "spiritual priesthood,"[17] which Luther had advocated. But the papal distinction of clergy and laity had returned even though Lutheranism teaches no such distinction but speaks of only one, common spiritual priesthood exercised by all Christians.

3. Christianity Consists More of Practice than Knowledge. The essence of practice is love of neighbor, first among Christians, then toward all people.

4. No Unnecessary Theological Controversies. Erroneous minds should be won back through an exemplary Christian life rather than through dogmatic quarrels. Controversy needs to be limited to real issues of life and thought.

5. A Thorough Reform of Theological Education. This is the most extensive component of Spener's manifesto. Not learning and scholarship, but spiritual formation into a pious life *(praxis pietatis)* should be the focus in the training of pastors. Students should read such mystical authors as John Tauler (1300–1361, a Dominican in Germany) and *The Imitation of Christ* of Thomas à Kempis (1380–1471, a German Augustinian monk). Both writers advocate a strong inner relationship with God and an external godly life. Theology is to be "a practical habit" *(habitus practicus);* "everything must be directed to the practice of faith and life."[18] This should also apply to professors of theology, who should become models for their students. Universities should create "academic collegia of piety" analogous to the collegia in congregations. There, professors should conduct Bible studies for the enhancement of a true Christian life. Finally, the curriculum for the training of pastors should stress practical areas such as preaching skills (homiletics), teaching children and adults (catechetics), and pastoral care, the "care for souls" *(Seelsorge).*

6. *Simple, Edifying Preaching.* Preachers should not be pompous, not use ornamental rhetoric, nor boast to be intellectuals. Sermons need to focus on faith and its fruits in life, as modeled in the preaching of John Arndt.

Spener often referred to Luther in his manifesto for reform. Moreover, he, like Luther, hoped to effect change through a reform of existing structures rather than through revolutionary substitutions. At issue was the call for a gathering of the truly pious people in the church, "a little church in the church" *(ecclesiola in ecclesia).*[19] Initially, hardly anyone criticized Spener's proposals for reform. Occasionally, the *Pia Desideria* were compared with Luther's Ninety-five Theses. On the other hand, Pietism did not spread like wildfire. Its conventicles could be found in a number of German territories, mostly in central and northern Germany. They also appeared in the Baltic states, especially in Riga, led by the superintendent (bishop) John Fischer (1636–1705), who knew Spener. In Scandinavia, the Swedish pastor Jacob Helwig (1631–1684) also instituted Spenerian Bible studies for the laity in Stockholm. Another follower of Spener, John Gezelius Jr. (1647–1718), propagated Pietist ideas as a teacher in the Finnish Academy of Abo but seemed to be too cautious to institute conventicles. But gradually the Lutheran leadership in Germany became suspicious of such gatherings. So Spener tried to show his Lutheran orthodoxy in a massive response to a deacon from Nordhausen, George Conrad Dilfeld, who had questioned the notion in the *Pia Desideria* that there is no true theology without the illumination by the Holy Spirit.[20] Spener's response was titled *Die allgemeine Gottesgelehrtheit aller gläubigen Christen und rechtschaffenen Theologen* (The common knowledge of God of all faithful Christians and honest theologians), published in Frankfurt in 1680. Spener cited numerous texts from Luther and orthodox theologians that true theology could not be based on natural, rational power but only on the gift of the Holy Spirit. In this sense, he used the central Lutheran doctrine of justification by faith to make his point and to silence his opponent.

But Spener's reform program in Frankfurt created a radical wing that no longer wished to contend with the faults of Lutheran orthodoxy. A group of Pietist pastors led by John Jacob Schütz refused to attend communion because many participants seemed unworthy. By 1682, they stayed away from Lutheran worship services. Schütz became more and more enticed by speculations about an invisible, spiritualist church as a sign of the end of the world, which would result in the conversion of the Jews and the fall of the papacy. He became a guest of some disciples of the radical mystic Jacob Böhme (1575–1624), whose works had become popular in an Amsterdam edition in 1682. Though not a Böhme spiritualist, Schütz did embrace radical aspects of Jewish and Christian eschatology. When some of Spener's disciples began to talk about the Lutheran church as the Babel hostile to true piety, the senior of the Frankfurt Ministerium resigned and accepted a call as electoral chaplain in Dresden in 1686; after four years, he moved to Berlin to become provost at St. Nicholai Church and a member of the Brandenburg consistory (territorial church council). He used these influential positions to support a centrist Pietism and to criticize Pietist radicals in letters, treatises, and books. This kind of Pietism, a peaceful movement of reform within the established church, was also in tune with the domestic policy of the Brandenburg rulers, who advocated political tolerance and religious peace. When the archconservative orthodox faculty of Wittenberg University alleged that Spener had contravened the Augsburg Confession in 263 cases, Schütz, the elder statesman and patron of Pietism, silenced his accusers in a clear defense of Pietism in harmony with the chief Lutheran Confession.[21] When Pietism seemed once again to become linked to *Schwärmerei,* as Luther had called left-wing enthusiasts, especially through the millennialist teachings of the Holstein pastor John William Petersen (1649–1726) and his wife, Eleanor von Merlau, Spener denounced these and other spiritualist notions. When he died at age seventy, "he had a reputation in the Lutheran church unmatched by any theologian after Luther and beyond him in the evangelical [Lutheran] church."[22]

The Halle Foundation

Spener had good friends and young supporters in Berlin, among them one who would become the pillar of Pietism, August Hermann Francke (1663–1727). Young Francke was the son of an influential politician who served as adviser of Duke Ernest of Sachsen-Gotha, known for his educational reforms after the Thirty Years' War. The young student and expert in Eastern languages, particularly Hebrew, shared this interest in education. Educated at the universities of Erfurt, Kiel, and Hamburg, Francke combined his love for languages with the study of theology, and he was called in 1685 to teach Bible and philosophy at the University of Leipzig. A year later, he created a "collegium for the love of the Bible" *(collegium philobiblicum)*, consisting of eight colleagues engaged in a linguistic exegesis of biblical texts; the group met every Sunday and did strictly scholarly work. Spener visited the collegium in 1687 and met Francke, who had an open mind for a more pious way to study the Bible. Spener had advised him to read the *Guida spirituale* (Spiritual guide) of the Spanish mystic Michael Molinos (1628–1696), a popular mystic who taught the total submission of the human will to the Spirit of God; Francke translated the Italian book into German.

August Hermann Francke

But Francke also began to feel an intensive inner tension between his theological learning and the yearning for spiritual certainty. In discussions with friends in Lübeck in 1687, he admitted that he had lost faith in the Lutheran Confessions, the Bible as word of God, indeed in God. Finally, he fell on his knees, begging God "for deliverance from such a miserable state." Suddenly, he felt born again. "Just like in a twinkling all my doubt was gone," he wrote later.[23] His "penitential struggle" *(Busskampf)* was over, and his Lübeck conversion became a prototype in Pietism, stressing the exact time and place of a transition from radical doubt to spiritual certainty.

Francke went to Hamburg to study with the biblical scholar John Winckler, an ardent disciple of Spener. He now was fully immersed in Arndt's pious praxis, and he no longer desired to study for the doctorate. Radical Pietists even showed him how three-year-old children could be spiritually instructed, an experience that helped shape Francke's lifelong dedication to religious instruction at all levels of life. His lectures at Leipzig University became more popular than other lectures by the theological faculty. Students and town folk formed small Pietist groups. When Lutheran orthodox theologians charged Francke with heterodoxy, he published a keen *Apologia* (defense) in 1689. But the city fathers issued laws against conventicles. Francke left for Erfurt to become an assistant pastor at the old Augustinian Church, now Lutheran. When he continued his Pietist activities (small groups, catechetical instruction for everyone, pastoral care beyond the parish), the city council dismissed him in 1691. Influenced by the Catholic elector of Mainz, they accused him of having caused religious and political dissension. Francke left and spent two months with Spener in Berlin, trying to regain his reputation as a reliable scholar and pastor. He succeeded. In 1692, he was called as pastor to St. George Church in Glaucha near Halle and also as professor of classical Greek and Eastern languages at the new university in Halle. Both positions were funded by the government in Berlin and by the Prussian elector.

Soon, Halle would become the hub of the spreading Pietist movement under the leadership of Francke. His Lutheran orthodox opponents tried in vain to link him to radicals, who, like at the time of Spener, claimed to have ecstatic visions and often proclaimed the end of the world. While conceding the validity of such a spiritual enthusiasm, Francke eventually disengaged from it, but he continued his small group meetings inside and outside of his suburban congregation and enjoyed an increasing audience for his sermons. Lutheran orthodoxy in Halle finally lost its power when the Prussian king, Frederick William I (1713–1740), visited Francke and gave him public support. In 1714, Francke was called as pastor to the large city church of St. Ulrich. A journey through South Germany in 1719 showed him how his ideas and programs had begun to shape Lutheranism. His efforts in his own parish became the model for other Pietist reform efforts. He successfully pleaded for keeping Sundays as holy days, after they had become days of heavy drinking and other social ills. When someone put a larger sum of money into Francke's alms box, he took it as a sign to create a school for poor and orphaned children. Soon the small school became a boarding school. When more money appeared, Francke bought a house next door to the parsonage and converted it into an orphanage.

By 1700, Francke headed a foundation consisting of a school system for students from every way of life. They became known as German schools. Francke also founded a school for the training of teachers. Finally, he added a bookstore and printing press to the orphanage to propagate the Halle reform program. It was generously supported by charities, especially by a rich nobleman, Freiherr Carl von Canstein (1667–1719), who headed a "Bible Institute" (Bibelanstalt) beginning in 1710, the first in the world (and called the Cansteinian Bible Institute since 1720). It became the center of Bible publications, later executed by Bible societies. Two million Bibles had been printed and distributed in the eighteenth century. When Francke died in 1727, the German schools had instructed about 17,500 children through four inspectors and about a hundred teachers (including eight females); the Latin schools had four hundred students, three inspectors, and thirty-two teachers. The training school for teachers (Pädagogium) had eighty-two students, twenty-seven teachers, and one inspector. Students received excellent medical care. One school physician, Christian Richter (1676–1711), founded a pharmaceutical factory with laboratories and a store for supplies. New drugs brought in good profits. Beginning in 1696, there was also a refectory called "free tables" (Freitische) that served free daily meals to more than a hundred students, who, in turn, often assisted in the program of teaching and care for orphans. Halle had become to Francke a new Jerusalem. Since 1701, a series of tracts appeared and were sent into the world, titled

Die Fusstapfen des noch lebenden und waltenden liebreichen und getreuen Gottes (The footsteps of the still living and ruling, loving, and loyal God).

Francke soon tackled the problem of theological education that Spener had identified as the greatest malaise of German Lutheranism. Every Thursday from 10:00 A.M. to 11:00 A.M., he lectured on the relationship of the Bible and Christian life. The time for this lecture was kept open in the academic curriculum at Halle University so that all students could participate. Francke concentrated on the interpretation of Paul's Pastoral Epistles, especially 2 Timothy and Titus. Twelve handwritten volumes of notes from students are still extant, disclosing the content and style of Francke's lectures. He himself published a distillation of these lectures from 1703–1727 in several treatises advocating a new curriculum for the training of pastors stressing Spener's ideals.[24] Future pastors were to be trained in biblical and practical theology, in catechetics, with less emphasis on philosophy. A new feature of the theological curriculum was a workshop called homiletical exercises, with practice preaching. Francke was assisted in his academic reforms and teaching by two valuable colleagues, Joachim J. Breithaupt (1658–1732), who published the first Pietist systematic theology in 1694, titled *Institutes theologicae* (Theological institutes). The other colleague was Paul Anton (1661–1730), who concentrated his teaching on practical theology stressing personal piety. The three Halle professors attracted students from all over Europe. Other professors blended in so that the theological faculty had become the attractive academic arm of Pietism in the midst of the other educational institutions of the Halle Foundation. Among the faculty was the popular theologian and hymn writer John A. Freylinghausen (1670–1739), Francke's son-in-law, who published the most popular hymnal of Pietism, *Geistreiches Gesangbuch* (A rich spiritual hymnal, 1704).

Francke and the Halle Foundation had the full support of the Prussian government. The Prussian kings employed military chaplains trained in Halle; they became the advocates and guardians of the morale of the soldiers. Pietism dominated in Königsberg, the center of Prussian-Brandenburg power. Halle theologians staffed the royal, elitist school, the Collegium Fredericianum. In 1726, the University of Königsberg was ordered by the king to align itself completely with the teaching and theology of Halle Pietism. Moreover, all other schools were to do the same. The Pietist director of the royal collegium, Albert Schultz (1692–1763), lobbied for compulsory education in Prussia and Lithuania. When the Prussian court agreed, the public schools became an extension of Pietist education in Halle. Thus, Pietism created the first public school system in Germany. Famous minds were trained in the royal collegium, among them the eminent philosopher Immanuel Kant (1724–1804) and John G. Herder (1744–1803), who pioneered a new, nonrationalist view of humanity.

Francke pursued his vision to extend the educational principles of Halle Pietism to every known corner of the globe. Pietism was to become an ecumenical movement of reform. In 1704, he made an ambitious, public proposal in the "Great Essay" for "a project for a universal seminary or construction of a garden in which one could expect a true improvement of all estates of life within and outside of Germany, indeed in Europe and all the other parts of the world."[25] Francke's vision was realized in some but not all areas of the world. Students came to Halle from the Baltic states, Scandinavia, the Hapsburg territories (especially from Czechoslovakia and Hungary), Russia, and England. One of Francke's disciples, Anton Wilhelm Böhme (1673–1722), became a court chaplain in England.

The Danish-Halle Mission was founded in Copenhagen to propagate Pietist Christianity in India. Francke himself maintained a correspondence with the organizer of Lutheranism in the United States, Henry Melchior Muhlenberg (1711–1787), a graduate of Halle. Even Cotton Mather (1663–1728), a radical Puritan rather than a Pietist, corresponded with the patriarch of Halle.[26] Since 1710, all the missionary efforts of the Halle Foundation were regularly published in the *Hallesche Berichte* (Halle reports). Following tradition, Halle pursued the conversion of pagans and Jews. But the whole missionary and ecumenical program was hampered by the strong political link to the Prussian kings. They viewed Pietism as an ideology used to enhance Prussian military nationalism. Their large military orphanage in Potsdam as well as the military academy in Berlin became the Prussian version of Pietism. Pious edification was used in military handbooks to create "Christian soldiers," exemplified by the treatise, printed in Halle and distributed in the army, "The Pious Soldier, that Is, a Thorough Instruction for the True, Blessed and Christian Men of War."[27]

Halle Pietism, like other reform movements, did not have the global support that Francke had in mind. He had dedicated coworkers but did not attract the massive support needed for a global distribution of his ideas. The Eastern collegium (*collegium orientale*), for example, had only five students, and the training in Eastern languages and culture did not really get off the ground. Francke's son, Gotthilf August Francke (1696–1789), tried to continue his father's work as best he could. But he did not have the charism of the Halle patriarch, a charming, bewigged cosmopolitan fluent in several European languages, a pied piper who attracted people of all ages. His vision, "change the world by changing people" (*Weltverwandlung durch Menschenverwandlung*) remained a utopian goal.[28] Halle University and its satellites would soon be shaped by another movement, broader and more inclusive than Pietism, the philosophy of the European Enlightenment.

Zinzendorf Piety

A third, more peculiar brand of Pietism is embodied in Count Nikolaus Ludwig of Zinzendorf (1700–1760). His Lutheran family had left for Saxony to avoid political persecution by the Catholic Hapsburg establishment. His father advocated Spener's Pietism at the electoral Saxon court. Reared by a noble and famous grandmother, Henriette Catharina of Gersdorf (1648–1726), young Zinzendorf became exposed to an intellectual Pietism grounded in the original biblical languages and in a commitment to global Christianity. "She knew no difference between the Lutheran, Reformed and Catholic religion but whatever had heart and touched her was her neighbor."[29] Zinzendorf also attested that he learned his "intimacy with the Savior" from his aunt, Henrietta of Gersdorf (1686–1761). At age ten, he matriculated at the royal collegium in Halle; after six years, his family forced him to enter law school at Wittenberg University to prepare for a political career. But his heart was not in it. He studied more theology, especially Luther, than law. His obligatory academic journey

Nikolaus Ludwig of Zinzendorf

(a requirement for young noblemen) took him to Holland and Paris. There, he befriended the Catholic archbishop who appreciated Zinzendorf's religion of the heart and tolerated a hymnal the young nobleman had published for Catholic Christians in 1727.

Already in this early phase of academic formation, Zinzendorf linked his love for languages and encyclopedias to his religious reflections. He loved to study the first massive encyclopedia, the *Dictionnaire historique et critique* (Historical and critical dictionary, 1697) of the French Enlightenment philosopher Pierre Bayle, a Protestant skeptic. In a curious twist of the mind, Zinzendorf viewed this work as proof that "natural reason" can only become atheistic because rationalism and religion cannot be reconciled. There cannot be any positive relationship between religion and rational thinking. "Whoever has God in the head becomes an atheist. . . . I would be an atheist without Jesus."[30] In this anti-intellectual mood, Zinzendorf concluded that faith and reason are enemies; faith can unite only with love.

When Zinzendorf was called in 1721 to join the electoral Saxon court as one of its many legal advisers, he turned his attention to the plight of Protestants in Silesia, then Hapsburg territory, pleading for their toleration, even traveling to Prague to make his case before the Catholic emperor. In his spare time, he tried to organize Pietists in Dresden, using an anonymously published weekly journal, *Sokrates in*

Dresden, to call for a renewal of moral standards. Some Pietist circles were known as members of a society called Philadelphia (or "brotherly love"). In one of them, Zinzendorf found his wife, Erdmuthe Dorothea of Reuss-Ebersdorf (1700–1756), beginning a "champion marriage" *(Streiterehe)* in 1722 for Christ.

Zinzendorf would not have made much history without his link to the Moravian Brethren, disciples of the well-known heretic Jan Hus (1369–1415), who had been martyred for his opposition to papal authority. Originally known for their fierce military defense of their cause against Rome, the Moravians became pacifists and were permitted by Zinzendorf to settle on his land, Berthelsdorf, at the Czech border. Their leader, Christian David (1691–1751), had experienced a Pietist conversion. He and about three hundred Moravians created a settlement of craftsmen and farmers in 1722, called Herrnhut (German: "protected by the Lord"). It was not easy for the group to live in the harmony of love aspired by Pietism. Hussite, Lutheran, Reformed (Calvinist), and radical ideas prevailed during the early years of Herrnhut. Finally, Zinzendorf used his authority as a nobleman and landlord to persuade the Moravians to accept a constitution for a Brotherly Association *(Brüderlicher Verein),* with forty-two rules, led by elders. The association was to imitate the first Christian communities, and its main purpose was "the winning of souls for Christ." Lay ministry was stressed, together with the creation of small circles, exhibiting "enduring love for all brothers and children of God in all religions."[31] Thus Spener's "little church in the church" was revived, with the strong emphasis on remaining Lutheran in accordance with the Augsburg Confession. Zinzendorf had himself certified as a Lutheran pastor in an examination in Stralsund in 1734, and he joined the clergy roster in Tübingen as pastor of Herrnhut in 1734. The theological faculty at the University of Tübingen also approved the new community as Lutheran.

But Zinzendorf soon engaged in theological reflections that tended to destroy the harmony between confessional Lutheranism and Herrnhut Pietism. His piety was guided by his childhood experience, which he labeled intimate acquaintance with the Savior, manifested in long conversations with Jesus. This kind of medieval, mystical adoration of Christ was soon mixed with feelings of guilt about a lack of spiritual loyalty to the Savior who expects total dedication in word and action. Zinzendorf remembered his dramatic experience with a painting of the crucified Jesus in 1719 at the Düsseldorf art gallery, painted by Domenico Fetis, who inscribed his work with the words that struck the young Pietist count: "This I did for you. What have you done for me?" Zinzendorf no longer viewed the Pietist penitential struggle as the center of Christian life. This struggle, he contended, had been experienced once for all by Jesus, the Lamb of God, who represented all of humankind. Thus, the pendulum swung further than necessary—a trait of Zinzendorf's mind. Now Pietism, with its stress on conversion, seemed suspect of undermining biblical and Lutheran Christology. "We really have no quarrel with the Lutheran religion, but we are the opposite of Pietism."[32] He even suspected John Arndt as a "false teacher."[33] Though Zinzendorf's views of Christ sounded like those of Luther to some, others had problems with his "doctrine of blood and wounds" *(Blut-und Wundenlehre)*. The leader of the Herrnhut congregation loved to sing a hymn with the words, "Let us view our gracious election in your [Jesus'] nails."[34] Baroque culture and style, with its emphasis on emotion and ornamentation, became the context of this typical Zinzendorf piety resulting at times in eccentric exaggerations. The intimate acquaintance with Jesus was viewed as analogous to intimacy in marriage. Just as husband and wife are erotically intimate with each other, so is the believer intimate with Jesus.

Zinzendorf's son, Christian Renatus (Latin: "born again Christian," 1727–1752) drove Herrnhut Pietism to grotesque extremes. Sunday worship became a theater consisting of instrumental music, erotic preaching, and exhibition of various pictures carried through the assembly to stimulate an intimate relationship with Jesus. During this time (1743–1749), the enthusiastic congregation founded the "order of little fools" *(Närrchen-Orden)*, based on 1 Cor. 4:10 ("we are fools for the sake of Christ"). This kind of playful baroque sentimentality also created a cult focused on the wound in Jesus' side (John 19:34). Members, who called it "the little side-hole" *(Seitenhölchen)*, were the faithful who would nest like "little birds in the air of the cross" *(Kreuzluftvögelein)*. Good Friday was celebrated as the birthday of the little side-hole. Time was spent in "sweet dallying" according to Matt. 11:35 (things revealed only to infants). Jesus was addressed as "little lamb" in the company of "Papa" (God) and "Mama" (the Holy Spirit).

These extreme forms of Herrnhut Pietism were finally stopped in 1750 by the Saxon court. Zinzendorf had often been away, traveling to various places, when his son was steeped in such a peculiar piety. The father eventually called this period of radical Pietism a time of sifting (from Luke 22:31: "Satan has demanded to sift all of you like wheat"). But neither this interpretation of his faults nor his nobility could avoid an enduring critique of Zinzendorf as a suspect Lutheran.

Such suspicion seemed justified because Zinzendorf had himself consecrated as bishop of the Moravian Brethren in 1736 by one of their bishops in Poland, Daniel Ernest Jablonsky. This move mediated the ancient honor of apostolic succession through the link of the Moravians with the medieval Hussites. Both Lutheran orthodoxy and Halle Pietism rejected such behavior as a revival of a hated Roman Catholic tradition. Lobbying against Zinzendorf at the Saxon and Danish courts, his opponents succeeded in having Zinzendorf dismissed from his position as adviser in electoral Saxony and even managed to have him exiled from the territory just after he had become a Moravian bishop. Traveling widely, Zinzendorf and a few of his closest coworkers founded a "pilgrimage congregation" (*Pilgergemeine*), small support groups that sometimes became congregations. They finally succeeded in creating two large congregations northeast of Frankfurt am Main in the territory of Wetterau, one in Marienborn and the other in Herrnhaag. By 1750, they represented a Pietist colony of about one thousand. Much of this success was due to Zinzendorf's public speaking; his published speeches appeared in 1738 in German, English, Dutch, and Czech.[35] They were frequently read in public by loyal Pietists. King Frederick William I of Prussia, perhaps as idiosyncratic in politics as Zinzendorf was in theology, liked the count and paved the way for some of his enterprises. Zinzendorf was allowed to return to Herrnhut in 1747 under two conditions: he must be examined by a territorial religious committee and he must have his episcopal authority subordinated to the Herrnhut council of elders. Zinzendorf agreed, and in 1749, he and the Moravian community were certified as legitimate adherents to the Augsburg Confession and as part of the territorial Lutheran church.

Zinzendorf's travels to London, where he lived for some time, also acquainted him with John Wesley (1703–1791), the founder of Methodism. Wesley came for a brief visit to Herrnhut in 1741 after he had encountered Moravians in 1735 during his journey to Savannah, Georgia. Young and uncertain about his mission to Native Americans, Wesley experienced a conversion in a Moravian meeting in London in 1738 and wanted to learn more about their center in Herrnhut. But he and Zinzendorf could not agree on what makes believers holy (sanctification). The British leader attributed more power than did the Pietist count to the will of sinful human creatures who sought conversion. Zinzendorf stressed Luther's view of radical sinfulness that could be redeemed by faith alone and not by any effort of human will. He also could not live with the notion that the Savior needed to do his work in the large revival meetings of the Methodist missionaries. "Even though ten thousand and twenty thousand come together, as in the recent English and American revivals, it is a mob; it is more than an honorable enterprise of listening. For hardly only a third of the twenty thousand may hear anything; the others are bored and nothing happens to them."[36] But Methodism and Herrnhut still had much in common. Both stressed a pure church free from political control and a piety dedicated to mission at home and abroad. The idea of "the little church in the church" was cherished by both, exemplified in the creation of small associations called "bonds" (*Banden*).

Zinzendorf distanced himself in his final years from the baroque sentimentality of his disciples, perhaps influenced by the cosmopolitan context in London, where he spent much time. He still adhered to a religion of the heart but spoke less of the intimacy with the Savior, as the Herrnhut community did. After the death of his wife in 1756, he married the daughter of a Herrnhut elder in 1757, herself an elder sister, Anna Nitschmann (1715–1760), who had accompanied him in his travels. They both died in the same year in Herrnhut, where he wanted to spend his final days. He was buried between the graves of his two wives. His successor in the leadership of Herrnhut was August Gottlieb Spangenberg (1704–1792), who wrote a massive biography of Zinzendorf, full of praise for the founder of the German Moravian community.[37] He emigrated to Bethlehem, Pennsylvania, where he shepherded the Moravian community for many years. He also produced a dogmatic handbook in 1779, *Idea fidei fratrum* (The faith of the brethren), which put Zinzendorf piety into the context of traditional dogmatics. It has been said that Spangenberg made Zinzendorf into a mild biblicistic theologian at the expense of his originality.[38] Christian Gregor (1723–1801) collected many of Zinzendorf's hymns and published them in a hymnal for use in Lutheran churches.

Zinzendorf tried to remain a confessional Lutheran even though his opponents viewed him as an outsider because of his peculiar ideas and practices. The creation of the Moravian community at Herrnhut and his consecration as its bishop in the apostolic succession of the Hussite tradition provoked people to think of Zinzendorf piety as another church, besides the Lutheran, the Reformed, and the Roman Catholic. Indeed, the Moravian Brethren did lobby for such an independence at the Prussian court, which granted it to them in a "general concession" *(Generalkonzession)* in 1742, while Zinzendorf was in the United States. But he opposed this action, contending that Herrnhut was only a part of a transconfessional community embodying the ideal of *philadelphia,* brotherly love. According to Zinzendorf, there was only one, ecumenical church in which various ways of education (Greek: *tropoi*) are used by God to save people for eternal life. In this sense, each church expresses a tropos disclosed in declarations of faith or confessions, such as the Lutheran Confessions. Because the Moravian church was not based on any specific confession but on the Augsburg Confession, it belonged to the tropos known as Lutheranism. To show his radical quest for Christian unity, Zinzendorf even went so far as to have Christ, the Savior, elected as the chief elder of the Moravian Brethren in London in 1741. For only Christ was to be the head of his church, whose ecumenical essence was expressed in the existence of many local, regional, national, and international tropoi. No single church was to claim the Savior for itself; all churches lived in the bond of *philadelphia,* his way of uniting all in love.

Thus, it can be said that Zinzendorf viewed Pietism as a reform movement within the church catholic, just as Luther and Melanchthon had understood Lutheranism to be a reform movement with the Roman Catholic Church. For to all three of them, the church had to remain united without becoming uniform. Zinzendorf tried to honor this ecumenical spirit of Lutheranism even though he seemed, at times, to have crossed into a theological no-man's-land with his theological reflections, rooted in a baroque sentimentality, and an ardent sense of mission, anchored in the cheerful conviction that the world is a better place when it establishes and maintains an intimate relation with the Savior.

Revival of the Parish

The community of the Moravian Brethren soon became a model of parish life as envisaged by Spener. It was adopted in its basic form again and again in later generations of Lutheranism. Worship was the center of the congregation. In Herrnhut, various forms of worship were developed and enjoyed. Besides attending the Lutheran church in nearby Berthelsdorf, the Moravians invented many other ways of worshiping in their own community, especially footwashing, a love (Greek: *agape*) meal, and Easter sunrise services at the cemetery. In addition, there were daily "singing hours" *(Singstunden)* in the evening. In one of those hours in 1728, someone suggested that the group might deliver a "watchword" *(Losung)* for those who could not attend, mostly the sick and the elderly. The watchword consisted of a brief Bible reading, a verse from a hymn, and a prayer. Beginning in 1731, these watchwords were published; they are read today in many languages all over the world.

The Moravian spiritual life was also well organized. Small groups were the order of the day and soon became a Lutheran tradition. The entire community was divided into bands *(Banden)*. Zinzendorf introduced this basic structure in order to remove an entrenched individualism, stressing personal spiritual security often based on a dramatic conversion. Zinzendorf, like Luther, rediscovered the ancient Christian notion of faith as something shared. When someone experienced a weakening of faith, indeed radical doubt, he or she could borrow, as it were, part of the strong faith of another. For faith is to be viewed as the power between persons rather than just in them. It takes two to have one strong faith that is nourished by the communication of word and sacrament, the power that joins people. The Herrnhut bonds consisted of eight to ten people of the same sex drawn together by their state of spiritual development (men and women could not be in the same bond). Each bond elected its own leader, who, together with other leaders, assembled weekly with Zinzendorf for advice and guidance. By 1730, there were thirty bonds, one hundred by 1734. Soon the bonds were abandoned and choirs were instituted. The *choirs* were quite diverse, each consisting of small children, boys, girls, young men, young women, married couples, widows, and widowers. Larger choirs also were created, combining some smaller ones, such as a choir consisting of women with small children, pregnant women, and older women. These small groups became supporters of individuals who needed pastoral care or Christian education to become mature Christians. Choirs developed their own worship services (with choir litanies) and study groups, such as Bible study. Poetry and music were cherished in Herrnhut.

Members of choirs with unmarried or widowed members lived in their own community called choir homes. During the large Sunday worship services, the choirs would sit in designated places. Even the graves in the cemetery were arranged according to choirs, with simple uniform stone slabs. The Moravian parish, consisting of its various choirs, considered itself an ecumenical and missionary community. It always tried to make contact with other groups of Christians who had discovered their intimate relationship with the Savior. Moravians liked to speak of a "chain of the children of God in the world."[39]

Zinzendorf put much effort behind this quest for Christian unity. That is why he traveled to many locations, especially in Germany, Switzerland, and Holland. But these efforts remained almost exclusively Pietist, making Pietism a leaven, as it were, in the church at large. Soon, a Pietist network existed in Europe extending in the west to Holland, in the north to Scandinavia and the Baltic, and in the east to Russia. University students became ardent supporters. They created a student congregation modeled after Herrnhut in 1728 at the University of Jena. Spangenberg was their pastor; he also became the director of a theological seminary in Barby. All these efforts tried to manifest the Pietist conviction that the global Christian church was but a parish.

Pietism, grounded in the renewal of the local parish, endured most successfully in Württemberg, whose intellectual center was the University of Tübingen. Its theological faculty opposed Pietism, led by the orthodox theologian Lukas Osiander II, who criticized the theological "Bible" of Pietism, Arndt's *True Christianity,* in a lengthy treatise in 1623 titled *Theologische Bedenken* (Theological reflections). In it, he questioned Arndt's loyalty to the Lutheran Confessions. When other theologians defended Arndt and Osiander responded, the Württemberg court in Stuttgart censored him and stopped the beginning literary feud. Soon, more and more pro-Pietist voices were heard, and Pietism began to penetrate into the Lutheran territorial church. A small group of pastors, led by Ludwig Brunnquell, paved the way by welcoming Spener's manifesto, the *Pia Desideria.* Brunnquell accepted the basic features of Spener's reform program in an "opinion" (*Gutachten*) of 1677, distributed as an unpublished manuscript in the church.[40] But his mystical and millennialist tendencies made him known as a radical, and he was dismissed from his pastoral office in 1679.

Spener liked and met Brunnquell, even though he disagreed with him regarding his speculations about the Antichrist and the end of the world. But while the theological faculty in Tübingen continued its opposition to Pietism, local parishes and the leadership of the territorial church were increasingly drawn to the reform movement. Moreover, Spener had stayed in contact with many pastors and lay leaders through a massive correspondence, offering advice and critique. When a few supporters of Spener became members of the Württemberg synod, they succeeded in issuing an edict titled *Über die Piestisterey* (Concerning Pietism) in 1694. The edict called for more tolerance of theological opinions and cautiously supported a practical reform program without, however, referring to Spener's small groups *(collegia pietatis)*. But nobody wanted to view Pietism as a separatist movement. Even a Tübingen theologian, John Wolfgang Jäger, told the Württemberg authorities in 1697 that "the Tübingen theology and Stuttgart [the seat of government] should not denigrate into a schism."[41] Pietism began to have more and more support in the territorial church.

The chaplain at the court of Duke Eberhard Ludwig, John Henry Hedinger (1664–1704), became a Pietist leader. He published a new edition of the Luther Bible in 1704 with annotations based on a Halle commentary by Francke. Though widely used, it was not formally approved by the church and became known as the Pietist Bible. But the Halle Bible Institute retained the Luther Bible without any references to Pietist views.

Pietists continued to lobby for parish reform and revival through numerous public assemblies, attracting local parishes to the Spener model of small groups for Bible study and spiritual renewal. Some migrating preachers, through enthusiastic references to a mystical, otherworldly life, found audiences ready to face the end of the world. A layperson from Heilbronn, John George Rosenbach, urged people in 1706 to submit to the penitential struggle first advocated by Francke in Halle. He created conventicles in private homes, at times in parsonages, with participants from all walks of life, including pastors and scholars. When such groups began to appear in Tübingen, church authorities investigated them and agreed to permit them but under the conditions that they be supervised and that they prohibit women from attending. There was fear of mob action in the light of some enthusiastic discussions about the end of the world. Because some Pietists had preached and written about an eternal gospel, speculating about the date of the end time, church authorities issued a declaration in 1705 allowing pastors to offer "private information" to people who requested it. An edict of 1706 warned of unorthodox Pietist *Schwärmerei*, as Luther once labeled the opposition within his own camp. When some radical Pietists demonstrated in the streets of Stuttgart in 1710, an edict of 1711 threatened stubborn separatists with expulsion from Württemberg but recommended patience and "gentle instruction" of those who erred without knowing it. Because conventicles consisted of peaceful and God-fearing people, only eager to improve parish life, they were tolerated. By 1743, the Pietist revival of parishes was acknowledged as a legitimate way of improving territorial Lutheranism. Duke Karl Frederick issued a final declaration written by the head of the church consistory, George Bernhard Bilfinger (1693–1750), who offered a compromise: required attendance at Sunday worship services and family prayers as well as permission to attend "special assemblies of various people for various spiritual exercises."[42] Pastors were to supervise such meetings or at least were to be informed about them. Known separatists and nonresident strangers were not to be admitted. Conventicles were to be limited to fifteen persons; they could use only officially approved literature, especially the Luther Bible; money could be collected; and there were to be no love feasts. Thus, open schism and secret separation were avoided for the sake of law and order. Württemberg Pietism now was legally approved. Small assemblies went to work to reform and to revive parish life. Although not all the ideas and structures of Herrnhut had been approved, the small groups of Bible study and spiritual renewal had become enduring features of parish life, even beyond the territory of Württemberg.

Two Württemberg minds shaped Pietist thought as a basis for parish revival: the Bible scholar John Albrecht Bengel (1687–1752) and the philosopher-theologian

John Albrecht Bengel

Frederick Christopher Oetinger (1702–1782). Bengel was educated in Tübingen but was soon drawn to Pietism, especially during his travel to Halle, where he listened to the sermons of Francke and admired the care of orphans. From 1729 until 1741, he served as the director of a preparatory school (a former monastery) for future theologians and pastors. Thereafter, he became a provost (bishop) near Stuttgart. But the love of his life was interpreting the Bible based on the original texts of Greek and Hebrew. First, he edited a Greek New Testament based on the latest scholarly work on textual variants. Then, he published a massive commentary on the New Testament, *Gnomon Novi Testamenti* (Pointer for the New Testament), geared to the work of pastors. Finally, he offered speculations about the end time through a massive interpretation of Revelation. Clear language, theological simplicity, and practical application of the biblical texts made the *Gnomon* very popular among pastors, who used it in Bible study and preaching. John Wesley provided an English translation, followed by a German translation of the original Latin edition in the nineteenth century.

Bengel's speculations about the end time were linked to a complicated numerological "apocalyptical key" based on Revelation 13:18, "the number of the beast . . . six hundred and sixty-six"; verse 20, the final reign of a thousand years; and verse 21, the vision of a new Jerusalem. Accordingly, the end time would begin on June 18,1836, the final year of the divine order of salvation. "If the year 1836 should expire without any noticeable change," mused Bengel with scientific sobriety, "there would have to be a main mistake in my system and one should discern where it occurred."[43] He viewed all these millennialist efforts as a continuation of Luther's eschatological interpretation of Christian history, which would end after six thousand years with the final thousand years of the reign of Christ.[44] Local parishes were drawn to such Lutheran Bible study, often with a sense of reform in order to meet the end of time with a good ecclesiastical conscience.

Oetinger made Bengel's speculations the basis for his own Pietism. He was also educated in Tübingen, had met the Pietist patriarch Francke in 1717, and kept in close contact with Zinzendorf in Herrnhut. Ordained and called to several parishes in Württemberg, Oetinger combined faithful pastoral duties with work on a "sacred philosophy" (philosophia sacra), trying to combine theology and natural science. At the same time, he was fascinated by metaphysics focusing on attempts to describe the supernatural realm of spirits, even the souls of the dead. Parishioners were intrigued by Oetinger's search for a spiritual meaning of the universe. In this regard, he was influenced by the Swedish mystic Emanuel Swedenborg (1688–1772), who spoke of a "new church," a fraternity of Bible students who had visions of life after death. His Church of the New Jerusalem had members in Sweden, France, and England. Oetinger used Swedenborg as a wedge against the growing rationalism associated with the European age of Enlightenment, typified in Germany by Immanuel Kant (1724–1804). But when Kant and other philosophers ridiculed the Swedenborg circle as "occult dreamers," Oetinger withdrew from Swedenborg's radical visions. Moreover, he was unwilling to violate the authority of the Bible with metaphysical speculations. At the same time, he tried to combine the study of the Bible with an investigation of nature to show that the natural and the spiritual realms represent a meaningful whole. Accordingly, the "book of nature" discloses a religious knowledge that, though darkened by evil, leads regenerated Christians to a progressive knowledge of divine revelation; its final phase would begin in 1836, as Bengel had taught in his interpretation of the Revelation of John.[45]

Oetinger always looked for parishioners who might have special experiences, indeed visions, that could be part of a "central vision" (Zentralschau) revealing the mysteries of the universe. He discovered such a mind in a farmer, Michael Hahn (1758–1829), who founded a specific community. Hahn's central vision was intensively mystical. He spoke of the "depth" of the "soul-body" that Christ joined in a miraculous way. But his community of followers did not survive.[46] Oetinger provided members with pastoral care. He himself spoke of a "communal sense" (sensus communis), evident in a common sense of truth that would precede the usual work of reason.

Pastor Oetinger always tried to find someone among the common folk who had such a sense, a wisdom of the street; it would be the pointer to what life would be in its living, biblically based knowledge of God. He felt that parish life was threatened by the division of reality into spiritual and physical realms in the philosophy of the

Enlightenment. Oetinger wanted Pietism to become the chief weapon in the struggle to preserve the local parish from sheer rationalism. His principal enemies were the German philosophers Gottfried W. Leibniz (1646–1716) and Christian Wolff (1679–1754). Leibniz tried to view reality as a chain of substances, called monads (Greek: *monas*, "one") each of which mirrored the infinite. Wolff simply denied anything that could not be proven by reason. Oetinger saw some positive aspects in Leibniz's system but wanted to view monadology as his version of life. "I will tolerate the Leibniz philosophy," he wrote in 1776, "after I have beheaded it and substituted its head with the idea of life."[47] This idea of life combines corporeal and spiritual components in what Oetinger defined as "corporeality" *(Leiblichkeit)*, which includes an immortal soul and does not separate soul and body as Enlightenment philosophers taught. Thus corporeality is physical and spiritual because it is rooted in a mystical relationship with Christ in its most perfect and final form. "To be corporeal of the flesh and blood of Jesus is the highest perfection; otherwise the fullness of God does not dwell corporeally in Christ. Corporeality is the end of the works of God."[48] This description of Christian human existence echoes the central christocentric teachings of Pietism despite Oetinger's love affairs with mystical, theosophical, and even parapsychological speculations that belonged to the climate of opinion of his day.

Württemberg Pietism preserved, strengthened, and expanded Spener's call for the revival of the parish through an active priesthood of all the baptized. The small groups of Bible study, prayer, and social reform were here to stay, even though at times at the expense of good liturgy and theology. Thus, the parish became and remained the "little church in the church," strengthening the witness of the gospel inside the church and moving members from the center to the front lines of the struggle between good and evil in the world. There were, of course, always peculiar and odd characters in some parishes, *Schwärmerei*, as Luther dubbed them. But they, like wild bees, never had enough power to produce the sweet honey of Lutheran parochial Pietism.

Radicals

New movements, be they for change, reform, or even revolution, tend to produce radical wings. The Reformation did and so did Pietism. Sometimes, radicals separate themselves from mainline institutions. Already, some of Spener's disciples withdrew from the church, led by the lawyer John Jacob Schütz in Frankfurt and by the theologian John William Petersen and his influential wife, Eleonor von Merlau Petersen, who propagated their ideas in Brandenburg-Prussia. Schütz linked his Spenerian Pietism with various mystical speculations associated with the medieval writings of the German Dominican John Tauler (1300–1361) as well as with other separatist groups, including the Petersen couple. He knew the Lutheran Confessions well but felt unable to be committed to them. Spener told him to read Tauler, and suddenly the medieval sermons of the German mystic became the basis for a new spiritual life. He gradually came to believe that Europe was too corrupt for pure Christians. A meeting with the British nonconformist Quaker William Penn (1644–1718) convinced him that a "holy remnant" of Christians should join Penn's "holy experiment" in Pennsylvania. Schütz founded a company that bought land there. His associate, Franz Daniel Pastorius (1651–1720), went to Pennsylvania in 1683 with thirteen families from Krefeld to found what was the first German settlement in North America, Germantown, near Philadelphia. Schütz stayed home to devote himself to a systematic elaboration of his mystical-spiritualist ideas. They centered in a mystical hierarchy of repentance, illumination, and union with God—with speculations of soul migration mixed with Jewish mystical ideas; expectation of a final "time of salvation" preceded by the conversion of the Jews and the fall of the Roman papacy (two enduring Pietist speculations). Schütz summarized his ideas about the end time in an anonymous treatise in 1684 titled "Discourse, Whether the Elect are Obligated to Belong by Necessity to a Contemporary Large Community and Religion."[49] It contended that the mandate for "brotherly love" (*philadelphia*) in the New Testament could be realized only in small groups and not in "a large crowd" (*grosser Haufe*). Consequently, the large German Lutheran church could not represent true Christianity. Schütz stuck to his convictions and died estranged from the church. The Frankfurt church officials decreed that he should be buried at night when only a few disciples would honor his separatist stance in the life of the church. But even the few remaining disciples soon disbanded and returned to the institutional church.

The Petersen couple concentrated on speculations about the end time. They were Pietist millennialists. Eleonora von Merlau, in particular, made a name for herself in the circles of Spener and Schütz by describing visions and dreams that her husband used in his numerous writings to announce the imminent advent of the thousand-year kingdom mentioned in Revelation 20. But when he preached in Lüneburg about the detailed revelations of his wife's visions, the church authorities prohibited preaching, charging him with false teachings, exemplified in the notion of a continuing revelation exceeding the gospel of Jesus. Peterson responded to every accusation with an extensive defense, flooding the theological book market with fifty-four publications; another hundred manuscripts were ready for publication when he died. Friends at the Berlin court secured a pension for him so that he was able to live the life of an independent author. An example of his defense of his wife's apocalyptic-erotic visions of Christ is his "Open Letter to Some Theologians and Divines

Regarding the Question Whether Christ Wanted to Reveal Himself to Human Beings Today through a Divine Appearance and Did Really Do So? Together with Evidenced Facts Told by a Noble Young Woman" (1691).[50] In the ensuing public debate, the Petersens adopted and defended their teachings about the end time (eschatology), stressing the salvation of everyone in the thousand-year kingdom marked by an "eternal gospel" (based on Col. 1:20 and Rev. 14:6). They also claimed to know Jesus in his "heavenly flesh." These speculations had appeared before in the Christian mystical-apocalyptic tradition.[51] Critics of Petersen's works, which included poetry, often quoted the sarcastic remark of the famous German theologian Albrecht Ritschl (1822–1889) that "the real Pietism in Petersen was his wife."[52]

Well known among radical Pietists was the church historian Gottfried Arnold (1666–1714). He was drawn to the Christian past during his studies at Wittenberg, the center of anti-Pietist Lutheran orthodoxy. But he also supported the reform program of Spener, whom he had known since 1689 through a visit in Dresden. Spener found a position for him as a private tutor in Quedlinburg, where Arnold pursued his studies and published a history of the ancient church, *The First Love of the Communities of Christ*.[53] The subtitle discloses its Pietist spirit: "A true portrait of the first Christians according to their lively faith and holy life . . . in a useful history of the church, sketched faithfully and impartially." Arnold's historiographical effort was motivated by the work of the Anglican historian William Cave, author of the book *Primitive Christianity or the Religion of the Ancient Christians in the First Age of the Gospel* (1672), which appeared in German translation in Leipzig in 1694. Whereas Cave narrated a straightforward account of ancient Christian thought and life, Arnold viewed the early years of Christianity with Pietist eyes: small communities of spiritual brothers and sisters without any differences of spiritual authority (no difference between rich and poor, and women also led worship); a better life in persecution before the creation of the Constantinian state church without persecution; and the spiritual decline of Christianity through ritual, hierarchy, and secularization. In short, Arnold portrayed the first three hundred years of Christian history as a golden age, followed by an enduring decline. The book was an instant success, and Arnold's scholarship earned him a professorship at the University of Giessen in 1697. But he left the academic chair a year later, justifying this step in an open letter disclosing his "disgust about the pompous, ambitious sophistry of academic life."[54]

Back in Quedlinburg, Arnold continued his studies, concentrating on the ancient ascetic Christian life. His hero was the monk Macarius (300–380), who lived and preached in the Egyptian desert. Arnold edited the sermons of this desert father, praising the celibate mystical ascetic life as the most important Christian model. In 1700, he published his historical vision in a voluminous study, the *Impartial History of the Church and Heresy*.[55] In it, the term *impartial* is used as the key to separate institutional Christianity, the church, from a true, spiritual community of faith, not tolerated by Christendom and labeled heresy. Thus, Arnold constructed a theology of history that viewed traditional church history as a decline, indeed a fall, from true faith and regarded those whom the church condemned as heretics as the representatives of true Christian history.

Lutheran readers of the book tended to identify the decline with Roman Catholicism, most visible in the papacy, and saw the preservation of true Christianity in what Catholicism condemned, most evident in the sixteenth-century Reformation. Read this way, Arnold's history of heresy contains the spirit of Protestantism, prefigured in pre-Reformation history and refined in post-Reformation mystical movements, especially the author's radical, mystical Pietism. But Arnold himself expanded the Catholic-Protestant scheme of history by identifying the decline with secularization, the fusion of church and state, and the creation of dogma enforced by an ecclesiastical hierarchy. These and other worldly compromises had become the terminal diseases in the centuries before Pietism. According to Arnold, the visible consequences of this life-threatening cancer in Lutheranism are the neglect of Luther's early views, the creation of religious territories, and the codification of faith in the Book of Concord, whose Formula of Concord drove away the spirit of freedom once so obvious in the work of the young Luther. He saw spiritual decline as well among heretics who, though much better than the church that condemned them, also had their faults. Arnold contended that some were too quarrelsome, others too tyrannical. He envisaged only those as healthy Christians who cherish ascetic, spiritual discipline and are born again, "those who are quiet in the land" (Ps. 35:20).

But the radical church historian surprised friends and foes in 1701, when he fell in love with the daughter of the Quedlinburg court chaplain and applied for a call in the ministry. Yet he refused to subscribe by oath to the Book of Concord, once again causing conflict in the church. Spener stuck to him, appealed to the tolerant Prussian court, and had him sent to the countryside as a pastor and inspector of schools. Arnold served his king well in his pastoral office, preaching, teaching, and writing for the edification of the common folk. But just a few days before his death, he experienced what he had so abhorred in his "impartial" church history. During the celebration of confirmation at the Day of Pentecost in 1714, the recruiters of the militarist king invaded the church, stopped the worship service, and kidnapped the male candidates for confirmation while they prepared themselves for communion at the altar. A final lesson of the spiritual decline produced by an unhealthy union of church and state!

Radical Pietists had difficulties surviving because territorial authorities prohibited the creation of separatist religious groups. But some of their leaders left their imprint on the pages of church history. One of them was theologian, physician, and alchemist John Conrad Dippel (1673–1734). He was first a defender of Lutheran orthodoxy but converted to Pietism when he met Gottfried Arnold and his disciples. While writing against orthodoxy as a Lutheran form of "popery," Dippel also devoted much time to the search for gold through chemical experiments in a kitchen in Berlin, a scientific fad known as alchemy (also a search for a universal way of solving the riddles of the world). His universal solution for establishing Christian unity was a written proposal naming the Prussian king as the bishop of a new church staffed only with men who denied all denominational or confessional ideas in favor of propagating only an inner piety of the heart. He titled the proposal *One Lord and One Flock, or Infallible Method to Bring All Sects and Religions into One, True Church* (1706).[56] Dippel was exiled, indeed arrested, for a brief time, and fled to Holland where he studied medicine and worked as a physician. When he returned to Hamburg, he was arrested for offending just about everyone in authority. After seven years in prison, he went to Stockholm, finally settled in Wittgenstein-Perleburg, tolerated by the local count. He met Zinzendorf in 1730 but labeled him "a spiritual machine who could not stop talking about God night and day."[57] The count's personal physician edited Dippel's works, *An Open Way to Peace with God and All Creatures*, published in 1747.[58] Dippel was the most radical disciple of Arnold, focusing on a totally "nonpartisan" *(unparteilich)* way of Christianity. Christ to him was only an "inner word," and the Lutheran orthodox notion of fusing the word of God with the Bible was to him a "bibliolatry." He replaced the Lutheran chief article of justification by faith, grounded in the normative evidence of Christ in the Bible, with the mystical-spiritualist teaching that Christ dwells in the believer as the "inner word" through mystical illumination rather than external communication. Scripture and historical tradition are only human witnesses of this illumination, which the spirit of God can grant to all who desire it with humility and penance.[59]

Another radical was Ernst Christoph Hochmann von Hohenau (1670–1721), a revival preacher who attracted people from all stations of life. Educated in Halle and impressed by the millennialist teachings of the Petersen couple, he announced in 1699 the beginning of the final thousand years in Frankfurt am Main. He denounced infant baptism, affirmed pacifism, and moved quickly from one place to another to avoid political persecution. People saw him in Switzerland, in Holland, and in Czechoslovakia, where he befriended other separatists such as the Mennonites and mystics. In *Glaubens-Bekenntnis* (Confession of faith), written in prison and published in 1702, Hochmann stressed the testimony of "experiencing the inner work of God" without any debate or doubt. Peculiar is his view of marriage, which he envisaged in five ascending phases: (1) animal-like, driven by sexual lust; (2) earthly with divorce, mirroring Roman and Jewish culture; (3) Christian with children within the community loved by Christ (Eph. 5:25); (4) virginal (Platonic) as a spiritual union;

and (5) a spiritual union of the soul with Christ as the bridegroom producing spiritual children.[60] Hochmann and other radical Pietists wanted to create an inward, spiritual Christian church without secular human laws. "Now surely there is the time when human statutes must be denied and God must be served in spirit and in truth."[61]

Some radical Pietists managed to establish small congregations. Belief in adult baptism united many who had read Arnold's *First Love,* which rejected infant baptism as unbiblical. They practiced immersion and, labeled heretics and demagogues, began to spread in the Palatinate, from there to Switzerland and eventually to the United States. Among them was Conrad Beissel (1690–1786), who founded a monastic community in Ephrata, Pennsylvania. Some of the German New Baptists *(Neutäufer)* survived as Church of the Brethren.[62] Pietists from Württemberg and vicinity stressed personal inspiration issuing in revelations.

Among them were students from Berlin and Halle as well as other dissatisfied Pietists who desired the closest possible contact with God. They called themselves "tools of God"[63] and eventually gathered under the leadership of John Frederick Rock (1678–1749), who founded small communities in various parts of Germany and Switzerland. Though persecuted, congregations of such "inspired" Pietists survived. A century later, they found support in a general Lutheran environment of awakening and renewal in Germany. A group of about one thousand emigrated to the United States, where they founded the Amana Society in Iowa in 1854 (based on Song of Sol. 4:8).

Millennialist speculations were revived again in a "congregation of Zion" in Ronsdorf near Elberfeld, founded by the merchant Elias Eller (1690–1750). The congregation was inspired by a young girl, Anna von Büchel, who claimed to have experienced "inner voices" announcing the advent of the final millennium. According to these voices, some believers would be "elected" and "sealed" by the Holy Spirit. While the congregation waited for the end of the world, its members worked in various trades, making good money and having a good reputation. It is interesting to note that the other leader of the congregation besides Eller was the preacher Daniel Schleiermacher, the grandfather of the famous Reformed theologian Friedrich Schleiermacher (1768–1834). But the preacher and Eller disagreed regarding relations to the Reformed synods; Schleiermacher was ousted from the congregation. In 1765, the congregation became a member of the Reformed synod.

Missionaries

Pietism had a vision for Christian unity and a zeal for foreign mission. Francke's Halle Foundation was to become the center for missionary training. One of his disciples, Anton Wilhelm Böhme (1673–1722), became the court chaplain in England and established a link with the "Society for Promoting Christian Knowledge," founded in 1699. English candidates for mission came to the "English house" in Halle and made Francke's vision known in the English-speaking world. The first Pietist missionaries were two graduates of the Halle Foundation, Bartholomew Ziegenbalg (1682–1719) and Henry Plütschau (1677–1646). In 1706, they were sent to the Danish colony in Tranquebar, India, sponsored by King Frederick IV, who wanted to have a mission there.[64] This Lutheran missionary effort continued and enhanced previous, though rare, attempts of foreign mission.[65] Ziegenbalg was

Jerusalem Church, Tranquebar, India

well qualified for the mission, having learned Tamil, the native language, as well as being ready to immerse himself in the Indian culture. He produced a Tamil grammar and translated the New Testament, Luther's catechisms, and a service book.

But he and Plütschau faced many difficulties. The Danish community had little interest in the mission, and the local Danish pastors cared only for the immigrated community consisting of politicians, army personnel, and businessmen. Resident Roman Catholics rejected the Lutheran missions. But the undaunted Ziegenbalg succeeded in his mission, which he based on five principles that later became the model for Pietist missionaries: (1) Christian education of children in a parochial school should concentrate on the word of God. (2) The word of God must be available in the native language. Accordingly, a disciple of Ziegenbalg, John Philip Fabricius, completed the work of his mentor by publishing a Tamil Bible in 1796; he also translated many hymns. (3) The communication of the gospel must conform to the thought and life of the people. Consequently, Ziegenbalg researched the religious beliefs in South India and sent the research results to Halle. But his work was not appreciated at home. He was told to eradicate Hinduism and not propagate its superstitions in Europe. His studies of polytheism and heathen practices were published after his death.[66] (4) The mission is personal conversion. Ziegenbalg refused to favor specific groups, like the poor or other groups singled out by charity. (5) A church must be organized as early as possible, served by converts trained as leaders. That is why in 1709 Ziegenbalg requested that one member of the mission should be given the right to ordain so that a church could be quickly organized. In 1733, the first Indian pastor was ordained, Aaron, who had converted from Hinduism and had served for fifteen years as a catechist.

Future pastors were carefully selected and trained. Gifts from Germany and Denmark helped Ziegenbalg and his missionaries build a church that he dubbed New Jerusalem. King Frederick IV inaugurated an annual grant to the church, and the Danish Mission College supported the Indian missionary program after 1714. When Ziegenbalg died, the church had 350 members, many genuine converts mixed with former Roman Catholics and former slaves.

The Tranquebar church maintained close contact with the Church of England. The Danish government and England sponsored the Christian mission to India through the Anglican Society for the Promotion of Christian Knowledge. The Halle Foundation provided missionaries stressing the ecumenical, not Lutheran, aspect of mission.[67] On his one and only leave, Ziegenbalg was well received by the king and the archbishop of Canterbury. His *Annual Letters* were widely read in England.[68] The Anglican Society for Promoting Christian Knowledge assisted in the printing of the Tamil New Testament. There was much Anglican interest to expand the Tamil mission to other Indian territories, even though the Danish government prohibited the use of money for mission outside of Tranquebar. Thus, the expansion of the mission became known as the English mission. It was supported by the East India Company (founded in 1600), and its ambassadors engaged their chaplains as missionaries. But

Graduating class of the Theological Seminary of the Leipzig Mission, Tranquebar, India

they, like their Danish counterparts, were more interested in colonization than true conversion. Thus, the ambassadors were not successful, partly because they also were unwilling to abide by the Lutheran missionary principles that opposed colonization. Consequently, the mission was left in the hands of the Lutheran Pietists. They even assisted in the pastoral care of troops and English subjects but met resistance from the East India Company, which feared a decline of profits if natives became better educated and could start their own businesses. It is remarkable that there was an Anglican English mission with decisive participation by German Lutherans.

Other missionaries continued Ziegenbalg's work in New Jerusalem. When the Danish government sold its colony to England in 1845, the Leipzig Missionary Society supported the Lutheran pastors. Later, the Church of Sweden assumed part of the support. The mission in Tranquebar eventually evolved into the Tamil Evangelical Lutheran Church. The Danish-Halle Mission was the first organized effort to create a Lutheran network of foreign mission, an endeavor of both church and state. By the end of the eighteenth century, eighty missionaries had been sent to India. The most successful Lutheran missionary was Frederick Schwartz (1726–1798), who became chaplain to the English community in Trichinolpoly, after ten years of work in Tranquebar. Then he moved to Tanjore, where he gained the confidence of all classes of society. He was a remarkable linguist, fluent in Tamil, Portuguese, Hindustani, and Persian, the language of the court. Even the East India Company erected a memorial to Schwartz in the Fort Church of Madras, and regional Indian leaders praised the dedication of this transplanted German Lutheran. His work was well summarized by a British officer: "The knowledge and integrity of this irreproachable missionary have retrieved the character of Europeans from imputations of general depravity."[69] At the time of Schwartz's death, the Tanjore Church had two thousand members. The church was, in a way, an ecumenical experiment, because Lutheran pastors conducted Anglican worship services without an Anglican ordination.

Another disciple of Francke, John Henry Callenberg (1694–1760), founded what was known as the "Jewish and Mohammedan Institute" (*Institutum Judaicum et Muhamedicum*) in 1728 in Halle. The missionaries were sent not only to Eastern Europe and the Middle East but also to Scandinavia (1734, 1742, and 1748). From Halle, they went to Denmark to convert Jews there.[70] Twenty missionaries were sent out by the end of the century. Francke himself had dreamed of a mission to China but could not manage to organize it.

Zinzendorf and the Moravian Brethren constituted the other arm of the first Lutheran missionary enterprise. The count traveled to the Baltic region (Riga and Reval), Amsterdam, London, Switzerland, and the West Indies. Moravians developed a domestic mission for Christian renewal and a foreign mission for conversion to Christianity. Zinzendorf himself was enthusiastic about a "mission to the heathens" (*Heidenmission*). He, like Francke, saw its first realization in the Danish colonies. An encounter with two Eskimos from Greenland and an African from St. Thomas (West Indies) were signals for him that he should make efforts to convert heathens. Moreover, a former African slave, who had been brought to Herrnhut, strengthened the Moravian missionary resolve. The first two Moravian missionaries, Leonhard Dober and David Nitschmann, were chosen by lot in 1732 and sent to the West Indies. Three more missionaries joined them a year later. In contrast to the Halle missionaries, the Moravians did not receive any special training regarding foreign languages and cultures; they just remained simple craftsmen, who, like the apostle Paul, earned their own living and shared their simple faith. By 1700, they had traveled to twenty-eight missionary regions in almost all parts of the world. After the first few years of foreign mission, Zinzendorf began to equip future Moravian missionaries with a Pietist theology based on the work of his son-in-law, Freylinghausen, *Grundlegung der Theologie* (Foundation of theology). Zinzendorf's goal was not the conversion of nations but of individuals who desired to be baptized. To create "first fruits" among the heathen, he contended, would be sufficient during the time of the mission to the end time. He also hoped that the true renewal of the church might begin overseas and help to shape Christianity at home. "Perhaps when all the lands where there are Christians now again become completely heathen, then the real hour [for mission] will come from Africa, Asia and America."[71] Zinzendorf's dream was a fresh start of Christianity abroad, which then would refresh the churches at home. Brotherly love, based on an intimate relationship with the Savior, was to be the common bond of mission and unity.

After the successful mission to South India and the West Indies, the Missionary College in Copenhagen commissioned a Norwegian Lutheran pastor, Hans Egede (1686–1758), to begin the work of conversion in Greenland.[72] He and his family lived there for fourteen years. Egede had great difficulties learning the native language; he was quite hostile to "soothsayers" who had greater religious influence than he did; and he was only able to baptize infants until, finally, adults began to convert. After much hardship caused by the weather and Eskimo culture, he finally succeeded in creating a small community of Christians, especially after he and his wife had devoted themselves to the care of the sick during the smallpox epidemic of 1733; she died of the disease a year later. Egede was greatly aided in his mission when his son, Paul, joined him as a helper in 1734. The younger Egede had grown up in Greenland and spoke the native language fluently. He began a spiritual revival at Disko Bay after establishing the Christian settlement of Christianshaab in 1734. Before his death in 1784, Paul Egede produced a translation of the New Testament and an Eskimo grammar.

When Zinzendorf heard of the Greenland mission while visiting Copenhagen in 1731, he pledged the support of the Moravians. Their first missionaries arrived in Greenland in 1733, led by Christian David, a carpenter with a mind of his own. He disagreed with the prevalent notion that converts also needed to be colonized and live like Danes. On the other hand, the Danish government saw itself as the guardian of the Lutheran mission to Greenland, embodied in the orthodox Lutheran pioneer Egede. Conflict seemed inevitable. The Moravians questioned Egede's sincerity as a true apostle because he also colonized Eskimos for the Danish crown. The Moravians opposed such a mission and tried hard to establish places of gathering ("stations") where converts could experience a spiritual separation from pagan culture. They wanted to convert Eskimos to a heartfelt faith and not just make them good citizens. But in the end, the Danish mission of Egede and other missionaries prevailed.[73] He saw no reason to change native moral habits while the Moravians insisted on their renouncing "superstitious" pagan ways of life. They felt that rational teaching about God and obedience of divine law through a foreign government was ineffectual. At issue was a conversion of the heart based on an abhorrence of sin.

Moravians also tried to expand their mission from St. Thomas in the West Indies to Dutch Guyana. But they had little success, exemplified by George Dähne, who lived for two years in a hut in the forest among wild animals and hostile natives. After six years, he succeeded in converting and baptizing an old woman. Gradually, other natives converted.

Hindsight discloses that Pietism did not sustain its ecumenical and missionary thrust. Its Halle Foundation was meant to become a world center of foreign mission. Many missionaries were trained there and sent out into the world. But Francke's vision of changing the world by changing individuals was a utopian goal. He and Zinzendorf did not realize how difficult it was to persuade existing territorial Lutheran churches to join with apostolic boldness the adventure of Christian mission. Some of those who were sent out did indeed endure and succeed. But European Lutheranism was too entangled in political territorialism to branch out into an ecumenical mission. Thus, one must accept the thesis that Pietist missionaries gradually became ineffective because Halle Pietism was adopted by the Prussian absolutist military state and became a Prussian state religion rather than a movement for universal reform and mission.[74] But the flow of missionaries from Halle never stopped during the eighteenth and nineteenth centuries. Francke was particularly concerned about the mission to North America, and the Halle Foundation provided Lutherans with good leadership in the New World.

Link to the New World

North and South America became a cherished region for Europeans who desired change, adventure, and religious freedom. Many migrated to this world of unlimited opportunities between the arrival of Christopher Columbus in 1492 and the establishment of the United States of America in 1776. Thereafter, migration to South America was curtailed by an enduring colonialism, whereas North America adopted a constitution of liberty that permitted a flow of immigration with few limitations. Lutherans appeared first in 1528 in South America in a region now known as Venezuela.[75] A small colony of settlers was established there by the Welser banking house in Augsburg through the courtesy of Emperor Charles V, who owed the bank money and repaid it by granting the right to exploit land in South America. Some Lutherans were among the settlers. But the colony collapsed, and no Lutherans seem to have survived.

The emigrants' farewell to their native land

In North America, the name "Lutheran" appeared in the area now known as Florida in 1564. But the name was applied to French Calvinist Huguenot settlers by the Catholic Spanish authorities, who regarded all Protestants as Lutherans. When Sweden and Holland established settlements in what are now known as New York and Delaware, Swedish Lutherans founded New Sweden in the Delaware Valley in 1638. Some Lutherans also appeared in New Holland (now New York) but were not allowed by the Dutch Calvinists to import a Lutheran pastor. It was the English governor who granted religious freedom in the Dutch colony in 1664. Consequently, Lutherans received a pastor, Jacob Fabritius, from Silesia, Germany, who organized a congregation in New York and spoke of a great future for Lutherans but succumbed for a while to alcohol and an erratic life. He transferred his ministry to congregations in Delaware. His work in New York was continued by Pastor Bernard Arnzius, who hailed from Amsterdam and worked with Lutheran congregations for twenty years until his death in 1691.

Similar circumstances prevailed in the Swedish colony in Delaware, where Lutheran congregations were established and led by two Swedish pastors, Reorus Torkillus and John Campanius. But the loss of the Swedish colony to the Dutch in 1655 did not leave several hundred Swedish and Finnish Lutheran settlers without a pastor. The Dutch governor of New Amsterdam allowed the Finnish pastor Lars Lock to serve Lutheran congregations in Delaware even though he was known to be "more inclined to look into wine than into the Bible."[76]

Despite such and other weaknesses, Fabritius and Lock continued to serve congregations until they died of old age. When their home churches stopped sending pastors, laypeople (men only) began to lead worship services among almost one thousand Lutherans in Delaware. Finally, Sweden sent two more pastors in 1697, Andrew Rudman and Eric Bjork. They were to represent the Church of Sweden, which regarded the mission in Delaware as a district of the archdiocese of Uppsala. Rudman worked in Philadelphia, Bjork in Wilmington. Both began to repair and build churches. The Swedish Lutheran mission was now well established.

It continued in New York when Rudman ordained a young man from Philadelphia, Justus Falckner, who was a student of Francke in Halle, but hesitated accepting a call in the New World. With the ordination of Falckner, the Halle Foundation became linked to North America. He was its migrating preacher, traveling to Dutch Reformed and Lutheran congregations in Manhattan, Albany, and Athens, New York, and Hackensack, New Jersey. "I preach three times a week," he wrote to Francke in Halle, "My few auditors are mostly Dutch in speech, but in extraction they are mostly High Germans, also Swedes, Danes, Norwegians, Poles, Lithuanians, Transylvanians and other nationalities."[77]

Soon, two thousand Germans had arrived at the Hudson River, about a third being Lutheran. A Palatinate Lutheran pastor, Joshua Kocherthal, had come with them, to assist Falckner in his ministry, now extended to Germantown, Newburgh, and Rhinebeck. When Falckner died in 1723, Pastor William Christopher Berkenmeyer was sent from Hamburg to New York. He had to work with fourteen congregations within about 150 miles, encountering "pretenders" (preachers without ecclesiastical endorsement) and difficulties in organizing clusters of congregations. But the lines of authority were not very clear. Some parishioners sided with him, others with the pretenders, who defended their call as God-given without having to confirm it by the authorities of the institutional church. This debate on the ordained ministry was the first of many to come. An appeal to the Church of Sweden for help was denied. So Hamburg again sent two more pastors, Michael Christian Knoll in 1732 and John August Wolf two years later. The former organized a parish with several congregations in New York; the latter did so in Oldwick, New Jersey. Berkenmeyer served a parish on the upper Hudson, including congregations in Albany and Athens. Soon, there was controversy over the use of German and Dutch in worship services. The German faction called a German pastor, John L. Hofgut, who turned out to be an impostor; the Dutch portion organized a "classical assembly" modeled after the Dutch Reformed Church in Holland; and another German pastor, John F. Fries, organized a German congregation in Philadelphia, succeeding Berkenmeyer after his death in 1751.

The Halle Foundation, now headed by Francke's son, Gotthilf August Francke, took matters into its own hands and sent one of its best graduates, Henry Melchior Muhlenberg, to pacify and organize the quarreling Lutherans in America. He quickly became the "church father" of Lutheranism in the United States.[78] Faced with quarrels over language, tradition, and mission, he tried his best to reconcile the various factions of Lutherans. Hamburg sent two more pastors to assist him: John Christopher Hartwick and Peter N. Sommer. By 1787, thirty-one ministers tried to work with congregations consisting of about one hundred thousand members, more than half residing in Pennsylvania.[79] Named after the tolerant Quaker William Penn (1644–1718), the new state was to become a "holy experiment," according to its founder.[80] Soon, English would dominate in worship services even though the German Lutherans played a larger part in colonial

Henry Melchior Muhlenberg

America than the Dutch or Scandinavians. Muhlenberg encountered many Palatines, who migrated in large groups to New York and the Carolinas, accepting the invitation of their compatriot, Pastor Kocherthal. Palatines and other Germans also believed rumors about the New World as an ideal part of the globe, filled with milk and honey, with "roasted pigs" flying into mouths.[81] Many immigrants agreed to sell themselves as indentured slaves until they had paid their travel with their work, thus redeeming themselves; they were called "redemptioners." British authorities became concerned with the massive influx of Germans in Pennsylvania. Even the wise and tolerant Benjamin Franklin (1706–1790) shared these concerns. "Why should the Palatine boors be suffered to swarm into our settlements," he asked in 1751, "and, by herding together, establish their language and manners to the exclusion of ours?"[82]

Lutherans also soon settled in Baltimore, Maryland, an attractive harbor near Philadelphia and New York. Many came from ships landing in Charleston, South Carolina. Among them were about three hundred Salzburg Lutherans, part of thirty thousand who had been exiled in 1731 by the Roman Catholic archbishop, Leopold Anthony von Firmian. "I would rather have thorns and thistles on my fields than Protestants in my land," he fumed.[83] Most of these Salzburg refugees settled in Germany. But those who had come to America were welcomed by the British Methodists in Georgia and soon organized a thriving settlement called Ebenezer on poor soil near Savannah.

By 1750, Lutherans could be found almost everywhere on the east coast of the American colonies, ranging from Nova Scotia to South Carolina. They had endured much suffering during their sea voyages, some of which lasted for weeks and caused incredible hardship. Bad meat and filthy drinking water made many sick; storms created panic; and organizers of journeys cheated their clients. Immigrant life was hard, and congregations were led by few pastors, often laypeople, or by pretenders (as Berkenmeyer had called them), vagabond preachers who pretended to have a call to the ordained ministry. In 1733, Pennsylvania Lutherans began a correspondence with the Halle Pietists, led by Francke's son, Gotthilf, and Pastor Frederick M. Ziegenhagen, the representative of Halle's mission in London. Twenty-four mission pastors were sent to North America, especially Pennsylvania, during the second half of the eighteenth century. The *Hallesche Berichte* (Halle reports) from America became quite popular and were used to recruit and finance missionaries. Muhlenberg wanted a legitimate Lutheran ministry in order to dislodge charlatans who just wanted to make easy money from poor immigrants. He and other pastors began to tutor candidates for the ministry, stressing the use of biblical languages (Greek and Hebrew) and systematic theological reflection. Candidates also spent time in a congregation, learning to lead worship with word and sacraments. After a brief examination, they would be licensed to work in a congregation for one year. Finally, they would be ordained in a "classical assembly" of pastors and congregations, at times uniting Lutheran and Reformed congregations. Halle was not in favor of such unions, but Zinzendorf was. He even chaired a series of meetings in 1742 in

Philadelphia. It was his vision to unite all non-Roman Catholics in a "congregation of God in the spirit." The effort soon collapsed, and only the Moravian Brethren remained. Moreover, Philadelphia Lutherans opposed Zinzendorf's liberal ecumenical strategy and called for a confessional Lutheran union of Germans and Swedes. The Halle missionaries supported this effort, saying they lived in "Christian harmony" and regarded Muhlenberg as their "elder brother."[84]

Encouraged by such sentiments, Muhlenberg called for an official assembly of German Lutherans in Philadelphia on August 26, 1748, labeled as the most important event in the history of Lutheranism in America, the foundation of the "ministerium of North America."[85] The meeting was attended by six pastors and lay representatives from ten congregations in Pennsylvania. But only ministers were permitted to vote; laypeople were consultants. The attendees discussed the conditions of congregations and schools, approved a form of worship, and ordained a young man from Halle. The meeting described itself as "the united preachers of the Evangelical Lutheran congregations of German nationality in these American colonies, especially in Pennsylvania." In 1781, the assembly adopted the name Evangelical Lutheran Ministerium in North America. Gotthilf Francke in Halle was very pleased with the first meeting of the Ministerium. Future meetings included Swedish Lutheran clergy. Muhlenberg was its most revered president, also known as senior (a Lutheran title for oversight in Germany). Nothing was to be decided without approval from Germany, the Pietist "spiritual fathers and patrons." The constitution of 1781 established geographical districts or conferences of "pastors who live nearest together." The first satellite of the Ministerium was formed in 1784 in Albany, New York. Others would follow, foreshadowing the organization of synods. Muhlenberg and the Ministerium agreed to adopt the Dutch model for organizing local congregations, a modified version of John Calvin's church organization in Geneva, calling for four offices: pastors, teachers, elders, and deacons. The Lutheran congregations in the American colonies were to be headed by a church council, sometimes called consistory, consisting of the pastor, lay elders, and deacons. The congregation elected the pastor and all its officers by a majority vote. St. Michael's Church in Philadelphia was the first to adopt such a constitution. It called for six elders and six deacons as well as trustees to take care of property, a distinction of spiritual and temporal realms. Elders served for three years, deacons for two. Women could not vote. Such an organization of Lutherans in America signaled a difference with constitutional arrangements in Europe, where clusters of congregations still were called dioceses, headed by bishops in Scandinavia or superintendents in Germany.[86] Moreover, European Lutheranism was embedded in a territorial state church system under the authority of territorial princes. The Pietist Muhlenberg did not insist on a strict adherence to the Lutheran Confessions in matters of church polity, and he seemed to be quite comfortable with the Dutch Reformed model of church organization, which excluded the title "bishop," whereas the Lutheran Confessions kept it (Augsburg Confession 28).

Life in Lutheran congregations in colonial America was shaped by the hardship of the frontier culture. When pastors were available, they were often paid in kind rather than in cash. Muhlenberg recorded in his journals that ten farmers brought ten different products: a sausage, a piece of meat, a chicken, a loaf of bread, eggs, tea, sugar, honey, apples, and partridges.[87] At other times, he received clothes, shoes, Rhine wine, wood, fish, and even money.[88] Public worship was not the Mass, as the Lutheran Confessions recommend, but a service of prayer, hymns, Scripture lessons, confession or absolution, preaching, and regular, though not weekly, celebrations of the Lord's Supper. Pietist pastors were quite diverse in their arrangement of services but used the Amsterdam and London worship order with additional rubrics. Some German congregations used translations of the Anglican *Book of Common Prayer,* and a few Swedish parishes also used the order of the Mass of the Church of Sweden. Muhlenberg recommended liturgical variety without anything "papistical."[89] A pastor in North Carolina reported, "We preach in black suit and collar, usually, however, without a gown."[90] Few churches exhibited crucifixes or other decorations. Swedish Lutherans were the first to use organ music. "Sermons, often prepared in the saddle, averaged between three-quarters of an hour to a full hour in length."[91] Preaching and catechizing were closely related. The Lord's Supper was often "explained" in sermons and in Sunday school but celebrated only six to eight times a year, sometimes only twice. Muhlenberg once preached on the Lord's Supper to a Lutheran and Reformed assembly "in the manner of Queen Elizabeth I," known for her diplomacy. "It was the Lord that spake it; He took the bread and brake it; And what the Word did make it, That I believe and take it."[92] Parishioners were asked to prepare themselves through confession of sins and absolution. "Unworthy" members were excluded from the Lord's Supper, especially when they were involved in "sporting and dancing" or disclosed unbelief. Muhlenberg also encouraged a mission to the Indians without any success. "Negroes" were used as slaves, often listed as "part of the inventory of the parsonage."[93] Muhlenberg refused the gift of a slave, but his son, Peter, did not.[94] Parochial schools spread even though they were difficult to maintain because of lack of resources and teachers. Lutheran pastors tended to stay away from politics but took positions on decisive issues. Muhlenberg initially sided with England in the War of Independence, then tried to remain neutral.[95] But his son, Peter, left his parish in Woodstock, Virginia, to serve as a colonel and lieutenant-general in the Revolutionary army.

Among colonial American Lutherans, there were some signs of the conflict between orthodox and Pietist Lutherans in Europe. The consistory of Amsterdam sent only pastors who vowed to expound the doctrines contained in the Book of Concord. The Ministerium of North America required candidates for ordination to preach and teach only "what harmonizes with the Word of God and the Confessions of the Evangelical Lutheran Church."[96] Orthodox opponents of Pietism were not invited to the first sessions of the Ministerium of North America because, as Muhlenberg put it, "they decry us as pietists without reason."[97]

Defenders of orthodoxy said that Pietists were "no true Lutherans and dangerous," or "crypto-Herrnhuter" (secret Moravians).[98] When charged with false teaching in 1761, Muhlenberg defended himself as a loyal adherent to the Lutheran Confessions, and he was remembered for having said often that the orthodox preachers tried to adhere to the unaltered Augsburg Confession with unaltered hearts.[99] Eventually, he became tired of having become the focus of controversy. "Pennsylvania will miss me sorely when I die," he mused, echoing the language of Luther, "for I am almost like a privy to which all those with loose bowels come running from all directions to relieve themselves."[100] In the end, it was Pietism, not orthodoxy, that shaped the hearts and minds of Lutherans in North America.

Pietism encountered the ravage of the Thirty Years' War in which Lutheranism was saved through the decisive military intervention of the Lutheran Swedish king, Gustavus Adolphus II (1594–1632), who was killed in action.[101] Pietism also shared its time with the powerful age of Enlightenment, which concentrated on the earthly life rather than the afterlife.[102] Philosophers like René Descartes in France (1596–1650), David Hume in England (1711–1776), and Immanuel Kant in Germany (1724–1804) envisaged a world with a distant God, indeed often without God, marked by "free thinking," total religious tolerance, and a universal civility. Kant summed up this new way of thinking in a popular formulation: "Enlightenment is the exit of man from his immaturity brought about by his own fault. Maturity (*Mündigkeit*) is the ability to use one's own mind without being led by another mind."[103] Kantians thought that going to church was being immature, unen-

Gustavus Adolphus II, King of Sweden

lightened, indeed superstitious. But the majority of Lutherans in Germany and Scandinavia remained loyal to the church by adhering either to orthodox pure doctrine or by propagating the Pietist experience of personal rebirth.

Opposites attract. The great German philosopher of history, George W. F. Hegel (1770–1831), born Lutheran, transcended the rationalism of the Enlightenment to an idealistic view of world history. Accordingly, he perceived the sequence of time in terms of a trinitarian dialectic consisting of a thesis, antithesis, and synthesis.[104]

Some Lutheran Hegelians considered orthodoxy as the thesis, Pietism as the anti-thesis, and a merging of the two as an inevitable synthesis they dubbed the "age of awakening." It encompasses a renewal of Protestant life and thought in Europe and in the United States, exemplified by Methodism, a strong ethical component, and a zeal for mission at home and abroad.[105] Among Lutherans, there was a confessional awakening, a new interest in Lutheran roots.

6

Diversification
1817–1918

A Confessional Awakening

By 1817, the tercentenary of Luther's Reformation, European Lutheranism was confronted by changes in all aspects of life. Technological discoveries enabled improvements in communication and commerce, such as the steam locomotive, the telegraph, and electric lighting. People referred to this period as the industrial revolution, a revolution that created a growing difference between the poor and the rich. National capitalism grew, based on the economic theory of a "free market system" by Adam Smith (1723–1790).[1] The Declaration of Independence in the United States in 1776 and the French Revolution of 1789 propagated individual and national rights. The Congress of Vienna in 1815 condemned the tyranny of Napoleon yet affirmed the "holy alliance" of the monarchies of England, Prussia, Austria, and Russia as guardians of peace. The followers of Karl Marx (1818–1863), calling themselves Socialists and Communists, favored the abolition of monarchies and the rule of the proletariat.[2] Philosophers filled minds with various ideas and theories. Some announced the end of Christianity; others merely ignored it. Friedrich Nietzsche (1844–1900), the son of a Lutheran pastor, declared that God was dead, calling for a replacement of Christian values with a rationalist, secular ethics.[3] Charles Darwin (1809–1882) entertained and upset people with his theory that humans evolved from apes.[4] Alphonse de Gobineau envisaged human races dominated by a superior white Nordic race called Aryans, who would enslave inferior Semites.[5] Richard Wagner (1813–1883) adapted ancient German myths in operas to celebrate a master race, but many Lutherans clung to the inspired music of Johann Sebastian Bach (1685–1750).[6] They observed with great misgivings the increasing Roman Catholic devotion to Mary, enhanced by the "infallible dogma" of 1854, which affirmed her immaculate conception.[7] Another cause of apprehension was the pope's increasing power and influence. Lutherans were deeply offended by the dogma of papal infallibility at the First Vatican Council in 1870. When the Prussian king, Frederick William I, authorized Prince Otto von Bismarck to control Catholicism through stringent laws, the attempt failed (in the famous cultural struggle or *Kulturkampf* of 1872–1879). Rome mustered sufficient popular support to defeat his efforts. So even three centuries after Luther's reformation, Catholicism was still a formidable opponent of Lutheranism in his homeland.

Scandinavian Lutheranism continued its close relationship to the state, begun in the sixteenth century when the Reformation replaced Catholicism. Norway, a part of Denmark until 1814 and then a part of Sweden until it gained independence in 1905, nurtured its own Lutheran leadership with the help of the University of Oslo. Other, non-Lutheran churches had been tolerated since 1878. In Sweden, such tolerance had been established in the revised Constitution (1809). Finland, annexed by Russia in 1809 and independent since 1917, also favored Lutheranism as a state religion after decades of religiously inspired patriotic renewal movements.[8] Prussian Lutherans faced a severe crisis when King Frederick William III, quite enamored of Enlightenment philosophy, proposed the merger of Lutheran and Reformed churches in order to consolidate his power as supreme bishop of the territory. A royal commission was to bring the merger about in 1817 as a fitting memorial to Luther's Ninety-five Theses of 1517. But a conservative faction (known as *alt-lutherisch*, "old Lutheran") rejected the union as a tyranny imposed by the king. He tried to keep them in the union, using imprisonment and military occupation, but to no avail. Finally, the king withdrew his absolute rule and allowed them to form their own church, the Evangelical Lutheran Church in Prussia; it existed until 1904 when it joined the "union" of 1817.[9]

The defeat of the king's proposed merger prompted some Lutherans to call for a new Lutheran commitment to Luther and the Lutheran Confessions. The well-known lay theologian and Luther scholar John George Hamann (1730–1788) had much impact on this confessional awakening.[10] On October 31, 1817, Pastor Klaus Harms, the most popular preacher in Northern Germany, published his own Ninety-five Theses in Kiel. Harms called for loyalty to Luther, to the Augsburg Confession, and to a German Lutheranism cleansed from all Reformed (Calvinist) elements, especially in regard to the interpretation of the Lord's Supper.[11] The movement gained momentum in 1830, the tercentenary of the Augsburg Confession, when the high school teacher and later theologian at Marburg University, August F. C. Vilmar (1800–1868), called for a renewal of the church based on a strict confessionalism. Theologians and pastors joined the movement in the northeast, in Silesia, where territorial rulers had legislated a union between Lutherans and Calvinists.

Soon, the confessional awakening spread through Germany, centering at the University of Erlangen, the enduring stronghold of conservative confessional Lutheranism. A model parish for Neo-Lutheranism was organized by Pastor Wilhelm Löhe (1808–1872) in 1837 in Neuendettelsau, a small Bavarian town. There, he

Wilhelm Löhe

organized a diaconate along with affiliated homes, hospitals, and educational institutions; created a rich liturgy in a new order of worship (*Agende* of 1844); and established a mission society with links to North America, South America, and Australia. A prolific author, Löhe summarized his catholic ecclesiology in a widely read study.[12] He is the Neo-Lutheran who linked the ecumenical substance of the Lutheran Confessions with the call for mission at home and abroad. "Mission is nothing else but the one church of God in its movement."[13] He also viewed mission as an organic development toward the end time, and he speculated about its meaning and timing, in contrast to Augsburg Confession 17, which rejects such speculation.[14] Thus the so-called sacramental Lutheran, who was buried dressed in an alb, did an eschatological side-stepping, angering his constituency, especially in the United States.

The confessional awakening ruined the enforced union of Lutherans and the Reformed in Silesia. When it was enforced, many Lutherans emigrated to the United States with the help of Löhe and others, especially Frederick C. D. Wynecken (1810–1876), who had traveled in North America and organized strong support for Lutheran immigrants. Some Lutheran groups went to Australia. When King Frederick William IV of Prussia used military force to keep the hated union alive, lobbyists finally persuaded him to tolerate the return to confessional Lutheranism. In 1841, Prussian Lutheran conservatives organized the Evangelical Lutheran Church in Prussia. Neo-Lutheranism was kept alive through the publication of an enduring periodical created by the Erlangen theologian Gottlieb Harless (1806–1879), *Journal für Protestantismus und Kirche*.

Neo-Lutheran theology was nurtured in the Erlangen school by such minds as Harless and Löhe. It stressed the regeneration of the individual Christian through the church and its means of salvation, word, and sacrament. Erlangen theologians contended that the Lutheran Confessions had rediscovered and preserved the central orthodox aspects of Christianity. In this sense, Löhe viewed the Lutheran church as the model among other churches because it possessed the full truth. Such language sounds like the language of Vatican II (1965), which regards the Roman Catholic Church as the "fullest" expression of the church of Jesus Christ, with other churches only approximating such an expression.[15] But in contrast to Catholicism, the Erlangen School argued that Lutheranism discloses its power and authority in the parishioners whose pastors have sanctified them through word and sacrament.

Thus, Harless summarized the fullness of the church in its ethics as the testimony of life regenerated by word and sacrament.[16] But he opposed rituals, especially genuflection at the sight of consecrated eucharistic elements. When the Bavarian ministry of defense in 1838 ordered soldiers to genuflect at Corpus Christi processions, no matter whether they were Catholic or Protestant, Harless strongly opposed the order and lost his position at Erlangen University; he joined the Leipzig theological faculty. The controversial military order was withdrawn in 1844.[17] Though centered in a theology of regeneration (rebirth, sanctification), Neo-Lutheranism differed from Pietism with its focus on individual repentance and conversion. In contrast, the confessional awakening in nineteenth-century Germany was marked by liturgy centered in the Lord's Supper, and by ethics grounded in church piety. Neo-Lutherans occasionally quarreled over the definition of office and authority in the church, trying to find a middle way between Pietism and Catholicism.[18] Some advocated the notion of the church as an institution of salvation founded by the apostles but without a subsequent sacramental hierarchy (Roman Catholic and Greek Orthodox). Others argued for a definition of the church as a community organized by believers with the assistance of the Holy Spirit in word and sacrament. Neither side could claim victory.

Neo-Lutheranism was both confessional, in the sense of loyalty to the Lutheran Confessions, and confessing, in the sense of public, political activity. In Prussia, Bavaria, and other German territories, confessional Lutherans refused to accept the union with the Reformed, imposed by the king. In Catholic Bavaria, they rejected political moves to become a minority party among Catholics. Confessing Lutherans tried to see their church as an ecumenical and social model.[19]

In Scandinavia, Lutheranism experienced an awakening that was not strictly confessional, though influenced by German Neo-Lutheranism. Its source was

Nikolaj F. S. Grundtvig

Pietism, mediated by traveling Moravian preachers and by individual churchmen who appreciated and propagated Christian liberty. Nikolaj F. S. Grundtvig (1783–1872), a Danish pastor, led a reform movement beginning in 1830 that would leave a permanent imprint on Lutheranism.[20] He was Denmark's most influential educator, poet, and theologian, weaving ancient Nordic traditions into Danish religious life. Grundtvig saw the free ecumenical spirit of Lutheranism grounded in the ancient apostolic tradition as the force to unite Christianity and culture through education. He contended that the Apostles' Creed was the baptismal creed for all churches, the living word that Jesus communicated to his apostles. Accordingly, baptism and the Lord's Supper are the living words, the fundamental elements of the church. Grundtvig taught that biblical confessional formulations, especially John 3:16, were forerunners of the Apostles' Creed and should interpret the Bible, not vice versa.[21] Though involved in some controversies, Grundtvig and Grundtvigianism shaped all of Danish culture through

preaching, hymns (fifteen hundred from Grundtvig!), and tracts in adult education classes. Thus, Danish citizens were taught to view their native language and their common history as the ingredients of a school for life, whose graduates would be the political and economic pillars of Denmark.

The leader of the awakening in Norway was Hans Nielsen Hauge (1771–1824), a lay preacher and businessman who underwent a conversion experience; his preaching and writings called for a spiritual discipline of selfless love. Because Norwegian law prohibited street preaching and assemblies outside the state church (conventicles), Hauge was frequently arrested but remained loyal to the official church. He was a confessional Lutheran in the sense that he

Hans Nielsen Hauge

believed Christian discipline was to be based on a proper distinction between law (revealing sin) and grace (disclosing salvation in Christ).[22]

In Sweden, Pastor Lars Levi Laestadius (1800–1861) and the lay preacher Carl Olof Rosenius (1816–1868) created a religious revival calling for moral regeneration and mission at home and abroad. Laestadius experienced a conversion in 1844 and

found many followers in Swedish Lapland. Rosenius was strongly influenced by writings of Luther and German Pietism. He founded the journal *Pietisten* in 1834 and called for social reforms that eventually gained the approval of the state church.

In Finland, a general awakening was created by the itinerant preaching of the farmer Paavo Ruotsalainen (1777–1852), called "the prophet of the wilderness." His sermons about repentance and the need for intensive praying found many sympathetic ears among the clergy and the laity. Some of his disciples echoed much of Pietism with its call for conversion; others linked their experience with the Lutheran confessional tradition. Many pastors revived the use of private confession as a means of conversion, due to Ruotsalainen's influence, thus

Carl Olof Rosenius

bringing the movement closer to the state churches.[23]

German confessional and liberal Lutherans tried to be united against any threat of a union with the Reformed. So they founded the *Allgemeine Evangelisch-Lutherische Konferenz* or Common Evangelical Lutheran Conference in 1867, which met in 1868 in an assembly of fifteen hundred people in Hannover. A main issue of the conference was the meaning of Augsburg Confession article 7 in relation to church leadership. But the discussion on what is sufficient for unity created more tension than unity. Some Union Churches (Lutheran-Reformed) persisted in a number of territories throughout the nineteenth century. In Prussia, the old Union of 1817 continued with an emphasis on administrative cooperation, when the diplomatic skills of Duke Otto von Bismarck created a model church polity in 1876. A new constitution centered on four positions that shaped future developments: (1) establishing parish councils responsible for directing the work of the local congregation; (2) convening an annual district synod meeting to coordinate the work of the local congregations; (3) establishing a provincial synod to meet every third year; and (4) forming a general synod (in Greek, *synodos*, "assembly"), headed by a synod council, to meet every sixth year. New hymnals, containing streamlined forms of worship, accompanied these congregational reforms.

Neo-Lutherans on the continent were quite aware of the power and influence of the Anglo-Catholic Oxford Movement (organized in 1860) as well as of Methodism in England, where eight million people had joined the reform movement by 1900. The Anglo-Catholic Oxford Movement was begun by Anglican theologians who advocated a revival of the teachings of the early church fathers. They propagated these teachings in a series of tracts, contending that Roman Catholicism was more faithful to the ancient tradition than was Protestantism. Some, therefore, converted to Catholicism. Others remained Anglican, dubbed "Anglo-Catholic."[24] On the other hand, the religious awakening was also to stem the tide against secularism, especially its most threatening feature, Marxist Socialism, with its call for a radical transformation of society. But the confessional awakening never became a successful reform movement, dealing realistically with the problems of church unity and sociopolitical ills. Intellectuals and the common folk continued to become more and more estranged from the church. The efforts of theologians like Vilmar and pastors like Löhe hardly affected more than local or regional Lutheranism. The literature of the movement consisted of unattractive devotional tracts and complex theological writings. At its best, the confessional awakening created pockets of a Neo-Lutheran spirituality, affirming but not fully realizing Lutheran unity with some ecumenical dimensions. Löhe exported his zeal for Christian unity and mission to North America, where Lutheran immigrants continued to nurture the growth of Pietism and its link to a confessional awakening.

Inner Mission

The continuing concern for practical Christianity created the Inner Mission movement in Germany and to a lesser degree in Scandinavia. The movement wanted to deal with problems at home, to be a "home mission" as some called it, in addition to the "foreign mission" and its task of converting non-Christians abroad.[25] The Inner Mission was preceded by a general concern for a realization of the biblical call for love of neighbor, diaconal service. Lutheran Pastor John F. Oberlin (1740–1826) in Waldbach, Alsace, advocated working for social justice by creating schools, savings banks, and agricultural societies. Another Lutheran pastor, John Falk (1768–1828), devoted his life to the care of families and children in need. He created foster homes, small communities for religious instruction and "houses of recovery" *(Rettung-*

shäuser) where impoverished youth were rehabilitated; the best known was the "Luther Court" *(Lutherhof)* in Weimar. The Lutheran pastor in Kaiserswerth (near Düsseldorf), Theodor Fliedner (1800–1864), advocated antipoverty programs, prison reform, and an active role for women in the new industrial society. Influenced by Methodism in England, he founded hospitals for the poor as well as founding the first deaconess house in

The deaconess house at Kaiserswerth

Kaiserswerth, a training center for a church vocation specializing in education and pastoral care as an alternative for women, who were excluded from ordination.[26] When he died, there were numerous motherhouses for deaconesses, among them one in Pittsburgh and another in Jerusalem. Florence Nightingale (1820–1910), the English pioneer of hospital nursing and of care for the wounded in the battlefield, resided for some time in the Kaiserswerth motherhouse in 1851.

The Inner Mission movement found its most effective expression in the work of John H. Wichern (1808–1881), a Lutheran pastor nurtured by Pietism and a theology of social action.[27] Concerned about the social conditions in Hamburg, he began to gather starving children and in 1833 established an educational center for juvenile delinquents known as the "rough house" *(Rauhes Haus).* Graduates became "brothers," who went into the streets to save other boys from a life of depravity and poverty. Tracts with the title "Flying Leaflets from the Rough House" appeared beginning in 1844 and made Wichern's work known in Germany and abroad.

Joining the politically conservative faction in Prussia, Wichern laid out his plan for Inner Mission in Germany at the first national "Church Day" *(Kirchentag)* in Wittenberg in 1848, a national assembly of churches. In an emotional speech, he told the delegates that a strategy of love, not violence as advocated

John H. Wichern

by Marxists, was needed to renew society. A central committee was organized; Wichern was appointed in 1856 to organize a mission with the assistance of the royal Department for Domestic Affairs. The king saw in him a trusted adviser and appointed him as head of the Prussian prison system, with the special task of caring

for the poor within the royal ministry of justice. But a complex bureaucracy and increasing health problems slowed Wichern down. In the end, secularists (later known as Social Democrats) rather than the Inner Mission movement would shape German politics and culture.

After 1881, the Inner Mission was directed by Pastor Frederick Bodelschwingh (1831–1910).[28] Because he had been a childhood playmate of the future Prussian emperor Frederick III, he always had access to the Prussian court and received support for his programs. He was impressed by Löhe's work of parish renewal in Neuendettelsau and by the healing ministry of the Lutheran pastor in Bad Boll, John Christopher Blumhardt (1805–1890), the son of a well-known Pietist missionary in

Frederick Bodelschwingh

Basel.[29] For Bodelschwingh, both of them became models of mission. As assistant pastor at a German Lutheran congregation in Paris, he worked with rag-pickers, servant girls, and street sweepers. During his ministry in Dellwig an der Ruhr in the poor section of the Rhineland, he lost all four of his children in two weeks during an epidemic of whooping cough. The tragedy changed his life. "I realized," he recorded later, "how hard God can be against human beings, and that made me more compassionate towards others."[30] In 1872, he

was appointed as the head of the Rhenish-Westphalian center for epileptics near Bielefeld; it was staffed by deaconesses and was named Bethel, later known as the city of mercy. In 1877, he added a brotherhouse, caring for homeless men on the road, and in 1882 he founded "work camps" (Arbeitskolonie) in nearby Wilhelmsdorf, where social outcasts and people with mental illness found therapy through work. "Work instead of alms" was Bodelschwingh's motto. Unlike Wichern, he refused to advocate a Christian state and sought cooperation for justice among all political parties. When he was elected to be a member of the Prussian Provincial Diet (Landtag), he became its political gadfly, always lobbying for the recognition and rehabilitation of the victims of society, ranging from people with mental illness to the homeless. At

Gertrude Reichardt, the first deaconess

the same time, Bodelschwingh also turned his attention to

foreign mission by founding the Mission Society for German East Africa (today Tanzania). It was headquartered in Bethel and became known later as the Bethel Mission. He was convinced that everyone could become a Christian and that all ills could be cured by the mercy of God, based on his favorite biblical saying (later inscribed on his tombstone): "Since it is by God's mercy that we are engaged in this ministry, we do not lose heart" (2 Cor. 4:1). In 1890, he added a theological school (later known as *Theologische Hochschule*) to the Bethel institutions of mercy. The school was to train pastors, combining, in contrast to traditional education at universities, academic and practical work. The latter was a kind of internship, consisting of work in the various institutions of the Inner Mission. The school was certified by the government in 1905. Father Bodelschwingh, as people liked to call him, combined theology with pastoral care and an almost charismatic sense for programs and their link to institutions and finances.

His work was continued by his son Frederick, known as Bodelschwingh Jr. (1877–1946), who led the German Inner Mission into the next century. The movement did not succeed in integrating the Lutheran struggle for social justice with the efforts of the state to alleviate the suffering caused by the industrial revolution. Wichern's vision and Bodelschwingh's program, though favored by the Prussian monarchy, did not become an integral part of political justice. They were sidelined by politics. The court chaplain, Adolf Stöcker (1835–1909), a member of the church union and a sworn enemy of Marxist Socialism, did not support the religious Inner Mission but founded the Christian-Socialist Labor Party in 1878, assisted by economist Adolf Wagner (1835–1917), who favored patriarchal charity programs rather than any change of the existing social order. Stöcker expanded his influence by founding the Evangelical (Protestant) Congress in 1890, attracting to it the Prussian intellectual elite and anti-Semitic factions. He was concerned that a Christian social movement would be too liberal. Another popular Lutheran pastor in Frankfurt, Frederick Naumann (1860–1919), who advocated better wages for the working class, tried to revive Wichern's vision within the congress. But Stöcker refused to accept any compromise and founded the Free Ecclesiastical-Social Conference in 1897, consisting only of right-wing members of the Lutheran state church. Finally, Stöcker founded the Christian-Socialist Party (no longer the Labor Party), which lost its particular stance when political liberals began to dominate it.

The Inner Mission movement in Germany can be seen as part of an earlier broad philosophical revival labeled romantic. It stressed "light, life and love," as the major voice of the romantic philosophy put it, Johann Gottfried Herder (1744–1803).[31] Herder was Lutheran superintendent in Weimar, concerned with rescuing the world of human feelings and experience from the eighteenth-century rationalism that dominated the European Enlightenment. Romanticists liked to speak of the moral personality of Jesus, of religion as the best part of humanity, and of life filled with a sense of divine happiness. Love was the fundamental ingredient of life in the world as the creation of God. Wichern viewed it as the power that linked family, government, and church as agents of Christian salvation. He was influenced by the Erlangen theologian Frederick J. Stahl (1802–1861), a leader in the Conservative Party and defender of the notion that humanity is socially organized by divine "orders of salvation" evident in the "estates" (Latin: *status*) of economy, church, and politics.[32] Because all baptized Christians are part of these orders, they must revitalize them through Christian love, expressed as the power of the priesthood of all believers, which must improve the conditions of this world. In this context, the church is linked to the world as an "association" *(Verein)* that issues new moral power as "living Christianity." The major voice of this romantic morality was Richard Rothe (1799–1867), a Lutheran professor of ethics in Bonn and Heidelberg, who viewed the church as the beginning of a development of associations leading to a final "community" *(Gemeinschaft)* reflecting the intentions of Christ, the Savior. "The community, grounded in the Savior, must begin its development under the form of the church," ending in a perfect religious and moral association.[33]

Such idealistic and romantic sentiments did not win the day in an increasingly secularized culture in the nineteenth century. German Lutheranism was partially successful in continuing the Pietist drive to individual conversion and social action. The Inner Mission did much for social justice, at times with the strong support of the state, like in Prussia. In Norway, an initially small drive for inner mission by advocates of church renewal led to the creation of a central committee in 1891. It was to direct an increasing number of associations, clubs, and societies working with delinquent youth, sailors, and the poor. But the love for small, local, and regional associations soon shaped all of church life so that Lutheranism in Norway looked like a club system hardly matched in other countries.[34] But the designation of "association" in Norway was not theologically grounded in an order of salvation as was *Verein* in Germany. In Denmark, an Inner Mission was organized in 1861 by the Lutheran pastor Vilhelm Beck (1829–1901), who helped the state church to focus on home mission; he founded thirty inner mission houses by 1872. In Austria, the Inner Mission Society was organized in 1874 with a variety of institutions, including a motherhouse for deaconesses, located in Gallneukirchen near Linz. The Lutheran pastor William A. Passavant (1821–1894) created the first network of Inner Mission institutions in North America, beginning with the first Lutheran hospital in Pittsburgh in 1849. He also expanded Inner Mission concerns from

William A. Passavant

the care for the victims of society to all activities of the church ranging from education to architecture.[35]

The Inner Mission movement did not succeed in transforming society through an active priesthood of all believers, who, in Wichern's vision, would create Christian nations, or, according to Bodelschwingh, become a political partner of the state for the sake of social justice. The movement provided significant enduring care for the victims of society in various parts of the world where there is a Lutheran presence. Lutheran advocates for inner mission succeeded in expanding the classic Lutheran view of the continuing reform of the church to the need to reform society. But despite the work of the inner mission, linked to constitutional, liturgical, and ethical attempts to reform the church, many Lutherans still shied away from active involvement in the church and in society.

Toward Institutionalization in North America

By 1817, North American frontiers had been opened by improved transportation and the shameful persecution of Native Americans, so-called Indians. New York Lutherans founded the Committee on Home Missions in 1823 led by the head of Hartwick Seminary, Ernst L. Hazelius (1777–1853), a former Moravian. The drive for home mission was linked to the growth of church organization. The Ohio Synod was constituted in 1818, followed by the Maryland-Virginia Synod in 1820. Petty controversy delayed further organization into a general synod. Some conservative Lutherans opposed mixed

Samuel S. Schmucker

marriages with the Reformed (Calvinists) as being like mating cows with horses.[36] Others quarreled over leadership: obedience to synods was a new form of papacy![37] When the General Synod was finally organized in 1820, it was led firmly for fifty years by the Lutheran pastor-theologian Samuel S. Schmucker (1799–1873), son of a Pietist cleric and graduate of Princeton Seminary.[38] His goal for Lutheranism in North

America was threefold: (1) establishing a seminary to provide well-educated pastors; (2) establishing a college as the foundation for general knowledge and specialization focused on philosophy and theology; and (3) establishing the composition of a Lutheran systematic theology, a dogmatics. The General Synod realized the first two parts of his vision by founding Gettysburg Seminary in 1826 and Gettysburg College in 1832, both in Pennsylvania.

Gettysburg Seminary

Schmucker himself produced the dogmatics in 1834, in a work titled *Elements of Popular Theology.*

Although synods affirmed a strict adherence to the Lutheran Confessions, especially the Augsburg Confession, the General Synod was guided by Schmucker's distinction between adherence to "the fundamental doctrines of the Bible" and the Augsburg Confession, which contained these doctrines in a "substantially" correct way.[39] This view was staunchly defended by the *Lutheran Observer,* a journal edited by Benjamin Kurtz, a student of Schmucker. Another journal, the *Lutheran Standard,* defended a more conservative view, charging that disciples of Schmucker preferred revivals to strict confessional loyalty. The literary controversy was also influenced by the question of whether English or German should be the proper language in church activities, especially public worship. Some Lutherans favored the observance of Sabbath rules; others lobbied for temperance in the face of alcoholism at the frontier. Almost all Lutherans tolerated slavery. But pastors in Hartwick, New York, created the Franckean Synod (honoring the famous German Pietist), which opposed slavery and even ordained an African American pastor, Daniel Payne, who later became a bishop in the African Methodist Episcopal Church.[40] The synod also required total abstinence from alcohol.

Lutherans came to the New World from Germany and Scandinavia, their departure motivated by political, economic, and religious reasons. The Congress of Vienna in 1815 facilitated the rise of such political superpowers as Prussia, Austria, and Russia. Some Prussian Lutherans left in order to escape the king's mandate to unite Lutherans with Calvinists. Others emigrated because the industrial revolution disrupted the old social order, such as the guild system and traditional farming. The pressure of the machine age, the struggle between state churches and Pietism, or simply a sense of adventure made many Lutherans leave for a country where there was radical religious liberty. Scandinavian pastors soon appeared alongside German preachers in the East and South. The first U.S. Danish pastor was Claus L. Clausen (1820–1863), who was ordained at the call of a Norwegian congregation, primarily to serve Norwegians in Muskego, Wisconsin, in 1843.[41] Immigrants from Norway were called Sloopers, after supposedly sleek ships that were actually small and tubby. It was a term of honor restricted to one small party that came from Stavanger in 1825; it included a number of Quakers. The 1825 event signaled the beginning of mass immigration from Norway. The lay preacher Elling Eielsen (1804–1863) was the first Norwegian pastor ordained in 1843, working among Haugeans in the Fox River Valley, Illinois.[42] The Church of Sweden sent a missionary to the Swedish settlement in Andover, Illinois, Lars P. Esbjorn (1808–1870), who, after some controversy with other Swedish Lutherans, organized the Augustana Synod.[43]

The rapidity of Lutheran institutional expansion is illustrated by the fact that nearly sixty synods were organized between 1840 and 1875.[44] U.S. Lutherans also sent missionaries to Canada, which had a small contingent of Lutherans before 1776. Missionaries created other communities in Ontario and Nova Scotia.[45] The growth of Lutheranism in the United States was plagued by constant controversy linked to ethnic and doctrinal differences. Periodically, grandiose yet unrealistic proposals were made to unite Protestants against Catholics. William H. Muhlenberg (1798–1877), the grandson of the patriarch of North American Lutheranism, joined the Episcopal Church and called for an evangelical-catholic attitude, also favored by some Lutherans as a self-definition of their loyalty to the Lutheran Confessions. But by and large, ethnic Lutherans could melt in neither a cosmopolitan nor theological melting pot. Philip Schaff (1819–1893), a Swiss native with solid theological training in Germany and a post as Reformed professor at the Mercersburg Seminary in Pennsylvania, told German audiences that U.S. Lutherans in were divided into three groups: Neo-Lutherans linked to the Gettysburg Seminary and representing an Americanized German Lutheranism, "Old Lutherans" defending confessionalism and rejecting Reformed teachings, and "Moderate" or "Melanchthonian Lutherans" disclosing a willingness to compromise for the sake of Christian unity.[46] There was a dire need to establish solid doctrinal norms in order to clarify the proper Lutheran stance between revivalists and confessionalists.

Schmucker made a valiant attempt to avoid further controversy by proposing a revision of the Augsburg Confession in order to adjust it to "American Lutheranism." He was supported by Benjamin Kurtz; by Samuel Sprecher, his brother-in-law and president of Wittenberg College in Springfield, Ohio; and initially by the General Synod. The proposal was mailed to the pastors of the General Synod without identifying the sender and was titled *Definite Synodical Platform, Doctrinal and Disciplinarian, for Evangelical Lutheran Synods: Constructed in Accordance with the Principles of the General Synod.*[47] Its introduction listed five errors in the Augsburg Confession: (1) the approval of the ceremony of the Mass, (2) the approval of private confession and absolution, (3) the denial of the divine obligation of the Christian Sabbath, (4) the affirmation of baptismal regeneration, and (5) the affirmation of the real presence of the body and blood of the Savior in the Holy Communion. Schmucker simply removed what he considered to be Roman Catholic remainders in the Augsburg Confession. But in fact, he did much more: he rejected the biblical and ecumenical view of baptism especially cherished by Luther, as rebirth by water through the Holy Spirit (Titus 3:5). He also rejected the confessional Lutheran assertion of Christ's real presence in the Lord's Supper; his view was closer to the Calvinist, indeed the Zwinglian, view. No wonder, then, that Schmucker created a firestorm of opposition. A majority of Lutheran synods refused to share his views even though they could be interpreted as a call for Christian unity among Protestants, excluding Catholics as sectarians. Besides, no one had ever revised the Augsburg Confession after Melanchthon's draft or adopted his altered version. Schmucker was soundly defeated and resigned as president of Gettysburg Seminary in 1864.

When one of his most severe critics, James A. Brown, was elected seminary president, the Pennsylvania Ministerium became so divided that it agreed to establish another seminary in Philadelphia, headed by Professor Charles P. Krauth (1823–1883), the conservative, confessional voice at Gettysburg Seminary. In Philadelphia, he became the leader of the conservatives. Faced with a lack of unity among synods, he proposed a new organization, eventually known as the General Council, and presented a set of theses titled "The Fundamental Principles of Faith and Church Unity" together with a "Fraternal Appeal" of the General Synod in 1867 in Fort Wayne, Indiana, calling for the acceptance of the "unaltered" Augsburg Confession, "without equivocation or mental reservation."[48] But the delegates remained divided over the terminology of confessional subscription. Some synods wanted more discussion in Free Conferences. But other synods called for a position paper on four points: millennialism (or chiliasm), altar fellowship, pulpit fellowship, and secret or "unchurchly societies" (such as Freemasons). The General Council responded only to the questions of altar and pulpit fellowship in its Galesburg Rule of 1875. It was narrow-minded and far from ecumenical: "Lutheran pulpits are for Lutheran ministers only. Lutheran altars are for Lutheran communicants only." Exception can be made "by the conscientious judgment of pastors."[49] Accordingly, Lutheranism was no longer viewed as a reform movement within the church catholic, as the Lutheran Confessions claim, but as a legal entity whose laws and officials control the power of word and sacrament.

But synods still pursued their own interests in ecclesiastical fellowship, motivated more by common interests than confessional loyalty. Some Midwestern synods, led by the Ohio and Missouri Synods, held Free Conferences and formed the Synodical Conference in 1872. Now, Lutherans of German background were organized in three federations: the General Synod of 1820, the General Council of 1867, and the Synodical Conference of 1872. The Civil War (1861–1865) also divided Lutherans. Five Southern synods withdrew from the General Synod: North Carolina, South Carolina, Virginia, Western Virginia, and Georgia. Even after the war, Southern Lutherans remained segregated, forming the United Synod, South, in 1886. Moreover, additional immigration from Europe led to the formation of distinctly ethnic synods consisting of Danes, Norwegians, and Finns, as well as immigrants from Iceland and Slovakia, then still a territory of the Austro-Hungarian Empire. Many synods turned their attention to foreign and domestic mission rather than to pursuing Lutheran or Christian unity at home. Jews, African Americans, and Native Americans (including Inuits, or Eskimos, in Alaska) became targets of the "home mission."[50]

The institutionalization of Lutheranism in North America included the creation of educational institutions, especially seminaries, colleges, and universities. Synods in the Midwest established a dozen new seminaries and eighteen colleges between 1875 and 1900.[51] Practical and confessional interests dominated in the training of pastors. Charles P. Krauth in Philadelphia and C. F. W. Walther (1811–1887) in St. Louis represented the conservative confessional stance. Milton Valentine (1825–1906), president of Gettysburg Seminary, spoke more liberally of the "Catholic Lutheranism of the Augsburg Confession."[52] A controversy over predestination preoccupied conservative confessional minds without any consensus.[53] Norwegian Lutherans debated a number of controversial issues, such as the nature of conversion.[54] Swedish Lutherans battled over decentralization, favored by a revival movement inspired by Rosenius and his disciple Paul P. Waldenstrom; the dissidents became nonconfessional biblical fundamentalists.[55] There also was complaint that the Lutheran "school mania" of the period weakened the quality of seminary and college education.[56] Some synods organized parochial schools; a majority, especially in the South, favored the Sunday school movement.

But the drive for some form of Lutheran unity persisted, usually ending in merger attempts, often bypassing the question of confessional unity. The Eastern synods, General Synod, General Council, and United Synod, South, representing the Muhlenberg tradition, continued to negotiate. They agreed on a common form of worship in 1888, eventually resulting in a common hymnal in 1917.[57]

Free Conferences and mutual visits to conventions paved the way to a merger into the United Lutheran Church in America in 1918. Scandinavian immigrants formed the United Norwegian Church in America in 1890, with a dissident group known as the Lutheran Free Church organized in 1897. Three Midwestern synods (Wisconsin, Minnesota, and Michigan) formed the Joint Synod of Wisconsin in 1892. The Slovak Evangelical Lutheran Church of the U.S.A. was organized in 1902 and joined the Synodical Conference in 1908.

Lutherans in Canada did not yet find the road to mergers but remained separated in the various geographical regions, often linked to churches in the United States. Most influential was the United Norwegian Lutheran Church in America, especially in Saskatchewan.[58] When the Federal Council of the Churches of Christ in America (which became the National Council of Churches in 1950) was formed as a Protestant interdenominational organization, only the General Synod joined. It did so on the conditions that the council affirm a "scriptural doctrine of the Godhead" and "principles of evangelical Christianity."[59] Lutherans also shared the prevalent Protestant polemical attitude to Roman Catholicism, viewing it as an enemy to Christian and U.S. freedom. Lutherans seemed to feel comfortable with synodical polity. This form of institutionalization was guided by the principles of conformity with the word of God and adaptation to existing social conditions.[60] Compared to other Christians, Lutherans felt doctrinally superior, perhaps because they were linked to the European Reformation, which caused a schism over dogma and polity. Few non-Lutheran immigrants joined Lutheran churches, and if they did, it was through marriage with a Lutheran. Though willing to be Americanized, few Lutherans held political office. They staged a big quadricentennial celebration of the Reformation (1517–1917) under the shadow of the Good Friday declaration of war with Germany (April 8, 1917). Numerous publications on Luther appeared.[61] There was much ritual talk about rededication, confessional loyalty, and bold witness. Even the end of the Roman apostasy was expected, with the hope that "a kind of Pentecostal era" was just ahead.[62] "Rome was the only topic on which Lutherans could agree."[63]

The Missouri Way

In 1839, seven hundred Saxon Lutherans protested against rationalism and migrated to St. Louis (and Perry County), Missouri, led by the Dresden pastor Martin

Stephan. They elected him as their bishop, promising complete submission to his rule.[64] But Stephan's adultery and mismanagement of finances almost eradicated the Lutheran colony. A new leader, Pastor C. F. W. Walther (1811–1887), set the tone for the future of the synod by calling for "a true church" loyal to the Lutheran Confessions.[65] However, the synod was organized in four bodies: (1) the Saxons from Missouri, (2) Löhe's missionaries, (3) Wilhelm Sihler and colleagues who withdrew from the Ohio Synod, and (4) Frederick C. D. Wynecken and colleagues who withdrew from the General Synod. All of them wanted to preserve Lutheranism from Americanization. In a joint declaration of 1846, they affirmed acceptance of the Lutheran Confessions "as the pure and unadulterated explanation and presentation of the Word of God."[66] Another group of German immigrants from the Saginaw Valley, Michigan, joined the new coalition, which constituted itself as a synod in Chicago in 1847. Remembering the treachery of Bishop Stephan, the twenty-five congregations adopted a strictly congregationalist constitution that ascribed ultimate authority to congregations with the synod as an "advisory body."[67]

C. F. W. Walther

The new synod was eager to propagate its conservative confessional stance through three journals: *Der Lutheraner,* first published by Walther in 1844; *Lehre und Wehre* (Doctrine and defense) in 1855; and *Lutheran Witness* in 1882. Concordia Seminary in St. Louis became the theological center headed by Walther. Another seminary was established in Springfield, Illinois, in 1875. Both institutions advocated an aggressive Lutheran confessional and biblicist stance. When the controversial *Definite Platform* of Schmucker appeared in 1855, the synod dismissed it as a "mixture of rationalism, enthusiasm *(Schwärmerei)* and Roman Catholicism"; it was neither American nor Lutheran.[68]

Soon, the first of the synod's many quarrels over Lutheran unity occurred about the issue of polity. In 1866, the Buffalo Synod defended the view that the clergy should make all decisions in the synod. Missouri leaders defended their congregationalist stance, which Buffalo partisans labeled "anabaptistic, democratic stupidity."[69] A majority of pastors and congregations of the Buffalo Synod did join the Missouri Synod. But the quarrel continued when Löhe and the Iowa Synod objected to Walther's view of ordination based on the theory of transference, namely, that the congregation could transfer its ministry to an individual member of the priesthood of all believers by calling him to be their pastor. Löhe, on the other hand, maintained that only pastors and synods could ordain. Walther, who shared with Löhe and others the view of the ordained ministry as a divine institution, called Löhe's position "hierarchical," reflecting Roman Catholicism. The two synods also quarreled over confessional subscription. The Iowa Synod understood the Lutheran Confessions as historical documents without ultimate authority. Moreover, a distinction needed to be made between essential and nonessential matters illustrated by the two parts of the Augsburg Confession. So-called open questions would allow further insights into the Christian truth. Walther and the Missouri Synod rejected such a view. They advocated an unconditional subscription to the Lutheran Confessions contained in the Book of Concord because they were in full harmony with the Bible. Consequently, no differences should exist among Lutherans regarding any teachings, especially about the Antichrist, Sunday observances, and the end time (chiliasm)—three popular causes for speculation that find little, if any, attention in the Lutheran Confessions. In short, they argued, there are no open questions. Tension increased when the Missouri Synod expelled one of its district presidents who allegedly affirmed chiliasm; he was accepted by the Iowa Synod. But both sides had to concede how difficult it was to settle all questions through biblical references. Certain theological or exegetical problems are disclosed in the Bible and should not divide the church. Yet the whole issue of biblical authority and interpretation remained and was to appear again in the future.

Only the Wisconsin Synod agreed completely with the Missouri views on biblical and confessional authority. The Minnesota Synod shared similar views after being unable to tolerate the "un-Lutheran" practices of the General Council. It declared theological unity with the Missouri Synod in 1871. The Illinois and Missouri Synods reached a similar agreement in 1872. The Norwegian Synod had a chair of theology at Concordia Seminary in St. Louis from 1859 to 1876. But when the first occupant of the chair, Professor Lauritz Larsen, tried to persuade his fellow-Norwegians to accept the Missouri view on slavery, his synod opposed it. For Missouri taught that, though slavery is sinful, God nevertheless permitted it in order to bring both master and slave to faith in Christ, followed by Christian love. A large majority of Norwegian Lutherans called for the abolition of slavery. But all these synods now in the orbit of the Missouri Synod were willing to join the Synodical Conference of 1872 because it preserved the autonomy of member synods and the confessional paragraph of its constitution echoed the Missouri spirit: "The Synodical Conference acknowledges its adherence to the canonical Scriptures of the Old and New Testaments as the Word of God, and to the symbolical books of the Evangelical Lutheran Church constituting the Book of Concord of 1580 as its own." Moreover, the conference elected the now well-known Missouri churchman Walther as its president. The chief objective of the conference was the "union of all Lutheran synods in America in one orthodox Lutheran church."[70]

The Missouri Synod expanded its influence after 1882 when 250,000 Germans and 105,000 Scandinavians arrived in the United States.[71] Congregations were established in the East, especially in Buffalo, New York City, and Baltimore. But congregants had to use German in their worship services because the synod wanted to remain German. Moreover, the use of English was associated with doctrinal laxity and a liberal unionism without a strict loyalty to the Lutheran Confessions. An 1887 sermon illustrates this point of view, lamenting the fact that English does not transmit "pure doctrine" as well as German; that the heritage of such doctrine may need to be transmitted to "descendants who will perhaps use English—Should this not move us to pray earnestly, 'Dear God, grant the Word may also be preached pure and unadulterated also among those who speak English, as it is among us.'"[72] The English Conference was established in 1890 but did not become a nongeographical English District until 1911. But English was the language used in foreign mission in cooperation with the Leipzig Mission Society. India, Latin America, and Australia became mission fields, but they were understood as "home missions abroad," which sounds like an oxymoron but reflected the desire to have strict doctrinal control by the home headquarters. The synod meant by *mission* not only the conversion of "heathens" and Jews, but also the propagation of its own brand of pure doctrine among other Christians, including Lutherans. Thus, a small Saxon German-speaking congregation in London founded two other congregations and three parochial schools in the city.[73] Parochial schools were seen as principal means of conversion and spiritual formation. "Next to the pure doctrine our schools are the greatest treasure we have."[74] In addition to the schools, the Walther League of 1894 focused on keeping loyalty to the synod among young men; this league competed with the Luther League of 1895, which consisted of members of various other Lutheran church bodies.

The most intensive controversy between the Missouri and other Lutheran synods dealt with the doctrine of predestination. It began in the Synodical Conference among pastors who thought that Reformed (Calvinist) views had infiltrated Lutheranism in America. These views, centering in Calvin's theory of *double predestination* (that God elects some for salvation and others for damnation), had been debated already in the sixteenth century, resulting in the Lutheran admonition to "flee and avoid all abstruse, specious questions and discussions."[75] The topic of election was one in a series discussed at the meeting of the Western District of the Missouri Synod in 1877. The main theme already disclosed the uncompromising Missouri position: "*Soli deo gloria* ('glory be to God alone'). That only through the teaching of the Lutheran Church God alone is given all honor; this is an irrefutable proof that the teaching of the Lutheran Church is the only true one."[76]

President Walther's own explication of predestination sounded Calvinistic to some theologians: God chooses "a certain number of persons unto salvation"; they will be saved "and besides them none [*sic*] others"; and although God "foresaw some good in them," they were not chosen by their merits, "for as the Scriptures teach, all good in man originates with Him."[77] Walther criticized his opponents at the next meeting of the Western District in 1879, causing the most conservative theologian of the Missouri Synod, Frederick A. Schmidt, to counterattack in a theological journal, titled *Altes und Neues* (The old and the new). It described the Missouri position on divine election as antibiblical, anticonfessional, and "crypto-Calvinist" (a designation used against the Melanchthonian Philippists in the sixteenth century).

Schmidt, a Norwegian who had taught at Concordia Seminary, joined the Joint Synod of Ohio, which became the stronghold for the anti-Missouri position. Its president, Matthias Loy (1828–1915), an admirer of Walther, now also opposed him. A colloquy of theologians of the Synodical Conference in Milwaukee in 1881 ended with total enmity between Schmidt and Walther. Because Schmidt and his followers had called Walther and the Missouri Synod crypto-Calvinists, Walther and his disciples called the Ohian opponents synergists (Greek: *synergomai*, "to come together," saved by cooperation of good works and divine grace) and semi-Pelagians (linked to the Irish monk Pelagius, who opposed Augustine's view of strict predestination and was condemned as a heretic in 418).

Such name-calling only fueled the controversy, because crypto-Calvinism identified an old enemy within the Protestant camp and Pelagianism one outside of it, namely, Roman Catholicism. Yet both sides in the predestination controversy claimed to stand on solid Lutheran ground identified with the doctrine of justification by faith alone. They claimed to be in harmony with second-generation Lutheran theologians in the seventeenth century, who viewed predestination "in view of faith" (in Latin, *intuitu fidei*).[78] The Missourians emphasized that God predestines *unto* faith by grace and the merit of Christ. Their opponents stressed the notion that God predestines *in* view of faith foreseen by God. They accused the Missourians of leaving everything to God, undermining the human element of faith. In turn, they were charged of ascribing too much to the human cooperation with God, undermining divine grace. Thus, theological hairsplitting was added to polemical name-calling.

Walther's treatise of 1881 tried to provide guidance and evidence concerning what and who in the controversy was Lutheran.[79] The Formula of Concord (article 11) and Rom. 8:28-30 constituted the disputed texts. Even though both sides seemed to agree that divine predestination is never based on human merit, the Missouri Synod insisted on complete agreement on verbal formulations. Such agreement was to be based on thirteen Missouri theses that simply stated Walther's position in another way. The Joint Synod of Ohio stated its stance in four theses reflecting the work of Walther's most ardent opponent, Matthias Loy.[80] The four theses restated the *intuitu fidei* position of the seventeenth-century theologians, namely, that election occurs in view of faith and is not the cause of it. Pastors and congregations on both sides defected. The Joint Synod of Ohio canceled its membership in the Synodical Conference. The Norwegian Synod did the same when the Synodical Conference refused to let the Norwegian chief critic of the Missouri position, Frederick A. Schmidt, speak at the Chicago assembly of the conference in 1882. But a majority of the Norwegian pastors agreed with Walther, even though Scandinavian Lutherans did not subscribe to the Formula of Concord, which was created after a German controversy.

The Missouri Synod enforced its stance on pure doctrine by prohibiting its members from joining liberal religious organizations such as the Freemasons.[81] This was a charitable association of architects and artists working on buildings, with the center in a lodge where specific rituals were held, often labeled secret, based on biblical stories and a rationalist view of God as the creator of a mysterious universe. The Freemasons first met in a lodge in London in 1717 for the purpose of "concord and harmony." Eventually, they taught a whole system of mysteries based on various speculations about God and the world; they attracted an intellectual elite and older men who were often the pillars of society. Many pastors joined and enjoyed the company of men with good connections in business and politics. The chief Missouri theologian after Walther, Francis A. Pieper (1852–1931), declared that "secret societies, such as Odd Fellows, Freemasons, etc. are incompatible with the Christian Church."[82] But such a judgment was not enforced because many pastors belonged to lodges and did not view membership as a church-dividing issue. Pieper certainly spoke for the entire synod when he declared that "whoever contests our doctrinal position contends against the divine truth."[83] Moreover, the journal *Lehre und Wehre* consistently contended that there is no development of doctrine since the Reformation. Its editors adopted a crude theological fundamentalism and constantly pointed out the deviations of non-Missouri Lutherans from the divine truth deposited in the Missouri Synod.

But many pastors on all sides tried to be tolerant and called for conferences on debated issues. Members of the Midwestern German synods held five such conferences between 1903 and 1906. Although Missouri theologians attended, they never agreed with any principles proposed by other theologians, often consigning their position, but graciously not their souls, to hell. By 1929, it had become clear that the Missouri Synod suspected all other Lutheran synods of false teaching. Its convention voted to withdraw from all intersynodical conferences and referred to other synods as "our opponents."[84]

European Theological Schools of Thought

While the American situation developed, in Europe the most influential theologian after the Enlightenment was the Reformed Friedrich Schleiermacher (1768–1834), who tried to counter the rationalism of Enlightenment philosophy with a theology based on pious experience. Though not Lutheran, he experienced the kind of Lutheran Pietism taught by the Moravians when he studied at one of their seminaries.[85] He intended to attract intellectuals who favored rationalist principles, "the cultured despisers of religion [Christianity]." Everyone is religious, he contended, and it is with awe that everyone senses a divine power. This awe is expressed in a feeling (Gefühl) of dependence on a God who is greater than any power known on earth.

All human beings, Schleiermacher declared, have an innate sense and taste for the infinite, and Christians have Jesus Christ as their model, the one who experienced the most powerful consciousness of God, demonstrated in the Gospel of John. This Christocentric consciousness is incorporated in the church, which is a living community nurtured by the Holy Spirit rather than just an institution. Schleiermacher's claim of the existence of an innate religiosity transcended the views of opposing parties in Lutheranism. He was quite liberal in the sense that he expanded biblical and trinitarian notions to include the mysterious arena of romantic-mystical experience. Thus, rationalism and Pietism could be united in what Kantian philosophers called phenomenology, external facts whose ultimate meaning remains a mystery, a postulation, an assumption of freedom, immortality, and God. As a result, Schleiermacher's disciples could, with Kant, assert that one lives with the stars above and with a moral consciousness within oneself—both beyond rational explanation.

Schleiermacher was the first of a theological elite that shaped German Lutheran theological thought for the century before the end of World War I in 1918. Soon, his focus on individual and corporate religious experience was combined with intensive reflections on historical development and a critical use of sources. This theological school of thought, linked to historical criticism, had its home in Tübingen, where gifted minds were trained in a "foundation" (Stift) founded by Duke Ulrich of Württemberg in 1539. Promising students studied at the university and received a generous stipend to live in the *Stift* and specialize in theology and philosophy with the help of tutors. Almost all famous German theologians and philosophers of the nineteenth century were graduates of the *Stift*. The most influential among them was George W. F. Hegel, who completed his doctoral studies of theology in Tübingen in 1790. His original, virtually eccentric, ideas about God and historical reality focus on the notion that personal experience (the "subjective spirit") and rational observation (the "objective spirit") merge in the "absolute spirit" of God, a dialectic of what he called thesis, antithesis, and synthesis. Within this vision, Hegel saw Christianity as the culmination of the absolute spirit, thus as the "absolute religion" and as the fountain of universal truth evoking universal love and true freedom.[86]

The Tübingen school of Lutheran theology generated several scholars who, with Hegelian confidence, began to rewrite the history of Christian doctrine as a clue for viewing contemporary Christianity and its future. Ferdinand Christian Baur (1792–1800) attempted to demonstrate how seemingly contradictory developments in the history of Christianity are held together by basic dogmatic convictions grounded in the doctrine of God's incarnation in Jesus and in the doctrine of God's reconciliation with sinful creatures.[87]

Albrecht Ritschl (1822–1889), one of Baur's disciples who taught in Berlin, the hub of German culture, used the dialectical method to demonstrate the power of the Christian faith. He contended that Christianity is grounded in God's incarnation in Jesus and in the dogma of the Trinity, the two pillars that have endured throughout time. Both point to a universal Christian morality evident in the teachings of Jesus, who will usher in the "kingdom of God." It is an "objective" reality guaranteed by dogma, and it is a "subjective" reality experienced in moral action. Christianity exists in the dialectic of both these realities.[88]

Adolf von Harnack (1851–1930) was the most prominent among the Tübingen historians of dogma, teaching in Berlin. As a disciple of Ritschl, he tried to show how Greek ideas had dominated early Christianity ("Hellenization") and how attention had shifted from the teachings of Jesus to his person. Accordingly, the essence of Christianity, the original teachings of Jesus, had been buried in a dogmatic, liturgical, and ecclesiastical process, evident in Roman Catholicism and Greek Orthodoxy. So Harnack issued a Protestant call for a revival of Christianity according to three essential teachings of Jesus: (1) the reign of God and its coming, (2) God the Father and the infinite value of the human soul, and (3) the higher righteousness and the commandment of love.[89]

Another German theological school of thought was one that studied Christian origins in the context of other religions, the "school of the history of religions" (*religionsgeschichtliche Schule*). Representatives of this school studied at various universities, especially in Berlin, Heidelberg, and Göttingen. Its best-known scholar was

Ernst Troeltsch (1865–1923). Siding with Schleiermacher and opposing Marx, he contended that religion, not just socioeconomic forces, build culture, and he tried to show the interaction between religion and culture in a massive historical study.[90] It viewed Christianity in terms of classified groups as they reacted to their surrounding society: churches, sects, and mystical groups. This classification became quite popular. In the context of his work, Troeltsch also criticized the Lutheran distinction between law and gospel, linked to the "two-kingdoms-ethic," because the distinction impeded Lutherans from involvement in social and political action; it made for quietist, obedient citizens. "Thus Lutheran Christian individualism has retired behind the line of battle of all external events and outward activity, into a purely personal spirituality."[91]

The most radical historian was David F. Strauss (1808–1874), who initiated a long controversy with the publication of his biography of Jesus.[92] He distinguished between what he called the Christ of faith and the Jesus of history. It is difficult, Strauss argued, to distinguish the one from the other, because the Bible's language is clothed in myths. He defined *myth* as the expression of an idea in the form of a historical account. Accordingly, Christ was manufactured by believers who make dogmatic claims, such as the resurrection, without convincing evidence. Strauss concluded that Christianity has no more power to convince than atheism.

Such radical views were dubbed "left-wing Hegelianism," because they employed Hegel's dialectic as a critique of religion in favor of "scientific objectivity." "Right-wing Hegelianism" lifted up the power of ideas and tended to neglect any "scientific proof." Left-wing Hegelianism also was in line with the Marxist denial of the existence of God. Ludwig Feuerbach (1804–1872), another left-wing Hegelian, concluded further that all theology is anthropology, that God is the result of human projection, making divine an idea of something absolute and calling it "god."[93]

The Erlangen school represented the conservative Lutheran elite, defending the inspiration of the Bible, the orthodoxy of the Lutheran Confessions, and personal spiritual experience. An important voice of this school of theological thought was John K. von Hofmann (1810–1877), who defended the traditional medieval and Reformation notion of "salvation history" *(Heilsgeschichte)*. This notion asserts that the Bible reveals a process of promise and fulfillment, from the time of creation to the last day, which is disclosed in the testimony of faithful readers of the Bible who are born again when they encounter the word of God in it. In this sense, Hofmann wanted to present, as his work is titled, defensive tracts of a new way of teaching old truth.[94]

The notion of an organic development of salvation history, centered in Christ, was used by Gottfried Thomasius (1802–1875), who wanted to defend the ancient Christian and classic Lutheran doctrine of the interpenetration of the human and divine natures of Christ *(communicatio idiomatum).* Because the historians had shown that the oldest evidence of a Christology was Phil. 2:5-11 (centering in "emptying"; Greek: *kenosis*), Thomasius spoke of a "kenotic Christology" to describe the human and divine aspects of the incarnation. Jesus knew himself to be God but gave up ("emptied") the "divine form of existence" and "gave it over to the human form."[95] It was a fine way to combine historical and doctrinal views of Christ, but it failed in the end to attract and remained an isolated attempt to mediate between the Erlangen and Tübingen schools.

The most prominent Erlangen scholar was Adolf von Harless, who was spiritually formed by Pietists in Halle, where he experienced an old-fashioned conversion after meditating on John 5:44 ("How can you believe when you accept glory from one another and do not seek the glory that comes from the one who alone is God?") and John 7:16-17 ("Jesus answered them [the Jews], 'My teaching is not mine but his who sent me. Anyone who resolves to do the will of God will know whether the teaching is from God or whether I am speaking on my own'"). He declared that his personal experience of biblical truth corresponded to the Lutheran Confessions, which summarize the common faith of a Christian community. They are the necessary organizing principles of Christian theology that must be grounded in an ecclesiastical community and cannot be based just on individual insight. Here, Harless distinguished between church and churchdom, the former being the divinely established saving order, the latter disclosing a historically conditioned legal order. That may be a reason why later a proverb was coined, stating a mandate expressed in a German word game, *Suchet das Heil zu Erlangen* ("seek to gain your salvation," *erlangen* meaning "to gain").[96]

Some German Lutheran theologians tried to mediate between the radical historicists of Tübingen and the conservative confessionalists of Erlangen. Among them was the Tübingen theologian Isaac A. Dorner (1809–1884), a student of Baur, who tried to show that the incarnation of God in Christ is interwoven with human history and thus shapes every human being in the certainty of faith.[97]

Another influential mediator was the Marburg theologian Wilhelm Herrmann (1846–1922), a student of Ritschl, who focused on the question of certainty in the midst of historical uncertainty in the modern world. Christian certainty, he contended, comes with a steady communion with God, grounded in faith and evoking moral character.[98]

In Denmark, Lutheran theology was shaped by conservative church leaders like Hans L. Martensen (1808–1884), a professor who became bishop of Zeeland in 1854. He had written a systematic theology and ethics.[99] His opponent was the theologian and philosopher Søren Kierkegaard (1813–1855), who sharply criticized the church establishment as well as the Grundtvigian awakening.[100] He viewed the life of faith as "exceptional existence" in the world and the experiencing of the "paradox" illustrated in the story of Abraham sacrificing Isaac (Genesis 22).[101] In treatises, books, and journals, Kierkegaard described, like a "screeching seagull," what he called the true initiation into Christianity by way of a "borderline existence" always close to the abyss. Every Christian must face the abyss, Kierkegaard argued, just as he himself had faced it when he broke his engagement to Regina Olson in 1840. Humanity suffers from a spiritual "sickness unto death" that had overwhelmed the Danish church and its pompous ritual. Kierkegaard left the church in 1854, accusing its leaders of being fraudulent hypocrites.

Søren Kierkegaard

Regarded as an eccentric, he did not gain broad recognition as a philosopher until the end of World War I in 1918 when existentialists discovered him as one of their main philosophical sources.[102]

Two theological movements advocated specific ideas regarding the church and Christian life. Confessional, conservative theologians at Lund in Sweden defended the view of the church as a liturgical assembly led by pastors who are ordained into their office as God-willed. Some pastors and many laypeople joined a Bible and tract movement begun by the Lund pastor Henrik Schartau (1757–1825). He was a Pietist eager to link the Lutheran Confessions to spiritual formation, using the image of "father–children" to describe the life of congregations.[103]

Despite the diversity of theological thought in the nineteenth century, it must be noted that most theologians, especially in German Lutheranism, wanted to be scientific theologians. Moreover, they wanted to show how Christianity can be reconciled with contemporary views. Elite theologians wanted to become partners with elite philosophers, as was the case with Wilhelm Dilthey (1833–1911). Being the son of a Lutheran pastor, he studied theology but switched to philosophy in order to wrestle with the problem of interpretation, or hermeneutics (from the Greek name of the god Hermes, the messenger of other gods, or from the verb *hermeneuō*, "to bring to speech, to interpret"). How does the human spirit fare in the constellations of history? Dilthey rejected the deterministic, often mechanical approach of Enlightenment philosophers and proposed various theories of hermeneutics, distinguishing between natural science and humanistic studies *(Geisteswissenschaft)*.[104] At issue was "historical thinking," with a concentration on the Bible and the history of Christian doctrine. Such thinking involved the totality of existence in time as the realm where God becomes immanent, that is, the incarnation of God, who is historically real in Jesus and theologically relevant in Christ. Theologians wanted to demonstrate that the Christ of history is also the Christ of faith, even though the so-called historical

Jesus could not be fully ascertained. Nineteenth-century theologians worked hard to show how human and divine self-consciousness are identical in Jesus Christ and how the relationship of faith with him establishes personal, ecclesiastical, and even cultural identity (through Christian moral action). These theologians were quite optimistic in their enterprise of weaving salvation history into world history, as Hegel had done with great certainty. Kierkegaard is the lonely voice warning of such an enterprise, thus foreshadowing a deconstructive way of Christian reflection in the context of world wars and genocides.

Beyond Europe and North America

Movements like the Awakening and Inner Mission in Europe, as well as Lutheran migration to North America, strengthened the drive for global mission first attempted by Pietists. But their missionary work became just one part of an enthusiastic global program, announced by its zealot, William Carey (1761–1834), an English Baptist cobbler, in a sermon of 1792 on Is. 54:2-3 ("Lengthen your cords and strengthen your stakes").[105] The nineteenth century became a century of missions. Anglicans, Methodists, and Baptists led the way. Various national and regional missionary societies supported and propagated the call to evangelize in heathen lands, later called developing countries (those outside of North America and Europe).

German Lutheran churches first supported the Reformed Basel Society in Switzerland (1819). Berlin became a hub for foreign mission in 1824, supported by the church at large, by noble families who wanted to create "faithful witness to the gospel in a faithless age," and by about eight hundred women's auxiliary societies. Pastor John Gossner (1773–1858) transformed the effort into the Gossner Society in 1829. The Barmen-Rhenish Society (1829) began German efforts to support the work of the Church of England and its society in London. These and other societies tended to duplicate their work.

The initial Lutheran cooperation with Anglicans and the Reformed (Calvinists) created problems that characterized much of foreign missions. Some graduates of Lutheran mission seminaries refused to work for the Basel Society because they declined to have Holy Communion with the Reformed. Other Lutheran missionaries had similar problems with the Anglicans. German church authorities found the mission societies to be too independent and organized an Evangelical Lutheran Mission Society in Saxony in 1836. Conservative confessional theologians in Erlangen called for one united Lutheran foreign mission. Wilhelm Löhe, the influential reformer in Bavaria and North America, propagated a foreign mission that was to be catholic and sacramental. The director of the Dresden mission, Karl Grau (1814–1864), tried his best to unite the various Lutheran efforts in foreign mission but failed.

Each of the Lutheran Scandinavian countries had its own missionary societies doing work mainly in Scandinavian colonies: the Danish Missionary Society (founded in 1821), the Norwegian Mission Society (1842), the Swedish Mission Society (1835), and the Finnish Mission Society (1859). In North America, the various Lutheran Church bodies organized missionary societies to support the work of their particular ethnic home churches. Lutherans shared with other Protestants an initial optimism regarding the future of a Christian world. They joined a global Protestant evangelism (without cooperation with Roman Catholics), whose agents tried to tell converts that to be Christian transcended the folk church and colonial political power. But to a great extent, they also supported colonialism and exported Christian disunity. When the German imperial court provided financial support in 1913, some colonial missions experienced uncomfortable tensions between mission and nationalism. World War I, then, simply paralyzed many missions after 1914.

Asia and the Pacific

German Lutheran Pietists had made good beginnings in India. The Leipzig Mission continued the work of the Pietist mission in Tranquebar and in the Tamil Evangelical Lutheran Church, assisted by Swedish Lutherans since 1849; they organized a separate Swedish diocese in 1901. German Gossner Society missionaries went to the Indian highlands, settling in Ranchi. They were quite successful there after 1857 because they did not change the existing social order and related well to the people in their varying situations.[106] In 1841, the first U.S. Lutheran missionary, John C. F. Heyer (1793–1873), expanded a small mission begun by the North German (Bremen) Mission Society in Rajahmundry; he was sent by the Ministerium of Pennsylvania.[107] His work was enhanced by the medical missionary Dr. Anna S. Kugler from Philadelphia. She offered health services in 1883 and attracted many influential women and men as coworkers. A Swedish mission began in 1877 in the southern province of Madhya Pradesh.[108] Two Scandinavian missionaries, the Dane Hans P. Boerresen (1825–1901) and the Norwegian Lars O. Skrefsrud (1840–1910), joined the small mission of the German Gossner Society and began working in 1867 among the Santals, an aboriginal tribe located in Bihar (west of the Ganges River) and in Assam (northeast).[109]

Lutheranism began in 1861 in Indonesia, a Dutch colony in Southeast Asia until it gained independence as a republic in 1949, encompassing more than three thousand islands—the largest being Sumatra and Borneo. Rhenish missionaries worked there led by Ludwig I. Nommensen (1814–1918), who learned the tribal Batak language and immersed himself in Batak culture. Quite successful in his mission, he created schools for all ages, trained Batak missionaries who founded their own society in 1899, and brought deaconesses from Germany in 1891. The mission eventually became a sizable church, the Protestant Christian Batak Church (Huria Kristen Batak Protestan), which included all Lutherans.[110]

Lutherans appeared in Australia (a federal parliamentary state since 1901) in 1838 when the Berlin Gossner Society sent a group of pastors, laypeople, and artisans to work among Aborigines in a region now near Brisbane. But the settlers also wanted to have their own ethnic German church and called two outspoken confessional pastors from Dresden, who, together with opponents of the Church of the Prussian Union, founded a Lutheran Church in Australia in 1838 in Port Adelaide. They were financially supported by the Baptist director of the South Australia Company, who wanted German settlers and liked their pastor August L. C. Kavel (1798–1860). They were joined by another Prussian group led by Pastor Gotthard D. Fritzsche (1797–1863). Kavel created a church constitution based on the New Testament model of elders, a Presbyterian-Calvinist order. After a quarrel over millennialism, the Kavel and Fritzsche disciples united in a church of about eight hundred members. In 1864, the Kavel line became the Immanuel Synod and the Fritzsche line the South Australia Synod. They were united in a "confessional union" and began a mission among Aborigines, the Dieri, in the northeast corner of South Australia. The South Australia Synod started its own mission in 1877 in the Aranda country near Alice Springs. Their Finke River Mission, as they called the new venture, became quite successful when the immigrant scholar Karl Strehlow (1871–1922) and his son, Theodore, provided volumes on Aranda culture, the Dieri tribe, and translations of Christian catechetical materials for all ages. The Immanuel Synod was revived in its missionary work by a Löhe missionary from Neuendettelsau, John Flierl (1858–1947), who worked among the Aborigines on the Cape York Peninsula, which developed into the Hope Valley Mission in 1886 near Cooktown, north of Cairns.[111]

Lutheranism in New Zealand originated with some German Lutherans in 1843 and with the arrival of Missouri Synod pastors in the 1890s. A visit of the Concordia Seminary professor Augustus L. Graebner in 1902 helped ease the feeling of isolation and strengthened the mission to the Maoris. One of the Maori converts was trained at the seminary in Springfield, Illinois. After graduation in 1912, he worked as a missionary among his people. Danish Lutheran settlers formed eight congregations in New Zealand at the turn of the century. Again, Lutherans organized segregated churches, one for themselves and another for native converts.[112]

A Lutheran mission was started in 1886 in Papua New Guinea by the German Neuendettelsau and Rhenish Mission Societies. At that time, the British, Dutch, and Germans were the ruling colonial powers there, and the area has been an independent parliamentary state since 1975. The German missionary in Australia, Flierl, began work in the German colony near Finschhafen. His partner, Christian Keyszer

(1856–1937), adopted the method of converting groups, like a village or a whole tribe, by consent before doing individual baptisms. After 1908, native missionaries were sent out.[113]

The Lutheran mission in China (since 1949, the Communist People's Republic) joined other missionary efforts begun in the seventeenth century by Greek Orthodox, Catholic Jesuit, and Protestant missionaries. Dutch Reformed and Anglican missionaries worked in China beginning in 1624; the Anglican Robert Morrison (1782–1834) translated the Bible into Chinese in 1818. The Lutheran missionary Karl Gützlaff (1803–1851), trained in Berlin and sent by the Dutch Society, translated the Bible into Siamese (Thai) and propagated a China mission through popular travelogues in Europe. After 1846, other German missionaries went to Canton, to the province of Kwangtung, and to the northeastern port city of Tsing-tao. A Norwegian Lutheran Mission Society was organized in 1890, whose missionaries joined those from the American Hauge Synod in 1892.[114] Scandinavian and American Lutheran missionaries went to the central provinces. Soon, missionaries and merchants were identified with the higher privileged members of society. The Boxer Rebellion of 1900, spawned by traditionalists and nationalists, persecuted missionaries as unwelcome foreigners.[115] The Church of the Lutheran Brethren sent missionaries to the mainland provinces of Honan and Hupeh and established a church there in 1902.[116]

Lutheranism in Hong Kong (a British Crown Colony since 1847, now again part of China) began in 1847 with two missionaries of the Rhenish Society, Heinrich Koster and Ferdinand Genähr.[117]

The first Lutheran missionaries came to Japan (a parliamentary state with a symbolic emperor since 1947) in 1892: two Americans from the American Lutheran United Synod, South; a Dane; a Finnish pastor with his wife; and another woman worker. The Americans started in Saga, and the Finns worked in Tokyo.[118]

In Korea (since 1948 divided into North and South Korea), the Lutheran missionary in China, Gützlaff, tried to evangelize but failed. Eventually, Presbyterian and Methodist missionaries were well received.[119]

Africa

The oldest African state, Ethiopia (an empire from 1889 until 1974, when it became a Socialist state), became known to Lutherans through a layperson from Lübeck, Peter Heyling (1607–1652), who worked at the royal Ethiopian court as a physician and lawyer. He translated part of the New Testament into Amarigna (Amharic), but he had few followers. In 1837, his work was continued by John L. Krapf (1810–1881). Though not immediately successful, Krapf communicated a lively vision of mission in Africa. With the help of the Swedish mission, two converts established congregations, bought land, and established headquarters in Jima, a Muslim town in the province of Kefa. Another convert and freed Oromo slave, Onesimus Nesib (c. 1856–1931), translated the New Testament, Luther's Small Catechism, and hymns into Oromo. Two women assisted him. By 1897, the entire Bible was translated. Eventually, a mission was established in Addis Ababa by Onesimus's friend, the Swedish missionary Karl Cederquist (1854–1919), who founded a school where future leaders of the country were educated. When Emperor Haile Selassie introduced modern education in 1916, Cederquist was permitted to organize schools, congregations, and medical programs.[120] The oldest Lutheran church in Africa, preceded by mission work in South Africa since 1820, is the Evangelical Church of Eritrea (a former province of Ethiopia, now independent, bordering the Red Sea), begun in 1866 and headquartered in Imkullu, near Massawa, until 1891, then in Asmara and Tseazega. A Bible movement secured many converts. The Swedish Mission of Bible Friends joined the missionary effort in 1911.[121]

In Kenya (a British colony until independence in 1964), the German Lutheran missionary Krapf worked for the Anglican mission because he spoke Swahili and other native languages. The opening of the Suez Canal in 1869 created intensive contact with Europe.[122]

Lutheranism was introduced in Madagascar (a French territory until 1958, sovereign since 1960) through the Norwegian Missionary Society in 1866. Anglicans had prepared the way since 1818, and after a brief period of persecution, Christianity spread. Norwegian Lutherans were able to establish a network of missions and schools, including a seminary in Fianarantsoa.[123]

German missionaries from the Berlin, Bethel, and Leipzig Mission Societies brought Lutheranism to Tanzania (named Tanganyika until 1964) in 1890, led by the outstanding Leipzig missionary Bruno Gutmann (1876–1966).[124] He always worked with African traditions rather than against them.

Moravians visited southern Africa in 1737, but their missionary efforts did not succeed. In 1857, Carl H. Hahn (1818–1895) was sent by the Rhenish Mission Society to the Hereros. Assisted by the church in Finland, he organized a congregation in Cape Town. Martin Rautanen continued the mission among the Ovambos for fifty years, resulting in the creation of medical programs and establishing a printing press in 1901.[125]

In western Africa, Danish missionaries began their work in 1837 on the Gold Coast, joined by Moravian converts from Jamaica in 1843. Lutheran missionaries from the United States were sent to Liberia, led by David A. Day in 1874. Since 1847 German missionaries worked in Togoland (a German protectorate until 1918, French territory until it became the Togo republic in 1960) among the Ewe, whose convert Andreas Aku (1863–1931) guided Lutheranism into the modern era.[126]

Lutheranism came to the Middle East (also known as the Bible Lands: Israel, Jordan, and Lebanon) in 1841, when Anglicans and Prussian Lutherans founded the

German Christ Church, Jerusalem

Evangelical Bishopric in Jerusalem. Candidates would subscribe to the Augsburg Confession and the Thirty-nine Articles. The first bishop was Solomon Alexander, a native German Jewish convert. After 1885, the joint bishopric was dissolved and became Anglican. In 1851, Fliedner brought four deaconesses to Jerusalem to organize a hospital, a school, and an orphanage. Such institutions also were established in Constantinople (1852), Smyrna (1854), Alexandria (1857), Beirut (1860), and Cairo (1885). A Jerusalem Mission Society was organized in 1852. The German missionary John L. Schneller (1820–1896) and his wife worked with orphans, later housed in the famous Syrian Orphanage. The German Lutheran Chapel was built in Jerusalem in 1871, renamed the Church of the Redeemer in 1898, dedicated by the German emperor. The Swedish Jerusalem Society organized a hospital with eighty beds and a school in 1902, where 280 Jewish and Arab children were educated.[127]

The Lutheran Orient Mission began working among the Kurds in Iran (then named Persia and ruled by a king, the Shah) in 1911. The chief missionary was the Norwegian-American pastor and physician Ludwig O. Fossum (1879–1920). Similar missions were launched in Syria in 1898 by the Danish Oriental Mission and in Turkey by Germans who organized a Lutheran church in 1843 and a school in 1850.[128]

South America

German Lutherans came first to Brazil (a part of the Portuguese empire until 1889). A lone Hessian Lutheran writer, Hans Staden, appeared in the sixteenth century, writing about the native people in 1557. About five thousand German settlers came to farm near Sao Leopoldo after 1823. When many German settlers joined others from Europe to find a new life in Brazil, German churches organized them into congregations. The Prussian Synod helped to organize the Rio Grande Synod in 1886, followed by the Lutheran Church of Brazil in 1905, the Evangelical Synod of Santa Carina-Parana in 1911, and the Central Brazilian Synod in 1912. German Mission Societies tried to continue the mission to natives but had difficulties distinguishing between mission and colonization. The Missouri Synod opened its own seminary in Porto Alegre in 1903 to preserve pure doctrine from ecumenical cooperation that might lead to unionism. One of its pastors, C. Richard Oertel, traveled to the Island of Pine and organized three Lutheran congregations among Germans and Americans in 1911, one of them in Havana, Cuba (then a republic under U.S. tutelage); some nonpracticing Cuban Catholics also joined.[129]

Lutherans also began a mission in Puerto Rico in 1898, led by a college student from the U.S. Augustana Synod, Gustav S. Swenson, who learned Spanish, opened a mission center, and conducted bilingual (English and Spanish) worship services since 1899; he later became a pastor. His work was continued by the Augustana missionary Albert Ostrom until 1931.[130]

Danish settlers and traders brought Lutheranism to the Virgin Islands, especially to St. Thomas, a center of trade. Moravians had been there since 1730. When slaves were freed there in 1841, Lutherans provided for their education, supported by the government (since 1917, an unincorporated territory of the United States). The first choir at the Danish service in St. Thomas was black.[131]

Next to Brazil, Lutheranism became popular in Guyana (a British territory until independence in 1970) after the formation of the first Lutheran church, named Ebenezer, in 1743. A regular pastor was called in 1878, John R. Mittelholzer (1840–1913), a native trained by the London Mission Society. He negotiated Ebenezer's membership in the East Pennsylvania Synod of the General Synod in the United States. Since 1918, the United Lutheran Church in the United States made Guyana its mission field.[132]

Lutherans also were found early in Suriname (a Dutch colony in the north, independent since 1975) when they organized a church in 1741 under the jurisdiction of the Lutheran Consistory in Amsterdam, Holland. Reformed and Lutheran pastors were sent to serve in the Evangelical Lutheran Church in Suriname. Moravians founded a seminary there in 1902 that educated Lutheran and other Protestant candidates for ministry.[133]

A German-speaking Lutheran congregation was founded in Peru (a Spanish colony until 1824, still struggling for democratic reform) in 1899 by Swiss and German settlers. Pastors were provided by the Evangelical Church of the Old Prussian Union, which also sent pastors to a Lutheran congregation formed in the 1870s in Caracas, Venezuela (a Spanish colony, independent since 1830).[134]

Lutheran roots in Argentina (a Spanish colony until independence in 1813, but unstable through military dictators) began in 1843, when the Bremen Mission Society sent Pastor August L. Siegel to serve a newly formed congregation in Buenos Aires. The group created German colonial settlements along the Parana River and in the Santa Fe province. Pastors from neighboring areas (Paraguay, Brazil, and Chile) formed a conference in 1863 that became the basis for the German Evangelical La Plata Synod of 1900 headquartered in Buenos Aires.[135]

Lutheran presence in Chile (a Spanish colony until independence in 1826, but unstable through military dictators) goes back to German settlers in Valparaiso in

1822 and in Santiago in 1845. About seven hundred German families were served by two pastors who had come on their own after the European Revolution of 1848. After 1863, a growing number of congregations were supplied with pastors from the Prussian Lutheran Union Church, which declared in 1900 that the Chilean congregations were part of the Prussian Union.[136]

Lutheranism in Paraguay (a Spanish colony until independence in 1811) began in 1893 with the formation of a German church. In 1909, the government granted land to immigrants who wanted to convert Indians. But Mennonites dominated this mission effort.[137]

A congregation of Lutheran settlers was also formed in Montevideo, Uruguay (a Spanish colony, independent since 1830), in 1857. It became part of the Evangelical Church of the River Plate in Argentina.[138]

The Impact of the Great War

World War I (1914–1918) had tragic consequences for Lutheranism. German Lutherans were virtually totally isolated from other Lutherans, indeed other Christians. In North America, other Americans viewed Lutherans as enemies. Lutheran missions around the world encountered difficulties but continued as orphaned missions maintained by other Protestant missionaries from the United States, Canada, Australia, and Sweden. The power of nationalism and the force of colonialism severely tested Lutheran ecumenicity; and Lutheranism failed the test.

Two events symbolize the failure. First, two Christian leaders separated by the war, Pastor Frederick Sigmund-Schultze of the German Lutheran Union Church and the English Quaker Henry Hodkin, planned to create a witness to peace through the formation of the International Covenant of Reconciliation. It was never realized because of a lack of interest by Protestant Christians in Germany and England. Second, almost at the same time, the Lutheran chaplain at the Prussian court preached at a worship service for delegates enthusiastic about the war on the biblical passage "If God is for us, who is against us?" (Rom. 8:31). He made it clear, to the delight of Emperor William II, that God was on the side of Germany in its war against England. There is a diabolical spiritual abyss between these two events.[139]

The witness to peace in the German philosophical and theological tradition gave way to a focus on war as an essential part of the divine orders of creation with an "immeasurable cultural value."[140] Lutheran sermons completely supported the war effort and urged congregations to be patriotic, indeed firm in their hatred of the enemy. Preachers throughout Germany urged the parishioners "to stir up the spirit of hatred linked with God's holy spirit, the spirit of glowing faith and the love of the fatherland." A special order of worship recommended the use of patriotic language and nationalist songs.[141] A Lutheran pastor in Dortmund, Gottfried Traub

(1869–1956), left his ministry to become the director of the German Fatherland Party *(Deutsche Vaterlandspartei)*, a political satellite of the Covenant of German Protestants *(Deutscher Protestantenbund)* of 1909, consisting of a radical patriotic group of militarists favored by the Prussian military leaders. Traub even managed to survive in the political struggle after the war by supporting various political causes, including the cause for the rebuilding of German Lutheranism after 1918.

All Lutheran leaders, especially the intellectual elite, participated in the war propaganda. The most famous of all Lutheran scholars, Adolf von Harnack, composed the official solemn call for war by Emperor William II. The popular theologian Reinhold Seeberg (1859–1935) drafted the "Declaration of the University Professors of the German Empire" in 1914, contending that there is no difference between the spirit of German scholarship and Prussian militarism. "Both are one and we belong to it. This spirit does not only live in Prussia but is the same in all the territories of the German empire."[142] Theologians of all stripes signed the declaration; students enthusiastically volunteered for military duty. They did so as members of patriotic fraternities or similar organizations such as "the migrating birds" *(Wandervögel)* who became a special regiment in the German army; most of them were killed on the western front on the Flemish battlefield.

German Lutherans also linked the quatercentenary of the Reformation (1517–1917) with the war propaganda. Martin Luther's hymn "A Mighty Fortress," was sung at so many occasions to boost the war effort that it could hardly be distinguished anymore as a religious hymn in its own right. In numerous speeches and tracts, Luther appeared as a battle hero dressed in iron armor and praised in music and song.

When the war ended with the secret flight of Emperor William II to the Netherlands, German Lutherans quickly adopted the postwar legend, created by the optimistic nationalists, that imperial Germany remained "not conquered in the battle field," but was betrayed by a mutinous home front. As the Prussian Union Church leaders put it in their penitential triad of November 9, 1918: "We have lost the war; Germany is not lost; the empire must still be ours."[143]

The end of the war also brought an end to the long period of the domination of Lutheranism by territorial princes (stipulated at the Peace of Augsburg in 1555) as the highest authority *(summus episcopus)*. Diverse postwar political parties, especially Socialists, demanded the separation of church and state. So the Lutheran churches had to work out new constitutional arrangements in 1919. Most used an episcopal-synodical polity, headed by elected officials, usually called bishops or superintendents, who worked with executive committees known as "church councilors" *(Oberkirchenrat)*. In 1921, territorial churches banded together in the German Evangelical Covenant of Churches *(Deutscher evangelischer Kirchenbund)* in order to have more power in negotiations with the government, especially regarding religious education. The first negotiated law of 1918 stipulated that religious instruction is part of the curriculum provided by teachers approved and supplied by the church. Later, provisions were made for voluntary attendance in cases of opposition to the traditional confessions of a territory, thus avoiding any enforcement of religion in the schools. Such a liberal political climate enabled completely new religious groups, like the Jehovah's Witnesses, headquartered in Barmen, to gain a foothold in Germany.

Lutherans in North America generally supported Germany in regard to the war with England, also reviving old U.S. suspicions about the colonial power of Great Britain. "This war," wrote Theodore E. Schmauk, the leader of the General Synod, in 1914, "is the result of the British plan of destroying Germany's foreign commerce and relations, and of doing away . . . with a rival."[144] Some synods, like the Wartburg Synod in Iowa (of the General Council), prayed for a German victory, even singing German patriotic songs. Most Lutherans prayed for the welfare of their relatives in Germany. Even the Missouri Synod, traditionally reluctant to enter politics, published strong denunciations of the United States' "atrocious trade in arms" for the sake of its lust for profit that made its neutral stance "hypocritical murder."[145] Such an attitude was easier to maintain before 1917, when the nation entered the war. Then, U.S. Lutherans prayed for peace and reflected about the reasons that God allowed their nation to be drawn into the war.

But they also became exposed to the anti-German sentiments expressed by their neighbors. U.S. Germans were called enemy-sympathizers; German street names were removed; and German artists were not permitted to perform music or exhibit fine arts. Indeed, occasionally, German books were burned in public. A Baptist church in Oklahoma refused to celebrate Easter because they viewed it as "a German heathen custom." A real issue was the fact that German Lutheran pastors had to swear an oath of allegiance to the emperor (the Kaiser), because he was by law the head of the Lutheran Church. The oath ended with the promise, "I will preach the Word as His Gracious Majesty dictates." The Missouri Synod officially condemned this oath, also on behalf of "the American Lutheran Church."[146]

But anti-German propaganda increased with the intensity of the war. Nebraska closed hundreds of Lutheran (mostly Missouri Synod) parochial schools; some were burned. The state's Sedition Act of 1918 required the licensing of all preachers and teachers in a local district. The act was used against Lutherans such as the teacher Robert T. Meyer, who was convicted of teaching German to a ten-year-old boy. Only the Supreme Court prevented him from going to jail.[147] Worship services were interrupted. Pastors were sometimes daubed with yellow paint, made to kiss the flag, and ordered to buy war bonds; a few were tarred and feathered like black slaves had been half a century before. The well-known revivalist Billy Sunday (1862–1935) fueled the national hysteria with the saying, "If you turned hell upside down you'd find 'Made in Germany' stamped at the bottom of it." Missouri Synod officials were furious about the slanderous charge that every church in St. Louis sang a hymn of hate every Sunday.[148]

Luther Monument, Washington, D.C.

But U.S. Lutherans tried to show solid support of their adopted country during the war even though almost all printed media, including the *New York Times,* denounced the use of German in the schools as disloyalty. Public and private pressure led to better Lutheran cooperation. The New York Reformation Committee of 1917 became the Lutheran Bureau, which became one of the stepping-stones to the formation of the National Lutheran Council in 1918. Lutherans united in self-defense. Many synods, including Scandinavian ones, held a protest meeting against the Nebraska Council of Defense and signed a statement of complaint. Non-German Lutherans had come to feel the pressure of the war propaganda by the guilt of association, for being Lutheran. But there also was a reluctance to cave in to the government's pressure to enlist all organizations, including churches, in the war effort through Red Cross donations, war bonds, and even sermon suggestions.

Here, Lutherans put down their confessional foot, insisting on their traditional ways of free preaching of the law and the gospel and the administration of the sacraments. Some Lutherans criticized the president's call for a national day of prayer as a threat to religious liberty. Others, however, were eager to ornament their churches with flags depicting the armed services and with honor rolls for those killed in action, and they allowed government announcements during the worship services. Many Lutheran men volunteered to fight in the war. Their home churches provided for their spiritual care beyond the work of the few Lutheran military chaplains. The Missouri Synod formed an Army and Navy Board. Sixty-thousand Lutheran men, all of them laypeople, successfully lobbied the government to build and equip Lutheran centers in or near military training camps. The Lutheran United Inner Mission was organized in 1917 to maintain contact with the Red Cross and the Federal Council's Wartime Commission, the government's link to churches. Most Lutheran church bodies agreed to organize one central agency in 1918, called the National Lutheran Commission for Soldiers' and Sailors' Welfare. Because plans were under way to form a United Lutheran Church, the Missouri Synod did not join the new commission, charging them with a false unionism. But the laypeople in the Lutheran Brotherhood of America (later an insurance company) cooperated with the commission. Its president was the New York City Pastor Frederick H. Knubel (1870–1945), who would later also head the United Lutheran Church in the United States.

The commission established an office in Washington, D.C., and built a network of wartime services, ranging from regular contact with every Lutheran in the armed forces to care for interned aliens. The office also published numerous accounts about Lutheran servicemen in the daily press and in church publications. An appeal for finances yielded $1,350,000, much more than had been recommended in a proposed budget. When the war ended, the reports about the devastation in Europe and about the paralyzing effect on global missions motivated many Lutheran leaders to create an agency for all Lutherans in North America to provide help. The complex deliberations finally resulted in the establishment of the National Lutheran Council in 1918. Its statement of purpose mentioned gathering statistical information, representing Lutherans through publicity, coordinating activities related to all phases of life, and maintaining proper relations between church and state.[149]

The reconstruction of life in postwar Europe became the first task of the council; it collected $1,800,000 for this purpose by 1920.[150] Again, there was opposition from the defenders of pure doctrine. The Missouri Synod refused to participate because it argued that only full agreement in doctrine should be the basis for the work of the council. Similarly, the leading theologian of the Iowa Synod, J. M. Reu, charged that aid should not be given to those who were judged to be not sufficiently orthodox. The Iowa Synod left the council in 1920 and established its own way of aiding European Lutherans. The council reacted with a constitutional compromise: "that it is the right of the Bodies [members synods] themselves to determine the extent of cooperation."[151]

World War I was an ecumenical blessing in disguise for Lutheranism in non-European areas of the world. Already before the war, in 1910, the first international conference on missions in Edinburgh agreed to build a cooperative Protestant network based on the notion that mission was ecumenical, not denominational. The war tested this notion when German and British authorities took over some of their colonial territories. Despite political and military hostilities between Germany and England, Lutherans and Anglicans cooperated by continuing missionary work without proselytizing. German Lutherans took care of Anglican missions, and British missionaries did the same for Lutheran missions. For example, when Germans were interned in India, the National Missionary Council supported the continuation of the Gossner Lutheran mission under oversight of the Anglican bishop Foss Westcott for the duration of the war without any attempt of turning Lutherans into Anglicans.[152] In Tanzania, Africa, British missionary agencies served as trustees of the German mission until it came back into service after 1918.[153]

The war was a neuralgic event that could be felt throughout the whole body of Christianity. But whenever Christians suffer, they are better witnesses. Lutherans are no exception. Despite internal problems, such as confessional unity, Lutherans began to see the error of their ways after being exposed to the hell of war. Nationalism, patriotism, and colonialism lost their status in the list of virtues and became vices in the face of devastation, suffering, and untimely death. In the end, the war closed much of the distance between Lutherans in the supposedly civilized West (Europe and North America) and in the rest of the world. Yet the distance between Protestants and other Christians, especially Roman Catholics and Eastern Orthodox, still prevailed everywhere. The strong, popular movement of missions in the nineteenth century still lacked its basic ingredient, Christian unity. Lutherans also remained divided despite the appreciated lessons of World War I. The mandate of the Lutheran Confessions to distinguish between nonessentials *(adiaphora)* and essentials (the gospel in word and sacraments) was largely ignored. Political territorial fences in Europe still separated Lutherans from fruitful cooperation; ethnic divisions prevailed in North America; and colonial/economic interests remained a strong ingredient of foreign missions.

7

New Ventures

1918–

Pioneering the Ecumenical Movement

After World War I, a sense of the unity of humankind began to influence the notion of Christian unity. There was a longing for world peace and international cooperation. Many international organizations were founded to promote world peace. Students advocated peace. The Student Christian Movement of 1895 was in the forefront of a new drive for Christian unity and mission as a basis for peace. Christian leaders joined this drive, having become frustrated with the scandal of Christian divisions in every part of the world. Christian missions suffered from a lack of Christian unity. The Swedish Lutheran archbishop of Uppsala, Nathan Söderblom (1866–1931), was

athan Söderblom, Bishop of Sweden

the first Christian leader to transform the longing for unity into a realistic program.[1] The neutrality of his homeland was a positive factor in his ecumenical endeavors. "Lord, give me humility and wisdom to serve the great cause of the free unity of Thy church," the young Söderblom wrote in his diary during an international student conference in New Haven, Connecticut, in 1890. The petition became the motto of his life and work. After ordination in 1890 and work as a hospital chaplain, he accepted a call to become the pastor of the Swedish-Norwegian congregation in Paris. There, he pursued his lifelong interest in non-Christian religions by studying Persian religion. In 1901, he was called to a professorship at Uppsala University and a pastorate at Trinity Church. Soon, the Young Church movement, concerned with reform, found in him an aggressive leader. He and his wife held informal Monday evening meetings at their home where the Young Church discussed the future of Lutheranism in Sweden. When Uppsala Socialists invited him to speak during a general strike, he offered them his church to discuss labor issues.

Söderblom made his first proposal for Christian unity in 1908, during the state visit of King Edward VII of England, calling for closer ties with the Anglican Church. In an essay published by a major Stockholm newspaper, Söderblom proposed common missionary action by Anglicans and Lutherans in South India. He also linked his missionary proposal to a quest for intercommunion in both churches. The U.S. Lutheran Augusta Synod supported the sharing of Holy Communion with the Anglicans. But this drive for mission and unity provoked criticism from various quarters in Sweden. Some bishops and colleagues in the university chided Söderblom for siding with the Young Church movement. Others found a lack of Christian substance in his studies of other religions. Many Lutherans criticized his association with Marxist workers. A bleeding stomach ulcer, Söderblom's lifelong burden, only increased his difficulties in Uppsala. Consequently, he welcomed the call from the German University of Leipzig to be a guest professor from 1912 to 1913. The position confirmed Söderblom's international reputation as a scholar and provided him with an opportunity to continue his studies of the history of religions.

After he was appointed archbishop in 1914, he published a public work, *Appeal for Peace,* printed in seven languages (Söderblom was fluent in Swedish, French, German, and English), urging European church leaders not to identify their faith with national causes and to sign a declaration, "For Peace and Christian Fellowship." But only church leaders from neutral countries and some from the United States signed the declaration. German Lutherans defended their lack of cooperation with the excuse that the war was a defensive war and could only end with an honorable peace for Germany. So Söderblom's efforts were reduced to the welfare of prisoners of war and, at the end of the war, to the support of suffering children and minority groups. As the head of the Swedish branch of the World Alliance of Churches for Promoting International Friendship, founded in 1914, he issued an appeal to assist Austrian and German children; using letters, personal contacts, and the telephone, he brought seventeen hundred children for a summer to Sweden in 1919. He hoped that a league of nations would secure external peace and that a league of churches would provide an international base for a spiritual revival. It was his vision to unite Christians first for social action in a war-torn world despite their doctrinal differences; then they might organize an ecumenical council of churches to overcome their divisions.

The World Alliance of Churches for Promoting International Friendship supported Söderblom's ecumenical vision. The Anglican bishop George Bell became an active supporter of the archbishop. Söderblom produced a "Manifesto" in 1917, signed by him and leading clerics from neutral countries (Denmark, Norway, Sweden, the Netherlands, and Switzerland), calling for a durable peace. It evoked the first signs of cooperation from clerics in Germany. The Anglican archbishop William

Temple called for an international Christian conference to deal with Söderblom's idea. Söderblom immediately began to send out invitations to such a conference in Stockholm. He selected three different groups: official church bodies, or official representatives of churches; World Alliance leaders in different countries; and a number of individual clerics. The invitations did not recommend a specific program, but the conference was to reflect the method of Red Cross meetings between enemies such as Germans and Russians. Accordingly, participants from neutral countries would start exploring the willingness of delegates from hostile countries to agree to talk and, if so, assure in some way that the meetings would be profitable for the hostile parties.

But despite such care and caution, only the neutral churches responded positively. The German, Austrian, French, and Finnish churches declined the invitation; they wanted to postpone any international conference until the end of the war. But Söderblom decided to hold a Neutral Church Conference in Uppsala in 1917, with about thirty-five participants from the Netherlands, Switzerland, Denmark, Norway, and Sweden. The conference dealt with the topics of unity, life in society, and international law. The central topic, unity, was defined in strong Lutheran terms as unity by faith in the crucified Christ. So grounded, the conference declared, Christians need to cooperate without becoming uniform.

Söderblom continued to invite participants to an international conference, including the Greek Orthodox and the Roman Catholic churches. Several Orthodox churches agreed to participate, but the Vatican in Rome declined the invitation. But Söderblom was able to gather about sixty members of the World Alliance International Committee from fourteen countries at Oud Wassenaar near the Hague, Netherlands, in 1919. The German, British, and U.S. delegations were the largest. Former enemies, such as Germans and French, united as Christians. Söderblom was so moved by the signs of reconciliation that he spontaneously started the German hymn "Nun danket alle Gott" ("Now Thank We All Our God").[2] Söderblom doggedly continued his intensive personal campaign for international Christian unity, speaking at Oud Wassenaar about an ecumenical council built around the two oldest centers of Christianity, the patriarch of Constantinople and the archbishop of Canterbury (because Rome had declined to participate). The other branches of Christianity, "evangelical-Catholic" churches, should be represented through elected members according to their significance and the contributions they could make. If the conference were held in Uppsala, Söderblom would cover all expenses. It would concentrate on developing a strategy for common action regarding the renewal of society and the organization of an international Christian entity. Söderblom was authorized to plan for such a conference, with other members of the alliance. Nine delegates from the United States, Switzerland, and Sweden met at the

Paris conference. After delicate negotiations with various church leaders from Europe and North America, an agreement was reached to hold a preparatory meeting in Geneva in 1920. There, ninety delegates from fifteen countries called for a Universal Conference of the Church of Christ on Life and Work, which was to be headed by Söderblom and held in Stockholm in 1925.

More than six hundred participants from thirty-seven countries and ninety-one churches attended, including a delegation of the Greek Orthodox Church (but without any Roman Catholic participation). It was truly Söderblom's conference. He had prepared it meticulously, and its agenda reflected his focus on the church's relation to the world ranging from economic to educational problems. For eleven days, delegates met in intensive sessions to discuss six topics: (1) the church's obligation to the world in view of God's purpose for the world, (2) the church and economic and industrial problems, (3) the church and social and moral problems, (4) the church and the mutual relations of nations, (5) the church and Christian education, and (6) methods of practical and organizational cooperation between Christian communions. Despite tensions, Söderblom's vision of a supranational, universal Christian fellowship prevailed. The final official message of the conference reflected Luther's theology of the cross. "Under the cross of Jesus Christ we reach out our hands to one another. . . . In the Crucified and Risen Lord alone lies the world's hope."[3]

Söderblom was elected chair of the Continuation Committee of the conference in order to assure the progress of cooperative efforts among the churches. In 1927, a World Conference on Faith and Order was held in Lausanne, Switzerland, to deal with doctrinal and structural differences. More than four hundred delegates from over 127 churches attended. Seven topics were on the agenda: a call to unity, the church's message to the world—the gospel, the nature of the church, the church's common confession of faith, the church's ministry, the sacraments, the unity of Christendom, and the place of different churches in it.[4] But tensions about the nature of the church, ministry, and sacraments prevented any quick consensus. Two different views of the unity of the church dominated: the Anglican view of the church as "organic union" and the church as a "federation" consisting of various "confessional" communions. The Orthodox felt excluded by such a distinction, whereas Lutherans and the Reformed found themselves in a comfortable proximity. The Lutheran delegates, including Söderblom, cautioned that true unity, especially visible church unity, needed much more work; thus, no vote should be taken in Lausanne on this conflictive topic. Söderblom had to leave the conference for pressing work in Sweden. Later, he joined the judgment of others that "doctrine divides, service unites." But the final estimate of his ecumenical efforts was positive. "I have seen a glimpse of the united church," he declared after the Lausanne conference, "a distant goal, from which Christendom cannot be turned away."[5]

Söderblom devoted the last years of his life to world peace and the study of world religions. He received the Nobel Prize for peace in 1930; Alfred Nobel (1833–96) had been a member of his parish. His work on world religions was honored in the famous Gifford Lectures at Edinburgh University shortly before his death. Their title, *The Living God,* summarized Söderblom's enduring vision of a mystical unity of humankind.[6] His theological view of a progressive revelation in the world's major religions, culminating in the revelation in Jesus Christ, made him the target of Lutheran orthodox theologians, who considered him a "teacher of heathenism." His pioneering ecumenical work was not so much grounded in the Lutheran Confessions as it was in the radical liberal "school for the history of religions" *(religionsgeschichtliche Schule),* derived from Schleiermacher and other theologians. Nevertheless, Söderblom was the father of the ecumenical movement, because without him there would not have been any global, organized ecumenism.[7]

Until the beginning of World War II (1939–1945), Lutherans continued to be strong supporters of the ecumenical movement. But already at the second World Conference for Faith and Order in Edinburgh in 1937, the Lutheran delegates had come in greater numbers from outside of Europe (North America, India). German and Scandinavian Lutherans did manage to band together for ecumenical work in the Lutheran World Convention of 1923 in Eisenach, Germany, providing a link to postwar ecumenical work through the Lutheran World Federation of 1947. In North America, only the United Lutheran Church and the Augustana Synod pursued relations with non-Lutheran Christians. The United Lutheran Church's Washington Declaration of 1920 called for ecumenical cooperation as long as Lutherans would not be forced to compromise their stance.[8] So grounded, it and the Augustana Synod sent delegates to the ecumenical conferences in Stockholm (1925) and Lausanne (1927). Other Lutheran synods in the United States, especially in the Midwest, did not send delegates and accused ecumenically minded Lutherans of a false unionism. In response to the European Lutheran World Convention, the United Lutheran Church asked Abdel R. Wentz (1883–1976), in consultation with German church leaders, to draft a statement of principles that would allow Lutherans to participate under the condition of representing church bodies, not themselves, as co-opted individuals.[9] But burdened by the heavy biblicism of the Lutheran Church–Missouri Synod, Lutheran ecumenical discussions in North America did not contribute much to the ecumenical movement. Intra-Lutheran disagreements were stated in 1938 in the Baltimore Declaration of the United Lutheran Church and the Sandusky Declaration of the American Lutheran Church. But by 1940, the enduring American Lutheran question remained unanswered: Does confessional unity require theological uniformity? In contrast, European Lutherans wrestled with the question to what extent the ecumenical stance of the Lutheran Confessions compelled Lutheran churches to lead the ecumenical movement. A growing agreement with this view drew more and more Lutherans.

When the next Conference on Life and Work met at Oxford in 1937, the German government of Adolf Hitler (1889–1945) barred the attendance of the German Lutheran delegation. It did so again when the Conference on Faith and Order met in Edinburgh in 1937. Only the young pastor and theologian Dietrich Bonhoeffer (1906–1945) was able to attend because of his complex position as a consulting member of the Conference on Life and Work and as a double secret agent of the counterespionage department of the German army, with contacts in the British Secret Service; he was martyred by the Hitler regime in 1945.[10] During World War II, some contacts with German Lutherans could be maintained through the dedicated efforts of Hans Schönfeld, a Lutheran pastor and economist who headed the research institute of the Universal Christian Council for Life and Work in Geneva. His coworker was the Swedish pastor and theologian Nils Ehrenström, who used his stance of Swedish neutrality to maintain contact with persecuted churches. But it was not before the end of World War II that the pioneering participation of Lutherans was once again assured.

Dietrich Bonhoeffer

The Struggle with Tyranny

The ecumenical movement was crudely interrupted by World War II (1939–45) and its ideological power struggles grounded in Italian Fascism, headed by Benito Mussolini (1883–1945), German National Socialism (Nazism, from *Nationalsozialismus*), led by Adolf Hitler, and Russian Communism, directed by Joseph Stalin (1879–1953). Although the war involved countries all over the globe, Lutheranism was directly affected by Nazism and Communism in Europe. German Lutherans and, to a lesser degree, Scandinavian Lutherans encountered anti-Christian Nazism before and during the war. After the war, Lutherans in Russia, Eastern Europe, and East Germany faced atheistic Communism until its collapse in 1989.

Lutherans faced a new political situation in Germany after 1918, when territorial princes lost their veto power over the church as "supreme bishops" *(summi episcopi),* a power that the Peace of Augsburg had granted them in 1555. Germany was now governed by representatives of various political parties. The territorial churches formed a "League of Churches" *(Kirchenbund)* to negotiate a mutually satisfying relationship between church and state. The state granted religious freedom to the Lutheran United and Reformed churches, and an executive committee of the churches organized to guard this freedom and negotiate other changes when necessary. When the president of Germany, Paul von Hindenburg (1847–1934), officially transferred his office to Adolf Hitler in 1933, German Lutherans were confronted with a government hostile to their Judeo-Christian tradition. The National Socialists (Nazis) promised to create a new Germany. They had gained their power with the rise of nationalism after Germany's defeat in World War I and the resulting dire economic conditions. The Nazi party rode the wave of nationalism with great success. Two elite Lutheran theologians, Paul Althaus at Erlangen University and Emanuel Hirsch (1888–1972) at Bonn University, played into Nazi hands when they called for a halt of all German ecumenical work with Christians in the countries that won the war against Germany.[11] Interest in religion declined in the wake of the ongoing secularization of the new political situation. Adopting a racist stance grounded in the old myths of a Nordic superrace of Aryans, the new German government coordinated all sectors of public and private life to engage in a struggle against Communism and Judaism, its perceived enemies. Communists were viewed as the Slavic menace that threatened racial purity and Western culture; Jews were blamed for Europe's economic woes and seen as greedy subhuman Semites.

The Nazi government at first diplomatically asserted its support of "a positive Christianity," meaning religious freedom except when public security is threatened.

But the Nazi party had made it clear that security meant the elimination of "the Jewish-materialistic spirit at home and abroad."[12] Hitler himself told visitors in his home at Obersalzberg near Berchtesgaden that he read daily Christian devotions, as did Otto von Bismarck, and made decisions based on the German New Testament of Luther.[13] Nazi-oriented Lutherans, known as "German Christians" *(deutsche Christen)*, supported the ideology of the Nazi party, contending that the new Germany would be inspired by a "Luther-Spirit" *(Luthergeist)* that would unite all racially pure Germans. The German Chris-

Adolf Hitler shaking hands with German Christian Reichs-leiter Christian Kinder at the Reich Party Conference

tians called for the organization of a "church of the realm" *(Reichskirche)*, headed by a bishop appointed by Hitler and combining the twenty-eight territorial Protestant churches of Germany. In a document titled "Platform" (1932), they applauded Hitler for reviving "heroic piety" linked to Martin Luther; agreed with the policy against "racial mixing," especially concerning relations with Jews; called for a revival of "inner mission" as a protection of Germany from "the incapable and inferior"; and desired an "evangelical church" rooted in nationalism rather than cosmopolitanism. The platform viewed its program as the fulfillment of the intentions of the Reformation of the sixteenth century.[14]

Hitler appointed a Prussian Nazi pastor, Ludwig Müller, as *Reichsbischof*. Under the pressure applied by the German Christians, an opposition "emergency league"

Bishop Müller with Nazi party officials on the steps of the Rathaus, Wittenberg, Germany

(Notbund) of pastors was organized, headed by the Berlin pastor Martin Niemöller, a submarine commander and World War I hero.[15] The naval hero tried to persuade Hitler to be tolerant toward the church and the synagogue. Hitler, of course, declined, had Niemöller arrested in 1937, and kept him in the concentration camp in Dachau, from which he was freed by U.S. troops in 1945. In 1934, 138 delegates from twenty-six territorial churches, among them the most distinguished Lutheran leaders, met in Barmen and established a "Confessing Church" *(bekennende Kirche)*. The delegates signed a confession, the Barmen Declaration, that affirmed six articles opposing the position taken by the German Christians: (1) the gospel of Jesus Christ as revealed in Scripture and the creeds of the Reformation, including the Lutheran Confessions, are the "impregnable foundation" of the church; (2) Jesus Christ is the

Martin Niemöller

only lord of the church; (3) he works through word and sacraments; (4) he does so without any special leaders other than him; (5) the state has no absolute power over the church; and (6) the church must be free for its mission in the world. The new measures of the government were repudiated as "false teachings."[16] Naturally, the Nazi government declared all actions of the Confessing Church illegal.

By 1936, Lutherans in Germany were split into two factions, with the majority supporting the government. Hitler tightened his hold on Lutherans by requiring an oath of allegiance, effective on his forty-ninth birthday, April 20, 1938. The oath required them "to be obedient to the *Führer*" and the laws of the state; refusal meant dismissal from the office of the ministry. Though they debated it, most Lutheran pastors signed the oath.[17] Those who did not sign were forbidden to exercise their public ministry and received no salary. Many pastors were jailed or drafted into the armed forces (which did have military chaplains, except in the air force).[18] The theologian Paul Tillich, for example, was sent to the concentration camp in Sachsenhausen but was released in 1939. He fled to the United States. Dietrich Bonhoeffer actively participated in a plot to assassinate Hitler. The plot failed, and Bonhoeffer and many others were executed in 1945.

In 1945, the surviving leaders of the Confessing Church met to establish the new Council of the Evangelical Church in Germany and issued the Stuttgart Declaration, confessing the inadequacy of their witness during the reign of Hitler. It confesses a "solidarity of guilt" concerning "the inestimable suffering inflicted on many peoples and lands. . . . Indeed we have fought for long years in the name of Jesus Christ against the spirit that found horrible expression in the National Socialist regime of force, but we charge ourselves for not having borne testimony with greater courage, prayed more conscientiously, believed more joyously and loved more ardently."[19]

Scandinavian Lutheranism also had to encounter the tyranny of Nazism. In Denmark, church and state organized passive and active resistance during the German military occupation in World War II. Danish bishops protested against the planned deportation of the Jews, expressed in a pastoral letter of September 29, 1943.[20] Finland experienced the Russian invasion of 1939 and German domination from 1941 to 1943. In Norway, Lutheran resistance against Hitler, though under different conditions, was more effective than in Germany. When Germans occupied Norway from 1941 to the end of the war, they set up a puppet government to keep Norway in check. But this government was opposed by a large number of Norwegians, led by bishops, pastors, and lawyers (law and gospel, so to speak).[21] Both sides based their arguments on Luther. The new Nazi Department of Church and Culture warned Lutheran clergy against resigning, on the grounds that Luther had taught obedience to every government because government was God-given. Bishop Eivind Berggrav (1884–1959), on the other hand, declared that what was at issue was an ancient Norwegian law dating from 1140, which stated that reverence for Christ was the source of all Norwegian law and justice. He added that the new military government was placing itself above the law by demanding absolute obedience to the state, a position Luther never held.[22]

Berggrav publicly identified Hitler as an embodiment of Niccolò Machiavelli's (1469–1527) tyrannical "prince" (*Führer* in his translation). In a lecture in 1941, Berggrav depicted tyranny's authority as a crazy driver of a runaway horse, implying that such a driver or horse might have to be destroyed in order to maintain the safety of the streets. He concluded that those who remained silent shared the guilt of disobeying Christ, for no government had the right to demand the souls of its citizens. Berggrav was put under house arrest from 1942 to 1945. When the government began seizing Jewish property, the church protested, declaring that all people had the same rights and that tyrannical governments need not be obeyed, according to the word of God and the Lutheran Confessions.[23] The puppet government was faced with the choice of either enforcing its law, which would result in a bloodbath in Norway, or leaving the church alone. It chose to leave the church alone, especially because all the bishops had resigned, as had a vast majority of pastors who were supported by their congregations. Only about sixty of the thousand pastors remained in office under the puppet government. The church renounced its allegiance to the state in 1942 and became a self-governing folk church until 1945.

After the defeat of Nazism, Lutherans had to cope with Communism. The Communist Russian East German puppet state, the German Democratic Republic, tried for more than four decades (1945–1989) to make Lutheranism an obedient servant. But the lessons of the Hitler regime remained very much alive among East German Lutherans. Consequently, they made very few compromises with the state and remained the strongest opponent of its political and ideological programs. In contrast to the period of Nazism, East German Lutherans retained their constitutional unity with West German Lutherans as long as possible. They were also linked to world Lutheranism and to the ecumenical movement. Neither the infamous iron curtain nor the Berlin Wall could destroy this relationship, even though it was a central target of the tyrannical state and its highly effective secret police, the "Stasi" (*Staatssicherheitsdienst*).[24] The ambitious ideological program during the first decade of Communist tyranny led to open resistance in the streets on June 16–17, 1953; the resistance was crushed by the East German police and the tanks of the Russian occupation forces. Thereafter, the state formally declared its tolerance of the church but informally tried to destroy the church through propaganda, restrictions, and education. The chief target was Lutheran youth. The state tried hard to attract Lutheran teenagers through education as political formation for atheistic witness. The Lutheran rite of confirmation was matched with a parallel rite, with "youth consecration" (*Jugendweihe*) in 1954. It was a rite of passage at about age fourteen in the context of ideological instruction, with a concluding ritual that celebrated the atheistic Communist "worldview" (*Weltanschauung*). This worldview stressed solidarity with "the working class" everywhere in the world and a "Socialist morality" as the basis for world peace.[25]

A majority of Lutheran teenagers participated in the pedagogical preparation and ideological celebration of the *Jugendweihe*. But more often than not, this youth program became a cover for Lutheran boys and girls, who, urged by their parents, remained loyal to the church; many of them even were confirmed. Open Christian resistance was extremely rare. There was one case of self-immolation by burning: the Lutheran pastor Oskar Brüsewitz covered his body with gasoline in front of a church in Zeitz, near Erfurt, Saxony, and burned himself to death on August 22, 1976, after a zealous missionary campaign against the government, which claimed that he was mentally disturbed, a charge not medically confirmed.[26] A whole department of the secret police was charged with the supervision and eventual elimination of the Lutheran Church, by far the largest of Christian churches in East Germany. Lutheranism was the one important "enemy territory" in the mind of the Stasi. But Lutheran resistance, often combined with peace movements, ecological and other organizations, was extensive and well led, pioneered by church leaders who had learned the lessons of Nazi tyranny, such as Bishop Otto Dibelius (1880–1967).[27]

After the creation of the Berlin Wall in 1961 and the constitutional isolation of East German Lutherans in 1968, the United Evangelical Lutheran Church had to form a West German and East German organization. But other links between east and west existed: East German Lutherans participated in ecumenical meetings, for example, in the Lutheran World Federation and the World Council of Churches. In the 1980s, contacts with the world beyond the wall and the iron curtain increased. Lutheran churches became centers of discussion and resistance, often camouflaged by concerts, peace discussions, and other ways that the government viewed as "democratic" and thus as tolerable. The Church Day (Kirchentag) of 1987 in East Berlin disclosed the strength of church resistance. Lutherans and others had formed a network named "arch" (Arche) to tackle the severe ecological problems in East Germany, where the exclusive use of soft coal had begun to destroy soil and air. Another network, "For Real Peace" (Konkret für den Frieden), advocated the opening of borders for global work on peace.

Seminarians from Wittenberg founded a "Working Team 'Liable Church'" (Arbeitskreis solidarische Kirche) in 1985, a labor union of church members, as it were, calling for better conditions under the Communist government. By the fall of 1989, Lutheran churches became centers of peaceful, nonviolent opposition to the state. Live candles became the symbols of the freedom movements. Lutherans (including Reformed churches) and Catholics created a central "round table" (Runder Tisch) in the Dietrich Bonhoeffer House in Berlin to integrate Christian grievances with non-Christian ones, thus combining ecclesiastical and secular opposition to the state. Their central concern was a more open and humane democratic Socialism. Worship services were held and were well attended, calling for reunification. Finally, a "soft October revolution" (so named by the news media), consisting of numerous nonviolent demonstrations and negotiations, achieved what seemed to be a miracle: the resignation and exit of the Communist leadership, neutrality of the Russian occupation army that was no longer ordered to uphold public peace, and free elections in a united Germany. The infamous Berlin Wall was crossed by both sides on November 10, 1989, the birthday of Martin Luther. German Lutheranism had become a powerful political agent in the German liberation from tyrannical

Communism. Thus, German Lutherans had redeemed, as it were, the sin of Lutherans under Nazism half a century earlier, when Lutheranism succumbed to the siren
song of the Hitler regime. In 1991, a reunited Lutheran church was organized to do
its mission in a free, united Germany.

In Hungary, resistance against Communism was linked to Bishop Lajos Ordass
(1901–1978).[28] He had to endure imprisonment, house arrest, and lack of support
by other Lutheran church leaders. During the Hungarian uprising, when the people
revolted in the streets against their government in the fall of 1956, Ordass broadcast
an international message for help on November 2. But the Russian army crushed the
revolt. Ordass was deposed as bishop and silenced by continual surveillance. Nevertheless, he continued contact with friends at home and abroad. He, like the Norwegian bishop Berggrav and the German theologian Bonhoeffer, was an unflinching
witness of Christ in his own historical situation.

The terrors of German Nazism and Russian Communism swept like a black
cloud over Lutheranism in Europe. The story of how Lutherans resisted and survived in various regions besides Germany and Russia may still have to be told when
collective memory has reached the proper distance for critical hindsight. Bishop
Ordass put it well when he said that his conviction by a tyrannical court was to him
like "a veil that hides God's will and renders it incomprehensible" yet was still beneficial to him.[29]

Theological Trends

The reign of Nazism in Germany traumatized Lutheran theology. Truly confessional
theologians belonged to the Confessing Church based on the Barmen Confession of
1934. Although any public teaching of theology had been suspended; bishops, pastors, and congregations managed to maintain their spiritual health through conferences, books, and family connections. The clergy, if not drafted into Hitler's army,
tried to survive, with sporadic but diminishing contact with the outside world. The
surviving and most influential theologian during and after World War II was the
Swiss Reformed pastor Karl Barth (1886–1968).[30] Heavily involved in the resistance
against Hitler and principal author of the Barmen Confession, Barth was forced to
retire from teaching at Bonn University and accepted a professorship at Basel University in his native land. As a young pastor, he became completely disappointed
with the liberal theology of the nineteenth century shaped by Schleiermacher and
turned to the Bible for help. Its strange new world revived for him the simple insight
that all theology must be christocentric, based exclusively on the unique revelation
of God in Christ. He elaborated his new stance in a commentary on Paul's Letter to
the Romans in 1922.[31] Its publication was like groping in a dark church for a steady

hold, Barth said, and accidentally yanking the bell rope, bringing the whole town running. The book attracted a whole new generation of young pastors and theolo-

gians. Denying any convenient "point of contact" *(Anknüpfungspunkt)* between divine and human entities, Barth spoke of God as the "wholly Other" who is known exclusively by self-disclosure in Christ; an "impassable gulf" separates humanity and God. Such new language, echoing Kierkegaard's notion of the paradox and the radical experience of survival, was soon labeled dialectical theology. Together with two close friends, the Swiss pastor Eduard Thurneysen and the German theologian Frederick Gogarten (1887–1967), Barth argued his

Karl Barth

position in two new journals, *Zwischen den Zeiten* (Between the times) and *Theologische Existenz Heute* (Theological existence today), simultaneously with a point-by-point systematic exposition in the *Church Dogmatics.* But after the victory of Nazism in Germany, he withdrew from German colleagues, accusing Lutheranism as a spiritual collaborator of the new Teutonic ideology. All his massive work, he contended, was but a way to refute anything but "christological concentration," for, as he put it in his childlike mood, the whole point of theology is contained in a sigh of two words, "Oh, yes!" *(Ach, ja),* a kind of doxological relaxation in the face of God's revelation in Christ.[32] The combination of such simplicity with a sagacity to unmask any liberal notion as a compromise of the word of God made Barth the "church father of the twentieth century."[33]

Accompanying the movement of Barthians was another theological trend created by the Lutheran Marburg New Testament scholar Rudolf Bultmann (1884–1976).[34] A hip disease prevented him from being drafted in World War II; the exemption enabled him to do enduring scholarly work. When he presented the lecture "New Testament and Mythology" to members of the Confessing Church in 1941, he distinguished between "existence" (reality) and "myth" in the New Testament, calling for "demythologizing"; a long controversy ensued. To make the New Testament "message" (Greek: *kerygma*) believable to contemporary folk, Bultmann contended, one must abandon its unreal, mythical worldview: a three-storied structure of life, with the earth in the center, heaven above, and hell below, assuming that supernatural forces determine all of human life and thought.

Influenced by the German existentialist philosopher Martin Heidegger (1889–1976), Bultmann distinguished between an actual way of "being there" *(Dasein)* and an imagined way of "existing" *(Vorhandensein).* Something is real when it exists for me, Bultmann insisted with Luther, who also stressed the reality of

Christ when one is addressed by him or receives him in Holy Communion ("given for *you*"). In short, God is real when experienced existentially through the decisive word of salvation in Christ (again echoing Luther's view of biblical authority as a communication, word and sacrament, pertaining to oneself). Bultmann called such existence under the word an "authentic life" that cannot be created by myths. They are the form in which authentic life appears, but for such life to be an "ever-present reality," one must have faith in Christ, who is ever present in his word. Bultmann rejected such mythical doctrines as "Christ paid for our sins," or even the difference between the crucifixion and resurrection of Jesus. "The New Testament presents the event of Jesus Christ in mythical terms . . . side by side with the historical event of the crucifixion is the definitely non-historical event of the resurrection."[35] Bultmann tried to guard himself against the accusation of denying the resurrection of Jesus by the casuistic distinction of history as objective, verifiable event *(Historie)* and as subjective, experienced reality *(Geschichte)*. But opponents still viewed him as a destroyer of traditional teachings cherished in Lutheranism, such as the resurrection of Christ and the redemption of believers through his ministry; the language of existentialism just did not wash with church authorities.

In 1952, Bultmann was formally accused of heresy by Bavarian leaders of the United Evangelical Lutheran Church in Germany (VELKD), but he was not invited to a hearing to defend himself. Nothing came of it except the formation of two ultra-conservative movements, one named No Other Gospel and the other, Church Gathering for Bible and Confession in Bavaria. Twenty years later, the presiding bishop of the VELKD, Eduard Lohse, expressed regret in the name of his church to Bultmann. Two years before his death, the Marburg theological warrior expressed his great pleasure to have been acknowledged by Lohse as a Lutheran theologian.[36] Bultmann gained increasing support through his writings and lectures in Europe and North America, especially by nonordained intellectuals; his *Theology of the New Testament* appeared in nine editions between 1953 and 1984. He desired to be, above all, a contemporary Lutheran. His existentialist exegetical theology endured, with compromising variations, as a major theological trend in the twentieth century.

Lutheran theology wrestled once again with the question of the contemporary meaning of faith in Jesus Christ. At issue was a new hermeneutics. Some of the representatives of this new hermeneutics wanted to make sure that any existentialist view of the word of God in the Bible does not diminish its salvific power. Accordingly, the accomplished exegete and Luther scholar Gerhard Ebeling (1912–) spoke of Jesus as a "word event" *(Wortgeschehen)*. The New Testament scholar Ernst Fuchs (1903–) used the term "language event" *(Sprachereignis)*.[37] Other Lutheran theologians, led by Wolfhart Pannenberg (1928–), linked the quest for the meaning of the word of God with the interpretation of the totality of history. The whole meaning of history, he contended in his seminal work *Revelation as History*, is foreshadowed, as it were, in Jesus' message of the imminent end of time, in his "eschatology" (Greek: *eschaton*, "end").[38]

The revival of interest in history and its eschatological goal contributed to the rise of a Lutheran liberation theology within African and Latin American contexts. How could anyone being justified by faith alone tolerate, indeed even live with, a racism radiant in the South African notion of *apartheid,* the strict segregation of European and African Christians? The Brazilian theologian Walter Altmann argued the thesis that Luther and the Reformation insights must become revolutionary mandates for justice.[39] Christians must persuade the state to implement its God-given mandate to be just in the ancient sense of social and economic equity.

Traditional theological trends also prevailed, often labeled "confessional theologies."[40] It is best represented by the Erlangen scholar Werner Elert (1885–1954). He contended that the Lutheran form of structure of law and gospel is the basic insight into human existence, "the evangelical point of departure" *(der evangelische Ansatz).* Life, he wrote, must be viewed as either under the law and thus the wrath of God, or under the gospel as the center in the circle of faith. Nothing can bridge law and gospel except Christ, who did so in death and resurrection. According to Elert, Lutheranism represents the best, if not the only, way to construct the internal and external dynamic of the Christian life. This stance earned him the title *Lutheranissimus.*[41]

The Lundensian school in Sweden offered a broader and more ecumenical confessional theology, best represented by Gustav Aulén (1879–1977), Anders Nygren (1890–1978), and in Denmark by Regin Prenter (1907–1980). Aulén tried to show how the assertion of Christ as the only source of salvation from evil is the leitmotif of Christian history, analogous to the musical motifs in some operas of Richard Wagner. Aulén did his "motif research," as some have called it,[42] with the conviction that basic Christian themes reverberate in the history of Christian doctrine. His colleague Nygren wrote the history of two powerful motifs of love, expressed in Greek as *agape* and *eros:* selfless love and self-love. The Danish scholar Prenter revived Luther research at the University of Aarhus with a motif study of Luther's view of the Holy Spirit.[43]

Anders Nygren

The German-American Paul Tillich (1886–1965) returned to the question of the meaning of religion, especially the relationship of Christianity to religious pluralism. Christian theology must have a philosophical basis, he contended, in order to be defended as a religion in its own right. In attractive terms, Tillich defined faith as

Paul Tillich

"ultimate concern" that raises ultimate existential questions. These questions are in "correlation" to specific answers that are grounded in God, "the ground of being." Thus, the certainty of death leads to the certainty of the resurrection—but only as a symbol of everlasting life; the event of the resurrection of Jesus is only known by faith in him. Such language and argumentation made Tillich quite popular among minds curious, but not certain, about Christianity. But on the other hand, it removed him far from traditional Lutheran confessional theology.[44]

In the midst of such trends of theology, traditional work remained like an old-fashioned flower in the midst of an experimental garden. Some Lutheran theologians expanded their Barthian base, reworking the classical Lutheran stance grounded in justification by faith as part of an ecumenical trinitarian theology. This kind of work is well demonstrated by two Lutheran students of Karl Barth, Eberhard Juengel (1933–) in Tübingen, Germany, and Robert W. Jenson (1930–) in the United States. Both try to offer classic doctrine in a new dress, Juengel in complex ontological terms and Jenson with a broad ecumenical vision, including Greek Orthodox ideas.[45] Jenson also teamed up with Carl E. Braaten (1929–), originally a Tillich disciple, to advocate an "evangelical-catholic" stance in public teaching events, in their journal *Pro Ecclesia* (For the church), and in a massive edition of *Christian Dogmatics,* in cooperation with other U.S. Lutheran theologians. Two other Lutheran theologians, Ted Peters and Philip J. Hefner, tried to link theology with modern science.[46] To that extent, Lutheran theology became part of a strong wave of theological pluralism. But both may still be viewed, even by Lutherans, as voices almost drowned in the cacophony of theological pluralism.

The theological pluralism of the twentieth century may have prevented an intended international consensus, revealed in the Fourth Assembly of the Lutheran World Federation in Helsinki, Finland, in 1963.[47] It was the intention of the assembly to find a Lutheran consensus on justification in order to advance an initiated formal dialogue with Rome. The study document "On Justification" noted common work in biblical studies and liturgical functions. Accordingly, the time might have come when "the Gospel can be proclaimed without the word 'justification'"; drafters spoke of a broader and richer understanding of grace than was used with such terms as "by faith alone" *(sola fide)* and "by grace alone" *(sola gratia).* The ministry of word and sacrament needed to be better linked with "the new obedience" in Augsburg Confession 6; the divine judicial (forensic) act of forgiveness also effects a new life; and forgiveness leads to renewal. But delegates could not agree with the new proposals and only received the study document rather than approving it. The debates disclose dissatisfaction with the language, structure, and tone of the study document. The resulting document from Helsinki, "Justification Today," tried to link Luther to the modern world by suggesting that the contemporary question is not about "a gracious God" but about the "meaning of life." It was further suggested that life should be filled with the faith that Christ lives through the church in a God-less world, calling for "a new courage to be" (a formulation found in Tillich's work). In short, justification today means that faith in Christ conquers meaninglessness and forms the church for service in the world.

Celebrating the eucharist during the 1963 Assembly of the Lutheran World Federation

Subsequent discussion among Lutherans around the world disclosed a consensus about the dissatisfaction with the Helsinki document, especially by African and Asian Lutheran churches. They spoke of the still existing gap between the language of the sixteenth century and contemporary needs. The kinder part of the opposition spoke of further discussion that had not been possible in a "mere ten days" in Helsinki; the harsher critics found the Helsinki statement unacceptable. Lutheran ecumenical optimists hoped for a better way of restating justification through the ongoing Lutheran-Catholic dialogue.[48]

Lutheran theological trends in Europe were more visible and influential, perhaps because of the significant place of Lutheranism in Germany and Scandinavia. Lutheran theology in North America was very much nurtured and shaped by European sources. The theological reconstruction of American Lutheranism was also linked to the public theology of non-Lutheran (often Reformed-Calvinist) scholars and teachers, especially Reinhold Niebuhr (1892–1971), who taught applied Christianity at Union Seminary in New York, and his brother H. Richard Niebuhr (1894–1962), who taught at Yale Divinity School.[49] The Niebuhrs, both in their specific ways, expressed anger and sadness over the bland, ineffective role of Protestant churches in public life. Lutherans could also easily be seen in the kind of theological environment described by H. Richard Niebuhr as an epitaph for an apparently apathetic Christianity: "A God without wrath brought men without sin into a kingdom without judgment through the ministrations of a Christ without a cross."[50]

The Lutheran World Federation

When the first Lutheran World Convention met at Eisenach in 1923, hopes for Lutheran unity increased. But World War II interrupted any further attempts to strengthen global unity. After World War II, but before the founding of the World

First Lutheran World Convention, 1923

Council of Churches in 1948, four Lutheran concerns became the pillars for the organization of the Lutheran World Federation (LWF) in Geneva: (1) rescue for the needy, (2) common initiatives for mission, (3) joint efforts in theology, and (4) a common response to the ecumenical challenge.[51] German, Scandinavian, and U.S. Lutherans became the prime movers in creating a federation meeting for the first time in Lund, Sweden, in 1947. The first LWF executive secretary (later title: general secretary), Sylvester Michelfelder, a pastor of the American Lutheran Church, created a future pattern of work in a Handbook for National Committees and Study Committees, proposing fifteen areas of activities: theology, education, evangelism, stewardship, world missions, inner missions, men, women, youth, students, ecumenical relations, international affairs, interchurch aid, publicity, and publication.

The constitution of LWF did not emphasize doctrinal unity but stressed its nature as a "free association of Lutheran churches"; it would not interfere with their complete autonomy and would be only an "agent: in such matters as they assign to it [LWF]."[52] Such language was designed to make it possible for the Lutheran Church–Missouri Synod to become a member of LWF, but it did not do so. Assemblies met at intervals of five to six years. Global politics, such as the creation of small nations in Africa, and cultural problems, such as racial apartheid in South Africa,

Sylvester Michelfelder designed the LWF flag, shown here at the Augusta Victoria Hospital in Jerusalem (1953).

burdened the work of LWF. In its brightest and best moment, LWF combined theological sagacity and constitutional power as it condemned two white churches in South Africa because they did not reject apartheid. The situation was labeled "a state of confession" *(status confessionis),* a matter of confessional integrity. The Lutheran Confessions allow variations in matters of polity, worship, and doctrine without, however, sacrificing "the pure teaching of the holy gospel." When this gospel is denied to people because of race, LWF contended, the church must oppose such a denial even if it involves "matters of indifference" *(adiaphora),* as some had called racial segregation.[53] Consequently, the Sixth LWF Assembly in Dar es Salaam in 1977 urged member churches in South Africa to admit nonwhites as legitimate, equal members under the gospel. "Churches which have signed the confessions of the church . . . also commit themselves to accept in their worship and at the table of the Lord the brothers and sisters who belong to other churches that accept the same confessions."[54] Intense debate erupted after the resolution of the Sixth Assembly. But at its next assembly in Budapest, Hungary, in 1984, LWF stuck to its guns and suspended the membership of the two South African churches that had continued to exclude natives from worship. The Evangelical Lutheran Church in Southern Africa (Cape Church) and the German Evangelical Church in southwest Africa,

The signing of the LWF charter at the first assembly in Lund, Sweden (1947). Abdel Wentz is seated at the far left.

also known as Namibia, were suspended. Such action was intended "to serve as a help for those churches to come to clear witness against the policy of apartheid and to move to visible unity of the Lutheran churches in Southern Africa."[55] It was not until 1991 that the two suspended churches changed their position and were reinstated by the LWF council, which formally lifted the suspension.[56]

Another problematic issue for LWF was the behavior of member churches in Communist countries, especially East Germany and Hungary. Whereas few, if any, compromises were made in East Germany, the Lutheran church of Hungary faced severe leadership problems in the 1970s and 1980s. Bishop Lajos Ordass was removed from office, suffered a long prison term, and was put under house arrest.[57] Colleagues and friends, who had fled to Norway, organized an Ordass Foundation committed to saving his writings and honoring his witness. His church shifted into a diaconical relationship with the state, meaning that it gave no resistance to its Communist tyranny.[58] The new cooperative bishop was Zoltan Kaldy (1914–1987),

who also was a member of the Communist Hungarian parliament. There was considerable debate in LWF when Kaldy was elected its president at the Seventh Assembly in Budapest in 1984; it was customary to elect the church leader in the host country. The final message of the Budapest Assembly disclosed the LWF's darkest hour, because it asserted "that in the church of Christ we can have confidence in each other and can build bridges between people across political and ideological boundaries."[59] Kaldy died suddenly in 1987.

The Ecumenical Centre in Geneva (opened 1964) houses the LWF, the WCC, and other organizations.

One of the inspired dramatic events in the history of LWF was the acceptance of one of the younger churches and its new Lutheran confession, born in mission as the Huria Kristen Batak Protestan in Indonesia (see chapter 6). First organized by the Rhenish mission in 1861, the church and its indigenous leaders accepted only the Bible and the three ecumenical creeds as their norms of faith, convinced that a more detailed confession would hinder cooperation for the cause of Christ. Batak Lutherans also sought to distance themselves from their Dutch and German roots during the dictatorship of Adolf Hitler in Germany. The conflict had begun to affect their homeland when the Dutch authorities imprisoned German missionaries after 1940 on the grounds that they

Participants from the Huria Kristen Batak Protestan · the Minneapolis Assembly, 1957

were part of the enemy that had invaded the Netherlands. Having learned of the struggle among Lutherans in Germany that culminated in the 1934 Barmen Declaration against tyranny, the Bataks proceeded to create their own confession and constitution, declaring themselves a Protestant body grateful to the Lutheran tradition. A large church of about two million members, it is served by bishops (also called ephorus, from the Greek *ephoros,* "overseer"), pastors, teacher-preachers, deaconesses, and Bible women.

A Batak confession was drafted without any Western influence in 1951, titled *Confession of Faith of the Huria Kristen Batak Protestan.*[60] The preamble calls the confession a continuation of the three ancient ecumenical creeds. The confession is the basis "which must be preached, taught and lived" and the norm for rejecting and opposing false doctrine and heresy, contrary to God's word. It is particularly concerned with the power of non-Christian beliefs, which must be rejected. Article 1 affirms God in words echoing the Nicene Creed. Rejected are divine names like "Grandfather," belief in spirits derived from such a name; in "lucky days, fortune-telling and reading fate in the lines of one's hands." Article 2 affirms the Trinity and rejects speaking about only God (Maha Esa) and subordinating the Son and Holy Spirit to the Father. Article 3 affirms "the special acts of the triune God." Again using the language of the Nicene Creed about God and Christ, "he is our intercessor in heaven." Rejected are the Roman Catholic doctrines of Mary as "interceding for us with God"; the notion of the priest sacrificing Christ in the Mass; the primacy of the pope as "vicar of Christ on this earth." Also rejected is "the human conception that the Lord Jesus is comparable with the prophets of the world"; that the Holy Spirit "can descend upon man through his own power without the Gospel"; that the use of medicine is unnecessary because the invocation of the Holy Spirit might be suffi-cient; or any prophecy in the name of the Holy Spirit by people who claim to be filled by the Spirit. Article 4 affirms the Word of God in the Bible as sufficient for the Christian life. "The Holy Scripture is the beginning and end of all thought, wisdom and activity in the congregation (church) and with the believers." Article 5 speaks of the origin of sin, attributing it to the devil, who led people into transgression. Arti-cle 6 affirms original sin, which enslaves all persons. Rejected is the notion about newborn children without sin; that sin is only caused by poverty, penury, or distress; and that the human heart "is at the time of birth pure as blank paper." Article 7 speaks of redemption from sin through Christ alone by grace and faith, which God regards as righteousness.

Article 8 affirms several things. First, it affirms that the church is the assembly of believers in Christ called by the Holy Spirit. Rejected are the ideas that the church can be established through the "caprice" of people; that anyone in the church has the right to rule the church ("the Church is not a democracy but a Christocracy"); that the church is a "state church"; that ancestral customs *(adat)* rule the church; or that organization alone imparts life into the church. Second, it affirms that the church is holy because Christ has sanctified it, not because church members are holy. Rejected is the idea that people become holy through good works, or that "pessimism" and "schism" are results of sin, which is still in members. Third, it affirms the universal church, consisting of every variety of culture with various ceremonies and orders. Rejected is any consideration of the church as merely national without any fellow-ship with other churches. Fourth, it affirms that the church is one in a "spiritual," not "secular unity." Fifth, it affirms that the true signs of the church are the true preach-ing of the Gospel; the right administration of two sacraments; and the exercise of church discipline to combat sin.

Article 9 affirms the servants of the church, stressing the administration of min-istry according to the offices of Christ, prophet, priest, and king. Ministers are to preach inside and outside the church, celebrate baptism and Holy Communion, do pastoral care, and preserve pure doctrine. All this work must be done by a proper call. Article 10 affirms the two sacraments. Immersion is not necessary in baptism; Holy Communion must be done with both elements, bread and wine. Article 11 affirms church order based on the word of God. Required church festivals are the birth, death, resurrection, and ascension of Jesus, and Pentecost. Article 12 affirms secular government grounded in God for the sake of opposing evil and creating jus-tice. Church and state must be separate. A tyrannical government must not be obeyed, according to Acts 5:29. Article 13 affirms Sunday and rejects the require-ment of a Saturday-Sabbath taught by Seventh Day Adventists, who had a successful mission in Indonesia. Article 14 speaks about food, affirming all food as good and rejecting fasting as a way to become holy. Article 15 deals with faith and good works, which must be done as "fruits of faith," exemplified by the Ten Commandments. Article 16 deals with remembering the dead. They will be judged and strengthen the hope in the communion with God. Rejected are the notion of a soul surviving, influencing the living, and remaining in the grave, as well as the Roman Catholic teaching of purgatory and praying to the souls to receive power from them. Article 17 affirms angels as divine messengers to help believers. Article 18 affirms a final judgment through Christ, ordering salvation and torment. Rejected are attempts to compute the end time (millennialism) and the notion that there is still a period of grace after death.

The Batak confession was patterned after the Augsburg Confession. It is the only parallel ever produced for the Augsburg Confession and was recognized as such by

The Institute for Ecumenical Research

LWF in 1952, when it granted membership to the Batak church.[61] Two significant decisions advanced the ecumenical commitment of LWF: (1) the establishment of a Lutheran Foundation (Institute) for Inter-Confessional Ecumenical Research in Strasbourg, France, in 1963; and (2) a new constitution, adopted at the Eighth Assembly of LWF in Curitiba, Brazil, in 1990. The Strasbourg foundation was particularly geared toward a dialogue with Rome because Vatican II had sent promising signals. The foundation would be staffed by scholars from Germany, Scandinavia, North America, and developing countries, making up a team of at least four ecumenists with expertise in various theological disciplines.

In 1974, the foundation succeeded in creating an ecumenical advance on the conflictive issue of intercommunion or eucharistic hospitality between Lutherans and Catholics. A statement by its Institute for Ecumenical Research, Strasbourg, France, on Lutheran-Roman Catholic intercommunion, titled *Eucharistic Hospitality,* evaluated results of ecumenical dialogues on the eucharist and concluded with the recommendation for "occasional acts of intercommunion."[62] Such acts would be mixed marriage, ecumenical events, and congregational situations under the conditions that both sides know of the ecumenical advances in regard to the sacrament of Holy Communion. The Catholic bishop of Strasbourg did, "in a carefully substantiated directive," permit "under certain conditions" the reciprocal participation of couples of mixed marriages in both Catholic and Protestant eucharistic celebrations. But after a few years of such practice, Rome stopped it.[63]

The new LWF constitution of 1990 was developed after a long debate about the question of whether LWF should be viewed as a communion rather than a federation. The basic change involves Section II on the "nature and functions," which speaks of LWF as a "communion of churches which confess the triune God, agree in the proclamation of the Word of God and are united in pulpit and altar fellowship." But the move toward "communion" proved unacceptable to some Lutheran churches, especially the Lutheran Church–Missouri Synod, which is not listed as a member church.[64]

LWF did try to combine its work for Lutheran and Christian unity with a responsibility for the world and its problems, working together with the World Council of Churches. In the 1970s, LWF joined the quest for human rights, triggered heavily by the political situations in Latin America, with its military dictatorships. Luther's doctrine of the two kingdoms was revisited and reviewed. Accordingly, the group taught that "in the area of the secular realm Christians and non-Christians cooperate together on the basis of reason; it is thus not outside God's kingdom."[65] The rights of women and other minorities were considered in various LWF assemblies. A resolution of human rights was adopted in Dar es Salaam in 1977, declaring "that it is our task as Christians to

First meeting of the International Congress on Luther Research (Denmark, 1956)

promote, together with those who have different beliefs, the realization of full freedom of thought, conscience and religion. . . . Above all, voices must be raised against the misuse of power by the powerful where they ignore or circumvent the rights of the weak."[66] Concrete assistance to victims of poverty, injustice, and disease was provided by the Lutheran World Service, which, at times, had resources of more than $100 million. The group has made efforts for peace in the Holy Land and elsewhere since the 1980s, perhaps a final blow to "Lutheran quietism," a traditional lack of interest in political matters.[67] LWF has tried to be, with increasing success, an advocate for Lutheran ecumenical identity and Christian realism.

Ecumenical Dialogues

Sixteenth-century Lutheranism established liberal ecumenical norms for dialogue in order to achieve Christian unity once again. Roman Catholicism, the Reformed (Zwinglian-Calvinist) communions, and even remote Greek Orthodoxy would be the principal partners in dialogue. Philipp Melanchthon was the chief Lutheran ecumenical proponent who had formulated the conditions for dialogue in the Augsburg Confession's article 7, namely, to agree on word and sacraments.[68] But no agreements were possible in the sixteenth century. A Lutheran-Catholic team tried hard at

Regensburg in 1541 but failed; there was no other dialogue until the end of Vatican II in 1965 in Baltimore. Several intensive Lutheran-Reformed attempts to overcome the impasse concerning the Lord's Supper also failed; progress was made in Germany when the Prussian king, Frederick William III, forced a marriage, as it were, in the Prussian Union, which achieved a confessional consensus in 1835 in the Rhine provinces and in Westphalia. Melanchthon tried to make contact with Constantinople but failed. Lutheran theologians in Tübingen exchanged letters with Patriarch Jeremiah II between 1574 and 1581; the patriarch refused to make any concessions.[69]

Individual national Lutheran church bodies and LWF became partners in ecumenical dialogues in the twentieth century with the rise of the ecumenical movement. The dialogues were conducted on bilateral (with two partners) and multilateral (several partners) levels. Some of these dialogues were international, sponsored by LWF; others were national, organized by individual churches and national councils of churches.

Lutheran–Roman Catholic Dialogue

It began in 1965 in Baltimore with a U.S. team whose extensive work (1965–1993) and method became models for other dialogues: two annual meetings of about four days, with research papers and discussion; publication of findings offering "a common statement," disagreements, and selected papers. The team postponed thorny subjects but did not leave them untreated. The topics disclose this kind of planning: (1) the status of the Nicene Creed as dogma, (2) baptism, (3) eucharist, (4) eucharist and ministry, (5) papal primacy, (6) teaching authority and infallibility, (7) justification by faith, (8) the saints and Mary, and (9) Scripture and tradition.[70]

The LWF and the Vatican Secretariat for Promoting Christian Unity created an international Joint Lutheran–Roman Catholic Study Commission, which first met in 1967 and produced *The Malta Report* on the gospel and the church, ending with a quest for mutual recognition of the ministerial office and occasional intercommunion (especially for mixed marriages). A second dialogue group dealt beginning in 1973 with the 450th anniversary of the Augsburg Confession in 1980 and the 500th anniversary of Luther's birth in 1983. Then it turned to a dialogue on the eucharist, the ministry, community, and unity.[71] A third dialogue, 1986 to 1993, dealt with the church and justification, followed by a fourth dialogue on apostolicity.

Dialogue in Scandinavia was conducted on community, the Lord's Supper, ministry, baptism and church membership, episcopacy and marriage-family. A German dialogue dealt extensively with "church fellowship in word and sacrament."[72] The dialogue encouraged educational publications on Luther, no longer a "heretic" but a "father of the church."[73] Cardinal Willebrands formally told LWF in 1970 that Luther made demands later fulfilled by Vatican II.

In 1971, the Roman Catholic diocese of Cologne requested Rome to lift the ban from Luther on the 450th anniversary of his condemnation in Worms. Nothing formally needed to be done, according to experts on canon law, because Luther, once dead, no longer was under the jurisdiction of the earthly church. Rome called him "a teacher we have in common" *(ein gemeinsamer Lehrer)*, echoing a title given to the most revered of all Catholic "fathers of the church," Thomas Aquinas (c. 1223–1274).[74]

Such posthumous rehabilitation of the Wittenberg reformer was linked to a breakthrough on his famous doctrine of justification by faith. Based on the work of dialogues, especially the North American one, a consensus had been reached on justification in 1995, known as the Joint Declaration on the Doctrine of Justification, followed by hope for further progress toward unity but also by a theological firestorm in Germany against the consensus. But the declaration was solemnly and jointly celebrated on October 31, 1999, Reformation Day, in Augsburg, Germany. Both churches agreed that the doctrine of justification is an "indispensable criterion which constantly serves to orient all the teaching and practice of our churches to Christ"; all mutual condemnations were revoked.[75] Looking at the failure of the LWF to reach a Lutheran agreement on justification in Helsinki in 1963 and at the consensus of 1995, it can be noted that the latter accomplished what the Lutheran Confessions envisaged: justification as an ecumenical, not Lutheran, criterion for Christian unity. Dialogue is on the way to assessing the power of the consensus on justification in dealing with the great obstacle to Christian unity, papal infallibility.

Lutheran–Reformed Dialogue

Despite efforts to unite Lutherans and Swiss Reformed (Zwinglian and Calvinist), no Protestant doctrinal agreement was reached in the sixteenth century. Colloquies at Marburg in 1529, at Maulbronn in 1564, and at Montbeliard in 1586 revealed irreconcilable positions. Some progress was made in Germany in the Prussian Union of 1817, with a workable constitution in 1876. Lutheran and Reformed immigrants to the United States formed a "church association" *(Kirchenverein)* in 1841. In Hungary, pulpit and altar fellowship were established in 1835, but the two churches remained separate. In Austria, a small Reformed minority formed an administrative union with the Lutheran Church in 1891.

After World War II, efforts toward unity intensified. A number of dialogues recorded doctrinal agreement based on the respective confessions: in the Netherlands in 1956, in the Federal Republic of Germany (West Germany) in 1959, in France in 1964. These European dialogues dealt with biblical authority, the presence of Christ, baptism, and the Lord's Supper. A significant breakthrough was made in Germany at Arnoldsheim *(Theses)* in 1957 and finally, on a European level, at Leuenberg in 1973. Intensive dialogues were conducted in the United States, leading to theological reconciliation and to full communion (altar-pulpit fellowship and mutual ministry). After much critical research and heated controversy in the 1960s and 1980s, constructive proposals were offered.[76] An agreement was reached in Ethiopia in 1974 and in Indonesia in 1984, followed by an organized new federation or communion of Protestant churches. By and large, full communion was achieved on a world level, thus overcoming the division of the sixteenth century.[77]

Lutheran–Anglican Dialogue

Lutheran and Anglican contacts increased in global missions. Moreover, the Anglican view of the historic episcopate is sufficiently flexible for dialogical adjustments. It has been defined by the Lambeth Quadrilateral of 1888, together with the four norms of church unity (the Bible, the Apostles' and Nicene Creeds, the sacraments) as "locally adapted in the modes of administrations to the varying needs of the nations and peoples called of God into the unity of his church." The first bilateral dialogue was begun in 1909 between the Church of England and the Church of Sweden. By 1939, both sides reached a basic consensus in the sharing of ministry, sacraments, and the consecration of bishops. Dialogues were also held between Anglicans and Lutherans in Finland (1933–1934) and the Baltics (Latvia and Estonia, 1936–1938), again with a consensus on a common episcopal ministry and eucharistic hospitality. Similar dialogues were organized between Anglicans and Lutherans in Denmark, Norway, and Iceland, resulting in eucharistic hospitality in 1950. In 1964, the dialogue was extended to West Germany, including Reformed and United (Lutheran and Reformed) churches. It entered a second phase from 1987 to 1988, ending with the *Meissen Statement* of 1988. These dialogues were amplified by an international dialogue sponsored by LWF and the Lambeth Conference in 1970, resulting in the *Pullach Report* (1972) and the *Helsinki Report* (1983). The former did not reach an agreement regarding the historic episcopate; the latter did. In the United States, the dialogue with the Episcopal Church–USA consisted of three phases: 1969–1972, 1976–1980, and 1983–1995.[78]

The end result was a declaration of full communion based on a controversial distinction between *apostolic succession* and *historic episcopate* recommended by the World Council of Churches: the former is "an expression of the permanence and, therefore, of the continuity of Christ's own mission in which the church participates"; the latter is "the succession of bishops [that] became one of the ways . . . in which apostolic tradition of the Church was expressed . . . episcopal succession is a sign, though not a guarantee, of the continuity and unity of the Church."[79] The declaration of full communion was elaborated into the *Concordat of Agreement* between the Evangelical Lutheran Church in America and the Episcopal Church–USA, formally adopted in 2000.[80] The dialogue between the Anglican Church of Great

Britain and Ireland and the Lutheran Church in the Nordic and Baltic regions achieved a basic consensus in *The Porvoo Common Statement* of 1994 but from a different perspective.[81]

Lutheran–Orthodox Dialogue

Lutherans and Orthodox made sporadic contacts when Lutherans migrated to Russia under Czar Peter the Great (1672–1725). In 1914, the Swedish archbishop Nathan Söderblom invited the Orthodox churches to join the ecumenical movement. A significant number of Orthodox leaders participated in the Life and Work Conference in Stockholm in 1925. Regional dialogues were conducted by German Lutherans in the 1950s, by Finnish Lutherans in the 1970s, by Bulgarian and Romanian Lutherans and Reformed in 1979. Dialogue in the United States began in 1967 with various Orthodox churches. In 1973, a trilateral dialogue began (Lutheran, Reformed, and Orthodox), ending in 1989. The dialogue results were summed up in a final report titled *Christ 'in us' and Christ 'for us' in Lutheran and Orthodox Theology.* The main topics of all these dialogues concentrated on Scripture and tradition, creeds, Holy Spirit, communion, and ethics. From 1978 until 1981, LWF conducted a dialogue at the world level on the theme "participation in the mystery of the church"; after five meetings, this continued in 1991 with the topic of "authority in and of the church."[82]

Lutheran Dialogue with Other Denominations

In 1986, the LWF began theological conversations with Baptists, who originated as an opposition group against Anglicans in the sixteenth century. After four annual sessions, significant differences remained on the questions of authority, sacraments, and the church. National dialogues in Germany (1980–1983) and the United States (1979–1981) disclosed the same differences. But both denominations withdrew mutual condemnations with the understanding that both churches are grounded in the gospel.[83]

The LWF and the World Methodist Council conducted dialogue from 1977 to 1984, beginning in Dresden, Germany, in 1979 with the theme "The Authority of the Bible and the Authenticity of the Church." A second round was held in Bristol, England, in 1980, on "Justification and Sanctification." A third round in Oslo, Norway, in 1981, discussed "Holy Spirit and Church"; a fourth meeting was held in Lake Junaluska, North Carolina, in 1983. The final session in Bossey, Switzerland, in 1984 summarized the results: a proposal for full fellowship in word and sacrament, unity in service, and use of theological results to work for Christian unity. In the United States, dialogues were conducted by the National Lutheran Council and the United Methodist Church from 1977 to 1987 on baptism and episcopacy, the latter remaining a stumbling block on the path to unity.[84]

Four brief encounters between Lutherans and conservative evangelicals took place in the United States from 1979 to 1981 but without any substantial agreements beyond the ecumenical creeds.[85]

Nine Lutheran–Jewish meetings have been held since 1964 in the wake of the Holocaust and the 500th anniversary of Luther's birth in 1983. Lutherans tried to overcome anti-Semitism, linked to Luther's anti-Jewish outbursts and the tradition of a mission to Jews, both of which the denomination has firmly and formally rejected.[86]

Lutheran dialogues for Christian unity have been numerous and rich with evidence, based on the Lutheran Confessions, that to be Lutheran means to be ecumenical. Dialogues have paved the way to one of the most significant ecumenical advances in the United States in 1999: the full communion of the Evangelical Lutheran Church in America (ELCA) with the three main Reformed churches (Presbyterian Church [USA], Reformed Church in America, and United Church of Christ), the Episcopal Church–USA, and the Moravian Church (which has Lutheran Pietist roots). Although the Lutheran Church–Missouri Synod participated in many dialogues, it never voted in favor of any agreements. The various dialogues have engendered much historical and theological research, often through effective national and international teamwork.[87] Lutheranism will never be without dialogues, if it remains loyal to its confessional base that it is sufficient for Christian unity to have full communion, that is, agreement in faith, sacramental fellowship, and a common ministry. Some Lutherans try to increase this confessional condition for unity by advocating consensus in doctrine or polity. Others simply operate with a denominational ideology that disregards confessional identity and favors some kind of social-activist fellowship. Both are tempted to be institutionally secure rather than spiritually free. It is an enduring temptation linked to the fear that the freedom of the gospel may make life too difficult. That is a reason why there are ministries of security and defense in the world but not any ministries of freedom.

Global Constellations

Lutherans can be found almost everywhere in the world. Totaling about sixty-four million, they are most numerous in Europe, with a population of about thirty-seven million, and increasing most rapidly in Africa, which has about 10.5 million.[88] Among them is the fastest-growing Lutheran church, the Ethiopian Evangelical Lutheran Church Mekane Yesus, with 3.3 million members, having added almost eighty thousand members in the year 2000. The second largest Lutheran church in Africa is the Evangelical Lutheran Church in Tanzania, with 2.5 million members. Its most famous leader, Josiah Kibira (1925–1988), served as LWF president from 1977

Bishop Josiah Kibira

to 1984. Almost half of the Lutherans in Africa are in east Africa and Madagascar. Immigrant churches dominate in South Africa and Namibia. Smaller missionary churches are found in Zimbabwe and Botswana. In western central Africa, the largest community of Lutherans is in Cameroon, with about 255,000 in three churches. In west Africa, smaller Lutheran churches in Ghana, Nigeria, and Liberia are growing.

Lutherans in Africa live in the midst of wars, starvation, and rapid political changes often precipitated by military tyrants. Many small churches have merged with larger ones in order to become more effective in their missionary, educational, and social work. All African Conferences have been held since 1955, sponsored by the LWF Department of Missions (since 1977, renamed to the Department of Cooperation because the designation "mission" had become very offensive in developing countries). Racial segregation has been abandoned. Lutheran theologians have joined other Christian theologians in calling for ecumenical cooperation in strengthening theological education and focusing on "a theology of justice."[89] In this regard, the Lutheran "two kingdoms doctrine" attracted African minds because it does not divide the sacred from the profane but views the world holistically as an interaction of the two realms. Worship, too, with its emphasis on the participation of the whole congregation, blended into African spirituality, which stresses the communal life. Moreover, Lutherans in Africa cannot avoid dialogue with other Christians and other religions, such as Islam. Finally, the quick growth of congregations caused a lack of pastors; often, one pastor serves several large congregations, thus the need for recruitment for ministry.[90]

Celebrating the centennial of the Lutheran Church in northern Tanzania (October 1993)

Lutheran churches in Europe recorded the greatest losses (about two hundred thousand in the year 2000), especially in Germany (with the exception of Bavaria), Sweden, Denmark, and Finland. Slight increases were noted in Norway, Great Britain, and Austria. Germany has the highest number of Lutherans in a single country, nearly fourteen million. In Scandinavia, the population is almost entirely Lutheran. The largest church (also worldwide) is the Church of Sweden, with 7.4 million members, followed by the churches in Finland (4.6 million), Denmark (4.5 million), Norway (3.8 million), and Iceland (about 250,000). Besides these state or folk churches are "free" churches of various sizes. Belgium has the smallest Lutheran French-speaking church in Europe (about three hundred), France the largest (258,000). Smaller churches exist in Ireland, the Netherlands, and the United Kingdom (England). There are minority churches in Austria (with a small Reformed group, 340,000), in Switzerland (about five thousand), and in Italy (seven thousand). Italian Lutherans were finally granted equal status with the Roman Catholics in 1993.

Many parishioners have been alienated in the state or folk churches. But they remain members so that their children are baptized, confirmed, and married. They attend worship on Christmas Eve and expect a fine ritual funeral. Moreover, the relationship between church and state is no longer uniform in Europe, as it was arranged by the Peace of Augsburg in 1555, which ascribed the state dominion over the church. Churches have become more independent. In Germany, they legislate for themselves; they have unlimited freedom in the election of officers; and they negotiate their portion of church tax. In Scandinavia, independence from the state is on the rise. In Sweden, the Lutheran Church declared itself free from the state in 2001, with cooperation only in funding through taxes. There are discussions about the power of the bishops in Denmark, whether they can withdraw the credentials of ordained pastors.[91] The churches in Germany and Scandinavia also have complete legal freedom in how to use the church tax collected by the state. It is used not only for salaries and maintenance of structure, but also rather for new creative programs in education and diaconical work as well as for aiding the development of poor countries. Another problem for European state churches is the influx of non-Christian religions, such as Islam and Hinduism. Thus, the established Lutheran Church may foreshadow the fate of European Lutheranism. "It is like a porous tile. It stands out clearly from its surroundings, but is being permeated by seepage from quite a number of ideological and religious currents fashionable in our city."[92]

In eastern and southeastern Europe, Lutheran churches seemed stronger under Communist tyranny than they are after liberation from oppression. In East Germany, Lutherans were not a state church but a church in dispersion (diaspora), a minority church. Parishioners worked together with other groups, often political ones without Christian commitments, to advocate for alienated minorities. After the liberation in 1989, such cooperation faded away, and the pressure of Western ways increased. East German Lutherans were united with West Germans. The Lutheran churches in Hungary, Croatia, the Czech Republic, the Slovak Republic, Slovenia, Romania, Yugoslavia (with new territorial arrangements), and the Russian Federation and Commonwealth of Independent States are minority churches. The largest church (about five hundred thousand) is in Hungary. The new Evangelical Lutheran

Church in Russia is slowly growing, with about 250,000 members. A small church in Ingria, Russia (sixteen thousand members), has had altar and pulpit fellowship with the Lutheran Church–Missouri Synod since 1998; it is a member of LWF, whereas the Missouri Synod is not.[93] The churches try to work together and with other non-Lutheran churches.[94] In the Baltics, Lutheranism also survived Communist oppression. Many Lutherans had emigrated to North America, settling in the midwestern United States and in Canada.[95] The largest church is in Latvia (250,000 members), followed by churches in Estonia (two hundred thousand members) and in Lithuania (thirty thousand members).

The Lutheran churches in Asia have a total of about 6.6 million members, having increased their membership by about two hundred thousand in the year 2000. The largest and fastest-growing church is the Huria Kristen Batak Protestan in Indonesia, with about four million members; almost a million have been added since 1999. It is the only Lutheran church that drafted a new version of the Augsburg Confession (1951). Other Asian Lutheran churches are slowly growing. All these churches face the difficult task of introducing the core of Lutheranism into new and diverse cultures. Lutheran churches in India have the second largest number of members (about 1.6 million); there is a dialogue with the ecumenical Church of South India, formed in 1947 without Lutherans. The third largest number of Lutherans is in Papua New Guinea (almost one million). All these churches are growing and do effective educational work in schools for all ages. Lutherans in the Philippines belong to the Lutheran Church–Missouri Synod, growing from a mission in 1967 to about twenty thousand members. A small group of Lutherans in Japan (about thirty thousand) also is linked to the Missouri Synod. Moreover, Lutherans are quite visible through two seminaries and a twelve-volume translation of Luther's works. So are the few Lutherans (about three thousand) in South Korea, with their own school and a twelve-volume translation of Luther's works (1989).[96] Lutherans in Malaysia, Taiwan, and Singapore were linked to Chinese Lutherans before World War II; those in Hong Kong have to live with the new Communist Chinese regime. Only a few thousand Lutherans are left in Taiwan and China. Their future is uncertain. About twenty-five thousand Lutherans belong to the Protestant church in Sabah (North Borneo).[97] LWF has conducted All-Asia Conferences since 1962, stressing theological education. The only Lutheran church in Australia has ninety-four thousand members; it is linked to the Lutheran Church–Missouri Synod. New Zealand has a minority of about thirteen hundred Lutherans.[98]

Israel has a tiny Lutheran church with several hundred members, and Jordan has a Lutheran church with about sixteen hundred members (among twelve million Christians in the Middle East). Supported by LWF, Lutherans from these two countries are involved in educational, medical, and refugee work.

Latin America contains about 1.1 million Lutherans. Fifteen thousand new members were counted in 2000; fourteen thousand of them joined the Church of the Lutheran Confessions (organized in 1949) in Brazil, pushing its membership to 714,000. The second largest church is the Evangelical Church of the River Plate, with forty-seven thousand members (including Lutherans from Paraguay and Uruguay). Linked to the Lutheran Church–Missouri Synod is the Evangelical Lutheran Church of Argentina (about thirty thousand members). Smaller Lutheran churches are in Bolivia, Chile, Colombia, Costa Rica, Ecuador, El Salvador, Guatemala, Guyana, Honduras, Mexico, Nicaragua, Panama, Peru, Suriname, and Venezuela. The Evangelical Lutheran Congregation La Epifania in Guatemala is the smallest Lutheran church, with 350 members. Lutherans in Latin America live in the midst of political, social, and ideological struggles, whose victims are landless farmers. The Pentecostal movement is most successful in attracting people in Latin America. LWF founded a theological seminary in 1965 near Buenos Aires; it merged in 1970 with a graduate school in Buenos Aires. The problem of justice in liberation theology has attracted Lutheran theologians.[99]

In North America, Lutheran churches have a membership of about 8.5 million; among them are about 290,000 in Canada. The largest church is the ELCA, with about 5.2 million members. The second largest is the Lutheran Church–Missouri Synod, about 2.6 million members. The third largest is the Wisconsin Evangelical Lutheran Church, about 414,000 members. Ten smaller Lutheran churches are in the United States: the Association of Free Lutheran Congregations (thirty-two thousand members), Evangelical Lutheran Synod (twenty-four thousand members), Church of the Lutheran Brethren (fourteen thousand members), Church of the Lutheran Confessions (eighty-seven hundred members), Apostolic Lutheran Church in America (seven thousand members), Lithuanian Evangelical Lutheran Church in Diaspora (five thousand members), Lutheran Churches of the Reformation (fifteen hundred members), the Protestant Conference (eleven hundred members), Conservative Lutheran Association (ninety members), and the Fellowship of Lutheran Congregations (446 members). Canada has three churches: the Evangelical Lutheran Church in Canada (about 192,000 members), the Lutheran Church–Canada (eighty thousand members), and the Estonian Evangelical Lutheran Church (twelve thousand members).

This Lutheran diversity, rooted in doctrinal, structural, and ethnic differences, can be viewed through the lenses of the popular yet controversial "frontier thesis" set forth in 1893 by the historian Frederick J. Turner (1861–1932). The development and force of the American character, he contended, is nurtured by the drive to the frontier, the new space to the West. In regard to religion, it could be said that whenever a religious group experienced internal strife, its conservative part left the mainline group and founded another "denomination" in the West, the frontier; simply stated, "Let's leave rather than debate holy issues."[100] Lutherans are part and parcel of this American experience.

World War I and the economic depression in the 1920s and 1930s made U.S. Lutherans once again conscious of the scandal of division among themselves and in relation to non-Lutheran Christians. Students gathered for discussions on Christian unity led by an effective campus ministry. There was also a liturgical renewal based on an appreciation of pre-Reformation worship patterns, now revived by the Society of St. James and the Society of St. Ambrose. In addition, there was again a theological quest for a proper understanding of biblical authority and Lutheran unity, the two enduring problems of Lutheranism in America. Various official statements on Lutheran unity were drafted between 1919 and 1940, disclosing two theological camps: one led by the Lutheran Church–Missouri Synod, advocating the unique authority of the Bible because it is the verbally inspired word of God, and the other led by the United Lutheran Church in America in the National Lutheran Council, asserting a proper balance between the authority of the word of God, disclosed in Hebrew prophets, and in the lives of Jesus and his apostles, and the Bible as a book. Both camps tried hard to create Lutheran unity.

Eight documents of Lutheran unity were tested by almost all of the synods between 1919 and 1940.[101] The "Brief Statement" of 1932 clearly stated the biblical fundamentalism of the Missouri Synod: "We teach . . . the verbal inspiration of the Scriptures. . . . They are in all parts and words the infallible truth also in those parts which treat of historical, geographical and other secular matters." After intensive internal debate over the next three decades, the Lutheran Church–Missouri Synod adopted this position at its New Orleans convention in 1973.[102] Such an uncompromising repristination occurred after successful attempts by an ecumenically minded group in the synod, led by faculty members at Concordia Seminary in St. Louis, to have altar and pulpit fellowship with the American Lutheran Church (1964–1973). But a conservative faction of the synod, under the direction of J. A. O. Preus (1920–1994; elected synod president in 1969), his brother Robert Preus (1924–1995), and Hermann Otten, editor of Lutheran News, gained the upper hand and persuaded a majority of delegates in New Orleans to dismiss the president of Concordia Seminary, John H. Tietjen, and forty-five faculty members. They formed their own seminary, called Seminex (for "seminary in exile"), as part of the ELCA Lutheran School of Theology in Chicago. Together with about one hundred thousand other exiles, they organized the Association of Evangelical Lutheran Churches, which merged with the ELCA in 1989.

The Missouri schism of 1973 was a sensational religious news story and a traumatic event for some Lutherans. Viewed from a broader, ecumenical perspective, it was a squabble in a conservative body that resulted in the departure of a splinter group. This event may not have refuted non-Lutheran images of U.S. Lutheranism "as a sleeping giant that began to wake up between the two world wars" or of being "the last best hope of Protestantism in the United States."[103] Some historical analysts have proposed that U.S. Lutherans might become what these images suggest by facing the challenge of their "church father," Henry Melchior Muhlenberg (1711–1787), who made the important distinction between an established church and a church defined and nourished by its mission.[104] Another suggestion has been that they listen to what one of the "fathers of the country," Theodore Roosevelt, told a large crowd of citizens at the rededication of Luther Place Memorial Church in Washington, D.C., on January 29, 1905, namely, that the Lutheran church could become "one of America's greatest." But his prediction could only be realized if they "meant business," as the dean of historians of U.S. Lutheranism observed seven decades later,[105] and he concluded that "meaning business" is related to a main question that still confronts Lutherans in North America.

One of the main questions confronting confessional Lutherans currently is not their unity—the Missouri Synod notwithstanding—but their particularity in the ecumenical scene. Lutheran unity, fifty years overdue, will come eventually because Missouri cannot forever escape the implications of its own confession. But meanwhile, a burden of concern rests upon those who see the ecumenical heart of the Lutheran confession of the gospel as God's Word to the whole world.[106]

Confession and Culture

Lutheranism began as a reform movement within the Roman Catholic Church. When pope and emperor tried to eradicate the movement through ban and edict, the new Lutherans put their reform proposals into action in territories where they found solid commitment to their cause by rulers and subjects. The Augsburg Confession of 1530, therefore, was not only a doctrinal statement but also a report of what was taught and done in the converted territories whose rulers had signed it. Accordingly, the confession first listed "Chief Articles of Faith" and then "Articles in Which an Account Is Given of the Abuses That Have Been Corrected."[107] Moreover, it issued an invitation to discuss differences with a commitment to Christian unity.

> If the other electors, princes and estates also submit a similar written statement of their judgments and opinions, in both Latin and German, we are quite willing, in complete obedience to Your Imperial Majesty, our most gracious Lord, to discuss with them and their associates—as far as this can be done in fairness—such practical and equitable ways as may unite us. Thus, the matters at issue between the parties may be presented in writing on both sides; they may be negotiated

charitably and amicably; and these same differences may be so explained as to unite us in one, true religion, since we are all enlisted under one Christ and should confess Christ.[108]

Lutherans understood themselves to be defenders of a genuinely catholic and ecumenical "human tradition" grounded in Scripture and in agreement with the ancient church fathers of the Western Roman Catholic Church, such as Ambrose and Augustine, and the early teachings of canon law (developed by Gratian in the twelfth century). That is why Rome should have no reason to oppose the reform movement and its work to correct abuses. "There is nothing here [in the Augsburg Confession] that departs from the Scriptures or the catholic church, or from the Roman church, insofar as we can tell from its writers."[109] Lutherans assumed that any Christian "human tradition" is not identical with the "one, holy Christian church," the assembly of believers grounded in word and sacraments. For any human, visible, and institutional expression of such a church is infested, as is any- thing human, with evil, defined in the Bible as the original sin expressed in the desire to be like God (Gen. 3:5). Because the church functions as a human assembly, it must be granted that "*in this life* many hypocrites and evil people are mixed in with them [the true believers]."[110] Thus, the true holy Christian church is confessed by faith but is in its historical, temporal form made up of "human traditions" linked to the diversity of daily human life known as "culture."[111] In this diversity of cultures, the unity of the church is seen in the communication of word and sacraments. It is not seen in a uniformity of "human traditions, rites or ceremonies instituted by human beings."[112] The confession of faith in the one true church must be linked to a realis- tic recognition of culture as an unavoidable power in the life of the institutional church. All schisms, before and after the Reformation, disclose sufficient evidence for such a conclusion.

The Reformation was not the first schism linked to the power of culture. Three other schisms had occurred in Christendom before the Reformation. First, Gentile and Jewish Christians broke their unity over the question of circumcision and food regulations (Acts 15). Despite a compromise for the sake of unity, Jewish Christians remained a separate church until the fifth century, when they disappeared after the establishment of Christianity as the official religion by Emperor Constantine the Great (c. 274–337). But other Jewish Christians still exist as a group that affirms Jesus as the Messiah without any relation to the Trinity. Then, there was a schism as the result of a conflict over the divinity of Jesus in the fourth century in Egypt. The Arians, named after their leader, Arius, rejected the divinity of Jesus and forced the church into a long conflict over the dogma of the Trinity. The Arians were expelled from the church but continued as a schismatic church among the Goths, a German tribe that settled in Asia Minor. Eventually, the Arians became a political group and disappeared, like the Jewish Christians, when Eastern Orthodoxy became a state religion. Finally, there was the tragic schism of Eastern and Western Christianity in 1054, when Roman Catholicism and Greek Orthodoxy condemned each other because of differences in doctrine and worship. Long-simmering doctrinal differences, especially about the Trinity, were exacerbated by divergent customs, Western insensitivity to the East, and ever-growing differences over papal authority. Different cultures seemed to produce irreconcilable churches. Eventually, Eastern Orthodoxy became estranged from the West and has only in the last century become involved in the ecumenical movement and, most recently, has begun a formal dialogue with the Roman Catholic Church.[113]

Lutheranism, born in the midst of a new, critical reading of history by humanists, developed a keen theological sense for the interaction of confession and culture. Roman Catholicism had succumbed to the temptation of institutional triumphalism by creating a Christian culture, medieval Christendom, that claimed authority even over emperors. Biblical views of the end time (eschatology) taught Luther, a revolutionary scholar of Holy Scripture, that the one, holy, true church as a visible institution will never be fully realized because of the power of sin in the world. But there are cultural expressions of that church linked to its risen, living Lord, Jesus Christ, through the eschatological lifelines of word and sacrament. These lifelines are the signs of Christian unity in the midst of a diversity of churches in the human tradition of history. As reformers, Lutherans offered their confession not just as a series of revised doctrines but as a vision of the church in a particular culture, focused on word and sacraments with different ways to organize the church and its ministry in the world. They did so as *Catholic* reformers, trying to preserve as much as possible of the ecclesiastical arrangements of Catholicism, but without its claim of universal authority and doctrinal infallibility. Accordingly, the true church could be found in a variety of human traditions, united in the task of communicating the gospel and in eucharistic hospitality.

The Marburg Articles of 1529 are an example of how Lutherans created a confession in the face of disagreements regarding the communication of word and sacraments, in this case Holy Communion.[114] The divisive issue concerning the presence of Christ in the eucharist is presented within a summary of the Christian faith in fifteen points, called articles: (1) the trinitarian God, (2) the divine incarnation in Jesus, (3) his resurrection, (4) original sin, (5) salvation from sin through faith in Christ, (6) faith as a gift of the Holy Spirit through the gospel, (7) justification by faith, (8) the external word as means to receive faith, (9) baptism, (10) good works, (11) confession of sin and absolution, (12) secular government instituted by God, (13) freedom in human traditions, (14) infant baptism, and (15) Holy Communion.

Zwingli and his team agreed with the Lutherans in all but the last of the fifteen articles. They could not agree as to whether "the true body and blood of Christ" are "bodily present" in the bread and wine. Zwingli contended that the body of Christ cannot be everywhere because bodies are limited in their location by space and time. Here, Zwingli was speaking as a disciple of Aristotle, who defined physical presence in this manner. Luther, on the other hand, argued that the power of the spoken word ("This is my body") brings the bodily presence into the consecrated elements of bread and wine. Both reformers piously "agreed" to let the matter rest and diligently pray for a "right understanding"; a consensus on such an understanding was not achieved for centuries. In 1993, Lutherans and the Reformed shifted their attention from the mode of Christ's eucharistic presence to its consequences: "community, witness, proclamation, and the mission of the church in the world as fruit of the celebration at the Lord's Table enabled by the triune God."[115] Hindsight suggests that Zwingli was a child of the ancient Greek culture whose major philosopher, Aristotle, could not accept the contradiction that a body could be in two locations at the same time. Luther rejected the power of this culture and believed in the power of the divine word in the Bible that Christ could be everywhere. Zwingli unwittingly accepted another contradiction in the Marburg Articles when he did not reject the ancient confession of the Nicene Creed, cited in article 1, that one God is three persons. But he was so entangled with the contradictory notion of a bodily presence of Christ in the eucharist that he overlooked the more important contradictory assertions of the dogma of the Trinity. Moreover, he, unlike Luther, was quite willing to change the meaning of the word "is" (this *is* my body) by translating it with "signifies" (this signifies my body) and concluding from such change that Holy Communion was only a memorial of Christ's death, not a sacrament transmitting salvation in Christ.

It was important to Luther to see a doctrinal disagreement in the context of the whole arrangement of doctrines so that one could discern the significance of a single issue. The Marburg Articles show how a specific way of thinking, linked to a historical culture, could divide Reformation communities. The Augsburg Confession and other Lutheran confessions do not describe just a single doctrine or other issue but the totality of Christian thought and life in a specific historical situation.

Accordingly, confessions have become descriptions of "historical forms of life" (*geschichtliche Lebensformen*) of Christianity rather than specific, individual convictions that can be distinguished from other convictions.[116] These historical forms show how doctrinal confessions and diverse cultures have always interacted. The Lutheran New Testament scholar Ernst Käsemann (1906–1998) contended that the New Testament canon contains so many different versions of early Christian life that the canon cannot ensure the unity of the church. He offered three observations as reasons for such a conclusion: (1) the four Gospels render four different images of Christ and his words; (2) the record of events about Jesus and the early church is too inadequate to present a reliable historical record; (3) the New Testament preserved not only an understanding of the work, words, and person of Jesus but also misapprehensions that emerge as crude contradictions. Nevertheless, there is unity through the Spirit of God, Käsemann believes with Paul (2 Cor. 3:1-4), despite many human claims of unity through the letter of the law. This unity through the divine Spirit is "confessed" in the midst of the confessional cacophony of New Testament voices.[117]

One could also show that this diversity of New Testament sources was shaped by cultural contexts, such as the Gospel of Matthew with its obvious Jewish Christian concerns, or the Gospel of John with its Greek stance. Moreover, there is no evidence that Christian schisms or confessional differences are based on the diversity of confessions in the New Testament. But they are based on the Pauline conviction, adopted by Lutheranism, that the unity of the church is expressed in a diversity of confessions as historical forms of Christianity reflecting cultural differences.

The Lutheran Confessions are documents of a record of reform proposals and their realization in German territories. The Lutheran reformers became convinced by their exploration of the Bible and of Christian history that the one, holy, catholic church is a reality of the Christian faith and not a possible goal of a political church strategy. Lutherans disclosed the many abuses of the medieval church as evidence of the danger and futility of such a goal. Thus, they became aware of the fact that the unity of the church cannot be attested by the uniformity of confessions as historical forms of Christianity. The unity of the church is evident in the various confessions through the communication of word and sacrament as the means of the Holy Spirit to keep Christians united by faith until the time when they no longer "see in a mirror dimly, but . . . face to face" (1 Cor. 13:12).

The history of Lutheranism shows how difficult it is to believe in Christian unity and to live in a world of organized ecclesiastical diversity. The Peace of Augsburg in 1555 created territorial churches by settling Lutherans with Lutheran territorial princes as their bishops. They, like power-hungry politicians everywhere, promoted confessional uniformity through enforced adherence to pure doctrine, ushering in an age of orthodoxy marked by a fusion of religion and culture. Pietists opposed this territorial uniformity with a call for individual penance, conversion, and engagement in mission. A devastating example of how a cultural environment shapes Lutheranism is shown in Lutheran catechetical instruction in the United States in the early nineteenth century. Although Luther's Small Catechism was used as a basis for instruction, Pietist or rationalist theologies were used to explain it. Pastors focused especially on confirmation at about age fourteen as the time when one would become a Christian. In fact, one influential pastor stated "that infant baptism without confirmation was only half of a baptism for the mature years and thus would not be sufficient for an adult to be accepted as a subject in Jesus' kingdom."[118]

The distinguished Pietist educator, Samuel S. Schmucker (1799–1873) in Gettysburg, wanted to create a Lutheranism as the spearhead of a militant Protestantism poised for battle with Roman Catholicism in the United States. To make Lutheranism more ecumenical, in the sense of leading a pan-Protestant movement in the nation, he proposed a revision of the Augsburg Confession by removing what he saw as Roman Catholic remnants, such as the "real presence" of Christ in Holy Communion and the liturgy of the Mass. Thus, Schmucker succumbed to the temptation to let culture dominate the confession and propose the foundation of a distinctly American Lutheranism. But his proposal failed in 1855. On the other hand, the reinterpretation of the Augsburg Confession in the Batak confession of Indonesian Lutherans in 1951 made it strong in a culture quite different from the German context of the sixteenth century. Schmucker weakened the heartbeat of the confession by his removal of its reformed Catholicism. The Batak Lutherans transplanted it into a new culture without damaging its ecumenical rhythm, indeed enhancing it as a base for mission.

There also arose a conservative confessionalism in Germany and in North America, exemplified by the Erlangen school of Lutheran theology and the Lutheran Church–Missouri Synod. This confessionalism defended the Lutheran Confessions as the best and only source of Christian truth. The confessionalist movement fused with nationalist causes, illustrated by the powerful German association founded in 1886 and known through their journal *Die christliche Welt* (The Christian world). Another very influential group was *Der evangelische Bund* (the Evangelical League), though more Protestant than Lutheran, for "safeguarding German political interests." This close association of Lutheranism, Protestantism, and culture became known as "cultural Protestantism" *(Kulturprotestantismus)*. Confessionalism was most clearly exhibited when it was merged with biblical fundamentalism in the Lutheran Church–Missouri Synod in 1973. Originally intended as a renewal of Lutheranism in the nineteenth century, the confessionalist movement virtually abandoned the renewal because it wanted to establish one historical expression of Christian truth, the Lutheran Confessions, as the only, forever enduring one.[119]

The interaction of confession and culture has thrown Lutheranism into dangerous curves in its drive through history.[120] Lutheran history is marked by capricious, at times desperate, attempts to create Lutheran unity or to enhance Christian unity as intended by the Augsburg Confession, the Lutheran Magna Carta. Critical hindsight shows an increasing tendency in LWF and contemporary Lutheranism to realize the ecumenical vision of the Lutheran Confessions and to cherish the particular freedom and doxological sense of life in the face of the joyful future of the gospel. There is a drive in global Lutheranism to strive for unity in diversity through the ecumenical paradigm of communion, an understanding of the many diverse Lutheran churches in the world as one body united in a common faith and mission.[121] But there is also another tendency that broods like a dark cloud over the history of Lutheranism. It is a zealous drive, evident in the first encounter of Lutheranism and Catholicism, to guard the gospel from abuse rather than to embody its freedom and joy. In the face of such evidence, Lutheranism must continually remind itself, in, with, and under the earthly relativity of time, that to be with Christ in word and sacrament is the only way to have "a foretaste of the feast to come."[122]

Conclusion

Forward to Luther?

At the founding assembly of the Lutheran World Federation (LWF) in Lund, Sweden, in 1947, President Anders Nygren (1890–1978) reminded the delegates that Luther had rediscovered the gospel as the power to lead Christians through the perils of the world to the joyful, never-ending union with Christ. This eschatological kernel of Luther's thought had been neglected in Lutheranism during decades of secularization, tyranny, and war, Nygren contended. "Our purpose is not to reiterate what the Reformers said, but to re-think our Gospel, the one and only Gospel, the whole Gospel, to study it anew, possibly from a new point of approach and to express [it] in the terms of today. . . . This therefore, must be our watchword: Always forward toward Luther."[1]

Thus, Nygren connected Luther with the theme of the assembly, "The Lutheran Church in the World Today." His appeal to Luther could be made only if Luther was not viewed as a famous German reformer but as an ecumenical voice calling for a return to the gospel. Nygren, a citizen of neutral Sweden, knew that resistance to Hitler's tyranny in Germany had been solidly linked to Luther by Bishop Eivind Berggrav in Norway and Bishop Hanns Lilje (1899–1977) in Germany. Berggrav had stated in 1946 that during the resistance in Norway (1941–1945), he relied on the New Testament and on Luther who "above all, was the very best remedy to expel all 'Lutheran' servility to the state and secular authorities, and to characterize Hitler undauntingly."[2] Lilje, who had been in prison from 1944 to 1945, told the LWF assembly in Lund that "a church is truly Lutheran only if it fearlessly proclaims the judgment of God over all nations and if it, above all, humbly and penitently submits to its judgment itself."[3] In addition, the Hungarian Lutheran bishop Lajos Ordass (1890–1978) was known for his opposition of Communism, and without mentioning Luther, he told the Lund assembly of the Christian obligation to be a witness to Christ even at the very brink of despair.[4]

Luther is neither the founder of a church nor the most reliable "father of the church." That is why only three of his writings were included in the Lutheran Confessions: two catechisms (*Small* and *Large*) and *The Smalcald Articles*. Some of his teachings are staunchly medieval (such as his views on women); others are unacceptable in Christian thought and life (such as his call for the persecution of the

Jewish people). But in his best and brightest reflections on the nature of the church he remains an invaluable teacher. Luther rediscovered and bequeathed to subsequent generations, Lutherans and non-Lutherans, a view of the church that is always

The Luther seal

to be reformed: in its teaching tradition, in its structure, in its pattern of worship, and in its moral obligations. For nothing can be unchanging for Christians, who are called the people of "the Way" (Acts 9:2), "aliens and exiles" (1 Peter 2:11), "strangers and foreigners on the earth" (Heb. 11:13-14). They are pilgrims called to be witnesses of Christ in the mean, often meantime, between his ascension and return at the end of time. That is why Luther viewed the church as the gathering beset by evil, the devil, but sustained by word and sacrament; it is a militant and cruciform church. "Therefore whoever desires to see the Christian Church existing in quiet peace, entirely without crosses, without heresy and without factions, will never see it thus, or else he must view the false church of the devil as the real church."[5] In such a situation, Christians must be "wise as serpents and innocent as doves," as Jesus told his disciples when they were terrorized in an incredible environment of evil like "sheep among wolves" (Matt. 10:16-25). Luther combined a serpentine sagacity for evil with dovelike, innocent joy of life in Christ. "Even though Christ commands his disciples in Matt. 10:16 to imitate doves in their simplicity, that is, to be sincere and without venom, He nevertheless urges them to be wise as serpents; that is, they should be on their guard against insincere and treacherous people, and they should be cautious, the way a serpent in a fight is said to protect its head with extraordinary skill."[6]

It would behoove Lutherans of all stripes to focus on "serpenthood" as an exercise of rethinking the gospel based on Luther's insights and experience. The paradigm of serpenthood is rooted in a missionary mandate of Jesus ("See, I am sending you out," Matt. 10:16). The image of the serpent has an interesting history. In the Bible, the serpent appears first as a symbol of evil, tempting Adam and Eve in the garden, promising them that they can be "like God" (Gen. 3:5), the most original sin, namely, to play God in violation of the First Commandment, "You shall have no other gods." Then the serpent becomes a symbol of healing, echoing Greek medicine depicted by the symbol of two serpents curled around a staff—a logo still used today. When the people of Israel encountered dangerous serpents on their way to the Holy Land, Moses erected a bronze serpent, and whoever looked at it stayed alive (Num. 21:9). Finally, Jesus himself is the serpent depicting eternal life. "And just as Moses lifted up the serpent in the wilderness, so must the Son of Man be lifted up, that whoever believes in him may have eternal life" (John 3:14-15).

Serpentine wisdom means to be "quick-witted" and "alert" (Greek: *frominos* in Matt. 10:16); and dovelike innocence means to be "pure" and "uncorrupted" (Greek: *akaraios*). Such purity is linked to the Holy Spirit, who comes like a dove from heaven at the baptism of Jesus (Mark 1:10). "Dovehood" also stresses humble service, reflecting what Jesus said to his disciples before he sent them out into the world. "Whoever wishes to be first among you must be your slave . . . just as the Son of Man came not to be served but to serve" (Matt. 20:27-28). But Jesus also warned the disciples not to be just like sheep in the mission field, but wise like serpents; otherwise they will just become food for wolves.

Effective, holistic Christian mission combines servanthood with serpenthood—selfless service with cold-blooded discernment and a sharp mind. Like good physicians, Christians need to learn to make a diagnosis of what reality is, not what it might be. The church must do a thorough reality check in the world with its enduring temptation to play God or to sacrifice loyalty to Christ at the altar of self-love in the face of persecution and oppression. Jesus called for serpenthood in the face of persecution (Matt. 10:17–25): interrogation by church and state, betrayal by one's own family, suffering the fate of Jesus on the cross. To be apostolic, that is, sent in mission means to be not only a selfless servant, uncorrupted and innocent like the proverbial dove, but also a streetwise Christian in a world full of bad religion and illusions. There is nothing wrong with humble servanthood, depicted as innocent dovehood. But cooing turtledoves are often shot down from the roof when they are making love, as any hunter of fowl knows. One can be a naive, untrained Christian charismatic who enjoys God. But one must also be a wise, alert Christian in the harsh reality of this world and learn the serpentine ways of winding through to those who are in need of help and faith.[7]

Luther's serpenthood detected, diagnosed, and cured a number of diseases in his world of Christendom. Lutheranism today needs the serpenthood first mandated as an instrument of mission in a non-Christian, often hostile environment. Thus, the most important Christian task today is a cold-blooded diagnosis of reality in a world much more complex than Luther's but still marked by the ancient encounter of Jesus and the "evil spirit" whose name is "legion" (Mark 5:9, "many"). Evil is usually first experienced as confusion (from "diabolical," Greek: *diaballein*, "to throw things around"). Accordingly, the first task in driving out evil (traditionally known as exorcism) is gaining clarity through a reality check, a diagnosis of what is real within and outside the church. For illusion is a favorite pastime of the devil. In this regard, Christians have the advantage, if they follow the biblical, eschatological tradition, of seeing things as people of the future belonging already by faith to another world with a more accurate vision of this world. They should be able to detect, diagnose, and struggle with evil without fear, certain in their conviction that God remains in charge.

Here, Luther's recovery of the ancient virtue of justice can be the first step in dealing with evil by balancing its burden and defusing its explosive power; it is the first
realistic step of distinguishing law and gospel, the driving power of confessional
Lutheranism. Its Christian realism is needed now as it was in Luther's time to prevent illusions of a Christian takeover of the world or some of its parts. As targets of
persecution within European Christendom, Lutherans can provide convincing evidence of how foolish, indeed idolatrous, it is to confuse law and gospel by trying to
establish the reign of God as a political reality in the world or to withdraw from the
world altogether. True serpenthood creates critical hindsight and realistic foresight
based on simple dovelike faith in the work of the Holy Spirit, who guides the disciples of Christ according to its promise, to "new heavens and a new earth, where
righteousness is at home" (2 Peter 3:13). Above all, Luther alerted all Christians to
the unavoidable experience of suffering, *Anfechtung,* as the most sobering aspect of
being a Christian in transit to another world.

It has been said that Lutheranism tries to steer a middle course between authori-
tarianism and anarchism, and that the preaching of the gospel and the administration of the sacraments are the best guarantees against these two errors.[8] Luther and
the Lutheran Confessions add the caveat, with a sense of serpenthood, that preaching be done "purely" and the administration be done "rightly," because no human
enterprise is safe from perversion through evil.[9]

Luther, however, is not the foundation of Lutheranism, even though Lutherans
themselves have, at times, claimed so with false pride. On the other hand, Luther is
one of the most visible signposts on the crowded road of the Christian tradition and
cannot be ignored—certainly not by Lutherans, who should know better than anyone else that the voice of the "Wittenberg nightingale" was in harmony with the tune
of the gospel.[10]

Chronology

	Lutheranism	The World
1483	Nov. 10: Birth of Martin Luther.	Superpowers are France, Spain, and England. Renaissance and Humanism. Power of the printing press. Birth of painter Raffael Santi.
1484–1500	Luther's schooling.	Secularized papacy. 1492: Columbus arrives in the "New World." Tobacco introduced. Albrecht Dürer paints *Apocalypse*.
1501–1505	Luther at law school.	1502: Elector Frederick of Saxony founds University of Wittenberg. First pocket watches made in Nürnberg.
1505	July 2: Luther's thunderstorm experience.	James Wimpfeling publishes first history of Germany *(Epitome)*.
1506	Luther takes monastic vows.	Pope Julius II orders construction of St. Peter's in Rome. Leonardo da Vinci paints *Mona Lisa*.
1507	Luther ordained.	Sigismund I becomes king of Poland. John Tetzel sells indulgences.
1509	Luther earns biblical baccalaureate.	Henry VIII becomes king of England. Birth of John Calvin.
1510–1511	Nov. to April: Luther in Rome.	Debate over the use of biblical Hebrew between the humanist Reuchlin and the Dominicans in Cologne.
1512	Luther earns doctorate. Joins faculty in Wittenberg.	Fifth Lateran Council in Rome.
1513–1517	Luther's first biblical lectures.	Pope Leo X. Balboa discovers the Pacific. Archbishop of Mainz and the Fugger

		Bank of Augsburg sell indulgences. 1516: Greek New Testament of Erasmus.
1517	Oct. 31: Luther's Ninety-five Theses against indulgences.	Pope Leo X increases number of Cardinals. John Tetzel sells indulgences.
1518	Luther's hearing by Cajetan in Augsburg. He appeals to be heard by a council.	Diet of Augsburg plans defense against Turks.
1519	Luther and Eck debate at Leipzig.	Charles I of Spain becomes Emperor Charles V. Zwingli begins Swiss Reformation. Magellan begins circumnavigation of the globe.
1520	Luther's four reform treatises. Luther burns papal bull in December.	Suliman II starts drive to the north. Bull *Exsurge Domine* against Luther.
1521	Luther condemned by Rome and the Diet of Worms. At the Wartburg. Radicals in Wittenberg.	Pope Leo X dies. Spain conquers Mexico.
1522	Luther's German New Testament. Returns to Wittenberg.	Dutch Pope Hadrian VI. Uprising of German knights.
1523	Luther's liturgical, social, and educational reforms in Wittenberg.	Pope Clement VII. Diet of Nürnberg postpones action until Rome convenes a council. Zwingli's reforms adopted in Zurich.
1525	June 13: Luther marries Katherine of Bora. Debate with Erasmus on free will.	Death of Frederick "the Wise." Anabaptists in Zurich. Peasant rebellion. Execution of Thomas Müntzer.
1527	Luther writes against Zwingli on the Lord's Supper.	Reformation spreads to Scandinavia.
1528	First Lutherans in Latin America (Venezuela).	1526–1529: Emperor Charles V devastates Rome during war against France.

1529	Luther's Large and Small Catechisms. Colloquy with Zwingli in Marburg.	Lutheran territories submit formal "protest" at Diet of Speyer. Turks besiege Vienna.
1530	*The Augsburg Confession.*	Catholic *Confutation*. Negotiations.
1531	Melanchthon's *Apology of the Augsburg Confession*. Lutheran Smalcald League.	Henry VIII breaks with Rome. Halley's comet linked to the end of the world.
1535	Luther meets with papal legate Vergerio regarding a future council.	Anabaptist "kingdom" in Münster defeated. Catholic Defense League.
1536	"Wittenberg Concord" on Lord's Supper.	Pope Paul III announces impending council. Denmark becomes Lutheran.
1537	Luther drafts *The Smalcald Articles.*	Scandinavia, Iceland, and the Baltic begin to adopt Lutheranism.
1540	Luther approves of the bigamy of Philip of Hesse, leader of the Smalcald League.	Pope ratifies Jesuit order. Turks conquer Hungary.
1543	Luther writes radical treatises against Jews.	Emperor lobbies for united Europe against Turks. Copernicus dies.
1545	Luther makes final revisions on his Bible translation.	1545–1563: Council of Trent. Diet of Worms agrees to truce with Turks.
1546	Feb. 18: Luther dies.	Smalcald war. Emperor invades Saxony.
1546–1570	Intra-Lutheran Controversies.	Maurice of Saxony's intrigue against emperor produces compromise.
1555	The Peace of Augsburg grants equal territorial rights to adherents of the Augsburg Confession.	1556: Emperor Charles V abdicates. Catholic "Counter Reformation."
1564	First Lutherans in North America (Florida).	Emperor Maximilian II rejects the decisions of the Council of Trent.

1580	*The Book of Concord.*	1558–1603: Elizabethan age in England. Francis Bacon. William Shakespeare.
1638	First Lutherans in Delaware and New York. Justus Falckner sent from Halle.	Gustavus Adolphus of Sweden prevents Lutheran defeat in Thirty Years' War (killed in 1632).
1648	Flowering of Lutheran orthodoxy.	End of Thirty Years' War. Peace of Westphalia. Age of Louis XIV (1643–1715) promotes economics, science, and the arts.
1675	Spener's *Pia Desideria.*	Age of Enlightenment. Growth of Hapsburg power under Leopold I.
1700	Beginning of Francke's Halle Foundation.	Rule of Peter the Great in Russia (died 1725). William III and Mary in England (1689–1702) establish Bill of Rights.
1706	First Lutheran missionary Ziegenbalg in Tranquebar, India.	War of the Spanish Succession. Nordic War (Sweden, Russia).
1722	Zinzendorf and the Moravians in Herrnhut.	Russia and England among superpowers. Music of George Frederick Handel.
1731	Expulsion of Salzburg Lutherans.	Emperor Charles VI yields East Indian colonial trade to England, which, in turn, agrees to his law to make his children, not those of his brother, inherit the crown ("Pragmatic Sanction").
1733	Lutheran mission to Greenland.	Rise of Prussia (Frederick William I, 1713–1740) as military power.
1748	Henry Melchior Muhlenberg organizes ministerium in Philadelphia.	Prussia and Austria become superpowers (Frederick the Great, Maria Theresia).
1760	Spread of Lutheranism in America.	Industrial Revolution in England. Charles Wesley and Methodism.

1770–1800	"Lutheran" philosophers Kant (died 1804) and Hegel (died 1831).	1776: American Revolution. 1789: French Revolution. Napoleon. Music of Mozart, Haydn, Beethoven. "Free market system" of Adam Smith (died 1790).
1817	Lutheran confessional awakening. Klaus Harms's Ninety-Five Theses. Quarrel over union of Lutherans and Reformed imposed by Prussian court. Formation of Evangelical Lutheran Church in Prussia.	1814–1815: Congress of Vienna rearranges political power in Europe. "Holy Alliance" of Russia, Prussia, and Austria. Technology of steam, electricity, and the telegraph.
1820	Formation of General Synod in America.	Portugal independent from Spain. Medical breakthroughs in France (1826: discovery of diphtheria).
1821–1859	Establishment and growth of Societies for Foreign Mission.	Introduction of custom dues for grain in Europe and North America.
1824	Death of Norwegian Pietist Hans Nielsen Hauge.	Greek rebellion against Turkey creates independent kingdom. First trade union in England.
1826	Samuel S. Schmucker heads First American Lutheran Seminary (Gettysburg, Pa.).	English migration to Canada and Australia.
1830	Grundtvig's influence in Denmark. Tercentenary celebration of *The Augsburg Confession*. Erlangen school. Mission to "third world" (developing) countries.	1830–1848: Flowering of Paris under the "citizen king" Louis Philip. 1834: Schleiermacher dies.
1837	Löhe's reforms in Neuendettelsau.	1837–1901: Age of Queen Victoria. Romantic philosophy and music (Byron, Göthe, Wagner).
1841	Formation of Evangelical Lutheran Church of Prussia.	"Opium Wars" between England and China. Hong Kong becomes independent.

1847	Formation of the Missouri Synod.	1845–1848: Mexican-American War. Texas, New Mexico, and California join United States.
1848	Inner Mission movement led by Fliedner, Wichern, and Bodelschwingh.	Communist Manifesto of Marx and Engels. Revolutionary uprisings in Paris, Berlin, and Vienna. 1848–1916: Franz Josef of Austria.
1855	Schmucker's Definite Platform and critique of *The Augsburg Confession*. Death of Kierkegaard.	Crimean War between Russia and Turkey. Russia loses influence in Europe.
1867	Fraternal Appeal of the General Synod in America for the acceptance of *The Augsburg Confession*.	1861–1865: Civil War in United States. 1864: Geneva Convention.
1872	Synodical Conference in America. Tübingen and Erlangen schools of theology.	Imperial Chancellor Bismarck tries to control German Catholicism. 1870: Vatican I promulgates papal infallibility.
1875	Galesburg Rule in America.	A new world of ideas from Darwin, Nietzsche, Gobineau.
1895	Lutherans help to organize the Student Christian Movement. Nathan Söderblom supports its efforts in Sweden.	Germany, France, and the United States negotiate agreements regarding colonies in Africa.
1908	Söderblom makes first proposal for Christian unity, beginning with Lutherans and Anglicans.	1905: Norway becomes independent. Influence of international Communism. 1905–1906: First revolution in Russia.
1910	Participation in first international Conference on Mission in Edinburgh.	United States becomes superpower after Spanish-American War (1898) and Theodore Roosevelt (President, 1901–1909).
1914	American Lutherans do not support Germany. University	1914–1918: World War I.

professors in Germany do with zeal. Söderblom becomes Archbishop of Uppsala. Makes Appeal for Peace in seven languages.

1917	Quatercentenary of the Reformation. Hymn "A Mighty Fortress" used for German war effort. Söderblom and other neutral churchmen issue Manifesto for Peace.	War in the air and with submarines. Breaking of diplomatic relations between United States and Germany. Russian Communist Revolution.
1918	Formation of National Lutheran Council USA.	1919: Peace of Versailles. Rise of Italian Fascism led by Benito Mussolini.
1923	Lutheran World Convention in Eisenach.	Adolf Hitler and Erich Ludendorff stage unsuccessful revolt in Munich. Hitler imprisoned (until 1924).
1925	Söderblom chairs ecumenical Conference on Life and Work in Stockholm.	Declaration of neutrality between Soviet Union and Japan.
1927	Faith and Order Conference in Lausanne, Switzerland.	Joseph Stalin becomes leader of Russian Communist Party.
1930	Söderblom awarded Nobel Prize for peace.	1929: "Black Friday" on New York Stock Exchange. Establishment of Vatican City in Rome. Reign of Mussolini begins.
1932	Formation of German Lutheran church in support of Hitler ("German Christians").	1933: Reign of Hitler begins.
1934	German Barmen Declaration of the "Confessing Church" opposing Hitler.	German totalitarian laws. Establishment of Secret Police. Mussolini and Hitler meet in Venice.
1938	German Lutherans divided. Martin Niemöller imprisoned.	Hitler enforces oath of allegiance. Annexation of Austria.

1939	Paul Tillich flees to the U.S. Dietrich Bonhoeffer joins resistance to Hitler.	1939–1945: World War II.
1941	Bishop Berggrav organizes resistance against German military occupation of Norway. Rudolf Bultmann begins to "demythologize" the New Testament in Marburg.	War extends to Africa. France capitulates.
1943	Bonhoeffer arrested as "spy."	Battle of Stalingrad signals Hitler's military defeat.
1945	German Stuttgart Declaration of guilt. Bonhoeffer martyred. Persecution begins in East Germany.	Germany capitulates. United States uses atomic bombs against Japan. Japan capitulates. Creation of the German Democratic Republic (East Germany). Formation of the United Nations organization.
1947	Formation of Lutheran World Federation.	Establishment of World Council of Churches. Creation of Jewish and Palestinian territories in the Middle East.
1951	Batak Confession of Faith.	Influence of atomic energy. Existentialist philosophy (Heidegger). Television.
1953	Influence of Karl Barth. "Lundensian School of Theology" (Aulén, Prenter). 1954: Death of Werner Elert.	Death of Stalin. Pope promulgates dogma of the bodily assumption of Mary. American–North Korean Armistice.
1963	Neuralgic LWF assembly in Helsinki on justification. Creation of Ecumenical Institute in Strasbourg. 1964: Jewish dialogue.	1962–1965: Vatican II. Vietnam War begins. President John F. Kennedy assassinated.
1965	Dialogue with Catholics in North America. International Lutheran-Catholic Joint Commission (Malta Report).	Cultural Revolution in China. Arab-Israeli Six-Day War. First successful human heart transplant. 1968: Martin Luther King Jr. assassinated.

1967: Lutheran-Orthodox Dialogue in North America.

1971	Luther called "common teacher" not "heretic" by Rome.

1969: American landing on the moon.

1973	Lutheran Church–Missouri Synod adopts "verbal inspiration of Scripture." Seminex and association of exiles.

Yom Kippur Arab-Israeli War. End of Vietnam War. 1974: President Richard Nixon resigns.

1977	Dialogue with Methodists. Anti-Communist Hungarian resistance. 1978: Bishop Ordass dies.

1978: Camp David Treaty between Egypt and Israel.

1983	Luther's 500th birthday.

Soviet Union shoots down Korean airliner.

1984	LWF ousts two "apartheid" churches (reinstated in 1991). Assembly in Budapest elects Communist Kaldy as president (died in 1987).

Famine in Ethiopia, Sudan, and Chad.

1990	LWF Constitution proposes "communion of churches" rather than "federation."

1989: Reunion of East and West Germany. Iraq invades Kuwait. 1991: Gulf War. Tunnel linking England and France completed.

1999	Celebration of Joint Declaration on the Doctrine of Justification with Catholics.

Pre-millennium expectations.

2000	Declaration of "full communion" of the Evangelical Lutheran Church in America with Episcopalians, the Reformed Church and the Moravians. Affirmation of the "historic episcopacy."

Sept. 11, 2001: Attack on World Trade Towers (New York City) and the Pentagon in Washington, D.C. Fear of international terrorism.

Notes

Preface

1. WA 8:685.50-11. LW 45:70-71.

2. RGG 4:531.

3. Eric W. Gritsch and Robert W. Jenson, *Lutheranism: The Theological Movement and Its Confessional Writings* (Philadelphia: Fortress Press, 1976).

4. A survey of various features of Lutheranism in Europe and America is provided by Altman K. Swihart, *Luther and the Lutheran Church, 1483–1960* (New York: Philosophical Library, 1960). A defensive account of the exemplary "morphology" of Lutheranism is offered by Werner Elert, *The Structure of Lutheranism*, 2 vols., trans. Walter A. Hansen (St. Louis: Concordia, 1962). A broad, general history, including non-Lutheran developments, was produced by Conrad John Immanuel Bergendoff, *The Church of the Lutheran Reformation: A Historical Survey of Lutheranism* (St. Louis: Concordia, 1967). A very helpful statistical survey is provided by E. Theodore Bachmann and Mercia Brenne Bachmann, *Lutheran Churches in the World: A Handbook* (Minneapolis: Augsburg, 1989).

5. Günther Gassmann, ed., *Historical Dictionary of Lutheranism,* in cooperation with Duane H. Larson and Mark W. Oldenburg (Lanham, Md.: Scarecrow, 2001).

6. Donald L. Huber, *World Lutheranism: A Select Bibliography for English Readers* (ATLA Bibliography Series 44; Lanham, Md.: Scarecrow, 2000).

7. *Encyclopedia of the Lutheran Church*, 3 vols., ed. Julius Bodensieck (Minneapolis: Augsburg, 1965).

1. Birth of a Movement, 1517–1521

1. See Niccolò Machiavelli's classic justification of tyrannical leadership in *The Prince* in *Chief Works and Others,* trans. A. H. Gilbert, 3 vols. (Durham, N.C.: Duke University Press, 1965).

2. So labeled by the Italian humanist Francis Petrarch (1304–1374). On this period of the papacy, see Yves Renouard, *The Avignon Papacy, 1305–1403,* trans. D. Bethell (Hamden, Conn.: Archon, 1970).

3. C. M. D. Crowder, *Unity, Heresy, and Reform, 1378–1460: The Conciliar Response to the Great Schism* (Documents of Medieval History 3; New York: St. Martin's, 1977). On Pisa, see Crowder, 41–64.

4. The medieval pope John XXIII is not listed in the official succession of popes. The true John XXIII served from 1958 until 1963.

5. How the sacrament of penance dominated Christian life has been shown by Thomas N. Tentler, *Sin and Confession on the Eve of the Reformation* (Princeton, N.J.: Princeton University Press, 1977).

6. See J. H. Dahmus, *The Prosecution of John Wyclif* (New Haven, Conn.: Yale University Press, 1952). On Jan Hus and Hussites, see OER 2:276–80; Peter Brock, *The Political and Social Doctrines of the Unity of the Czech Brethren in the Fifteenth and Early Sixteenth Centuries* (Slavistic Printings and Reprintings 11; Gravenhage: Mouton, 1957). The Moravian Brethren were named after one part of medieval Czechoslovakia, the dukedom of Moravia, which separated from the kingdom of Bohemia.

7. See OER 3:486–88. Donald Weinstein, *Savonarola and Florence: Prophecy and Patriotism in the Renaissance* (Princeton, N.J.: Princeton University Press, 1976).

8. See OER 3:418–20 and 2:264–72; William J. Bouwsma, *The Culture of Renaissance and Humanism* (AHA Pamphlets 401; Washington, D.C.: American Historical Association, 1973).

9. See Owen Chadwick, *The Reformation,* vol. 3 of *The Pelican History of the Church* (Harmondsworth, Eng.: Penguin, 1972), 39.

10. His full name was Thomas Hernerken from Kempen. See Gerard Groote, *Devotio Moderna: Basic Writings,* trans. J. Van Engen (The Classics of Western Spirituality; New York: Paulist, 1988).

11. Quoted in Chadwick, *Reformation,* 33. But critical research has shown that Luther refused to hatch the "egg" (Erasmus). See Bernhard Lohse, *Martin Luther's Theology: Its Historical and Systematic Development,* trans. R. A. Harrisville (Minneapolis: Fortress Press, 1999), 160–68.

12. Text in DS 430. See also "Lateran IV," in TRE 20:482, literature, 488–89.

13. See Ernest A. Moody, *The Logic of William of Ockham* (London: Sheed & Ward, 1935). On the link to the Reformation, see Erwin Iserloh, *Gnade und Eucharistie in der philosophischen Theologie des Wilhelm von Ockham: Ihre Bedeutung für die Ursachen der Reformation* (Veröffentlichungen 8; Wiesbaden: Steiner, 1956).

14. See "Fifth Lateran Council" (1512–1517) in OER 2:397–99. Original text in Giovanni D. Mansi, ed., *Sacrorum Conciliorum nova et amplissima,* 60 vols. (Paris, 1899–1927), 32:649–999.

15. A popular slogan since the thirteenth century. See TRE 28:390.

16. The slogan about the "sources" was frequently used; for example, in Philip Melanchthon's inaugural lecture of 1518: "If we direct our minds *to the sources* [in Latin: *ad fontes*] we will begin to understand Christ" (C. G. Bretschneider and H. E. Bindseil, eds., *Corpus Reformatorum: Philippi Melanchthons Opera* [Halle, 1834–], 11:23; italics mine). The reference to "vanity" is from the medieval best-seller *The Imitation of Christ* by Thomas à Kempis, quoted in Chadwick, *The Reformation,* 18. See also n. 10.

17. Luther research is massive. It has been collected in *Jahrbuch der Luther-Gesellschaft* before 1920 and in the *Lutherjahrbuch* since 1920; also in *Archiv für Reformationsgeschichte: Literaturberichte.* For historical details, see Martin Brecht, *Martin Luther,* trans. J. L. Schaaf, 3 vols. (Minneapolis: Fortress Press, 1990–93). Life, thought, and legacy are portrayed by Eric W. Gritsch, *Martin—God's Court Jester: Luther in Retrospect* (Ramsey, N.J.: Sigler, 1991).

18. Various sources suggest a traumatic experience, typical of young men. See the useful collection of documents on the young Luther by Otto Scheel, *Martin Luther: Vom Katholizis-*

mus zur Reformation, 2 vols. (3d ed.; Tübingen, 1917–21). See vol. 1, ch. 5. Quotations in WA.TR 4:440.9–10, 12–15. No. 4707, 1539. WA 8:573.30–574.2. LW 48:332. Summary of Luther's accounts in Gritsch, *Martin,* 6. On Luther's spiritual and academic formation see Marilyn J. Harran, *Martin Luther: Learning for Life* (St. Louis: Concordia, 1997).

19. Table Talk, 1539. WA.TR 4:440.12–19. No. 4707.

20. Table Talk, 1533. No. 495. WA.TR 1:220.9–17. LW 54:85.

21. See, for example, Ernest G. Schwiebert, *Luther and His Times: The Reformation from a New Perspective* (St. Louis; Concordia, 1950), 145.

22. Table Talk, 1537. No. 3556a. WA.TR 3:410.42–43. LW 54:234.

23. Letter to his father, 1521. WA 8:574.2, 7–8. LW 48:332.

24. Table Talk, 1531. No. 116. WA.TR 1:44.31–32. LW 54:14. Letter to George Spalatin, 1518. WA.BR 1:133.31–34, 37–39. LW 48:53–54.

25. Especially his interpretation of Paul. See Leif Grane, *Modus Loquendi Theologicus: Luthers Kampf um die Erneuerung der Theologie (1515–1518)* (Leiden: Brill, 1975), 60–62.

26. Sermon of November 15, 1545. WA 51:89.20–24. Luther seemed be concerned only about his spiritual struggle and recalled nothing about Rome as the center of Renaissance art.

27. Table Talk, 1531. No. 2255a. WA.TR 2:379.7–19. No. 4091. WA.TR 4:129.30–130.2. 1540. No. 5371. WA.TR 5:98.21–28.

28. "Infiltrating and Clandestine Preachers," 1532. WA 30/3:522.2–8. LW 40:387–388. On Staupitz, see David C. Steinmetz, *Misericordia Dei: The Theology of Johannes von Staupitz in Its Late Medieval Setting* (Studies in Medieval and Reformation Thought 4; Leiden: Brill, 1968).

29. This German word is difficult to translate, and I therefore use the original form. Luther sometimes rendered it in Latin as *tentatio* ("temptation"), but its textual meaning varies. It was one of Luther's favorite words to describe the attacks of Satan or the struggle with God.

30. Letter, 1518. WA.BR 1:525.10–13. LW 48:65–66.

31. The search for a date has created a literary jungle. Recent scholarship tends to date the breakthrough late, about 1517 or 1518. For a discussion of literature and the late date, see Brecht, *Martin Luther,* 1:221–237.

32. The lectures are in WA 56–57. LW 25–29. Only the later "Lectures on Galatians," 1535 are available in LW 26–27.

33. "Preface to the Latin Edition of Luther's Writings," 1545. WA 54:185.13–186.16. LW 34:336–337.

34. WA 7:25.34. 26.4–7. LW 31:351–352.

35. Preface in WA 1:152–153. ET of the longer 1518 version with commentary by Bengt Hoffmann, trans. and ed., *The Theologia Germanica of Martin Luther: Translation, Introduction and Commentary* (New York: Paulist, 1980).

36. Table Talk, 1532. No. 3232c. WA.TR 3:228.31–32. LW 54:193–194. The variant No. 3232b mentions *cloaca.* 228.23. Too much attention has been paid to this "tower experience." See Harry G. Haile, "The Great Martin Luther Spoof, or, Philosophical Limits to Knowledge," *Yale Review* 67 (1978): 236–46.

37. On indulgences, see TRE 1:347–64; OER 2:314–15.

38. 1. "Disputation on the Question of Human Power and Will without Grace," 1516. WA 1:142–151. 2. "Disputation against Scholastic Theology," 1517. WA 1:221–228. LW 31:5–16. 3. "Ninety-five Theses," 1517. WA 1:233–238. LW 31:19–33. It is not clear whether or not Luther nailed the theses to the door of the Castle Church even though the door served as a bulletin board for posting forthcoming academic disputations. See Erwin Iserloh, *The Theses Were Not Posted: Luther between Reform and Reformation,* trans. J. Wicks (Boston: Beacon, 1968); and Heinrich Bornkamm, *Thesen und Thesenanschlag Luther: Geschehen und Bedeutung* (Theologische Bibliothek Töpelmann 14; Berlin: Töpelmann, 1967). The best source collection is in Kurt Aland, *95 Theses: With the Pertinent Documents from the History of the Reformation* (St. Louis: Concordia, 1967).

39. "Heidelberg Disputation," 1518, especially theses 19–20. WA 1:361.32–362.3. LW 31:40. How the theses shaped Luther's entire theology has been shown by Walter von Loewenich, *Luther's Theology of the Cross,* trans. H. J. Bouman (Minneapolis: Augsburg, 1976).

40. Table Talk, 1540. No. 5070. WA.TR 4:641.20–642.2. LW 54:385.

41. "Sermon on Baptism," 1534. WA 37:661.20–26.

42. "Lectures on Galatians," 1535. WA 40/1:589.25–28. LW 26:387.

43. "Sermon on Gal. 3:23–29," 1531. WA 36:9.28–29.

44. "Lectures on Galatians," 1535. WA 40/1:509.27–28. LW 26:329.

45. "Disputation on Matt. 22:1-14," 1537. WA 39/1:283.18–19.

46. See the fragmentary outline of a treatise "On Justification," 1530. WA 30/2:657–676. How Luther's "article of justification" is related to "soteriology" (what God did in Christ for human salvation) has been shown by Wilhelm Maurer, "Die Einheit der Theologie Luthers," in *Kirche und Geschichte: Gesammelte Aufsätze,* ed. Ernst-Wilhelm Kohls and Gerhard Müller, vol. 1, *Luther und das evangelische Bekenntnis* (Göttingen: Vandenhoeck & Ruprecht, 1970), 11–21.

47. "Sermons on the Gospel of St. John," 1539. WA 47:66.21–24. LW 22:339. "Lectures on Psalms," 1532–1533. WA 40/3:337.11.

48. On "Copernican revolution," see Philip J. Watson, *Let God Be God: An Interpretation of the Theology of Martin Luther* (Philadelphia: Fortress Press, 1966), 33–34. Quotation in Table Talk, 1539. No. 4638. WA.TR 4:43.4. LW 54:359.

49. For a blow-by-blow account of these events, see James Mackinnon, *Luther and the Reformation,* 4 vols. (London: Longmans, Green, 1925–30), vol. 2, ch. 1. Also Brecht, *Martin Luther,* 1:202–21, 239–73.

50. "Obelisci" were marks in the critical appraisal of Graeco-Roman and biblical literature, indicating false and heretical texts. "Asterisci" were marks indicating the more valuable texts.

51. Letter to Spalatin, 1518. WA.BR 1:233.1–2. LW 48:56.

52. "Explanations of the Ninety-five Theses," 1518. WA 1:525–628. LW 31:79–252.

53. For the first time in a letter to Spalatin, 1517. WA.BR 1:118.16. See also LW 48:55, n. 12.

54. The title "elector" made Frederick one of seven princes who elected the Holy Roman Emperor, a designation of the symbolic ruler of the Christian world since the crowning of

Charlemagne by Pope Leo III in 800. The election of a Holy Roman Emperor was regulated by the golden bull of 1356 (a bull was a seal attached to a document; special designation for solemn papal announcements). Three ecclesiastical rulers (the archbishops of Mainz, Trier, and Cologne) and four secular princes (king of Bohemia, duke of Saxony, margrave of Brandenburg, and count of Palatinate) were designated as electors. Previously, the emperor evolved through power politics. When Maximilian died in 1518, the seven electors ended up in a tie vote, three favoring the election of Francis I of France and three favoring Charles I of Spain. Despite promised political favors, indeed attempted bribery, Frederick broke the tie by voting for Charles I who became Emperor Charles V in 1519. Consequently, Charles V would be careful not to offend Frederick. See Karl Brandi, *The Emperor Charles V: The Growth and Destiny of a Man and of a World Empire*, trans. C. V. Wedgwood (New York: Jonathon Cape, 1965), 5:111. How wise Frederick was with respect to Luther's reform movement has been analyzed by Paul Kirn, *Friedrich der Weise und die Kirche: Seine kirchenpolitik vor und nach Luthers hervortreten im jahre 1517* (Beiträge zur kulturgeschichte des mittelalters und der renaissance 30; Leipzig: Teubner, 1926).

55. On the Augsburg meeting, see Luther's own account, "Proceedings at Augsburg," 1518. WA 2:6–26. LW 31:259–292. Details in Gerhard Hennig, *Cajetan und Luther: Ein historischer Beitrag zur Begegnung von Thomismus und Reformation* (Arbeiten zur Theologie 2; Stuttgart: Calwer, 1966). Summary in Scott H. Hendrix, *Luther and the Papacy: Stages in a Reformation Conflict* (Philadelphia: Fortress Press, 1981), 52–70.

56. "Appeal of Friar Luther to a Council," 1518. WA 2:40.9–20. For the origin and meaning of Luther's conciliarism, see Christa T. Johns, *Luthers Konzilsidee in ihrer historischen Bedingtheit und ihrem reformatorischem Neuansatz* (Berlin: Töpelmann, 1966), 137–43.

57. Letter to Luther, 1519. WA.BR 1:267.9–10.

58. Luther's paper is found in WA 2:66–73. His conciliatory behavior has been shown by Hans-Günther Leder, *Ausgleich mit dem Papst? Luthers Haltung in den Verhandlungen mit Miltitz 1520* (Arbeiten zur Theologie; Stuttgart: Calwer, 1969). Quotation in Letter, 1519. WA.BR 1:313.17–18.

59. WA.BR 1:365.29–31.

60. Philipp Melanchthon (from the Greek *melan-chtonos*, "black earth," *Schwarzerd*, his native German name; the change of a native name into Latin or Greek was a fashionable humanist custom). See OER 3:41–44. On the beginnings of his career in Wittenberg see Clyde C. Manschreck, *Melanchthon: The Quiet Reformer* (New York: Abingdon, 1958), ch. 1; Wilhelm Maurer, *Der junge Melanchthon zwischen Humanismus und Reformation*, 2 vols. (Göttingen: Vandenhoeck & Ruprecht, 1967–69), 2, ch. 1.

61. Eyewitness accounts of the debate are in "The Disputation of John Eck and Martin Luther Held at Leipzig," 1519. WA 2:250–383. For Luther's own account, see WA 2:388–435. LW 31:309–325. For a good summary of issues, see Kurt-Victor Selge, "Die Leipziger Disputation zwischen Luther und Eck," ZKG 86 (1975): 26–40; and in Hendrix, *Luther and the Papacy*, 85–89.

62. For Luther's use of church history, see John M. Headley, *Luther's View of Church History* (New Haven, Conn.: Yale University Press, 1963), especially ch. 4.

63. "The Leipzig Debate," 1519. WA 2:161.35–38. LW 31:318. The detailed defense of the thesis is in "Lutheran Resolution about Proposition 13 on the Power of the Pope," 1519. WA 2:180–240.

64. The main source of the investigation was Luther's "The Babylonian Captivity," 1520, WA 6:497–573, LW 36:11–126.

65. See Brecht, *Martin Luther*, 1:338.

66. Letter to Spalatin, 1519. WA.BR 1:424.145–152. LW 31:325.

67. This designation appeared in an anonymous preface to the Basel edition of Luther's works. See John M. Todd, *Luther: A Life* (New York: Crossroad, 1982), 172–73. How printing affected the spread of the Reformation has been described by Louise W. Holborn, "Printing and the Growth of a Protestant Movement in Germany from 1517 to 1524," CH 11 (1942): 123–37.

68. For a chronological listing of publications and events between October 30, 1519, and April 2, 1521, see Georg Buchwald and Gustav Kawerau, eds., *Luther Kalendarium: Verzeichnis von Luthers Schriften*, 2d ed. (Leipzig, 1929), 12–19.

69. WA 2:685–697. LW 42:97–115. WA 6:157–169. LW 39:25–44. WA 10/2:375–406. LW 43:5–45.

70. "Trade and Usury," 1524. WA 6:58.13. LW 45:305. For a study of how Luther arrived at this compromise, see Wilhelm A. Schulze, "Luther und der Zins," *Luther* 42 (1971): 139–46.

71. "On the Papacy in Rome," 1520. WA 6:285–324. LW 39:55–104.

72. WA 7:621–688. LW 39:143–224. The second treatise was an ironic reply titled "Retraction." WA 8:247–254. LW 39:229–238.

73. The *four* rather than the three "great treatises" of 1520. It was (and still is) customary not to include the "Treatise on Good Works," presumably to stress the number "three."

74. WA 6:216.29–31. LW 44:38.

75. WA 6:249.2–6. LW 44:78.

76. WA 6:257.27–28. LW 44:90.

77. WA 6:276.1–4. LW 44:113.

78. WA 6:276.18–19. LW 44:114.

79. Listed in WA 6:415.19–427.29. LW 44:139–156. Such grievances had been submitted to German diets since 1456. See "Gravamina" in OER 2:190–91.

80. WA 6:408.11–15. LW 44:129.

81. WA 6:435.3–4. LW 44:166. WA 6:468.32–36. 469.13–17. LW 44:216–217.

82. WA 6:572.23–30. LW 36:124–125.

83. Text of *Exsurge Domini* in Carl Mirbt and Kurt Aland, eds., *Quellen zur Geschichte des Papsttums und des römischen Katholizismus* (Tübingen: Mohr [Siebeck], 1967), 1:504–13. ET in C. J. Barry, ed., *Readings in Church History*, 3 vols. (Westminster, Md.: Newman, 1960–65). On the Roman trial, see Paul Kalkoff, "Zu Luthers römischen Prozess," ZKG 25 (1904): 587–96.

84. WA. BR 2:177.71–75. LW 48:178–179.

85. Letter of October 11, 1520. WA. BR 2: 195.

86. Text against the bull is in WA 6:595–629. Text of the appeal for a council is in WA 7:74–151.

87. WA 7:181.1–8. LW 31:394–395.

88. Text of the bull in Mirbt and Aland, eds., *Quellen*, 513–15; English text in Barry, ed., *Readings in Church History.*

89. Paul Kalkoff, ed., *Die Depeschen des Nuntius Aleander vom Wormser Reichstage 1521* (Halle, 1886), 69. For the recorded proceedings with Luther at the Diet of Worms, see *Deutsche Reichstagsakten unter Kaiser Karl V. Jüngere Reihe,* edited by the Historische Kommission bei der bayrischen Akademie der (Gotha: Wissenschaften, 1893; photomechanical reprint, Göttingen, 1967), 2:449–661. See also Fritz Reuter, ed., *Der Reichstag zu Worms: Reichspolitik und Luthersache* (Worms: Stadtarchiv, 1971). Illustrated source materials appear in De Lamar Jensen, ed., *Confrontation at Worms: Martin Luther and the Diet of Worms* (Provo, Utah: Brigham Young University Press, 1973). Some eyewitness accounts are in "Luther at the Diet of Worms," WA 7:814–857. LW 32:103–131. Detailed narrative in Brecht, *Martin Luther,* 1:433–76.

90. WA.BR 2:298.6–10. LW 48:198.

91. "Luther at the Diet of Worms," 1521. WA 7:838.4–9. LW 32:112–113. Translation mine. The words "I cannot do otherwise, here I stand, God help me, Amen" are found in a later text.

92. Text of the edict is in *Deutsche Reichstagsakten,* 2:643–61; English text in Jensen, *Confrontation,* 75–111.

93. Letter of April 28, 1521. WA.BR 2:305.5–8. LW 48:201.

94. WA.BR 2:309.111–113. LW 48:209.

95. The inkwell story first appeared in 1650. See Ernest G. Schwiebert, *Luther and His Times* (St. Louis: Concordia, 1950), 518–19.

96. "The Magnificat," 1521. WA 7:538–604. LW 21:297–358. Sermons in "Church Postil," 1522. WA 10/1. The gigantic work of translation encompasses twelve volumes. WA.DB 1–12. See Michael J. Reu, *Luther's German Bible* (Columbus, Ohio: Lutheran Book Concern, 1934); Willem J. Kooiman, *Luther and the Bible,* trans. John Schmidt (Philadelphia: Fortress Press, 1961), chs. 7, 9; Heinz Bluhm, *Martin Luther: Creative Translator* (St. Louis: Concordia, 1965). See also Eric W. Gritsch, "Luther as Bible Translator," in *The Cambridge Companion to Martin Luther,* ed. D. K. McKim (Cambridge: Cambridge University Press, forthcoming).

97. Literal translation, or "the way they speak." "On Translating," 1530, WA 30/2, 637, LW 37:189.

98. Letter to Albrecht, December 1, 1521. WA.BR 2:406–408. LW 48:339–343.

99. "The Judgment of Martin Luther on Monastic Vows," 1521. WA 8:577.18–19. 605.15–18. 668.18–20. LW 44:388, 399–400.

100. "Against Latomus," 1521. WA 8:103.35–107. LW 32:229.

101. See the exposition of Rom. 4:7 in "Lectures on Romans," 1515–1516. WA 56:268.26–177.3, especially 269.21–22. LW 25:257–277, especially 258.

102. "A Sincere Admonition to All Christians to Guard against Insurrection and Rebellion," 1522. WA 8:67–687. LW 45:57–74.

103. See Eric W. Gritsch, *Thomas Müntzer: A Tragedy of Errors* (Minneapolis: Fortress Press, 1989).

104. "Eight Sermons at Wittenberg," 1522. WA 10/3:57.15–17. LW 51:96.

105. Details on the impasse between Elector Frederick and the princes advocating the implementation of the Edict of Worms are in Brecht, *Martin Luther,* 2:105–12.

106. "The Estate of Marriage," 1522. WA 10/2:276.26–29.283.1–16.287.14–289.17. LW 45:18, 25, 30–34. "Temporal Authority: To What Extent It Should Be Obeyed," 1522. WA 11:245–280. LW 45:77–129. See also Eric W. Gritsch, "Luther and Violence: A Reappraisal of the Neuralgic Theme," *Sixteenth Century Journal* 3 (1972): 37–55.

2. Growth and Consolidation, 1521–1555

1. On Luther's role in the installation, see Peter Brunner, *Nikolaus von Amsdorf als Bischof von Naumburg: Eine Untersuchung zur Gestalt des evangelischen Bischofsamtes* (Gütersloh: Mohn, 1961). On Luther's Wittenberg team, see Walter C. Tillmans, *The World and Men around Luther* (Minneapolis: Augsburg, 1959).

2. Letter of June 23, 1529, to Philip of Hesse. WA.BR 5:102.53–57. LW 49:231. On Sickingen and Hutten, see OER 4:55. 2:281–82.

3. WA 10/3:375–406. LW 43:11–42.

4. "Ordinance of a Common Chest," 1523. WA 12:11–30. LW 45:169–194, quote 176. See also Harold J. Grimm, "Luther's Contribution to Sixteenth Century Organization of Poor Relief," *Archiv für Reformationsgeschichte* 61 (1971): 222–33.

5. On the emergency, see "That a Christian Assembly or Congregation has the Right . . . to Call Appoint and Dismiss Teachers," 1523. WA 11:412.16–18. LW 39:310–311. In 1545, Luther and his Wittenberg team defended a traditional episcopal order. See Eric W. Gritsch, "Episcopacy: The Legacy of the Lutheran Confessions," *Concordat of Agreement: Supporting Essays,* ed. Daniel F. Martensen (Minneapolis: Augsburg Fortress; Cincinnati: Forward Movement, 1995), 109.

6. Quotations: "Concerning the Order of Public Worship," 1523. WA 12:37.29. LW 53:14. "An Order of Mass and Communion for the Church of Wittenberg," 1523. WA 12:211.20–22. 214.14–215.5. LW 53:26, 30–32. See also Karlfried Froehlich, "Luther's Hymns and Johann Sebastian Bach," *Encounters with Luther: Lectures, Discussions, and Sermons at the Martin Luther Colloquia,* ed. Eric W. Gritsch (Gettysburg, Pa.: Institute for Luther Studies, Gettysburg Lutheran Seminary, 1970–90), 4:1–27.

7. WA 19:537–41. ET in BC 371–75.

8. WA 15:48.27–30. 49.12–14. LW 45:372, 373.

9. WA.BR 3:394.24–25. LW 49:93.

10. The Rhenish gulden of 1536 had a buying power of $13.40 in terms of 1913 values (according to the calculations in Ernest G. Schwiebert, *Luther and His Times* [St. Louis: Concordia, 1950], 258). Luther received an annual salary of two hundred gulden and occasional gifts of food and clothes, but no royalties for publications. He might have belonged to the middle class by modern standards. See also Brecht, *Martin Luther,* 2:201–3.

11. WA.TR 3:211.18–19. "Table Talk," 1536. No. 3178a. LW 53:191.

12. See Roland H. Bainton, "Katherine von Bora," *Women of the Reformation in Germany and Italy* (Minneapolis: Augsburg, 1971), 23–43; Willem J. Kooiman, "Luther at Home," in *The Martin Luther Lectures,* vol. 3, *The Mature Luther,* ed. Roland H. Bainton et al. (Decorah, Iowa: Luther College Press, 1959), 59–75.

13. OER 4:103.

14. Preface to "Instructions for the Visitors of Parish Pastors in Electoral Saxony," 1528. WA 26:200.28–33. 201–240. LW 40:273–74.

15. Text of catechisms in BS 501–527. 546–733. BC 347–480. Quotation BS 553. BC 383:19. See also Eric W. Gritsch, "Luther's Catechisms of 1529: Whetstones of the Church," in Gritsch, ed., *Encounters with Luther,* 2:237–48.

16. This is the position of Gerald Strauss, *Luther's House of Learning: Indoctrination of the Young in the German Reformation* (Baltimore, Md.: Johns Hopkins University Press, 1978), 7, 307. See also Scott C. Dixon, *The Reformation and Rural Society: The Parishes of Brandenburg-Ansbach-Kulmbach 1528–1603* (Cambridge: Cambridge University Press, 1996), 207.

17. Marilyn J. Harran, *Martin Luther: Learning for Life* (St. Louis: Concordia, 1997), 222.

18. OER 4:103–105. 3:351.

19. See the tract so titled in Günther Franz, ed., *Thomas Müntzer: Schriften und Briefe* (Quellen und Forschungen zur Reformationsgeschichte 33; Gütersloh: Mohn, 1968); English text in Hans J. Hillerbrand, "Thomas Müntzer's Last Tract against Luther," *Mennonite Quarterly Review* 38 (1964): 20–36.

20. Quotation from "Against the Robbing and Murdering Hordes of Peasants," 1525. WA 18:357.21–360.28–31. LW 46:53–54. This was the view of Frederick Engels (1820–1911), cofounder of Marxism, and his disciples. See Abraham Friesen, *Reformation and Utopia: The Marxist Interpretation of the Reformation and Its Antecedents* (Wiesbaden: Steiner, 1974), chs. 7–9. Engel's view was adopted and advocated by the Academy of Sciences of the German Democratic Republic in 1983 in *Theses concerning Martin Luther, 1483–1983: The Luther Quincentenary in the German Democratic Republic* (Berlin: Zeit im Bild, 1983), 17.

21. See Ronald Sider, *Karlstadt's Battle with Luther: Documents in a Liberal-Radical Debate* (Philadelphia: Fortress Press, 1978). On Carlstadt in general, see OER 1:178–80.

22. This phrase is also the title of the treatise. WA 18:600–787. LW 33:5–295. Erasmus, "Diatribe or Discourse Concerning Free Choice" in Gordon E. Rupp and Philip S. Watson, eds., *Luther and Erasmus: Free Will and Salvation,* Library of Christian Classics 17 (Philadelphia: Westminster, 1969). See also Cornelis Augustijn, *Erasmus: His Life, Works and Influence* (Toronto: Toronto University Press, 1991).

23. WA 18:685.3–6, 14–16. LW 33:139.

24. See Luther's two treatises against Zwingli on the Lord's Supper in WA 19:482–523. WA 23:64–283. LW 36:331–361. LW 37:5–150. A third treatise sums up Luther's position in terms of a "Confession" in WA 26:261–509. LW 37:153–372.

25. Augustine used the phrase "visible word." See his commentary on John 3 in Tract 80, J. P. Migne, ed., *Patrologia: Series Latina,* 221 vols. in 222 (Paris, 1844–1904) 35, 1840.3. See also BC 220:5.

26. See the various accounts of the Marburg colloquy in WA 30/3:160–171. LW 38:5–89. Text of the "Schwabach Articles" in *Corpus Reformatorum*, ed. Carl B. Bretschneider and H. E. Bindseil (Halle, 1834–60), 26:151–59. See the detailed account in Martin Brecht, *Martin Luther*, trans. J. L. Schaaf, 3 vols. (Minneapolis: Fortress Press, 1990–93), 2:325–34.

27. Anabaptists and other dissenters within the Protestant Reformation have been identified as part of a massive "radical reformation." See the detailed work of George H. Williams, *The Radical Reformation*, Sixteenth Century Essays and Studies 15, 3d ed., rev. (Kirksville, Mo.: Sixteenth Century Journal, 1992). Williams notes that the Diet of Speyer in 1529 activated the Justinian Code against the Anabaptists, charging them with insurrection (359).

28. "Concerning Rebaptism," 1528. WA 26:154.6–14. 168.27–29. LW 40:239–240. 256. Sounds as if Luther's *sola scriptura* is complemented by *sola traditio!* See Eric W. Gritsch, "Martin Luther's View of Tradition," in *Quadrilog: Tradition and the Future of Ecumenism, Essays in Honor of George H. Tavard*, ed. Kenneth Hagen (Collegeville, Minn.: Liturgical, 1994), 61–75.

29. Early Anabaptist teachings were summarized in the "Schleitheim Confession," 1527, text in John C. Wenger, "The Schleitheim Confession of Faith," *Mennonite Quarterly Review* 19 (1945): 243–53. On Luther's polemics, see John S. Oyer, *Lutheran Reformers against the Anabaptists: Luther, Melanchthon, and Menius, and the Anabaptists of Central Germany* (The Hague: Nijhoff, 1964), ch. 4.

30. Table Talk, 1540. WA.TR 5:20.12–15. No. 5232b.

31. "Of the War against the Turks," 1529. WA 30/2:107–148. LW 46:157–205. Quotation WA 30/2:148.9–11. LW 46:204.

32. See Roland H. Bainton, "The Left Wing of the Reformation," *Journal of Religion* 21 (1941): 124–34; Eric W. Gritsch, "Luther und die Schwärmer: Verworfene Anfechtung? Zum 50. Todesjahr Karl Holl," *Luther* 3 (1976): 105–21.

33. See Karl E. Förstemann, ed., *Urkundenbuch zu der Geschichte des Reichstages zu Augsburg im Jahre 1530* (1833; reprint, Osnabrück, 1966), 1:1–9.

34. Letter of May 15, 1530. WA.BR 5:319.6–8. LW 49:297–298. Luther was at Coburg from April until October. See Gordon E. Rupp, "Luther at the Castle Coburg, 1530," *Bulletin of the John Rylands University Library* 61 (1979): 182–205.

35. Last revised in 1543, text in *Corpus Reformatorum* 21; ET in Clyde L. Manschreck, ed., *Melanchthon on Christian Doctrine: Loci Communes, 1555* (A Library of Protestant Thought; New York: Oxford University Press, 1965).

36. German and Latin text in BS 44–137; ET (from which I quote) in BC 30–105. Schwabach Articles in WA 30/3:81–91. ET in Robert Kolb and James A. Nestingen, eds., *Sources and Contexts of the Book of Concord* (Minneapolis: Fortress Press, 2001), 83–87. Torgau Articles in Karl E. Foerstemann, *Die Augsburgische Konfession, lateinisch und deutsch* (Gotha, 1896), 128–39. ET in Kolb and Nestingen, *Sources and Contexts*, 93–104. See also Wilhelm Maurer, *Historical Commentary on the Augsburg Confession*, trans. H. G. Anderson (Philadelphia: Fortress Press, 1986); OER 1:93–97; Eric W. Gritsch, "Reflections on Melanchthon as a Theologian of the Augsburg Confession," *Lutheran Quarterly* 12 (1998): 445–52.

37. See Eric W. Gritsch, "The Origins of the Lutheran Teaching on Justification," in *Lutherans and Catholics in Dialogue*, vol. 7, *Justification by Faith*, eds. H. G. Anderson, T. A. Murphy, and J. A. Burgess (Minneapolis: Augsburg, 1985), 167.

38. See the critical text edition of Herbert Immenkötter, ed., *Die Confutatio der Confessio Augustana vom 3. August 1530* (2d ed.; Münster Westfalen: Aschendorff, 1979). ET in Kolb and Nestingen, *Sources and Contexts*, 105–39. See also OER 1:408–10; Jill Raitt, "From Augsburg to Trent," *Lutherans and Catholics in Dialogue*, vol. 7, *Justification by Faith*, 200–217.

39. Raitt, "From Augsburg to Trent," 204.

40. Table Talk, 1530. WA.TR 4:495.7–9. No. 4780.

41. For the section on justification, see BC 120–73. Critique: BC 109–120, 174–294. BC cites much of the text of the *Confutation* in footnotes.

42. "Dr. Martin Luther's Warning to His Dear German People," 1531. WA 30/3: 282.33–283.1. LW 47:19.

43. "Commentary on the Alleged Edict of Augsburg," 1531. WA 30/3:387.3–9. LW 34:103–104. The philological origin of the saying has been investigated by Adolf Hauffen, "Husz eine Gans—Luther ein Schwan," *Prager deutsche Studien* 9 (1908): 1–28.

44. See OER 3:162–63.

45. See Brecht, *Martin Luther*, 3, 5. Paul Drews, *Die Disputationen Martin Luthers* (Göttingen, 1895).

46. Details in Brecht, *Martin Luther*, 126–34.

47. Text in BS 977–978. BC 595:13–596:16. Quotation BS 977:20. BC 595:14.

48. Text in *Corpus Reformatorum* 26, 357. Details on this and other controversial views of the eucharist in Ernst Bizer, *Studien zur Geschichte des Abendmahlsstreits im 16. Jahrhundert* (1940; reprint, Darmstadt: Wissenschaftliche Buchgesellschaft, 1962).

49. Text of the articles in BS 407–68. BC 297–328. Quotation BS 977:20. BC 301:1.

50. BS 471–498. BC 330–343. Text of Melanchthon's reservation in BS 463:6–464:4. BC 326:5.

51. BS 485:41. BC 337:41.

52. See OER 1:471. See Martin Schwarz Lausten, "The Early Reformation in Denmark and Norway, 1520–1559," in *The Scandinavian Reformation: From Evangelical Movement to Institutionalization of Reform*, ed. Ole P. Grell (Cambridge: Cambridge University Press, 1995), 12–41; by the same author, "Die Beziehungen zwischen Dänemark und der Universität Wittenberg in der Reformationszeit" in *Zwischen Wissenschaft und Politik: Studien zur deutschen Universitätsgeschichte*, ed. A. Kohnle and F. Engelhausen (Festschrift für Eike Wolgast zum 65 Geburtstag; Stuttgart: Calwer, 2001), 238–57; Niels K. Andersen, "The Reformation in Scandinavia and in the Baltic," *The New Cambridge Modern History*, vol. 2, *The Reformation, 1520–1559*, ed. G. R. Elton (Cambridge: Cambridge University Press, 1990) 134–60; Leif Grane and Kai Horby, eds., *Die dänische Reformation vor ihrem internationalen Hintergrund = The Danish Reformation against Its International Background* (Göttingen: Vandenhoeck & Ruprecht, 1990); E. H. Dunkley, *The Reformation in Denmark* (London: SPCK, 1948).

53. This is the conclusion of Niels K. Andersen, *Confessio Hafniensis: Den kobenhavensk Bekendelse af 1530* (Copenhagen: Gad, 1954); and of Martin Schwarz Lausten in OER 1:472.

54. Details on both in OER 3:199–200. 4:145–46.

55. Trygve R. Skarsten in OER 4:127. See the general narrative by Michael Roberts, *The Early Vasas: A History of Sweden, 1523–1611* (Cambridge: Cambridge University Press, 1968).

56. Details on Norway in OER 3:155–58. See also Kenneth E. Christopherson, "Norwegian Historiography of Norway's Reformation," Ph.D. diss., University of Michigan, 1985.

57. OER 3:157.

58. See OER 1:10–12. 2:106–8; Kaakko Gummerus, *Michael Agricola, der Reformator Finnlands,* Schriften der Luthergesellschaft 2 (Helsinki, 1941).

59. OER 2:301. For a general account of Lutheran beginnings, see Stefán Einarsson, "The Reformation," in *A History of Icelandic Literature* (New York: Johns Hopkins Press for the American-Scandinavian Foundation, 1957), 170–78; Jon Helgason, "Die Kirche in Island," in *Ekklesia,* 2 vols., ed. Friedrich Siegmund-Schulze (Gotha, 1934), 2:7–35.

60. See Luther's "Exhortation to the Knights of the Teutonic Order," 1523. WA 12:232–244. LW 45:141–158. On the order and its work in Prussia, see OER 3:360–61.

61. See OER 2:401–2. See also Egil Grislis, "Recent Trends in the Study of the Reformation in the City of Riga," *Journal of Baltic Studies* 7, no. 2 (1976): 145–69; Leonid Arbusow Jr., *Die Einführung der Reformation in Liv-, Est-, und Kurland* (Leipzig: Vermittlungsverlag, 1921); Reinhard Wittram, ed., *Baltische Kirchengeschichte: Beiträge zur Geschichte der Missionierung und der Reformation, der evangelisch-lutherischen Landeskirchen und des Volkskirchentums in den baltischen Landen* (Göttingen: Vandenhoeck & Ruprecht, 1956).

62. OER 2:70–71. See also Otto Pohrt, "Reformationsgeschichte Livlands: Ein Überblick," *Schriften des Vereins für Reformationsgeschichte 46.2* (1928).

63. OER 2:434–36. See also Antanas Musteikis, *The Reformation in Lithuania: Religious Fluctuations in the Sixteenth Century* (East European Monographs 246; Boulder: East European Monographs; New York: Columbia University Press, 1988); Zenonas Ivinskis, *Die Entwicklung der Reformation in Litauen bis zum Erscheinen der Jesuiten (1569),* Sonderdruck aus Forschungen zur osteuropäischen Geschichte 12 (Berlin, 1967).

64. OER 3:285.

65. OER 1:183. 3:87–88. See also Fredrick G. Heymann, "The Impact of Martin Luther upon Bohemia," *Central European History* 1 (1968): 107–30; Harrison S. Thomson, "Luther and Bohemia," *Archiv für Reformationsgeschichte* 44 (1953): 160–81.

66. OER 3:87.

67. OER 2:272. See also Andrew Pettegree, ed., *The Early Reformation in Europe* (Cambridge, Eng.: Cambridge University Press, 1993), 49–69; William Töth, "Highlights of the Hungarian Reformation," CH 9 (1940): 141–56; Mihaly Bucsay, *Der Protestantismus in Ungarn, 1521–1978: Ungarns Reformationskirchen in Geschichte und Gegenwart,* 2 vols. (Graz: Böhlau, 1977–79).

68. OER 4:171–172. LCW 319.

69. OER 1:104–7. See also Grete Mecenseffy, *Geschichte des Protestantismus in Österreich* (Graz: Böhlau, 1956).

70. "On the Councils and the Church," 1539. WA 50:615.28–30. 616.2–4. LW 41:133.

71. Table Talk, 1539. No. 4465. WA.TR 4:325.22–24. LW 54:343.

72. The Regensburg meetings were preceded by conversations in Hagenau and Worms in 1540. How conciliatory these negotiations were has been shown by Vinzenz Pfnür, *Die Einigung bei den Religionsgesprächen von Worms und Regensburg 1540/41: Eine Täuschung?* (Gütersloh: Mohn, 1980). On the compromise on justification and Luther's reaction, see Walther von Loewenich, *Duplex Iustitia: Luthers Stellung zu einer Unionsformel des 16. Jahrhunderts* (Wiesbaden: Steiner, 1972), 23–55.

73. Letter to Robert Barnes, 1531. WA.BR 6:179.26–29. LW 50:33. For details on this disastrous story, see Brecht, *Martin Luther* 3:205–15. See also John A. Faulkner, "Luther and the Bigamous Marriage of Philip of Hesse," *American Journal of Theology* 17 (1913): 206–31.

74. "Against Hanswurst," 1541. WA 51:469–572. LW 41:181–256.

75. Table Talk, 1542. No. 5488. WA.TR 5:184.4–7. LW 54:427–428.

76. "Luther's Will," 1542. WA.BR 9:573.60–62. LW 34:297.

77. Table Talk, 1540. No. 5010. WA.TR 4:611.12–16. LW 54:377.

78. "Against the Sabbatarians," 1539. WA 50:336.2–6. LW 47:96.

79. WA 53:523.1–526.16. 541: 30–33. 542.5–7. LW 47:268–272. 292. Lutheranism cannot be identified with this Luther. See reasons in Eric W. Gritsch, *Martin—God's Court Jester: Luther in Retrospect* (2d ed.; Ramsey, N.J.: Sigler, 1991), ch. 7; and Gritsch, "Luther, Lutheranism and the Jews," *Stepping Stones to Further Jewish-Lutheran Relationships: Key Lutheran Statements*, ed. H. H. Ditmanson (Minneapolis: Augsburg Fortress, 1990), ch. 8. See also Gritsch, "The Jews in Reformation Theology," in *Jewish-Christian Encounters over the Centuries: Symbiosis, Prejudice, Holocaust, Dialogue*, ed. M. Perry and F. M. Schweitzer (New York: Lang, 1994), 197–213.

80. Table Talk, 1542–1543. No. 5537. WA.TR 5:222.14–15.19–20. LW 54:448.

81. "Brief Confession Concerning the Holy Sacrament," 1544. WA 54:141–161; especially 141.17–18, 19–20. LW 38:281–319, 287–288. On Schwenckfeld's teaching, see Paul C. Maier, ed., *Caspar Schwenckfeld: On the Person and Work of Christ: A Study of Schwenckfeldian Theology at Its Core* (Assen: Van Gorcum, 1959), parts 2–3. See also Eric W. Gritsch, "Luther and Schwenckfeld: Towards Reconciliation by Hindsight," in *Schwenckfeld and Early Schwenckfeldianism*, Papers Presented at the Colloquium on Schwenckfeld and the Schwenckfelders, Sept. 17–22, 1984, ed. Peter C. Erb (Pennsburg, Pa., 1986), 401–14.

82. WA 54:299.5–7. LW 41:376.

83. "An Italian Lie Concerning Dr. Martin Luther's Death," 1545. WA 54:192–194. LW 34:365–366.

84. The most reliable of several records is Justus Jonas and Michael Coelius, "Concerning the Departure from This Mortal Life of the Reverend Dr. Martin Luther, 1546." Jonas was the Erfurt lawyer who had joined the Wittenberg faculty; Coelius was the court preacher of Count Albrecht of Mansfeld. Details in Brecht, *Martin Luther,* 3:369–82.

85. Recorded as Table Talk, 1546. No. 5677. WA.TR 5:317.12–318.3. LW 54:476.

86. Regarding the major changes of the interpretation of Luther, see Gritsch, *Martin—God's Court Jester,* ch. 12. See also the introduction of Luther to Catholics in a series of Catholic publications on major Christian figures by Gritsch, *Martin Luther: Faith in Christ and the Gospel—Selected Spiritual Writings* (Hyde Park, N.Y.: New City, 1996). Literature on

Luther is listed and evaluated in an annual publication titled *Lutherjahrbuch* (Göttingen, 1933–).

87. On the origins and history of the Luther rose, see Michael Freund, "Zur Geschichte der Lutherrose," *Luther* 42 (1972): 37–39.

88. Melanchthon's address is preserved in *Corpus Reformatorum* 11:726–34.

89. Text in Joachim Mehlhausen, ed., *Das Augsburger Interim von 1548* (Texte zur Geschichte der evangelischen Theologie 3, Neukirchen-Vluyn: Neukirchener, 1970). ET in Kolb and Nestingen, *Sources and Contexts*, 145–82. Quotation, 146. OER 2:319. See also "Interim" in TRE 16:230–37 and Joachim Mehlhausen, ed., *Das Augsburger Interim von 1548: Nach den Reichstagsakten deutsch und lateinisch* (Texte zur Geschichte der evangelischen Theologie 3; Neukirchen-Vlyn: Neukirchener, 1970).

90. The provisions of the treaty are listed and assessed in Karl Brandi, *Der Augsburger Religionsfriede vom 25. September 1555* (2d ed.; Leipzig, 1927). See also TRE 4:639–45. OER 1:91–93.

91. OER 3:456.

3. Confessional Identity, 1555–1580

1. This is Luther's thesis in the preface to "The German Mass and Order of Service," 1526. WA 19:72–113. LW 53:61–90.

2. See OER 1:275. See also Eric W. Gritsch, "Luther's Catechisms of 1529: Whetstones of the Church," in *Encounters with Luther: Lectures, Discussions, and Sermons at the Martin Luther Colloquia*, ed. Eric W. Gritsch (Gettysburg, Pa.: Institute for Luther Studies, Gettysburg Lutheran Seminary, 1970–90), 2:237–48.

3. BS 769:20. BC 487:7.

4. Text of both catechisms are in BS 501–27.545–733. BC 347–75.379–480.

5. BC 431:1; 388:13–15; 388:22; 392:48; 430:326.

6. BC 431:1; 433:24; 355:4; 355:6; 438:53, 58.

7. BC 440:2; 440:2; 455:111.

8. Luther accepted only two sacraments, baptism and Holy Communion, because he found only in them a "divinely instituted sign" (like water, bread, wine) and "the promise of forgiveness of sins" (made by Jesus). "The Babylonian Captivity of the Church," 1520. WA 6:572.23–30. LW 36:124–25.

9. BC 457:6, 459:24.

10. BC 460:35–461:36.

11. Quotations from BC 463:56, 464:56; 360:12; 466:84.

12. BC 474–475:75–79.

13. BC 476:87.

14. See *The Use of the Means of Grace: The Practice of Word and Sacrament* (Chicago: Evangelical Lutheran Church in America, 1998), 25. Also see Eric W. Gritsch, "Infant Communion: What Shape Tradition?" *Academy* 36 (1979): 85–108.

15. Quotations from BC 478:15; BC 478:18, 22. BC 479:32.

16. Luther, "Preface to the Large Catechism," 1529. BS 552:38–553:24. BC 382–383:19–20.

17. For Luther's distinction of law and gospel, see Eric W. Gritsch, *Martin—God's Court Jester: Luther in Retrospect* (2d ed.; Ramsey, N.J.: Sigler, 1991), ch. 5, especially, 94–98.

18. All the works are contained in *Corpus Reformatorum*, ed. C. B. Bretschneider and H. E. Bindseil (Halle, 1834–1860), vols. 1–28. Additional works have been edited later in *Supplementa Melanchthoniana: Werke Philipp Melanchthons, die im Corpus Reformatorum, vermisst werden*, 5 vols. (1910; reprint, Frankfurt: Minerva, 1968). See also Clyde C. Manschreck, *Melanchthon: The Quiet Reformer* (New York: Abingdon, 1958), and OER 3:41–45.

19. Quotations from BC 110:11; 114:15 and 116:32; 132:72, 73.

20. Quotations from BC 147:179; 171:358; 170:358.

21. Quotations from BC 174:7; 176:18, 20; 180:33; 180:34.

22. Quotations from BC 219:4; BC 219–220:5; BC 220:11.

23. Quotations from BC 222:1; BC 229:38; BC 229:39; BC 230:51.

24. Quotations from BC 234:9; 235:4.

25. BC 238:4–7.

26. Quotations from BC 238:10; 241–242:31.

27. BC 245:4.

28. Quotations from BC 249:7, 251:20, 257:66.

29. Quotations from BC 258:1, 262:25; 271:75; 276:94, 95.

30. BC 283:37.

31. Quotations from BC 290:13; 291:15.

32. See "Melanchthon" in TRE, 371–410; and Michael Rogness, *Philip Melanchthon: Reformer without Honor* (Minneapolis: Augsburg, 1969).

33. Text of the "Wittenberg Reformation" (*Wittenbergische Reformation*) in *Corpus Reformatorum* 5:579–606; quotation, 597.

34. Manschreck, *Melanchthon: The Quiet Reformer*, 15.

35. OER 4:174. Text of all decrees in Latin and English are in *Decrees of the Ecumenical Councils*, vol. 2, *Trent to the Vatican*, ed. N. P. Tanner (London: Sheed & Ward; Washington, D.C.: Georgetown University Press, 1990). For a standard history, see Hubert Jedin, *A History of the Council of Trent*, trans. E. Graf, 2 vols. (St. Louis: Herder, 1957).

36. DS 2803; English text in Frederick M. Jelly, "The Roman Catholic Dogma of Mary's Immaculate Conception," *Lutherans and Catholics in Dialogue*, vol. 8, *The One Mediator, the Saints, and Mary*, eds. H. G. Anderson, J. F. Stafford, and J. A. Burgess (Minneapolis: Augsburg Fortress, 1992), 263.

37. DS 3902; English text in *Papal Documents on Mary*, ed. W. J. Doheny and J. P. Kelly (Milwaukee, Wisc.: Bruce, 1954), 299–320.

38. Text of Vatican I in DS 3074. For details, see Maurice C. Duchaine, "Vatican I on Primacy and Infallibility," *Lutherans and Catholics in Dialogue*, vol. 5, *Papal Primacy and the Universal Church*, ed. P. C. Empie and T. A. Murphy (Minneapolis: Augsburg, 1974), 139–50.

39. See Carl J. Peter, "The Decree on Justification in the Council of Trent," in *Lutherans and Catholics in Dialogue*, vol. 7, *Justification by Faith*, eds. H. G. Anderson, T. A. Murphy, J. A. Burgess (Minneapolis: Augsburg, 1985), 219.

40. DS 1582.

41. Peter, "The Decree on Justification in the Council of Trent," 223.

42. See Martin Chemnitz (1522–1586), *Examination of the Council of Trent*, trans. F. Kramer, 4 vols. (St. Louis: Concordia, 1971), Eighth Topic, Concerning Justification, 147–99.

43. DS 792a–843.

44. OER 1:140. Bellarmine personally issued the order to prohibit Galileo from teaching that the earth circled the sun. See also James Brodrick, *Robert Bellarmino: Saint and Scholar* (1928; reprint, London: Burns & Oates, 1966).

45. See "Catholic Reformation" in OER 1:293.

46. OER 1:52. Agricola's Antinomian position and his controversy with Luther and Melanchthon are analyzed in Joachim Rogge, *Johann Agricolas Lutherverständnis unter besonderer Berücksichtigung des Antinomianismus* (Berlin, 1960). See also the introduction to Luther's treatise *Against the Antinomians*, 1539. LW 47:101–106.

47. OER 1:10. A wealth of primary documents from Late Reformation controversies appears in *Documents*, 181–244.

48. BC 50, XVIII:1–3.

49. OER 4:134. Details of the entire controversy in "Synergismus." TRE 19:229–35. See also Robert Kolb, *Nikolaus von Amsdorf (1483–1565): Popular Polemics in the Preservation of Luther's Legacy* (Niewkoop: De Graaf, 1978).

50. BC 56:27.

51. Ibid.

52. OER 2:501. TRE 21:725–30. See also Robert Kolb, "Georg Major as a Controversialist: Polemics in the Late Reformation," CH 45 (1976): 455–68.

53. Article 6 of the Augsburg Confession, BC 40–41.

54. OER 3:258.

55. BC 132:72.

56. RGG 2:1177–78 on Funck. See also OER 3:183–85 on Osiander.

57. "Interims" in OER 2:320. See also "Adiaphora," OER 1:4–7.

58. BC 44–45.

59. "Confession Concerning Christ's Supper," 1528. LW 37:367. "Large Catechism," 1529. BC 467:8.

60. See "Eucharist." OER 2:77. Details of the controversy in "Kryptocalvinisten." TRE 20:123–29. See also "Philippists." OER 3:258–61.

61. See "Consubstantiation." OER 1:418–19. *Altered Augsburg Confession*, Art. 10, text in *Corpus Reformatorum*, 26:357. Rare ET in J. M. Reu, *The Augsburg Confession: A Collection of Sources with an Historical Introduction* (Chicago: Wartburg, 1930), 398–419.

62. Manschreck, *Melanchthon: The Quiet Reformer*, 293.

63. For the development of the Formula of Concord, see OER 2:117–21; TRE 19:476–83. See also *Sixteenth Century Journal 8*, no. 4 (1977), the issue titled *The Formula of Concord: Quadricentennial Essays*; Robert Kolb, *Andreae and the Formula of Concord: Six Sermons on the Way to Lutheran Unity* (Saint Louis: Concordia, 1977); by the same author, *Confessing One Faith: Reformers Define the Church, 1530–1580* (Saint Louis: Concordia, 1991).

64. BC 486.

65. BC 526.

66. BC 527:3.

67. So listed in FC. BC 527:4–528:8.

68. BC 528–529:9.

69. BC 530:15.

70. BC 541:57.

71. BC 541:56.

72. BC 533:7.

73. BC 549:25.

74. BC 553: 49.

75. BC 564:13; 572:54.

76. BC 576:12.

77. BC 584:18; 585:20; 586:27.

78. Quotations from BC 587:1; 590:20; 591:24.

79. Quotations are from BC 599:35; 604:62–63; 606:75; 608:86; 608:89. Some theologians raised "blasphemous" questions regarding the presence of Christ in the Lord's Supper: "1. When and how does the body of Christ come to the bread or into the bread? 2. How near or how far away from the bread is it? 3. How is it hidden under the bread? 4. How long does the sacramental union last? 5. When does the body of Christ leave the bread again? 6. Does the body of Christ which we receive orally enter our bodies and stomachs and is it digested there? 7. Is it crushed and chewed with the teeth? 8. Is it a living body or a dead corpse, since we receive the body under the bread separately from the blood under the wine?" Book of Concord, ed. Theodore G. Tappert (Philadelphia: Fortress Press, 1959), 591, n. 4.

80. Chalcedon is now the Turkish town of Kadiköy on the Asiatic shore of the Bosphorus across from Istanbul, formerly Byzantium, Constantinople. See also "Chalcedon" in *The Westminster Dictionary of Church History,* ed. J. C. Brauer (Philadelphia: Westminster, 1971), 176.

81. BC 628:66.

82. BC 513:30.

83. BC 635:3.

84. BC 637:9; 637:10; 638:15.

85. See "Predestination" in OER 3:335.

86. BC 519:17.

87. BC 646:33.

88. BC 656–60. Extensive treatment of these and other groups in George H. Williams, *The Radical Reformation,* 3d ed. (Sixteenth Century Essays and Studies 15; Kirksville, Mo.: Sixteenth Century Journal, 1992).

89. BC 660:39.

90. BC 3. Catalogue of Testimonies in BS 1001–1135. ET in Robert Kolb and James A. Nestingen, eds., *Sources and Contexts of the Book of Concord* (Minneapolis: Fortress Press, 2001), 221–44.

91. BC 15:23.

92. BC 7. What follows is based on the declaration, *Lutheran Identity*, by the Institute for Ecumenical Research of the Lutheran World Federation in Strasbourg, France, published there in German and English on the fourth centennial of the FC (Strasbourg: Institute for Ecumenical Research, 1977).

93. *Lutheran Book of Worship* (Minneapolis: Augsburg, 1978), 124.

4. Orthodoxy, 1580–1675

1. Summaries and sources of Lutheran orthodoxy in OER 3:180–83. TRE 25:464–85. See especially James M. Estes, *Christian Magistrate and State Church: The Reforming Career of Johannes Brenz* (Toronto: University of Toronto Press, 1982; and H. E. Weber, *Reformation, Orthodoxie und Rationalismus*, 2 vols. (1937–51; reprint, Gütersloh, 1976).

2. See "Erastianism" in OER 2:59–60. Also John Figgins Neville, "Erastus and Erastianism," *Journal of Theological Studies* 2 (1901): 66–101. Ruth Wesel-Roth, *Thomas Erastus: Ein Beitrag zur Geschichte der reformierten Kirche und zur Lehre von der Staatssouveränität* (Lahr, Baden: Schauenburg, 1954).

3. TRE 8:307. This view was defended by Professor Hans Wandal (1624–1675).

4. RGG 6:1659–61.

5. Luther's views are summarized in Eric W. Gritsch, *Martin—God's Court Jester: Luther in Retrospect* (2d ed.; Ramsey, N.J.: Sigler, 1991), ch. 6. See OER 4:184–86 (includes the view of Melanchthon).

6. On the historical impact of Luther's political views, see Eric W. Gritsch, "Luther and the State," *Luther and the Modern State in Germany*, ed. J. D. Tracy (Sixteenth Century Essays and Studies 7; Kirksville, Mo.: Sixteenth Century Journal, 1986), 45–59; Gritsch, "The Use and Abuse of Luther's Political Advice," *Lutherjahrbuch* 57 (1990), 207–19.

7. BC 82:11.

8. BC 8.

9. *Gottes Wort und Luthers Lehr wird vergehen nimmermehr*. Memorial coin of 1617, commemorating the one-hundredth anniversary of the Ninety-five Theses. See Ernst W. Zeeden, *The Legacy of Luther: Martin Luther and the Reformation in the Estimation of the German Lutherans from Luther's Death to the Beginning of the Age of Goethe*, trans. R. M. Bethell (Westminster, Md.: Newman, 1954), 37, 47–48.

10. Quoted in TRE 3:794. For more on Lutheran orthodoxy, see *Documents*, 216–44.

11. TRE 3:794.

12. Quoted in OER 1:310.

13. Leonhart Hutter, *Compendium of Theological Loci* . . . (*Compendium locorum theologicorum* . . .). Latest edition was edited by Wolfgang Trillhaas (Berlin, 1961).

14. John Andreas Quenstedt, *Theologia didactico-polemica sive systema theologicum*, 1685. See also the detailed study of Quenstedt by Jörg Baur, *Die Vernunft zwischen Ontologie und Evangelium: Eine Untersuchung zur Theologie Johann Andreas Quenstedts* (Gütersloh: Mohn, 1962).

15. Johann Gerhard, *Loci theologici* (Theological loci), ed. E. Preuss (1610–22; reprint, Berlin, 1863–85).

16. John Musäus, *Introductio in theologiam, qua de natura theologiae naturalis, et revelatae, itemque de theologiae revelatae principio cognoscendi primo, scriptura sacra, agitur* (Introduction to theology, dealing with the nature of a natural and revealed theology, that is, with a revealed theology that must first be recognized in Holy Scripture, 1661).

17. His systematic theology is summarized in Balthasar Mentzer, *Synopsis theologiae analytico ordine comprehensae* (Synopsis of theology, comprehended by analytical order, 1610).

18. RGG 5:1067. On Brochmand, see RGG (4th ed., Tübingen: Mohr, 1998), 1:1768.

19. Brief sketch in Robert D. Preus, *The Theology of Post-Reformation Lutheranism: A Study of Theological Prolegomena* (St. Louis: Concordia, 1970), 54.

20. RGG 1:1587.

21. *Acroamaticum* is an Aristotelian term, used in the description of teaching as listening (Greek: *akroasdai,* "listening" in contrast to "questioning").

22. Quoted in Preus, *Theology,* 28.

23. Quoted in Preus, *Theology,* 263, from *Loci theologici,* II, 427.

24. RGG 3:775.

25. See Gritsch, *Martin,* 98, 109.

26. Abraham Calov, *Biblia illustrata,* II, 1034, quoted in Preus, *Theology,* 281.

27. Calov, *Biblia illustrata,* II, 1547, quoted in Preus, *Theology,* 283.

28. Quenstedt, *Systema,* I, C. 4, S. 2, qu. 15 (I, 157), quoted in Preus, *Theology,* 287.

29. Quenstedt, *Systema,* I, 57, quoted in Preus, *Theology,* 288.

30. From Quenstedt, *Systema,* I, 68, quoted in Preus, *Theology,* 294.

31. Johann Gerhard, *Loci theologici,* II, 36, quoted in Preus, *Theology,* 297.

32. From Abraham Calov, *Apodixis articulorum fidei,* 35, quoted in Preus, *Theology,* 298.

33. Abraham Calov thought that the famous translator of Scripture, Jerome (348–420), may have used a text without signs. *Criticus sacer,* I, 328, quoted in Preus, *Theology,* 387, n. 158.

34. Quoted in Preus, *Theology,* 309.

35. *Systema,* I, C.4, S. 2,q.12, quoted in Preus, *Theology,* 312–13.

36. David Hollaz, *Examen,* I, S.2, C. 1, q.39, quoted in Preus, *Theology,* 364.

37. Quenstedt, *Systema,* I, C.4, S.2, q.5, quoted in Preus, *Theology,* 340.

38. Preus, *Theology,* 342. Italics added.

39. David Hollaz, quoted in Preus, *Theology,* 398, n. 270.

40. Quenstedt, *Systema,* I, C.4, S.2, q.5, quoted in Preus, *Theology,* 353.

41. So Friedeman Bechmann in Preus, *Theology,* 258–59.

42. Quoted in Preus, *Theology,* 399, n. 290.

43. *Physica et ethica mosaica* (Mosaic physics and ethics), 1614.

44. Preus, *Theology,* 358–61.

45. The quarrel is sketched in Preus, *Theology,* 129. Details in Ernst Schlee, *Der Streit des Daniel Hoffmann* (Marburg, 1862).

46. So Luther in "Disputation on the Divinity and Humanity of Christ" (*Disputatio de divinitate et humanitate Christi*), 1540. WA 39/2:93.

47. WA 39/2:22. How close Gerhard is to Luther in this regard has been shown by Johannes Wallmann, *Der Theologiebegriff bei Johann Gerhard und Georg Calixt* (Tübingen: Mohr, 1961).

48. *Systema,* I, 69–75. Summarized in Preus, *The Theology of Post-Reformation Lutheranism,* 132.

49. The phrase is derived from Luther's Smalcald Articles, 1537. II, 1:5. BS 415. BC 301. See Valentin Löscher, *Timotheus verinus* (Wittenberg, 1718). Details in Friedrich Loofs, "Der articulus stantis et cadentis ecclesiae," *Theologische Studien und Kritiken* 90 (1917), 323–420.

50. *Hodosophia Christiana sive theologia positive,* 58, quoted in Preus, *Theology,* 262.

51. Abraham Calov, *Biblia novi testamenta illustrata,* II, 1035, quoted in Preus, *Theology,* 315.

52. Walther, *Harmonia biblica,* pp. 1–10, quoted in Preus, *Theology,* 350.

53. Dannhauer, *Hermeneutica sacra,* 409, quoted in Preus, *Theology,* 353.

54. See "Socinianism" in OER 4:83–87.

55. Calov, *Socinismus profligatus,* 79, quoted in Preus, *Theology,* 356.

56. David Hollaz, *Examen,* 992–95, quoted in Preus, *Theology.*

57. The proposal was made in a widely read treatise written for the French king, Henry IV, and titled *Eirenicum de pace ecclesiae catholicae* (Proposal for the peace of the church catholic), date unavailable. On Junius, see Christiaan de Jonge, *De irenische Ecclesiologie van Franciscus Junius (1545–1602)* (Bibliotheca Humanistica and Reformatorica 30; Niewkoop: De Graaf, 1980). OER 2:360.

58. Details about Calixt and the controversies about this point of view in TRE 7:555–58.

59. "*Irenik*" in TRE 16:269.

60. On the celibacy of priests, see the treatise *De coniugio clericorum,* 1621. On the toleration of Catholics, see *Discurs von der wahren christlichen Religion und Kirchen,* 1633. Calixt was well supported by Duke August and served as consultant to Duke Ernest of Gotha, who reorganized the churches of Franconia (Franken) on the basis of Calixt's ecumenical views. But the defeat of Lutheran princes at the Battle of Nördlingen in 1634 revitalized anti-Catholicism; it was not tolerated.

61. It is an unfinished work titled *Epitome theologiae moralis (Epitome of moral theology),* 1634.

62. His life and work are summarized in OER 1:271.

63. "Catalogue of Testimonies" (*catalogus testimoniorum*). BS 1104:5. Available only in Latin.

64. Latin version. BS 61:2. BC 43:2–3.

65. Apology of the Augsburg Confession, 13:5. BS 293:5. BC 219–220:5.

66. Preface to BC. BS 9:5. BC 10.

67. Augsburg Confession 7:2. German text. BS 61. BC 42.

68. Augsburg Confession 7:2.

69. Augsburg Confession 5:5. Latin version. BS 58. BC 41.

70. Augsburg Confession 7:3–4. BS 61. BC 42.

71. Lutheran Confessions, 79. "Third Commandment." BS 580. BC 396.

72. Formula of Concord 7:86. BS 1001. BC 608.

73. See the insightful Lutheran analysis of Wilhelm Dantine, *Justification of the Ungodly,* trans. Eric W. Gritsch and R. C. Gritsch (St. Louis: Concordia, 1968), especially Part I.

74. RGG 6:1138.

75. Formula of Concord 3:18. BS 935. BC 497.

5. Pietism, 1675–1817

1. Johannes Wallmann, *Der Pietismus*, ed. B. Moeller (Die Kirche und ihre Geschichte: Ein Handbuch; Göttingen: Vandenhoeck & Ruprecht, 1990), 13.

2. Wallmann, *Der Pietismus*, 13. There is a useful sketch of "Pietism" with bibliography in TRE 26:607–31. See also Ernest F. Stoeffler, *The Rise of Evangelical Pietism* (Leiden: Brill, 1971), and *German Pietism during the Eighteenth Century* (Leiden: Brill, 1973).

3. Original title: *Vier Bücher vom wahren Christentum* (Four books of true Christianity). ET: *True Christianity*, trans. Peter Erb (New York: Paulist, 1979). The book has been translated into many languages and accompanied many Lutherans on their way to other lands, especially the United States.

4. John Arndt, *True Christianity* (Philadelphia: Lutheran Bookstore, 1868), quoted in Wallmann, *Der Pietismus*, 18. See extensive excerpts in *Documents*, 249–58.

5. For a list of his works, see Wallmann, *Der Pietismus*, 17.

6. See OER 4:21–24.

7. *Praxis Arndiana: das ist, des Hertzens-Seuffzer über die 4 Bücher wahren Christentums Johann Arndts.* In 1677, Hoburg penned a sequel, *Arndus Redivivus, Das ist Arndischer Wegweiser zum Himmelreich* (Arndt come to life, that is, the Arndtian road-sign to the kingdom of God). The flowering of Lutheran devotional writing is sampled in *Documents*, 245–76.

8. Original title: *La pratique de l'oraison et meditation Chrétienne*, 1660. Spener titled it *Kurzer Unterricht von andächtiger Betrachtung* (Brief instruction for a pious view).

9. "Es ist jetzt stadtbekannt der Nam der Pietisten. Was ist ein Pietist? Der Gottes Wort studiert, und nach demselben auch ein heiliges Leben führt." Quoted in Wallmann, *Der Pietismus*, 8.

10. John Arndt, *Evangelienpostille*, 1616. Philip Jacob Spener, *Pia Desideria oder Hertzliches Verlangen nach gottgefälliger Besserung der wahren Evangelischen Kirchen* (1616); ET: *Pia Desideria*, trans. and ed. T. G. Tappert (Philadelphia: Fortress Press, 1964).

11. Spener, *Pia Desideria*, 43, 44. See excerpts from Spener in *Documents*, 282–92.

12. Ibid., 52.

13. Ibid., 59–60.

14. It should be noted that these verses do not speak of a conversion but of the "mystery" of God's decision to postpone the conversion of Israel whose calling is "irrevocable" (11:29). In this sense, divine judgments are "unsearchable" and "inscrutable" (11:33).

15. Spener, *Pia Desideria*, 89.

16. Ibid., 90.

17. Ibid., 92.

18. Ibid., 105.

19. This formulation first appears in Spener's letters to friends in 1676. See Wallmann, *Der Pietismus*, 50.

20. In the treatise *Theosophia Horbio-Speneriana* (Helmsted, 1679). John Henry Horb (1645–1695), to whom "Horbio" in the title refers, was Spener's brother-in-law and pastor in Trarbach; he was a strong supporter of Spener's proposals.

21. *Aufrichtige Übereinstimmung der Augsburgischen Konfession* (Honest agreement with the Augsburg Confession) (Berlin, 1695).

22. Wallmann, *Der Pietismus,* 59. Spener's chief works are collected in *Theologische Bedenken,* 4 vols. and an addendum, 1700–1702, 1711. See U. Sträter, "Von Bedenken und Briefen," *Zeitschrift für Religions- und Zeitgeschichte* 40 (1988): 235–50; K. James Stein, *Philip Jacob Spener: Pietist Patriarch* (Chicago: Covenant, 1986).

23. Quotations from the popular work *August Hermann Francke's Lebenslauf* (The life of August Hermann Francke) (1690–1691), quoted in Wallmann, *Der Pietismus,* 63.

24. The twelve volumes of student notes have been edited by F. De Boor, *Die paränetischen und methodischen Vorlesungen A. H. Franckes,* 2 vols. (Halle: Theologische Habilitation, 1968) and summarized by the same author in *Zeitschrift für Religions-und Geistesgeschichte* 20 (1968): 300–320. The main treatise is *Methodus studii theologici* (Method of the study of theology), 1723.

25. The text of the "Great Essay" (*Der grosse Aufsatz*) is found in Otto Podczeck, ed., *A. H. Franckes Schrift über eine reform des Erziehungs-und Bildungswesens als Ausgangspunkt einer geistlichen und sozialen Neuordnung der Evangelischen Kirche des 18. Jahrhunderts: Der grosse Aufsatz* (Sächsische Akademie der Wissenschaften; Berlin: Akademi, 1962), 23.

26. A surprising discovery made by Ernst Benz, "Ecumenical Relations between Boston Puritanism and German Pietism. Cotton Mather and August Hermann Francke," *Harvard Theological Review* 54 (1961): 159–93. On Scandinavia, Hapsburg, Russia, and England, see Wallmann, *Der Pietismus,* 77. On Prussia, see Richard L. Gawthrop, *Pietism and the Making of Eighteenth Century Prussia* (Cambridge: Cambridge University Press, 1993).

27. *Der fromme Soldat, das ist, Gründtliche Anweisung zur wahren Gottseligkeit für Christliebende Kriegsmänner;* Wallmann, *Der Pietismus,* 78.

28. Wallmann, *Der Pietismus,* 79. See Arthur J. Lewis, *Zinzendorf: The Ecumenical Pioneer* (Philadelphia: Fortress Press, 1962).

29. Ibid., 110. Quoted from the archives of Herrnhut in Wallmann, *Der Pietismus,* 119.

30. Quoted in Wallmann, *Der Pietismus,* 112.

31. Ibid., 114.

32. Ibid., 121.

33. In a speech at the synod of Hirschberg. in Wallmann, *Der Pietismus,* 121.

34. From a hymn of Martin Behm, "O Jesu Christ, meines Lebens Licht" ("Oh Jesus Christ, the Light of My Life"), stanza 11, cited in Wallmann, *Der Pietismus,* 121.

35. Zinzendorf's individual writings are identified in a bibliographical handbook, using abbreviated titles and numeration: D. Meyer, ed., *Bibliographisches Handbuch zur Zinzendorfforschung* [BHZ] (Düsseldorf, 1987), Teil A: "Schriften Zinzendorfs." Quote from *Berliner Reden* (Berlin speeches), BHZ A, 130, in a still unfinished edition of Zinzendorf's writings edited by D. Meyer.

36. *Zeister Speeches* (*Zeister Reden*), 1747. BHZ A, 175.

37. *Leben des Herrn Nikolaus Ludwig Grafen von Zinzendorf und Pottendorf* (The life of Lord Nikolaus Ludwig, Count of Zinzendorf and Pottendorf), 8 parts (1772; reprint, Hildesheim, N.Y.: Olms, 1971).

38. W. Jannasch, quoted in Wallmann, *Der Pietismus,* 123.

39. TRE 7:23.

40. Content summarized in Wallmann, *Der Pietismus,* 125.

41. Ibid., 127.

42. Ibid., 129.

43. Ibid., 135.

44. See Luther's *Reckoning Years of the World* (*Supputatio annorum mundi*), 1541. WA 53:22. Details in Eric W. Gritsch, *Martin—God's Court Jester: Luther in Retrospect* (2d ed.; Ramsey, N.J.: Sigler, 1991), 100.

45. See *Sechzig erbauliche Reden über die Offenbarung Johannis* (3rd ed.; Stuttgart: Brodhagsche Buchhandlung, 1835). See also Wallmann, *Der Pietismus,* 135–37.

46. TRE 14:383–84.

47. Quoted in Wallmann, *Der Pietismus,* 143.

48. Ibid., 143.

49. *Diskurs, ob die Auswerwählten verpflichtet seien, sich notwendig zu einer heutigen grossen Gemeinde und Religion zu halten* (Duisburg, 1684). See also Wallmann, *Der Pietismus,* 84.

50. Wallmann, *Der Pietismus,* 87.

51. The "eternal gospel" of the thousand-year kingdom was propagated by Joachim of Flora (1132–1202), a radical Italian Franciscan whose teachings were condemned in 1265. The notion of the "heavenly flesh of Christ" in heaven and in the eucharist was taught by the Lutheran spiritualist Kaspar Schwenckfeld (1489–1561) and rejected by Luther.

52. "Das eigentlich Pietistische an Petersen war seine Frau." See Albrecht Ritschl, *Die Geschichte des Pietismus,* 3 vols. (1880–1886; reprint, Bonn: Marcus, 1966), 2:248. See also Wallmann, *Der Pietismus,* 85.

53. *Die Erste Liebe der Gemeinden Christi* (Frankfurt am Main, 1696).

54. Quoted in Wallmann, *Der Pietismus,* 92.

55. *Unparteiische Kirchen-und Ketzergeschichte* (Frankfurt am Main, 1699–1700).

56. *Ein Hirt und eine Herde oder unfehlbare Methode, alle Secten und Religionen zur einigen wahren Kirche zu bringen;* see Wallmann, *Der Pietismus,* 97.

57. Quoted in Wallmann, *Der Pietismus,* 98.

58. Wallmann, *Der Pietismus,* 98.

59. See the helpful summary of John Conrad Dippel's theology and its place in the history of Lutheranism in Emanuel Hirsch, *Geschichte der neueren evangelischen Theologie im Zusammenhang mit den allgemeinen Bewegungen des europäischen Denkens,* 5 vols. (3d ed.; Gütersloh: Bertelsmann, 1964), 2:277–98.

60. Hochmann's life and thought have been sketched by Heinz Renkewitz, *Hochmann von Hohenau (1670–1721): Quellenstudien zur Geschichte des Pietismus* (2d ed.; Witten, 1969).

61. Renkewitz, *Hochmann von Hohenau,* 254.

62. See Donald F. Durnbaugh, *European Origins of the Brethren: A Source Book on the Beginnings of the Church of the Brethren in the Early Eighteenth Century* (Elgin, Ill.: Brethren, 1958).

63. Wallmann, *Der Pietismus*, 107.

64. See Arno Lehmann, *The Story of the Tranquebar Mission and the Beginnings of Protestant Christianity in India,* trans. M. J. Lutz (Madras: Christian Literature Society, 1956); H. M. Zorn, *Bartholomaeus Ziegenbalg* (St. Louis: Concordia, 1933).

65. In the sixteenth century, a Lutheran from Tübingen, Primas Truber, had tried to convert Croat Muslims but had been expelled by Catholic authorities.

66. *Genealogie der Malabrischen Götter* (Madras, 1867) and *Malabarisches Heidentum,* ed. W. Caland (Amsterdam: Müller, 1926).

67. TRE 16:105.

68. Translation of *Alte Briefe aus Indien,* ed. Arno Lehmann (Berlin: Evangelische Verlagsanstalt, 1957).

69. Quoted in Stephen Neill, *A History of Christian Missions,* vol. 6 of *The Pelican History of the Church,* 2d ed., rev. by O. Chadwick (New York: Penguin, 1986), 199.

70. Evidence supplied by Martin Schwarz Lausten, who has studied the unedited diaries of the missionaries in his work *De fromme og jöderne* (The Pious and the Jews) (Copenhagen, 2000).

71. Quoted in Wallmann, *Der Pietismus,* 119.

72. See L. Bobe, *Hans Egede: Colonizer and Missionary of Greenland* (Copenhagen: Rosenkilde and Bagger, 1952). How he and the missionaries of Lutheran Pietism enhanced Christian mission as a whole has been shown by Neill, *A History of Christian Missions,* 194–203.

73. TRE 14:260.

74. This is the thesis of Carl Hinrichs, *Preussentum und Pietismus: Der Pietismus in Brandenburg-Preussen als religiös-soziale Reformbewegung* (Göttingen: Vandenhoeck & Ruprecht, 1971), 231–300.

75. See E. Clifford Nelson, ed., *The Lutherans in North America* (2d ed.; Philadelphia: Fortress Press, 1980), 3.

76. Nelson, *Lutherans,* 11.

77. Quoted in Nelson, *Lutherans,* 14.

78. Helpful biography by Leonard R. Riforgiato, *Missionary of Moderation: Henry Melchior Muhlenberg and the Lutheran Church in English America* (Lewisburg, Pa.: Bucknell University Press; London: Associated University Presses, 1980). Muhlenberg's collected works are in *The Journals of Henry Melchior Muhlenberg,* 3 vols., trans. T. Tappert and J. W. Doberstein (Philadelphia: Lutheran Historical Society; Evansville, Ind.: Whipporwill, 1982).

79. Nelson, *Lutherans,* 37.

80. Penn announced his "holy experiment" in 1681. It was to establish total religious liberty. See TRE 28:36.

81. Nelson, *Lutherans,* 6.

82. Quoted in ibid., 8.

83. Quoted in ibid, 33.

84. So stated in a "Halle Report" in ibid., 49.

85. Nelson, *Lutherans,* 49.

86. Although both titles indicate "oversight," superintendents exercised this task in regard to church constitutions and church law; they became "auxiliary bishops," as it were. See Gassmann, *Historical Dictionary of Lutheranism*, 120.

87. *Journals of Muhlenberg*, 1:91.

88. Nelson, *Lutherans*, 62.

89. *Journals of Muhlenberg*, 1:193, 194.

90. Quoted in Nelson, *Lutherans*, 66.

91. Nelson, *Lutherans*, 68.

92. *Journals of Muhlenberg*, 1:307.

93. Nelson, *Lutherans*, 74.

94. *Journals of Muhlenberg*, 2:638.

95. Theodore G. Tappert, "Henry Melchior Muhlenberg and the American Revolution," CH 11 (1942): 284–301.

96. *Documentary History of the Evangelical Lutheran Ministerium of Pennsylvania and the Adjacent States* (Philadelphia: Board of Publication of the General Council of the Evangelical Lutheran Church in North America, 1898), 21, 175.

97. Quoted in Nelson, *Lutherans*, 64.

98. *Documentary History*, 11, 50; *The Albany Protocol: Wilhelm Christoph Berkenmeyer's Chronicle of Lutheran Affairs in New York Colony, 1731–1750*, trans. S. Hart and S. G. Hart-Runeman, ed. J. P. Dern (Ann Arbor, Mich., 1971), xlvi–xlvii.

99. *Journals of Muhlenberg*, 2:387; 3:427.

100. Ibid., 2:268.

101. See Charles R. Fletcher, *Gustavus Adolphus and the Thirty Years' War* (New York: Capricorn, 1963).

102. A helpful summary is in Ernst Cassirer, *The Philosophy of the Enlightenment*, trans. F. C. A. Koelln and J. Pettegrove (Princeton, N.J.: Princeton University Press, 1951).

103. Immanuel Kant, *Was ist Aufklärung?* (What Is Enlightenment?), ed. Norbert Kinsky (1784; Darmstadt: Wissenschaftliche Buchgesellschaft, 1973), 7:53.

104. See W. T. Stace, *The Philosophy of Hegel: A Systematic Exposition* (New York: Dover, 1955).

105. "Awakening" (*Erweckung*) has been defined by such trends. See Erich Beyreuther, *Die Erweckungsbewegung*, ed. K. D. Schmidt and E. Wolf (Die Kirche und ihre Geschichte: Ein Handbuch; Göttingen: Vandenhoeck & Ruprecht, 1963), a useful summary of international scope with bibliographical data.

6. Diversification, 1817–1918

1. Adam Smith, *An Inquiry into the Nature and Causes of the Wealth of Nations* (Great Books of the Western World 39; Chicago: Encyclopaedia Brittanica, 1955).

2. Karl Marx, *Capital, Communist Manifesto, and Other Writings*, ed. Max Eastmann (New York: Modern Library, 1932).

3. See Karl Jaspers, *Nietzsche and Christianity*, trans. E. B. Ashton (Chicago: Regnery, 1961).

4. Michael Ruse, *The Darwinian Revolution: Science Red in Tooth and Claw* (2d ed.; Chicago: University of Chicago Press, 1999).

5. Alphonse de Gobineau, "Essai sur l'inegalité des races humaines" (Essay on the Inequality of Human Races), 1853–55.

6. See Karl Geiringer, *Johann Sebastian Bach: The Culmination of an Era,* in collaboration with Irene Geiringer (New York: Oxford University Press, 1966).

7. DS 2803.

8. See Leslie S. Hunter, *Scandinavian Churches: A Picture of the Development and Life in the Churches of Denmark, Finland, Iceland, Norway and Sweden* (London: Faber and Faber, 1965). Also RGG 2:7 (Denmark), 4:1524–26 (Norway), 5:1595–99, 2:962 (Finland).

9. J. D. Loewenberg, ed., *The Persecution of the Lutheran Church in Prussia* (London, 1840).

10. Also known as Neo-Lutheranism *(Neuluthertum)*. TRE 24:327–41.

11. TRE 1:305, 345.

12. Wilhelm Löhe, *Three Books about the Church,* trans. and ed. James I. Schaaf (Philadelphia: Fortress Press, 1969), with an introduction to Löhe's life and work. Collected works in Klaus Ghanzeret, ed., *Wilhelm Löhe: Gesammelte Werke,* 8 vols. (Neuendettelsau, 1951–66).

13. Löhe, *Three Books,* 5:1, 96.

14. BC 50.

15. See *Dogmatic Constitution of the Church,* I, 8: "This Church [of Christ] . . . subsists in the Catholic Church which is governed by the successor of Peter"; and *Decree on Ecumenism,* I, 3: "It is through Christ's Catholic Church alone . . . that the fullness of the means of salvation can be obtained." From *Vatican Council II: More Postconciliar Documents,* ed. A. Flannery (Vatican Collection 2; Dublin: Dominican; Northport, N.Y.: Costello, 1975), 357, 456.

16. Gottlieb Harless, *Christliche Ethik,* 1843 (8th ed., 1893). RGG 3:76.

17. See "The Genuflection Controversy" (*Kniebeugungsstreit*) in RGG 3:1684.

18. Emanuel Hirsch, *Geschichte der neueren evangelischen Theologie im Zusammenhang mit den allgemeinen Bewegungen des europäischen Denkens,* 5 vols., 3d ed. (Gütersloh: Bertelsmann, 1964), 5:190–210.

19. Well demonstrated by John E. Groh, *Nineteenth Century German Protestantism: The Church as Social Model* (Washington, D.C.: University Press of America, 1982), ch. 5.

20. See Johannes Knudsen, *Danish Rebel: A Study of N. F. S. Grundtvig* (Philadelphia: Muhlenberg, 1955). See also the collection of essays in A. M. Allchin, D. Jasper, J. H. Schjorring, and K. Stephenson, eds., *Heritage and Prophecy: Grundtvig and the English-Speaking World* (Skrifter udgivet af Grundtvig-selskabet, 24; Aarhus, Denmark: Aarhus University Press, 1993).

21. TRE 14:285.

22. Demonstrated in his *Autobiographical Writings,* trans. J. M. Njus (Minneapolis: Augsburg, 1954). See also Andreas Aarflot, *Hans Nielsen Hauge: His Life and Message* (Minneapolis: Augsburg, 1979).

23. See G. Everett Arden, *Four Northern Lights: Men Who Shaped Scandinavian Churches* (Minneapolis: Augsburg, 1964) for sketches of Grundtvig, Hauge, Rosenius, and Ruotsalainen.

24. See Eugene Fairweather, ed., *The Oxford Movement* (Library of Protestant Thought; New York: Oxford University Press, 1964).

25. Sketch of the movement by Karl Kupisch, *Deutschland im 19. und 20. Jahrhundert,* ed. Kurt D. Schmidt and Ernst Wolf (Die Kirche in ihrer Geschichte: Ein Handbuch; Göttingen: Vandenhoeck & Ruprecht, 1966), 67–71. Also TRE 16:166–74. Jeremiah F. Ohl, *The Inner Mission: A Handbook for Christian Workers* (Philadelphia: General Council Publication House, 1911). Friedrich Mahling, *Die Innere Mission,* 2 vols. (Gütersloh: Bertelsmann, 1937).

26. Abdel R. Wentz, *Fliedner the Faithful* (Philadelphia: Board of Publication of the United Lutheran Church in America, 1936).

27. Martin Gerhardt, *Johann Hinrich Wichern,* 3 vols. (Hamburg: Agentur des Rauhen hauses, 1927–31). Gerald Christianson, "J. H. Wichern and the Rise of Lutheran Social Institutions," *Lutheran Quarterly* 19 (1967): 357–70.

28. See Margaret Bradfield, *The Good Samaritan: The Life and Work of Friederich von Bodelschwingh* (London: Marshall, Morgan & Scott, 1964). Collected works of Bodelschwingh in Alfred Adam, ed., *Friedrich Bodelschwingh: Ausgewählte Schriften,* 2 vols. (Bethel: Bethel-Verlag, 1958–64). Bernhard Gramlich, *Bodelschwingh, Bethel und die Barmherzigkeit* (Gütersloh: Mohn, 1964).

29. Blumhardt became world-famous through his exorcism of the demons he viewed as causes for mental illnesses. His blow-by-blow account of the cure of a woman named Gottliebin Dittus became a media event. His massive writings have been collected by Otto Bruder, ed., *Johann Christoph Blumhardt: Ausgewählte Schriften,* 3 vols. (Zürich, 1947–48). See also the biography by Friedrich Seebass, *Johann Christoph Blumhardt* (Hamburg, 1949).

30. Quoted in TRE 6:744.

31. For a summary of his ideas, see Hirsch, *Geschichte der neueren evangelischen Theologie,* 4:208–47. Quotation in TRE 16:170.

32. TRE 16:171.

33. Citations from Rothe's *Theologische Ethik* in RGG 5:1199.

34. RGG 4:1526.

35. See George H. Gerberding, *Life and Letters of W. H. Passavant* (Greenville, Pa: Young Lutheran, 1906), 195–96.

36. E. Clifford Nelson, ed., in collaboration with others, *The Lutherans in North America* (rev. ed.; Philadelphia: Fortress Press, 1980), 117.

37. Ibid., 118.

38. See Abdel R. Wentz, *Pioneer in Christian Unity: Samuel Simon Schmucker* (Philadelphia: Fortress Press, 1967). But Schmucker defined *unity* as an anti-Roman Catholic Protestant stance.

39. Samuel S. Schmucker, *Elements of Popular Theology, with Special Reference to the Doctrines of the Reformation* (Andover, Mass., 1834), iii–iv; quoted in Nelson, *Lutherans,* 130.

40. Nelson, *Lutherans,* 143. See also Douglas C. Stange, *Radicalism for Humanity: A Study of Lutheran Abolitionism* (St. Louis: Concordia, 1970).

41. See Enok Mortensen, *The Danish Lutheran Church in America: The History and Heritage of the American Evangelical Lutheran Church* (Studies in Church History, ser. 2, no. 25; Philadelphia: Board of Publication, Lutheran Church in America, 1967).

42. See Theodore C. Blegen, *Norwegian Migration to America, 1825–1860* (New York: Arno, 1969).

43. See G. Everett Arden, *Augustana Heritage: A History of the Augustana Synod* (Rock Island, Ill.: Augustana Book Concern, 1963).

44. Nelson, *Lutherans*, 175.

45. Ibid., 202–4. See also Mark A. Noll, *A History of Christianity in the United States and Canada* (Grand Rapids, Mich.: Eerdmans, 1992), 262–84.

46. Address to the "Association for Inner Mission" in Berlin in 1854. English text in August R. Suelflow, "Nietzsche and Schaff on American Lutheranism," *Concordia Historical Institute Quarterly* 23 (1951): 149–57. Long quotation in Nelson, *Lutherans*, 211–13. General treatment of tensions in Theodore G. Tappert, *Lutheran Confessional Theology in America, 1840–1880* (A Library of Protestant Thought; New York: Oxford University Press, 1972).

47. Philadelphia, 1855; text in Richard C. Wolf, *Documents of Lutheran Unity in America* (Philadelphia: Fortress Press, 1966). Five errors of the Augsburg Confession in Wolf, 103. See also the comparison of the Augsburg Confession and Schmucker's recension in Nelson, *Lutherans*, 222–23.

48. Wolf, *Documents*, 145.

49. Ibid., 170.

50. See Andrew S. Burgess, ed., *Lutheran World Mission* (Minneapolis: Augsburg, 1954); A. E. Thompson, *A Century of Jewish Missions* (Chicago: Revell, 1902); on "Negro Mission," see Dean Lueking, *Mission in the Making* (St. Louis: Concordia, 1964), 115–18; summary in Nelson, *Lutherans*, 279–84.

51. Nelson, *Lutherans*, 286–91.

52. Quoted in ibid., 308.

53. Nelson, *Lutherans*, 313–23.

54. Ibid., 323–24.

55. Ibid., 325–28.

56. Ibid., 294.

57. Luther D. Reed, *The Lutheran Liturgy: A Study of the Common Liturgy of the Lutheran Church in America* (rev. ed.; Philadelphia: Muhlenberg, 1959), 183–97; Nelson, *Lutherans*, 373.

58. Nelson, *Lutherans*, 364.

59. Quoted in ibid., 387, from the Minutes of 1911, 228.

60. See Robert Fortenbaugh, *The Development of the Synodical Polity of the Lutheran Church in America, to 1829* (Philadelphia: Fortress Press, 1926), 28.

61. An example is the work of J. M. Reu, *Thirty-five Years of Luther Research* (Chicago: Wartburg, 1917), summarizing the work of the Luther renaissance beginning with the famous Weimar Edition of the reformer's works in 1883.

62. Editorial in *Lutheran Standard*, October 13, 1917, 641.

63. Nelson, *Lutherans*, 395.

64. In a document called "Investiture." See Walter O. Forster, *Zion on the Mississippi: The Settlement of the Saxon Lutherans in Missouri, 1839–1841* (St. Louis: Concordia, 1953), 299–300; general history of the Missouri Synod in Walter A. Baepler, *A Century of Grace: A History of the Missouri Synod, 1847–1947* (St. Louis: Concordia, 1947); "Missouri-Synod" in RGG 4:1016–18.

65. See Lewis W. Spitz, *The Life of Dr. W. C. F. Walther* (St. Louis: Concordia, 1961); Nelson, *Lutherans*, 178–79.

66. Quoted in Nelson, *Lutherans*, 180.

67. Nelson, *Lutherans*, 180.

68. Ibid., 226.

69. Quoted in ibid., 248.

70. Quotations in ibid., 251.

71. Nelson, *Lutherans*, 255.

72. Lueking, *Mission in the Making*, 139.

73. Ibid., 187–88.

74. Stated at a meeting of the Missouri Synod in 1872. See A. C. Stellhorn, *Schools of the Lutheran Church—Missouri Synod* (St. Louis: Concordia, 1963), 176.

75. BC 655:93. The Lutheran point is that one must distinguish between the revealed will of God in Christ (promising salvation by faith) and the hidden will, which cannot be a subject of proper Christian theology. See BC 646:33. On the controversy, see Nelson, *Lutherans*, 313–22.

76. Quoted in Nelson, *Lutherans*, 315, n. 47.

77. Quoted in ibid., 316.

78. See the historical and contemporary importance of this "solution" in Eric W. Gritsch and Robert W. Jenson, *Lutheranism: The Theological Movement and Its Confessional Writings* (Philadelphia: Fortress Press, 1976), ch. 11, esp. 161–63.

79. C. F. W. Walther, *The Controversy Concerning Predestination*, trans. A. Crull (St. Louis: Concordia, 1881).

80. Both sets of theses can be found in Wolf, *Documents*, 199–204.

81. See *Freimaurerei* in RGG 2:1113–18.

82. Quoted in Nelson, *Lutherans*, 353. See also Theodore Graebner, *Dr. Francis Pieper: A Biographical Sketch* (St. Louis: Concordia, 1931).

83. Quoted in Nelson, 377.

84. Ibid., 447.

85. RGG 4:1422; Justo L. Gonzaléz, *A History of Christian Thought*, vol. 3, *From the Protestant Reformation to the Twentieth Century* (Nashville: Abingdon, 1975), 348. See also Martin Redeker, *Schleiermacher: Life and Thought*, trans. J. Wallhauser (Philadelphia: Fortress Press, 1973). Schleiermacher's most influential works are *On Religion: Speeches to Its Cultured Despisers*, trans. J. Oman (The Library of Religion and Culture; New York: Harper, 1958); and *The Christian Faith*, trans. H. R. Mackintosh, J. S. Stewart, et al. (Edinburgh: T. and T. Clark, 1928).

86. See the twenty-six volumes of his collected works: Georg W. F. Hegel, *Sämtliche Werke*, ed. H. G. Glockner, 26 vols. (Leipzig: Meiner, 1928). For a summary of his thought and influence, see Claude Welch, *Protestant Thought in the Nineteenth Century*, 2 vols. (New Haven, Conn.: Yale University Press, 1972–85), vol. 1, ch. 4. See also Gonzaléz, *A History of Christian Thought*, 3:362–64.

87. A summary of his work is found in Welch, *Protestant Thought*, 1:155–60. See also Peter C. Hodgson, *The Formation of Historical Theology: A Study of Ferdinand Christian Baur* (New York: Harper & Row, 1960).

88. Argued in Albrecht Ritschl's main study, *The Christian Doctrine of Justification and Reconciliation* (New York, 1900). See also David L. Mueller, *An Introduction to the Theology of Albrecht Ritschl* (Philadelphia: Westminster, 1969); and Philip J. Hefner, *Faith and the Vitalities of History: A Theological Study of the Work of Albrecht Ritschl* (New York: Harper & Row, 1966). For a summary of his thought, see Welch, *Protestant Thought*, vol. 2: ch. 1, and Gonzaléz, *A History of Christian Thought*, 3:374–77.

89. In Adolf von Harnack's popular tract *What Is Christianity?*, trans. T. B. Saunders (Fortress Texts in Modern Theology; Philadelphia: Fortress Press, 1957), 51. See also his classic work, *History of Dogma*, 7 vols. (London, 1896–99), summarized in his *Outlines of the History of Dogma*, trans. E. K. Mitchell (1893; Boston: Beacon, 1957). Sketch of his life and work in Welch, *Protestant Thought*, 146–52, 305–7.

90 Ernst Troeltsch, *The Social Teachings of the Christian Churches*, trans. O. Wyon, 2 vols. (New York: Macmillan, 1931). See also Welch, *Protestant Thought*, vol. 2, ch. 8.

91. Troeltsch, *Social Teachings*, 2:540.

92. David F. Strauss, *Leben Jesu*, 2 vols. (Tübingen, 1835–36), ET = *The Life of Jesus, Critically Examined*, trans. M. Evans (New York: Blanchard, 1855). For a detailed description of the intensive controversy, see Albert Schweitzer, *The Quest for the Historical Jesus: A Critical Study of Its Progress from Reimarus to Wrede*, trans. W. Montgomery (New York: Macmillan, 1968), chs. 7–9.

93. Ludwig Feuerbach, *The Essence of Christianity*, trans. G. Eliot (The Library of Religion and Culture. New York: Harper, 1957). See also Welch, *Protestant Thought*, 1:170–77.

94. Johann K. von Hofmann, *Schutzschriften für eine neue Weise, alte Wahrheit zu lehren*, 4 vols. (Erlangen, 1856–59).

95. Welch, *Protestant Thought*, 1:237.

96. On the Erlangen school, see Welch, *Protestant Thought*, 1:218–27.

97. See Welch, *Protestant Thought*, 1:273–82. Isaac Dorner's major work is *History of the Development of the Doctrine of the Person of Christ*, 4 vols. (Edinburgh, 1861–63).

98. Wilhelm Herrmann, *The Communion of the Christian with God*, trans. R. W. Stewart (1903; reprint, Philadelphia: Fortress Press, 1971). On Herrmann's theology, see Welch, *Protestant Thought*, 2:44–54.

99. English editions of Hans L. Martensen's works: *Christian Ethics*, 2 vols. (Edinburgh, 1882). German editions are *Die christliche Dogmatik* (Leipzig, 1856), and *Die christliche Ethik*, 3 vols. (Gotha, 1878). Summary of his work in Felix Flückinger and Wilhelm Anz, *Theologie und Philosophie im 19. Jahrhundert*, ed. Bernd Moeller (Die Kirche in ihrer Geschichte: Ein Handbuch; Göttingen: Vandenhoeck & Ruprecht, 1975), 65–66.

100. Søren Kierkegaard, *Attack on Christendom*, trans. W. Lowrie (Princeton, N.J.: Princeton University Press, 1968). See also Niels Thulstrup, *Kierkegaard and the Church in Denmark*, trans. F. H. Cryer (Copenhagen: Reitzel, 1984); and Edgar L. Allen, *Kierkegaard: His Life and Thought* (London: Nott, 1935). Summary in Welch, *Protestant Thought*, vol. 1, ch. 13.

101. Søren Kierkegaard, *Fear and Trembling*, trans. W. Lowrie (Princeton, N.J.: Princeton University Press, 1941).

102. See Gonzaléz, *A History of Christian Thought*, 3:372–73.

103. See Henric Schartau, *Henric Schartau and the Order of Grace: Biography by Henrik Hägglund and Fifteen Sermons by Henric Schartau*, trans. S. G. Hägglund (Rock Island, Ill.: Augustana Book Concern, 1928).

104. Wilhelm Dilthey's collected writings: *Wilhelm Dilthey Gesammelte Schriften*, 12 vols. (Leipzig: Teubner, 1914–36). See also Eric W. Gritsch, "Wilhelm Dilthey and the Interpretation of History," *The Lutheran Quarterly* 17 (1963): 58–69.

105. See Stephen Neill, *A History of Christian Missions*, vol. 6 of *The Pelican History of the Church*, 2d ed., rev. by O. Chadwick (New York: Penguin, 1986), 222–23; Kenneth S. Latourette, *A History of the Expansion of Christianity*, 7 vols. (New York, London: Harper & Brothers, 1937–45); Hans-Werner Gensichen, *Missionsgeschichte der neueren Zeit*, ed. Kurt D. Schmidt and Ernst Wolf (Die Kirche in ihrer Geschichte: Ein Handbuch; Göttingen: Vandenhoeck & Ruprecht, 1961).

106. Neill, *A History of Christian Missions*, 306. For Tranquebar see LCW, 217.

107. Nelson, *Lutherans*, 201–2. LCW, 205.

108. LCW, 207.

109. LCW, 213.

110. LCW, 227–28, 232.

111. See LCW, 253–55, and E. H. Proeve and H. F. W. Proeve, *A Work of Love and Sacrifice: The Story of the Mission among the Dieri Tribe at Cooper's Creek* (Point Pas, Aus., 1952).

112. LCW, 255.

113. LCW, 263–64

114. Nelson, *Lutherans*, 280.

115. Ibid., 159–60.

116. Ibid., 173. This Lutheran church originated in 1900 in Milwaukee, Wisconsin, consisting of a group of independent congregations linked to the Evangelical Lutheran Free Church of Norway.

117. Ibid., 169–70.

118. Nelson, *Lutherans*, 182, 280–81.

119. LCW, 187.

120. Ibid., 59–61.

121. Ibid., 64–67.

122. Ibid., 68–69.

123. Ibid., 72–74.

124. Ibid., 84. See also Ernst Jaeschke, *Bruno Gutmann: His Life, His Thoughts, His Work. An Early Attempt of a Theology in an African Context* (Makumira Publications 3/4; Erlangen: Verlag der Ev.-Luth. Mission, 1958).

125. LCW, 89, 100.

126. Ibid., 137, 145; Nelson, *Lutherans,* 202.

127. LCW, 273–75.

128. Ibid., 290, 293.

129. Ibid., 461, 474–75, 477, 482.

130. Ibid., 485.

131. Ibid., 486, 488.

132. Ibid., 510.

133. Ibid., 511–12.

134. Ibid., 526.

135. Ibid., 537–58, 540.

136. Ibid., 543.

137. Ibid., 547.

138. Ibid., 550.

139. Details and a sketch of German Lutheran attitudes during the war in Kupisch, *Deutschland im 19. und 20. Jahrhundert,* 92–97.

140. Ibid., 93, n. 5. Based on a paper on "eternal peace" presented by the Munich scholar of international law, Karl von Stengel, at the First Peace Conference in the Hague, Netherlands, in 1899.

141. Kupisch, *Deutschland im 19. und 20. Jahrhundert,* 95; quotation from a massive collection of war sermons.

142. Ibid., 94.

143. Quoted in ibid., 97.

144. Theodore E. Schmauk, "The Great War of Germany against Europe," *Lutheran Church* Review 33 (October 1914): 704. On U.S. Lutheran attitudes, see also Nelson, *Lutherans,* 395–405.

145. See Carl S. Meyer, ed., *Readings in the History of the Lutheran Church–Missouri Synod* (St. Louis: Concordia, 1964), 236.

146. Nelson, *Lutherans,* 397, n. 21.

147. Ibid., 398.

148. Ibid.

149. For a history of the council, see Frederick K. Wentz, *Lutherans in Concert* (Minneapolis: Augsburg, 1968).

150. Nelson, *Lutherans,* 405.

151. Ibid., 407.

152. Neill, *A History of Christian Missions,* 403–4.

153. LCW, 84.

7. New Ventures, 1918–

1. See Bengt Sundkler, *Nathan Söderblom: His Life and Work* (Lund: Gleerup, 1968).

2. Reported in Ruth Rouse and Stephen C. Neill, eds., *A History of the Ecumenical Movement, 1517–1968,* 2 vols. (3d ed.; Geneva: World Council of Churches, 1986), 1:532.

3. Quoted in Rouse and Neill, *A History of the Ecumenical Movement*, 1:548.For the work in Stockholm, see ibid., 1:548–50.

4. On Lausanne, see Rouse and Neill, *A History of the Ecumenical Movement*, 1:420–25.

5. Sundkler, *Nathan Söderblom*, 231.

6. Nathan Söderblom, *The Living God* (Edinburgh: T. and T. Clark, 1933).

7. That is the judgment of Rouse and Neill, *A History of the Ecumenical Movement*, 2:546.

8. E. Clifford Nelson, ed., in collaboration with others, *The Lutherans in North America* (rev. ed.; Philadelphia: Fortress Press, 1980), 439–42.

9. Ibid., 467.

10. On his ecumenical work, see Eberhard Bethge, *Dietrich Bonhoeffer: A Biography*, 2d ed., rev. by Victoria J. Barnett (Minneapolis: Fortress Press, 2000), 472–84.

11. Statement in the paper *Christliche Welt* (1931): 605; English excerpts in Bethge, *Dietrich Bonhoeffer*, 195–96. Bonhoeffer opposed the theologians' statement.

12. Quotation from the twenty-four-point party program of February 14, 1920. See Ernst C. Helmreich, *The German Churches under Hitler: Background, Struggle, and Epilogue* (Detroit: Wayne State University Press, 1979), 123.

13. Helmreich, *German Churches*, 139.

14. Details in ibid., chs. 6–7. English text of the platform in Franklin H. Littell, *The German Phoenix: Men and Movements in the Church of Germany* (Garden City, N.Y.: Doubleday, 1960), Appendix A. German text: "Richtlinien der Glaubensbewegung 'Deutsche Christen' vom 26. Mai, 1932," *Kirchliches Jahrbuch für die evangelische Kirche in Deutschland* (1933–44): 4–7.

15. See James Bentley, *Martin Niemöller 1892–1984* (Oxford: Oxford University Press, 1989).

16. German text in *Kirchliches Jahrbuch* (1933–44): 63–65; ET in Arthur C. Cochrane, *The Church's Confession under Hitler* (Philadelphia: Fortress Press, 1962), 238–42. See also Eric W. Gritsch, "Barth, Barmen and America: Lessons of Hindsight," *Katallagete* 10, 1–3 (fall 1987): 40–42; the issue was a special edition that included a copy of the original text of the declaration.

17. English text in Bethge, *Dietrich Bonhoeffer*, 600. On the debate, see Helmreich, *The German Churches under Hitler*, 227–32.

18. RGG 4:947–48.

19. Helmreich, *German Churches*, 421. German text in *Kirchliches Jahrbuch* (1945–48): 26–27.

20. See Martin Schwarz Lausten, *A Church History of Denmark* (Burlington, Vt.: Ashgate, 2001), 300.

21. See Bjarne Höye and Trygve M. Ager, *The Fight of the Norwegian Church against Nazism* (New York: Macmillan, 1943).

22. See Alex Johnson, *Eivind Berggrav: God's Man of Suspense*, trans. K. Jordheim with H. L. Overholt (Minneapolis: Augsburg, 1960).

23. Augsburg Confession 16:7; BC 50.

24. See Robert F. Goeckel, *The Lutheran Church and the East German State: Political Conflict and Change under Ulbricht and Honecker* (Ithaca, NY: Cornell University Press, 1990).

Excellent German study with many illustrations in Peter Maser, *Die Kirchen in der DDR* (Bonn: Deutsche Zeitbilder, 2000).

25. "The Ten Commandments of Socialist Morality" were proclaimed by Walter Ulbricht in 1958. See *The Evangelical Church in Berlin and the Soviet Zone of Germany*, trans. P. Lynch (Witten: Eckart, 1959), 7.

26. See Maser, *Die Kirchen in der DDR*, 116–17.

27. *Day Is Dawning: The Story of Bishop Otto Dibelius, Based on His Proclamations and Authentic Documents* (Philadelphia: Christian Education Press, 1956).

28. See Tibor Fabiny, *A Short History of Lutheranism in Hungary* (Budapest, 1997), 29–37; Laszlo G. Terray, *He Could Not Do Otherwise: Bishop Lajos Ordass, 1901–1978*, trans. E. W. Gritsch (Grand Rapids, Mich.: Eerdmans, 1997).

29. Terray, *He Could Not Do Otherwise*, 84.

30. Biographical details in Eberhard Busch, *Karl Barth: His Life from Letters and Autobiographical Texts* (Grand Rapids, Mich.: Eerdmans, 1976). See Barth's massive *Church Dogmatics*, 12 vols., trans. G. T. Thomson et al. (Edinburgh: T. and T. Clark, 1936–2000). Helpful summary in Justo L. González, *A History of Christian Thought*, vol. 3, *From the Protestant Reformation to the Twentieth* Century (Nashville: Abingdon, 1975), 432–40. Brief introduction and sample readings in Carl E. Braaten and Robert W. Jenson, eds., *A Map of Twentieth-Century Theology: Readings from Karl Barth to Radical Pluralism* (Minneapolis: Fortress Press, 1995), 21–50.

31. Karl Barth, *Epistle to the Romans*, trans. E. C. Hoskyns from the 6th ed. (London: Oxford University Press, 1968).

32. *Theologische Existenz Heute 47* (1936): 56.

33. TRE 5:25.

34. Rudolf Bultmann's collected essays are in *Kerygma and Myth*, ed. H. W. Bartsch (New York: Harper & Row, 1961). See also H. P. Owen, *Revelation and Existence: A Study in the Theology of Rudolf Bultmann* (Cardiff: University of Wales Press, 1957). See also González, *A History of Christian Thought*, 3:440–45. Best summary in German by Eberhard Hauschildt, "Rudolf Bultmann" in *Profile des Luthertums: Biographien zum 20. Jahrhundert*, ed. W.-D. Hauschildt (Die lutherische Kirche, Geschichte und Gestalten 20; Gütersloh: Gütersloher, 1998), 91–115.

35. Bultmann, *Kerygma and Myth*, 34.

36. Hauschildt, "Rudolf Bultmann," 103.

37. See the summary of their views with excerpts from their work in Braaten and Jenson, *A Map of Twentieth-Century Theology*, 130–46.

38. Ibid., 149–60.

39. See Walter Altmann, *Luther and Liberation: A Latin American Perspective*, trans. M. M. Solberg (Minneapolis: Fortress Press, 1992). On liberation theology, see González, *A History of Christian Thought*, 3:468–71.

40. Braaten and Jenson, *A Map of Twentieth-Century Theology*, 247.

41. Ibid., 248. For the systematic vision of such a life, see Werner Elert, *The Structure of Lutheranism*, 2 vols., trans. W. A. Hansen (St. Louis: Concordia, 1962).

42. TRE 21:54.

43. See Gustaf Aulén, *Christus Victor*, trans. A. G. Herbert (London: SPCK; New York: Macmillan, 1937); Anders Nygren, *Agape and Eros*, trans. P. S. Watson (Philadelphia: Westminster, 1953). Summary and excerpt of his work in Braaten and Jenson, *A Map of Twentieth Century Theology*, 249–51, 262–68. Regin Prenter, *Spiritus Creator*, trans. J. M. Jensen (Philadelphia: Muhlenberg, 1953). On the Lundensian school, see Gonzaléz, *A History of Christian Thought*, 3:445–47.

44. See Paul Tillich, *Systematic Theology* (3 vols., Chicago: University of Chicago Press, 1951–57). His work is sketched in Gonzaléz, *A History of Christian Thought*, 3:457–59. See also Braaten and Jenson, *A Map of Twentieth-Century Theology*, 211–12, 213–22.

45. See Eberhard Jüngel, *The Doctrine of the Trinity: God's Being Is in Becoming*, trans. H. Harris (Scottish Journal of Theology Monograph Supplements 4; Grand Rapids, Mich.: Eerdmans, 1976); *Justification: The Heart of the Christian Faith*, trans. J. F. Cayzer (Edinburgh: T. and T. Clark, 2001); Robert W. Jenson, *Systematic Theology*, 2 vols. (New York: Oxford University Press, 2001).

46. See Carl E. Braaten and Robert W. Jenson, eds., *Christian Dogmatics*, 2 vols. (Minneapolis: Fortress Press, 1984); Ted Peters, *God—The World's Future: Systematic Theology for a New Era* (2d ed.; Minneapolis: Fortress Press, 2000); Philip J. Hefner, *The Human Factor: Evolution, Culture, and Religion* (Minneapolis: Fortress Press, 1993).

47. *Proceedings of the Fourth Assembly, July 30–August 11, 1963* (Berlin and Hamburg: Lutheran World Federation, 1965). Summary in "Helsinki 1963," *Lutheran World 11* (1964): 1–36. Study document "On Justification" (New York: National Lutheran Council, n.d.).

48. "Justification Today," Document 75 in *Lutheran World 12*, 1 Supplement (1965): 1–11. On the worldwide reactions, see Abdel R. Wentz, "Lutheran World Federation," in *The Encyclopedia of the Lutheran Church*, ed. J. Bodensieck (Minneapolis: Augsburg, 1965), 2:1428–29. See also the summary in *From Federation to Communion: The History of the Lutheran World Federation*, ed. Jens H. Schjoring, Prasanna Kumari, and Norman A. Hjelm (Minneapolis: Fortress Press, 1997), 377–80. A German summary and analysis are offered by Albrecht Peters, "Systematische Besinnung zu einer Neuinterpretation der reformatorischen Rechtfertigungslehre," *Rechtfertigung im neuzeitlichen Lebenszusammenhang: Studien zur Neuinterpretation der Rechtfertigungslehre*, ed. W. Lohff and C. Walther (Gütersloh: Mohn, 1974), 107–25.

49. See Nelson, *Lutherans*, 457–61. On the Niebuhrs, see Gonzaléz, *A History of Christian Thought*, 3:455–57.

50. H. Richard Niebuhr, *The Kingdom of God in America* (New York: Harper, 1937), 193.

51. See *From Federation to Communion*, 6. On the origins of LWF, see E. Clifford Nelson, *The Rise of World Lutheranism: An American Perspective* (Philadelphia: Fortress Press, 1982).

52. Text of 1947 constitution in *From Federation to Communion*, 527–30.

53. On the matter of confessional integrity, see BC 637:10.

54. *From Federation to Communion*, 72.

55. Ibid., 73.

56. Ibid., 409.

57. See Terray, *He Could Not Do Otherwise*, and *From Federation to Communion*, 30–31.

58. For a devastating critique of this diaconical theology, see Vilmos Vajta, *Die "diakonische Theologie" im Gesellschaftssystem Ungarns* (Frankfurt am Main: Lembeck, 1987).

59. *Proceedings,* 11, cited in *From Federation to Communion,* 411. Summary of Kaldy's life and work in *From Federation to Communion,* 464–71.

60. English text in John H. Leith, ed., *Creeds of the Churches* (3d ed.; Atlanta: John Knox, 1982), 556–66. See also Gerhardus C. Oosthuizen, *Theological Discussions and Confessional Developments in the Churches of Asia and Africa* (Franeker: Wever, 1958); LCW, 232–35.

61. *From Federation to Communion,* 55.

62. *Eucharistic Hospitality,* Institute for Ecumenical Research (Strasbourg: Foundation [Institute] for Inter-Confessional [Ecumenical] Research, 1974). It was established by the Helsinki assembly in Helsinki in 1963. See *From Federation to Communion,* 380.

63. Quotation from *Eucharistic Hospitality,* 2:5. An analysis of this intercommunion is offered by Marc Lienhard, "Miteinander kommunizieren in gemischten Ehen," *Lutherische Monatshefte* 1 (1973): 49.

64. *From Federation to Communion,* 544.

65. Ibid., 328. Based on a team study headed by Ulrich Duchrow, ed., *Lutheran Churches—Salt or Mirror of Society? Case Studies of the Theory and Practice of the Two Kingdoms Doctrine* (Geneva: Lutheran World Federation, 1977).

66. *From Federation to Communion,* 331.

67. See the summary of critical discussion and a contemporary Lutheran view of peace by Eric W. Gritsch, "Christian Unity and Peace Making: A Lutheran Perspective," in *The Fragmentation of the Church and Its Unity in Peacemaking,* edited by J. Gros and J. D. Rempel (Grand Rapids, Mich.: Eerdmans, 2001), 16–33. See also *From Federation to Communion,* 340–41.

68. BC 42–43.

69. On the Lutheran-Catholic dialogue in the sixteenth century, see Raitt, "From Augsburg to Trent," in *Lutherans and Catholics in Dialogue,* vol. 7, *Justification by Faith,* edited by H. G. Anderson, T. A. Murphy, J. A. Burgess (Minneapolis: Augsburg, 1985), 200–217. On the Lutheran-Reformed dialogue, see *Dictionary of the Ecumenical Movement,* ed. N. Lossky (Geneva: World Council of Churches; Grand Rapids, Mich.: Eerdmans, 1991), 636. On relations to Orthodoxy, see George Mastrantonis, *Augsburg and Constantinople: The Correspondence between the Tübingen Theologians and Patriarch Jeremiah II of Constantinople and the Augsburg Confession* (The Archbishop Iakovos Library of Ecclesiastical and Historical Sources 7; Brookline, Mass.: Holy Cross Orthodox, 1982).

70. *Lutherans and Catholics in Dialogue,* 10 vols., edited by H. G. Anderson, P. Empie, T. A. Murphy, et al. (Minneapolis: Augsburg Fortress, 1965–93).

71. See *Growth in Agreement: Reports and Agreed Statements of Ecumenical Conversations on a World Level,* ed. H. Meyer and L. Vischer (New York: Paulist; Geneva: World Council of Churches): "The Malta Report" (1972); "All under One Christ" (1984); "Martin Luther: Witness to Jesus Christ" (1983); "The Eucharist" (1978); "Ways to Community" (1980); "The Ministry in the Church" (1981); "Facing Unity" (1985).

72. *Kirchengemeinschaft in Wort und Sakrament* (1984). See also *Communion, the Lord's Supper and the Ministry of the Church* (Oslo, 1982 and 1986); *Marriage and Family in the*

Christian Viewpoint, Ecumenical Convergence on Baptism and Church Membership, The Office of the Bishop (Stockholm, 1974, 1978, 1988).

73. See, for example, the joint Lutheran-Catholic study guide by Mark Edwards and George Tavard, *Luther: A Reformer for the Churches* (Philadelphia: Fortress Press; New York: Paulist, 1983) and the Catholic publication of Eric W. Gritsch, ed., *Martin Luther: Faith in Christ and the Gospel: Selected Spiritual Writings* (Hyde Park, N.Y.: New City, 1996).

74. On Luther's rehabilitation, see Eric W. Gritsch, "Luther: From Rejection to Rehabilitation," in *Promoting Unity: Themes in Lutheran-Catholic Dialogue,* ed. H. G. Anderson and J. R. Crumley (Minneapolis: Augsburg, 1989), 9–16. On the legal Catholic issues, see Erwin Iserloh, "Aufhebung des Lutherbannes? Kirchengeschichtliche Überlegungen zu einer aktuellen Frage," in *Lutherprozess und Lutherbann: Vorgeschichte, Ergebnis, Nachwirkung,* ed. R. Bäumer (Katholisches Leben und Kirchenreform im Zeitalter der Glaubensspaltung 32; Münster: Aschendorff, 1972), 69–80.

75. "Joint Declaration on the Doctrine of Justification" (Geneva and Rome: Lutheran World Federation and Pontifical Council for Promoting Christian Unity, 1995), quotation, Section 18; reference to condemnations, Section 41. More than 150 German Lutheran theologians opposed the consensus with radical polemical language. See the massive collection of the texts in *Dokumentation* (Evangelischer Pressedienst, November 1997 to March 1998, Frankfurt am Main).

76. "Full communion" is the final stage of dialogue. See *Ecumenism: The Vision of the Evangelical Lutheran Church in America* (Minneapolis: Augsburg Fortress, 1994); *Marburg Revisited: A Reexamination of Lutheran and Reformed Traditions,* ed. P. C. Empie and J. I. McCord (Minneapolis: Augsburg, 1966); *A Common Calling: The Witness of Our Reformation Churches in North America Today,* ed. K. F. Nickle and T. F. Lull (Minneapolis: Augsburg Fortress, 1993).

77. *Dictionary of the Ecumenical Movement,* 636–38. See also *A Reexamination of the Lutheran and Reformed Traditions,* 4 vols. (New York: National Lutheran Council, 1964–66). Full communion in the United States was achieved in 2000 between the Evangelical Lutheran Church in America and the Reformed churches (Presbyterian, Dutch Reformed, and United Church of Christ).

78. See the history of the dialogues in *Dictionary of the Ecumenical Movement,* 20–21. Text of *Pullach Report* in *Growth in Agreement: Reports and Agreed Statements of Ecumenical Conversations on a World Level,* ed. H. Meyer and L. Vischer (New York: Paulist; Geneva: World Council of Churches, 1984), 13–34; *Meissen Statement* in *Meissen 1988: Relations between the Church of England, the Federation of the Evangelical Churches in the German Democratic Republic, and the Evangelical Church in Germany in the Federal Republic of Germany* (London, 1988). Statements of the U.S. dialogue from 1969 to 1991 in *Growing Consensus: Church Dialogues in the United States, 1962–1991,* ed. J. A. Burgess and J. Gros (Ecumenical Documents 5; New York: Paulist, 1995), 173–338.

79. *Baptism, Eucharist and Ministry* (Faith and Order Paper 111; Geneva: World Council of Churches, 1982), par. 35, 36, 38.

80. The text in *Growing Consensus* (325–38) was revised before the formal Lutheran adoption; it is available at the headquarters of both churches.

81. Text in "Occasional Paper no. 3" (The Council for Christian Unity of the General Synod of the Church of England). See also Michael Root, "The Concordat and the Northern European Poorvo Statement: Different Paths to the Same Goal," in *A Commentary on "Concordat of Agreement,"* ed. J. E. Griffiss and D. F. Martensen (Minneapolis: Augsburg; Cincinnati: Forward Movement, 1994), 138–50.

82. See *Dictionary of the Ecumenical Movement,* 635–36; *Report of the Consultation of Lutheran/Orthodox Dialogues* (Geneva: Lutheran World Federation, 1975).

83. See a summary of the dialogue in *Dictionary of the Ecumenical Movement,* 83–84. German results in "Texte aus der VELKD (vereinigte evangelisch-lutherische Kirche Deutschlands)," *Lutherisches Kirchenamt,* 17 (1981); U.S. results in "Lutheran-Baptist Dialogue," *American Baptist Quarterly* 1:2 (December 1982): 103–12.

84 See *The Church: A Community of Grace,* final report of the LWF/WMC Joint Commission (Geneva, 1984). On the work in the United States, see *Growing Consensus,* 112–28.

85. *Growing Consensus,* 169–72.

86. See *Stepping Stones to Further Jewish-Lutheran Relations. Key Lutheran Statements,* ed. H. H. Ditmanson (Minneapolis: Augsburg Fortress, 1990).

87. See, for example, Joseph A. Burgess, ed., *Lutherans in Ecumenical Dialogue: A Reappraisal* (Minneapolis: Augsburg Fortress, 1990).

88. All statistics are from LWF *Information* 1 (Geneva: Lutheran World Federation, 2001). General survey of Lutheran churches in the world in TRE 21:607–17.

89. LWF *Information,* 8 (Geneva: Lutheran World Federation, 1999).

90. See the fascinating narrative of the Ethiopian convert Emmanuel Abraham, *Reminiscences of My Life* (Oslo: Lunde, 1995). See also the point of view of the Zimbabwe theologian Ambrose Moyo, "Whither Lutheranism? Lutheranism in Africa," *Word and World* 11 (1991): 257–64. On Tanzania, see Gerhard Mellinghoff, ed., *Lutherische Kirche in Tanzania: Ein Handbuch* (Erlanger Taschenbücher 39; Erlangen: Ev.-Luth. Mission, 1986). Per Larsson, *Bishop Josia Kibira of Bukoba in an International Perspective* (Nairobi, Kenya: Uzima; Dodoma, Tanzania: Central Tanganyika, 1992). Biographical sketch in *From Federation to Communion,* 457–63.

91. See Karsten Nissen, "Whither Lutheranism? Lutheran Churches of Western Europe," *Word and World* 11, no. 3 (1991): 253.

92. Nissen, "Whither Lutheranism?" 255.

93. *LWF Information* 16–17 (Geneva: Lutheran World Federation, 1998), 10.

94. Rainer Stahl, "Whither Lutheranism? An Eastern European Perspective," *Word and World* 11 (1991): 243–47. See also Fabiny, *A Short History of Lutheranism in Hungary;* Grete Mecenseffy, *Geschichte des Protestantismus in Österreich* (Graz: Böhlaus, 1956).

95. Nelson, *Lutherans,* 261.

96. TRE 21:614.

97. See a Japanese point of view by Yoshikazu Tokuzen, "Whither Lutheranism? An Asian Perspective," *Word and World* 11 (1991): 265–68. See also Benjamin P. Huddle, *History of the Lutheran Church in Japan* (New York: Board of Foreign Missions of the United Lutheran Church in America, 1958). On Papua New Guinea, see Christian Keysser, *A People Reborn,*

trans. A. Allin and J. Kuder (Pasadena, Calif.: William Carey Library, 1980). On Lutherans in ecumenical dialogue in India, see Herbert E. Hoefer, ed., *The Augsburg Confession and Ecumenism in India* (Madras: Gurukul Lutheran Theological College and Research Institute, 1980).

98. See Everard Leske, *For Faith and Freedom: The Story of Lutherans and Lutheranism in Australia, 1838–1966* (Adelaide, So. Australia: Openbook, 1966); Jean A. King, *The Lutheran Story: A Brief History of the Lutheran Church in New Zealand, 1843–1993* (Palmerston North, N.Z.: Lutheran Church of New Zealand, 1994).

99. See Walter Altmann "Whither Lutheranism? Notes from a Latin American Perspective," *Word and World* 11 (1991): 269–75.

100. See the summary of the thesis in *The Westminster Dictionary of Church History*, ed. J. C. Brauer (Philadelphia: Westminster, 1971), 344–47. See also the same dictionary's definition of *denomination* as a competitive religious group, 262–63. Frederick J. Turner, *The Frontier in American History* (New York: Holt, Rinehart and Winston, 1962). The link to the rise of denominationalism was established by William W. Sweet, *Religion on the American Frontier, 1783–1840*, 4 vols. (New York: Holt, 1931; Chicago: University of Chicago Press, 1939, 1946; New York: Cooper Square, 1964). How nonreligious factors have the greatest influence in the establishment of denominations has been shown by H. Richard Niebuhr, *The Social Sources of Denominationalism* (New York: Meridian, 1959).

101. See the list in Nelson, *Lutherans*, 459.

102. Quotation in James E. Adams, *Preus of Missouri and the Great Lutheran Civil War* (New York: Harper & Row, 1977), 20. On the debate and its tragic resolution, see also Frederick W. Danker, *No Room in the Brotherhood: The Preus-Otten Purge of Missouri* (St. Louis: Concordia, 1977); summary in Nelson, *Lutherans*, 530–35. The position of the Lutheran Church–Missouri Synod is not supported by the Lutheran Confessions, which teach "adherence to the prophetic and apostolic writings of the Old and New Testaments" (not to the total literature of the Bible). BC 527:3.

103. Nelson, *Lutherans*, 482; Winthrop S. Hudson, *American Protestantism* (Chicago: University of Chicago Press, 1961), 177.

104. See Todd W. Nichol, "Whither Lutheranism? A North American Perspective," *Word and World* 11, no. 3 (1991), 285. A treatment of various issues and possible solutions is offered in Carl E. Braaten, *The New Church Debate: Issues Facing American Lutheranism* (Philadelphia: Fortress Press, 1983).

105. Nelson, *Lutherans*, 359.

106. Ibid., 539–40.

107. BC 37 and 61.

108. Preface to the Augsburg Confession, BC 32:9–11.

109. Conclusion of Part One, Augsburg Confession, BC 59:1.

110. Augsburg Confession, 8:1, BC 43, italics added.

111. The designations *culture* and *cult* have the same root in the Latin verb, *colere*, meaning "to cultivate" a way of life including ritual and worship. That is why the Augsburg Confession speaks of ceremonies and human traditions as integral parts of daily living.

112. Augsburg Confession 7:3–4, BC 43.

113. See "Jewish Christians" in *The Westminster Dictionary of Church History*, 455–56; also "Arians," 58–59; "Eastern Schism," 746–47. On the evolving Lutheran confession, see TRE 19:420–26.

114. WA 30/3:160–71. LW 38:15–89. Text, 85–89.

115. *A Common Calling*, 50.

116. TRE 19:421.

117. Ernst Käsemann, "Begründet der neutestamentliche Kanon die Einheit der Kirche?" in *Exegetische Versuche und Besinnungen*, 2 vols. (Göttingen: Vandenhoeck & Ruprecht, 1960), 1:214–23.

118. See Arthur C. Repp Sr., *Luther's Catechism Comes to America: Theological Effects on the Issues of the Small Catechism in or for America Prior to 1850* (ATLA Monograph Series 18; Metuchen, N.J.: Scarecrow; Philadelphia: American Theological Library Association, 1982), 150.

119. See "Konfessionalismus" in TRE 19:430 and "Kulturprotestantismus" in TRE 20:230–43. Wilhelm Löhe defended "confessionalism" by introducing a controversial formula for subscribing to the enduring Christian truth disclosed in the Lutheran Confessions: they are not only true "insofar" *(quatenus)* as they agree with Holy Scripture but "because" *(quia)* they do, TRE 19:427.

120. On this interaction, see the classic study of H. Richard Niebuhr, *Christ and Culture* (New York: Harper, 1956).

121. See the global study of LWF, *Between Vision and Reality: Lutheran Churches in Transition*, ed. Wolfgang Greive, LWF Documentation No. 47 (Geneva: Lutheran World Federation, 2001).

122. Offertory in the celebration of Holy Communion from the *Lutheran Book of Worship* (Minneapolis: Augsburg, 1978), 66.

Conclusion: Forward to Luther?

1. Assembly proceedings cited in *From Federation to Communion: The History of the Lutheran World Federation*, ed. J. H. Schjoring, P. Kumari, and N. A. Hjelm (Minneapolis: Fortress Press, 1997), 426, 427.

2. Ibid., 29–30.

3. Ibid., 32.

4. Ibid., 31.

5. "The Symbols or Creeds of the Christian Church," 1538. WA 50:272.30–273.1. LW 34:215.

6. "Lectures on Genesis," 1535/36. WA 42:376. LW 2:163.

7. I know a teacher who suffered from an inferiority complex. He thought that all others were better teachers, and he became paralyzed in his vocation. He could no longer teach. After years of unsuccessful therapy, he switched therapists and got a second opinion. "I have a diagnosis for you. You do not have an inferiority complex. You *are* inferior." The reality

check made it possible for him to return to teaching, not as the best of all teachers, but as a wise one who discovered the power of weakness.

8. Martin E. Marty, "The Church and Its Polity," in *Theology in the Life of the Church*, ed. R. W. Bertram (Philadelphia: Fortress Press, 1966), 255–56.

9. Augsburg Confession 7:2, BC 43.

10. See Hans Sachs, *Die Wittenbergisch Nachtigall* (The Wittenberg nightingale) (Wittenberg, 1523). RGG 5:1265.

Bibliography

Aarflot, Andreas. *Hans Nielsen Hauge: His Life and Message.* Minneapolis: Augsburg, 1979.

Abraham, Emmanuel. *Reminiscences of My Life.* Oslo: Lunde, 1995.

Adam, Alfred, ed. *Friedrich von Bodelschwingh: Ausgewählte Schriften.* 2 vols. Bethel: Bethel-Verlag, 1958–64.

Adams, James E. *Preus of Missouri and the Great Lutheran Civil War.* New York: Harper & Row, 1977.

Aland, Kurt, ed. *95 Theses: With the Pertinent Documents from the History of the Reformation.* St. Louis: Concordia, 1967.

The Albany Protocol: Wilhelm Christoph Berkenmeyer's Chronicle of Lutheran Affairs in New York Colony, 1731-1750. Translated by S. Hart and S. G. Hart-Runeman. Edited by J. P. Dern. Ann Arbor, Mich.: n.p., 1971.

Allchin, A. M., D. Jasper, J. H. Schjorring, and K. Stephenson, eds. *Heritage and Prophecy: Grundtvig and the English-Speaking World.* Skrifter udgivet af Grundtvig-selskabet, 24. Aarhus, Denmark: Aarhus University Press, 1993.

Allen, E. L. *Kierkegaard: His Life and Thought.* London: Nott, 1935.

Altmann, Walter. "Whither Lutheranism? Notes from a Latin American Perspective," *Word and World* 11 (1991): 269–75.

———. *Luther and Liberation: A Latin American Perspective.* Translated by M. M. Solberg. Minneapolis: Fortress Press, 1992.

Andersen, Niels K. *Confessio Hafniensis: Den kobenhavnske Bekendelse af 1530.* Copenhagen: Gad, 1954.

———. "The Reformation in Scandinavia and in the Baltic." In *The New Cambridge Modern History.* Vol. 2, *The Reformation, 1520–1559.* Edited by G. R. Elton. Cambridge: Cambridge University Press, 1990. 134–60.

Arbusow, Leonid, Jr. *Die Einführung der Reformation in Liv-, Est-, und Kurland.* Leipzig: Vermittlungsverlag, 1921.

Arden, G. Everett. *Augustana Heritage: A History of the Augustana Synod.* Rock Island, Ill.: Augustana Book Concern, 1963.

———. *Four Northern Lights: Men Who Shaped Scandinavian Churches.* Minneapolis: Augsburg, 1964.

Arndt, John. *Evangelienpostille.* 1616.

———. *True Christianity.* Translated by P. Erb. New York: Paulist, 1979.

Arnold, Gottfried. *Die Erste Liebe der Gemeinden Christi.* Frankfurt am Main, 1696.

———. *Unparteiische Kirchen-und Ketzergeschichte.* Frankfurt am Main, 1699–70.

Asheim, Ivar, and Victor R. Gold, eds. *Episcopacy in the Lutheran Church? Studies in the Development of the Office of Church Leadership.* Philadelphia: Fortress Press, 1970.

Aslakssen, Cort. *Physica et Ethica Mosaica.* 1614.

Augustijn, Cornelis. *Erasmus: His Life, Works, and Influence*. Translated by J. C. Grayson. Toronto: University of Toronto Press, 1991.

Aulén, Gustaf. *Christus Victor*. Translated by A. G. Herbert. London: SPCK; New York: Macmillan, 1931.

Bachmann, E. Theodore, and Mercia Brenne Bachmann. *Lutheran Churches in the World: A Handbook*. Minneapolis: Augsburg, 1989.

Baepler, Walter A. *A Century of Grace: A History of the Missouri Synod, 1847–1947*. St. Louis: Concordia, 1947.

Bainton, Roland H. "The Left Wing of the Reformation." *Journal of Religion* 21 (1941): 124–34.

———. *Here I Stand: A Life of Martin Luther*. New York: Abingdon-Cokesbury, 1950.

———. "Luther on Birds, Dogs and Babies." In *Martin Luther Lectures*. Vol. 1, *Luther Today*. Edited by Roland H. Bainton and others. Decorah, Ia.: Luther College Press, 1957. 3–12.

———. "Luther's Attitude on Religious Liberty." In *Collected Papers in Church History*. Vol. 2: *Studies on the Reformation*. Boston: Beacon, 1963. 20–45.

———. "Katharine von Bora." In *Women of the Reformation in Germany and Italy*. Minneapolis: Augsburg, 1971. 23–43.

Baptism, Eucharist, and Ministry. Faith and Order Paper 111. Geneva: World Council of Churches, 1982.

Barry, C. J., ed. *Readings in Church History*. 3 vols. Westminster, Md.: Newman, 1960–65.

Barth, Karl. *Church Dogmatics*. Translated by G. T. Thomson et al. 12 vols. Edinburgh: T. and T. Clark, 1936–2000.

———. *Epistle to the Romans*. Translated by E. C. Hoskyns from the 6th edition. London: Oxford University Press, 1968.

Baur, Jörg. *Die Bekenntnisschriften der evangelisch-lutherischen Kirche*. 3d ed. Göttingen: Vandenhoeck & Ruprecht, 1930.

———. *Die Vernunft zwischen Ontologie und Evangelium: Eine Untersuchung zur Theologie Johann Andreas Quenstedts*. Gütersloh: Mohn, 1962.

Bentley, James. *Martin Niemöller 1892–1984*. Oxford: Oxford University Press, 1989.

Benz, Ernst. "Ecumenical Relations between Boston Puritanism and German Pietism: Cotton Mather and August Hermann Francke." *Harvard Theological Review* 54 (1961): 159–93.

Bergendoff, Conrad John Immanuel. *Olavus Petri and the Ecclesiastical Transformation in Sweden, 1521–1552: A Study in the Swedish Reformation*. 1928. Reprint, Philadelphia: Fortress Press, 1965.

———. *The Church of the Lutheran Reformation: A Historical Survey of Lutheranism*. St. Louis: Concordia, 1967.

Bethge, Eberhard. *Dietrich Bonhoeffer: A Biography*. 2d ed. Revised by Victoria J. Barnett. Minneapolis: Fortress Press, 2000.

Betts, R. R. "Poland, Bohemia and Hungary." In *The New Cambridge Modern History*. Vol. 2, *The Reformation 1520–1559*. Edited by G. R. Elton. 2d ed. Cambridge: Cambridge University Press, 1990. 198–222.

Between Vision and Reality: Lutheran Churches in Transition. Edited by W. Greive. LWF Documentation No. 47. Geneva: Lutheran World Federation, 2001.

Beyreuther, Erich. *Die Erweckungsbewegung.* Edited by K. D. Schmidt and E. Wolf. Die Kirche und ihre Geschichte: Ein Handbuch. Göttingen: Vandenhoeck & Ruprecht, 1963.

Bibliography of the Lutheran Confessions. Edited by D. Daniel and C. Arand. Sixteenth Century Bibliography 28. St. Louis: Concordia, 1988.

Bizer, Ernst. *Studien zur Geschichte des Abendmahlsstreits im 16. Jahrhundert.* 1940. Reprint, Darmstadt: Wissenschaftliche Buchgesellschaft, 1962.

Blegen, Theodore C. *Norwegian Migration to America, 1825–1860.* New York: Arno, 1969.

Bluhm, Heinz. *Martin Luther: Creative Translator.* St. Louis: Concordia, 1965.

Bobe, Louis. *Hans Egede: Colonizer and Missionary of Greenland.* Copenhagen: Rosenkilde and Bagger, 1952.

The Book of Concord: Confessions of the Evangelical Lutheran Church. Edited by T. G. Tappert. Philadelphia: Fortress Press, 1959.

The Book of Concord: Confessions of the Evangelical Lutheran Church. Edited by R. Kolb and T. Wengert. Minneapolis: Fortress Press, 2000.

Bornkamm, Heinrich. *Luther's World of Thought.* Translated by M. F. Bertram. Philadelphia: Fortress Press, 1958.

———. *Luther's Doctrine of the Two Kingdoms.* Translated by K. H. Hertz. Philadelphia: Fortress Press, 1966.

———. *Thesen und Thesenanschlag Luthers: Geschehen und Bedeutung.* Theologische Bibliothek Töpelmann 14. Berlin: Töpelmann, 1967.

———. *Luther and the Old Testament.* Translated by E. W. Gritsch and R. Gritsch. Philadelphia: Fortress Press, 1969.

Bouwsma, William J. *The Culture of Renaissance and Humanism.* AHA Pamphlets 401. Washington, D.C.: American Historical Association, 1973.

Braaten, Carl E., ed. *The New Church Debate: Issues Facing American Lutheranism.* Philadelphia: Fortress Press, 1983.

Braaten, Carl E., and Robert W. Jenson, eds. *Christian Dogmatics.* 2 vols. Minneapolis: Fortress Press, 1984.

———. *A Map of Twentieth-Century Theology: Readings from Karl Barth to Radical Pluralism.* Minneapolis: Fortress Press, 1995.

Bradfield, Margaret. *The Good Samaritan: The Life and Work of Friedrich von Bodelschwingh.* London: Marshall, Morgan & Scott, 1961.

Brandi, Karl. *Der Augsburger Religionsfriede vom 25. September 1555.* 2d ed. Leipzig, 1927.

———. *The Emperor Charles V: The Growth and Destiny of a Man and of a World Empire.* Translated by C. V. Wedgewood. New York, 1965.

Brecht, Martin. *Martin Luther.* Translated by J. L. Schaaf. 3 vols. Minneapolis: Fortress Press, 1990–93.

Brock, Peter. *The Political and Social Doctrines of the Unity of the Czech Brethren in the Fifteenth and Early Sixteenth Centuries.* Slavistic Printings and Reprintings 11. Gravenhage: Mouton, 1957.

Brodrick, James. *Robert Bellarmine: Saint and Scholar*. 1928. Reprint, London: Burns & Oates, 1966.

Bruder, Otto. *Johann Christoph Blumhardt: Ausgewählte Schriften*. 3 vols. Zurich, 1947–48.

Brunner, Peter. *Nikolaus von Amsdorf als Bischof von Naumburg: Eine Untersuchung zur Gestalt des evangelischen Bischofsamtes*. Gütersloh: Mohn, 1961.

Buchwald, Georg, and Gustav Kawerau, eds. *Luther Kalendarium: Verzeichnis von Luthers Schriften*. 2d ed. Leipzig, 1929.

Bucsay, Mihaly. *Der Protestantismus in Ungarn, 1521–1978: Ungarns Reformationskirchen in Geschichte und Gegenwart*. 2 vols. Graz: Böhlau, 1977–79.

Bultmann, Rudolf. *Kerygma and Myth*. Edited by H. Bartsch. New York: Harper & Row, 1961.

Burgess, Andrew S., ed. *Lutheran World Missions*. Minneapolis: Augsburg, 1954.

Burgess, Joseph A., ed. *Lutherans in Ecumenical Dialogue: A Reappraisal*. Minneapolis: Augsburg Fortress, 1990.

Busch, Eberhard. *Karl Barth: His Life from Letters and Autobiographical Texts*. Translated by J. Bowden. Grand Rapids, Mich.: Eerdmans, 1994.

Calixt, George. *De coniugio clericorum*. 1621.

———. *Discurs von der wahren christlichen Religion und Kirchen*. 1633.

———. *Epitome theologia moralis*. 1634.

Cassirer, Ernst. *The Philosophy of the Enlightenment*. Translated by F. C. A. Koelln and J. Pettegrove. Princeton, N.J.: Princeton University Press, 1951.

Chadwick, Owen. *The Reformation*. Vol. 3 of *The Pelican History of the Church*. Harmondsworth, Eng.: Penguin, 1972.

Chemnitz, Martin. *Examination of the Council of Trent*. Translated by F. Kramer. 4 vols. St. Louis: Concordia, 1971.

Christianson, Gerald. "J. H. Wichern and the Rise of Lutheran Social Institutions." *Lutheran Quarterly* 19 (1967): 357–70.

Christopherson, Kenneth E. "Norwegian Historiography of Norway's Reformation." Ph.D. diss. University of Michigan, 1985.

The Church: A Community of Grace. Final report of the Lutheran World Federation and World Methodist Council Joint Commission. Geneva: World Council of Churches, 1984.

Church History. Chicago, 1932–.

Cochrane, Arthur C. *The Church's Confession under Hitler*. Philadelphia: Westminster, 1962.

A Common Calling: The Witness of Our Reformation Churches in North America Today. Edited by K. F. Nickle and T. F. Lull. Minneapolis: Augsburg Fortress, 1993.

Communion, the Lord's Supper and the Ministry of the Church. Oslo, 1982 and 1986.

Corpus Reformatorum. 28 vols. Edited by C. B. Bretschneider and H. E. Bindseil. Halle, 1834–60.

Crowder, C. M. D. *Unity, Heresy, and Reform, 1378–1460: The Conciliar Response to the Great Schism*. Documents of Medieval History 3. New York: St. Martin's, 1977.

Dahmus, J. H. *The Prosecution of John Wyclif*. New Haven, Conn.: Yale University Press, 1952.

Danker, Frederick W. *No Room in the Brotherhood: The Preus-Otten Purge of Missouri.* St. Louis: Concordia, 1977.

Dantine, Wilhelm. *Justification of the Ungodly.* Translated by E. W. Gritsch and R. C. Gritsch. St. Louis: Concordia, 1968.

De Boor, F. *Die paränetischen und methodischen Vorlesungen A. H. Franckes.* 2 vols. Halle: Theologische Habilitation, 1968.

Deutsche Reichstagsakten unter Kaiser Karl V. Jüngere Reihe. Edited by the Historische Kommission bei der bayrischen Akademie der Wissenschaften. 1893. Photomechanical reprint, Göttingen, 1967.

Dictionary of the Ecumenical Movement. Edited by G. Wainwright. Revised edition. Grand Rapids, Mich.: Eerdmans, forthcoming.

Dilfeld, George Conrad. *Theosophia Horbio-Speneriana.* Helmsted, 1679.

Dilthey, Wilhelm. *Gesammelte Schriften.* 12 vols. Leipzig: Teubner, 1914–58.

Dixon, Scott D. *The Reformation and Rural Society: The Parishes of Brandenburg-Ansbach-Kulmbach 1528–1603.* Cambridge: Cambridge University Press, 1996.

D. Martin Luthers Werke. Kritische Gesamtausgabe [Schriften]. Weimar: Böhlau, 1883–. Briefwechsel. Weimar: Böhlau, 1930–1948. Deutsche Bibel. Weimar: Böhlaus Nachfolger, 1906–1961. Tischreden. Weimar: Böhlaus Nachfolger, 1912–1921.

Documentary History of the Evangelical Lutheran Ministerium of Pennsylvania and the Adjacent States. Philadelphia: Board of Publication of the General Council of the Evangelical Lutheran Church in North America, 1898.

Dorner, Isaac A. *History of the Development of the Doctrine of the Person of Christ.* 4 vols. Edinburgh: T. and T. Clark, 1861–63.

Drews, Paul. *Die Disputationen Martin Luthers.* Göttingen, 1895.

Duchaine, Maurice C. "Vatican I on Primacy and Infallibility." In *Lutherans and Catholics in Dialogue.* Vol. 5, *Primacy and the Universal Church.* Edited by P. C. Empie and T. A. Murphy. Minneapolis: Augsburg, 1974, 139–50.

Duchrow, Ulrich, ed. *Lutheran Churches—Salt or Mirror of Society? Case Studies of the Theory and Practice of the Two Kingdoms Doctrine.* Geneva: Lutheran World Federation, 1977.

Dunkley, E. H. *The Reformation in Denmark.* London: SPCK, 1948.

Durnbaugh, Donald F. *European Origins of the Brethren: A Source Book on the Beginnings of the Church of the Brethren in the Early Eighteenth Century.* Elgin, Ill.: Brethren, 1958.

Ecumenism: The Vision of the Evangelical Lutheran Church in America. Minneapolis: Augsburg Fortress, 1994.

Edwards, Mark U., and George Tavard. *Luther: A Reformer for the Churches—An Ecumenical Study Guide.* Philadelphia: Fortress Press; New York: Paulist, 1983.

Einarsson, Stefán. "The Reformation." In *A History of Icelandic Literature.* New York: Johns Hopkins Press for the American-Scandinavian Foundation, 1957.

Eisenstein, Elizabeth L. *The Printing Revolution in Early Modern Europe.* Cambridge: Cambridge University Press, 1983.

Elert, Werner. *The Structure of Lutheranism.* Translated by W. A. Hansen. 2 vols. St. Louis: Concordia, 1962.

Enchiridion Symbolorum. Edited by H. Denzinger and A. Schönmetzer. 37th ed. Freiburg: Herder, 1991.

Encyclopedia of the Lutheran Church. Edited by J. Bodensieck. 3 vols. Minneapolis: Augsburg, 1965.

Estes, James Martin. *Christian Magistrate and State Church: The Reforming Career of Johannes Brenz.* Toronto: University of Toronto Press, 1982.

Eucharistic Hospitality. Institute for Ecumenical Research. Strasbourg, 1974.

The Evangelical Church in Berlin and the Soviet Zone in Germany. Translated by P. Lynch. Witten: Eckart, 1959.

Fabiny, Tibor. *A Short History of Lutheranism in Hungary.* Budapest, 1997.

Faulkner, John A. "Luther and the Bigamous Marriage of Philip of Hesse." *American Journal of Theology* 17 (1913): 206–31.

Feuerbach, Ludwig. *The Essence of Christianity.* Translated by G. Eliot. The Library of Religion and Culture. New York: Harper, 1957.

Figgis, John Neville. "Erastus and Erastianism." *Journal of Theological Studies* 2 (1901): 66–101.

Fletcher, C. R. L. *Gustavus Adolphus and the Thirty Years War.* New York: Capricorn, 1963.

Flückinger, Felix, and Wilhelm Anz. *Theologie und Philosophie im 19. Jahrhundert.* Edited by B. Moeller. Die Kirche in ihrer Geschichte: Ein Handbuch. Göttingen: Vandenhoeck & Ruprecht, 1975.

Forde, Gerhard O. *Justification by Faith—A Matter of Death and Life.* Philadelphia: Fortress Press, 1982.

Forell, George W. *Martin Luther: Theologian of the Church. Collected Essays.* Edited by William R. Russell. Word & World Supplement Series. St. Paul, Minn.: Luther Seminary, 1994.

Förstemann, Karl E., ed. *Urkundenbuch zu der Geschichte des Reichstages zu Augsburg im Jahre 1530.* 2 vols. 1833–35. Reprint, Osnabrück: Biblio-Verlag, 1966.

Forster, Walter O. *Zion on the Mississippi: The Settlement of the Saxon Lutherans in Missouri, 1839–1841.* St. Louis: Concordia, 1953.

Fortenbaugh, Robert. *The Development of the Synodical Polity of the Lutheran Church in America, to 1829.* Philadelphia: Fortress Press, 1926.

Francke, August Hermann. *Methodus studii theologici.* 1723.

Franz, Günther, ed. *Thomas Müntzer: Schriften und Briefe.* Quellen und Forschungen zur Reformationsgeschichte 33. Gütersloh: Mohn, 1968.

Freund, Michael. "Zur Geschichte der Lutherrose." *Luther* 42 (1972): 37–39.

Friesen, Abraham. *Reformation and Utopia: The Marxist Interpretation of the Reformation and Its Antecedents.* Wiesbaden: Steiner, 1974.

Froehlich, Karlfried. "Luther's Hymns and Johann Sebastian Bach." In Gritsch, ed., *Encounters with Luther,* 4:1–27.

From Federation to Communion: The History of the Lutheran World Federation. Edited by J. H. Schjoring, P. Kumari, and N. A. Hjelm. Minneapolis: Fortress Press, 1997.

Gassmann, Günther. "Lutherische Kirchen." TRE 21:599–620.

———, ed. *Historical Dictionary of Lutheranism.* In cooperation with Duane H. Larson and Mark W. Oldenburg. Lanham, Md.: Scarecrow, 2001.

Gassmann, Günther, and Scott Hendrix. *Fortress Introduction to the Lutheran Confessions.* Minneapolis: Fortress Press, 1999.

Gawthrop, Richard L. *Pietism and the Making of Eighteenth Century Prussia.* Cambridge: Cambridge University Press, 1993.

Geiringer, Karl. *Johann Sebastian Bach: The Culmination of an Era.* In collaboration with Irene Geiringer. New York: Oxford University Press, 1966.

Gensichen, Hans-Werner. *Missionsgeschichte der neueren Zeit.* 3d edition. Edited by K. D. Schmidt and E. Wolf. Die Kirche in ihrer Geschichte: Ein Handbuch. Göttingen: Vandenhoeck & Ruprecht, 1976.

Gerberding, G. H. *Life and Letters of W. H. Passavant, D.D.* Greenville, Pa.: Young Lutheran, 1906.

Gerhard, Johann. *Loci theologici.* Edited by E. Preuss. 1610–22. Reprint, Berlin, 1863–85.

Gerhardt, Martin. *Johann Hinrich Wichern.* 3 vols. Hamburg: Agentur des Rauhen hauses, 1927–31.

Ghanzeret, Klaus, ed. *Wilhelm Löhe: Gesammelte Schriften.* 8 vols. Neuendettelsau, 1951–66.

Gobineau, Alphonse, de. *Essai sur l'inégalité des races humaines.* Paris, 1853–55.

Goeckel, Robert F. *The Lutheran Church and the East German State: Political Conflict and Change under Ulbricht and Honecker.* Ithaca, N.Y.: Cornell University Press, 1990.

González, Justo L. *A History of Christian Thought.* Vol. 3: *From the Protestant Reformation to the Twentieth Century.* Nashville: Abingdon, 1975.

Graebner, Theodore. *Dr. Francis Pieper: A Biographical Sketch.* St. Louis: Concordia, 1931.

Gramlich, Bernhard. *Bodelschwingh, Bethel und die Barmherzigkeit.* Gütersloh: Mohn, 1964.

Grane, Leif. *Modus Loquendi Theologicus: Luthers Kampf um die Erneuerung der Theologie (1515–1518).* Leiden: Brill, 1975.

———. *The Augsburg Confession.* Minneapolis: Augsburg, 1987.

Grane, Leif, and Kai Horby, eds. *Die dänische Reformation vor ihrem internationalen Hintergrund = The Danish Reformation against Its International Background.* Göttingen: Vandenhoeck & Ruprecht, 1990.

Greive, Wolfgang, ed. *Between Vision and Reality: Lutheran Churches in Transition.* LWF Documentation No. 47. Geneva: Lutheran World Federation, 2001.

Grell, Ole P., ed. *The Scandinavian Reformation: From Evangelical Movement to Institutionalization of Reform.* Cambridge: Cambridge University Press, 1995.

Grimm, Harold J. "Luther's Contribution to Sixteenth Century Organization of Poor Relief." *Archiv für Reformationsgeschichte* 61 (1971): 222–33.

Grislis, Egil. "Recent Trends in the Study of the Reformation in the City of Riga." *Journal of Baltic Studies* 7, no. 2 (1976): 145–69.

Gritsch, Eric W. "Wilhelm Dilthey and the Interpretation of History." *The Lutheran Quarterly* 17 (1963): 58–69.

———. "Luther and Violence: A Reappraisal of a Neuralgic Theme." *Sixteenth Century Journal* 3 (1972): 37–55.

———. "Luther's Catechisms of 1529: Whetstones of the Church." In Gritsch, ed., *Encounters with Luther*, 2:237–48.

———. "The Orthodoxy of Conflict: Luther's Ecumenism." In Gritsch, ed., *Encounters with Luther*, 3:115–23.

———. "Academia and Forum: Luther's Reformation in Wittenberg." In Gritsch, ed., *Encounters with Luther*, 4:214–28.

———. "Bold Sinning: The Lutheran Ethical Option." *Dialog* 14, no. 3 (1975): 26–32.

———. "Concord 1577: Faith Seeking Understanding through Controversy." *Dialog* 15, no. 2 (1976): 170–75.

———. "Luther und die Schwärmer: Verworfene Anfechtung? Zum 50. Todesjahr von Karl Holl." *Luther* 3 (1976): 105–21.

———. "Infant Communion: What Shape Tradition?" *Academy* 38 (1979): 85–108.

———. "Nine and One Half Theses on 'Luther's Success and Failure as a Reformer of the Church.'" Disputation with Albert Brandenburg at the Fifth International Congress for Luther Research, Lund, Sweden, 1977. In *Luther und die Theologie der Gegenwart*. Edited by L. Grane and B. Lohse. Göttingen: Vandenhoeck & Ruprecht, 1980. 97–111.

———. "The Origins of the Lutheran Teaching on Justification." In *Lutherans and Catholics in Dialogue*. Vol. 7, *Justification by Faith*. Edited by H. George Anderson, T. Austin Murphy, Joseph A. Burgess. Minneapolis: Augsburg, 1985. 162–72, 350–53.

———. "Luther and the State." In *Luther and the Modern State in Germany*. Edited by J. D. Tracy. Sixteenth Century Essays and Studies 7. Kirksville, Mo.: Sixteenth Century Journal, 1986. 45–59.

———. "Lutheranism." In *The Encyclopedia of Religion*. Edited by M. Eliade. New York: Macmillan, 1987. 61–64.

———. *Thomas Müntzer: A Tragedy of Errors*. Minneapolis: Fortress Press, 1989.

———. "Luther, Lutheranism, and the Jews." In *Stepping Stones to Further Jewish-Lutheran Relationships: Key Lutheran Statements*. Edited by H. H. Ditmanson. Minneapolis: Augsburg Fortress, 1990. 104–19.

———. "The Use and Abuse of Luther's Political Advice." Referate und Berichte des 7. Internationalen Kongresses für Lutherforschung, Oslo, 14–20. August, 1988. *Lutherjahrbuch* 57 (1990): 207–19.

———. *Martin—God's Court Jester: Luther in Retrospect*. 2d ed. Ramsey, N.J.: Sigler, 1991.

———. "The Views of Luther and Lutheranism on the Veneration of Mary." In *Lutherans and Catholics in Dialogue*. Vol. 8, *The One Mediator, the Saints, and Mary*. Edited by H. G. Anderson, J. F. Stafford, J. A. Burgess. Minneapolis: Augsburg Fortress, 1992. 235–48, 379–84.

———. "The Jews in Reformation Theology." In *Jewish-Christian Encounters Over the Centuries: Symbiosis, Prejudice, Holocaust, Dialogue*. Edited by M. Perry and F. M. Schweitzer. New York: Lang, 1994. 197–213.

————. "Martin Luther's View of Tradition." In *The Quadrilog: Tradition and the Future of Ecumenism—Essays in Honor of George H. Tavard.* Edited by K. Hagen. Collegeville, Minn.: Liturgical, 1994. 61–75.

————. "Episcopacy: The Legacy of the Lutheran Confessions." In *Concordat of Agreement: Supporting Essays.* Edited by D. F. Martensen. Minneapolis: Augsburg; Cincinnati: Forward Movement, 1995. 101–12, 219–22.

————. "Justification by Faith and Ecclesial Communion: Pointers from the Lutheran-Catholic Dialogue." In *Church and Theology: Essays in Memory of Carl J. Peter.* Edited by P. C. Phan. Washington, D.C.: Catholic University of America Press, 1995. 161–81.

————. "Martin Luther." In *Concise Encyclopedia of Preaching.* Edited by William H. Willimon and Richard Lischer. Louisville, Ky.: Westminster John Knox, 1995. 313–16.

————. "Reflections on Melanchthon as a Theologian of the Augsburg Confession." *Lutheran Quarterly* 12 (1998): 445–52.

————, ed. *Encounters with Luther: Lectures, Discussions, and Sermons at the Martin Luther Colloquia.* 4 vols. Gettysburg, Pa.: Institute for Luther Studies, Gettysburg Lutheran Seminary, 1970–90.

————, ed. *Martin Luther: Faith in Christ and the Gospel: Selected Spiritual Writings.* Hyde Park, N.Y.: New City, 1996.

Gritsch, Eric W., and Robert W. Jenson. *Lutheranism. The Theological Movement and Its Confessional Writings.* Philadelphia: Fortress Press, 1976.

Groh, John E. *Nineteenth Century German Protestantism: The Church as Social Model.* Washington, D.C.: University Press of America, 1982.

Groote, Gerard. *Devotio Moderna: Basic Writings.* Translated by J. Van Engen. The Classics of Western Spirituality. New York: Paulist, 1988.

Growing Consensus: Church Dialogues in the United States, 1962–1991. Edited by J. A. Burgess and J. Gros. Ecumenical Documents 5. New York: Paulist, 1995.

Growth in Agreement: Reports and Agreed Statements of Ecumenical Conversations on a World Level. Edited by H. Meyer and L. Vischer. New York: Paulist; Geneva: World Council of Churches, 1984.

Gummerus, Kaakko. *Michael Agricola, der Reformator Finnlands.* Schriften der Luthergesellschaft 2. Helsinki, 1941.

Haile, Harry G. "The Great Martin Luther Spoof, or, Philosophical Limits to Knowledge." *Yale Review* 67 (1978): 236–46.

Hall, S. "The Common Chest Concept: Luther's Contribution to Sixteenth-Century Poor Relief." *Social Thought* 5 (1979): 43–53.

Harless, Gottfried. *Christliche Ethik.* Erlangen, 1843. 8th ed., 1893.

Harley, William Nicholas. *Little Journeys with Martin Luther.* Columbus, Ohio: n.p., 1916.

Harnack, Adolf von. *Outlines of the History of Dogma.* Translated by E. K. Mitchell. London, 1893.

————. *What Is Christianity?* Translated by T. B. Saunders. Fortress Texts in Modern Theology. Philadelphia: Fortress Press, 1986.

Harran, Marilyn J. *Martin Luther: Learning for Life.* St. Louis: Concordia, 1997.

Hauffen, Adolf. "Husz eine Gans—Luther ein Schwan." *Prager deutsche Studien* 9 (1908): 1–28.

Hauge, Hans Nielsen. *Autobiographical Writings.* Translated by J. M. Njus. Minneapolis: Augsburg, 1954.

Hauschildt, Eberhard. "Rudolf Bultmann." In *Profile des Luthertums: Biographien zum 20. Jahrhundert.* Edited by W.-D. Hauschild. Die lutherische Kirche, Geschichte und Gestalten 20. Gütersloh: Gütersloher, 1998. 91–115.

Headly, John. *Luther's View of Church History.* New Haven, Conn.: Yale University Press, 1963.

Hefele, K. J. von. *A History of the Councils of the Church.* 5 vols. Edinburgh, 1871–96.

Hefner, Philip J. *Faith and the Vitalities of History: A Theological Study of the Work of Albrecht Ritschl.* New York: Harper & Row, 1966.

———. *The Human Factor: Evolution, Culture, and Religion.* Minneapolis: Fortress Press, 1993.

Hegel, Georg W. F. *Sämtliche Werke.* Edited by H. G. Glockner. 26 vols. Leipzig: Meiner, 1928.

Helgason, Jon. "Die Kirche in Island." In *Ekklesia.* Edited by Friedrich Siegmund-Schulze. 2 vols. Gotha, 1934. 2:7–35.

Helmreich, Ernst Christian. *The German Churches under Hitler: Background, Struggle, and Epilogue.* Detroit: Wayne State University Press, 1979.

Hendrix, Scott H. *Luther and the Papacy: Stages in a Reformation Conflict.* Philadelphia: Fortress Press, 1981.

———. *Tradition and Authority in the Reformation.* Collected Studies Series. Aldershot, England, and Brookfield, Vt.: Variorum, 1996.

Hennig, Gerhard. *Cajetan und Luther: Ein historischer Beitrag zur Begegnung von Thomismus und Reformation.* Arbeiten zur Theologie 2. Stuttgart: Calwer, 1966.

Herrmann, Wilhelm. *The Communion of the Christian with God.* Translated by R. W. Stewart. 1903. Philadelphia: Fortress Press, 1971.

Hertz, Karl H. *Two Kingdoms and One World: A Source Book in Christian Social Ethics.* Minneapolis: Augsburg, 1976.

Heymann, Frederick G. "The Impact of Martin Luther upon Bohemia." *Central European History* 1 (1968): 107–30.

Hillerbrand, Hans J. "Thomas Müntzer's Last Tract against Luther." *Mennonite Quarterly Review* 38 (1964): 20–36.

Hinrichs, Carl. *Preussentum und Pietismus: Der Pietismus in Brandenburg-Preussen als religiös-soziale Reformbewegung.* Göttingen: Vandenhoeck & Ruprecht, 1971.

Hirsch, Emanuel. *Geschichte der neueren evangelischen Theologie im Zusammenhang mit den allgemeinen Bewegungen des europäischen Denkens.* 5 vols. 3d ed. Gütersloh: Bertelsmann, 1964.

Hoburg, Christian. *Praxis Arndiana: Das ist, des Hertzens-Seufzter über die 4 Bücher wahren Christentums.* Amsterdam, 1642.

Hodgson, Peter C. *The Formation of Historical Theology: A Study of Ferdinand Christian Baur.* New York: Harper & Row, 1960.

Hoefer, Herbert E., ed. *The Augsburg Confession and Ecumenism in India*. Madras: Gurukul Lutheran Theological College and Research Institute, 1980.

Hoffmann, Bengt, trans. and ed. *The Theologia Germanica of Martin Luther: Translation, Introduction, and Commentary*. New York: Paulist, 1980.

Hofmann, John K. von. *Schutzschriften für eine neue Weise, alte Wahrhit zu lehren*. 4 vols. Erlangen, 1856–59.

Holborn, Louise W. "Printing and the Growth of a Protestant Movement in Germany from 1517 to 1524." CH 11 (1942): 123–37.

Hope, Nicholas. *German and Scandinavian Protestantism, 1700–1918*. 2d ed. New York: Oxford University Press, 1998.

Höye, Bjarne, and Trygve M. Ager. *The Fight of the Norwegian Church against Nazism*. New York: Macmillan, 1943.

Huber, Donald. *World Lutheranism: A Select Bibliography for English Readers*. ATLA Bibliography Series 44. Lanham, Md.: Scarecrow, 2000.

Huddle, B. Paul. *History of the Lutheran Church in Japan*. New York: Board of Foreign Missions of the United Lutheran Church in America, 1958.

Hudson, Winthrop S. *American Protestantism*. Chicago: University of Chicago Press, 1961.

Humanismus und Wittenberger Reformation: Festgabe anlässlich des 500. Geburtstages des Praeceptor Germaniae Philipp Melanchthon am 16. Februar 1997: Helmar Junghans gewidmet. Edited by M. Beyer and G. Wartenberg with H.-P. Hasse. Leipzig: Evangelische Verlagsanstalt, 1996.

Hunter, Leslie Stannard. *Scandinavian Churches: A Picture of the Development and Life of the Churches of Denmark, Finland, Iceland, Norway, and Sweden*. London: Faber and Faber, 1965.

Immenkötter, Herbert, ed. *Die Confutatio der Confessio Augustana vom 3. August 1530*. Münster Westfalen: Aschendorff, 1979.

Iserloh, Erwin. *Gnade und Evharistie in der philosophischen Theologie des Wilhelm von Ockham: Ihre Bedeutung für die Ursachen der Reformation*. Veröffentlichungen 8. Wiesbaden: Steiner, 1956.

———. *The Theses Were Not Posted: Luther Between Reform and Reformation*. Translated by J. Wicks. Boston: Beacon, 1968.

———. "Aufhebung des Lutherbannes? Kirchengeschichtliche Überlegungen zu einer aktuellen Frage." In *Lutherprozess und Lutherbann: Vorgeschichte, Ergebnis, Nachwirkung*. Edited by R. Bäumer. Katholisches Leben und Kirchenreform im Zeitalter der Glaubensspaltung 32. Münster: Aschendorff, 1972.

Ivinskis, Zenonas. *Die Entwicklung der Reformation in Litauen bis zum Erscheinen der Jesuiten (1569)*. Sonderdruck aus Forschungen zur osteuropäischen Geschichte 12. Berlin, 1967.

Jaeschke, Ernst. *Bruno Gutmann, His Life, His Thoughts, His Work: An Early Attempt at a Theology in an African Context*. Makumira Publications 3/4. Erlangen: Verlag der Ev.-Luth. Mission, 1958.

Jaspers, Karl. *Nietzsche and Christianiy.* Translated by E. B. Ashton. Chicago: Regnery, 1961.

Jedin, Hubert. *A History of the Council of Trent.* Translated by E. Graf. St. Louis: Herder, 1957.

Jelly, Frederick M. "The Roman Catholic Dogma of Mary's Immaculate Conception." In *Lutherans and Catholics in Dialogue.* Vol. 8, *The One Mediator, the Saints, and Mary.* Edited by H. G. Anderson, J. F. Stafford, and J. A. Burgess. Minneapolis: Augsburg Fortress, 1992. 263–78, 386–87.

Jensen, De Lamar, trans. *Confrontation at Worms: Martin Luther and the Diet of Worms.* Provo, Utah: Brigham Young University Press, 1973.

Jenson, Robert W. *Systematic Theology.* 2 vols. New York: Oxford University Press, 1997–99.

Johns, Christa T. *Luthers Konzilsidee in ihrer historischen Bedingtheit und ihrem reformatorischem Neuansatz.* Berlin: Töpelmann, 1966.

Johnson, Alex. *Eivind Berggrav: God's Man of Suspense.* Translated by K. Jordheim with H. L. Overholt. Minneapolis: Augsburg, 1960.

Jonge, Christiaan de. *Die irenische ecclesiologie von Franciscus Junius (1545–1602).* Bibliotheca Humanistica and Reformatorica 30. Niewkoop: De Graaf, 1980.

Jüngel, Eberhard. "Justification Today." *Lutheran World* 12, no. 1 (1965): 1–11.

———. *The Doctrine of the Trinity: God's Being Is in Becoming.* Translated by H. Harris. Scottish Journal of Theology Monograph Supplements 4. Grand Rapids, Mich.: Eerdmans, 1976.

Kalkoff, Paul. *Die Depeschen des Nuntius Aleander vom Wormser Reichstag 1521.* Halle, 1886.

———. "Zu Luther's römischen Prozesses." ZKG 25 (1904): 587–96.

Kant, Immanuel. *Was ist Aufklärung?* Edited by Norbert Kinsky. 1784. Darmstadt: Wissenschaftliche Buchgesellschaft, 1973. ET = *Foundations of the Metaphysics of Morals and What Is Enlightenment?* 2d ed. The Library of Liberal Arts. Translated by L. W. Beck. New York: Macmillan; London: Collier Macmillan, 1990.

Käsemann, Ernst. "Begründet der neutestamentliche Kanon die Einheit der Kirche?" In *Exegetische Versuche und Besinnungen.* 2 vols. Göttingen, 1960. 1:214–23.

Keysser, Christian A. *A People Reborn.* Translated by A. Allin and J. Kuder. Pasadena, Calif.: William Carey Library, 1980.

Kidd, B. J. *Documents Illustrative of the Reformation.* Oxford: Oxford University Press, 1967.

Kierkegaard, Søren. *Fear and Trembling.* Translated by W. Lowrie. Princeton, N.J.: Princeton University Press, 1941.

———. *Attack on Christendom.* Translated by W. Lowrie. Princeton, N.J.: Princeton University Press, 1968.

King, Jean A. *The Lutheran Story: A Brief History of the Lutheran Church in New Zealand, 1843–1993.* Palmerston North, N.Z.: Lutheran Church of New Zealand, 1994.

Kirn, Paul. *Friedrich der Weise und die Kirche: Seine kirchenpolitik vor und nach Luthers Hervortreten im jahre 1517.* Beiträge zur kulturgeschichte des mittelalters und der renaissance 30. Leipzig: Teubner, 1926.

Knudsen, Johannes. *Danish Rebel: A Study of N. F. S. Grundtvig.* Philadelphia: Muhlenberg, 1955.

Kolb, Robert. "Georg Major as a Controversialist: Polemics in the Late Reformation." CH 45 (1976): 455–68.

———. *Andreae and the Formula of Concord: Six Sermons on the Way to Lutheran Unity.* St. Louis: Concordia, 1977.

———. *Nikolaus von Amsdorf (1483–1565): Popular Polemics in the Preservation of Luther's Legacy.* Nieuwkoop: De Graaf, 1978.

———. *For All the Saints: Changing Perceptions of Martyrdom and Sainthood in the Lutheran Reformation.* Macon, Ga.: Mercer, 1987.

———. *Confessing One Faith: Reformers Define the Church, 1530–1580.* St. Louis: Concordia, 1991.

———. *Luther's Heirs Define His Legacy: Studies on Lutheran Confessionalization.* Collected Studies CS539. Brookfield, Vt.: Variorum, 1996.

Kolb, Robert, and James A. Nestingen, eds. *Sources and Contexts of the Book of Concord.* Minneapolis: Fortress Press, 2001.

Kooiman, Willem J. "Luther at Home." In *The Martin Luther Lectures.* Vol. 3, *The Mature Luther.* Edited by Roland H. Bainton et al. Decorah, Ia.: Luther College Press, 1959. 59–75.

———. *Luther and the Bible.* Translated by J. Schmidt. Philadelphia: Fortress Press, 1961.

Kupisch, Karl. *Deutschland im 19. und 20. Jahrhundert.* Edited by K. D. Schmidt and E. Wolf. Die Kirche und ihre Geschichte: Ein Handbuch. Göttingen: Vandenhoeck & Ruprecht, 1966.

Kusukawa, Sachiko. *Philip Melanchthon: Orations on Philosophy and Education.* Cambridge Texts in the History of Philosophy. Cambridge: Cambridge University Press, 1999.

Labadie, Jean de. *La pratique de l'oraison et méditation Chrétienne.* 1660.

Larsson, Per. *Bishop Josia Kibira of Bukoba in an International Perspective.* Nairobi, Kenya: Uzima; Dodoma, Tanzania: Central Tanganyika, 1992.

Latourette, Kenneth Scott. *A History of the Expansion of Christianity.* 7 vols. New York, London: Harper & Brothers, 1937–45.

Lausten, Martin Schwarz. "The Early Reformation in Denmark and Norway, 1520–1559." In *The Scandinavian Reformation: From Evangelical Movement to Institutionalization of Reform.* Edited by Ole P. Grell. Cambridge: Cambridge University Press, 1995. 12–41.

———. "Dänemark." In TRE 8:300–317.

———. "Denmark." In OER 1:471–74.

———. *De fromme og jøderne.* Copenhagen, 2000.

———. "Die Beziehungen zwischen Dänemark und der Universität Wittenberg in der Reformationszeit" in *Zwischen Wissenschaft und Politik: Studien zur deutschen Universitätsgeschichte.* Festschrift für Heike Wohlgast zum 65. Geburtstag. Edited by A. Kohnle and F. Engelhausen. Stuttgart: Calwer, 2001. 238–57.

———. *A Church History of Denmark.* Burlington, Vt.: Ashgate, 2001.

Leder, Hans-Günter. *Ausgleich mit dem Papst? Luthers Haltung in den Verhandlungen mit Miltitz 1520.* Arbeiten zur Theologie. Stuttgart: Calwer, 1969.

Leff, Gordon. *William of Ockham: The Metamorphosis of Scholastic Discourse.* Manchester: Manchester University Press; Totowa, N.J.: Rowman and Littlefield, 1975.

Lehmann, Arno. *It Began at Tranquebar: The Story of the Tranquebar Mission and the Beginnings of Protestant Christianity in India.* Translated by M. J. Lutz. Madras: Christian Literature Society, 1956.

Leith, John H., ed. *Creeds of the Churches: A Reader in Christian Doctrine, from the Bible to the Present.* 3d ed. Atlanta: John Knox, 1982.

Leske, Everard. *For Faith and Freedom: The Story of Lutherans in Australia, 1838–1996.* Adelaide, So. Australia: Openbook, 1996.

The Leuenberg Agreement and Lutheran-Reformed Relationships: Evaluations by North American and European Theologians. Edited by W. G. Rusch and D. F. Martensen. Minneapolis: Augsburg, 1989.

Lewis, Arthur J. *Zinzendorf: The Ecumenical Pioneer.* Philadelphia: Fortress Press, 1962.

Lienhard, Marc. "Miteinander kommunizieren in gemischten Ehen." *Lutherische Monatshefte* 1 (1973): 49.

Littell, Franklin H. *The German Phoenix: Men and Movements in the Church in Germany.* Garden City, N.Y.: Doubleday, 1960.

Loewenberg, J. D., ed. *The Persecution of the Lutheran Church in Prussia.* London, 1840.

Loewenich, Walther, von. *Duplex Iustitia: Luthers Stellung zu einer Unionsformel des 16. Jahrhunderts.* Wiesbaden: Steiner, 1972.

———. *Luther's Theology of the Cross.* Translated by H. J. Bouman. Minneapolis: Augsburg, 1976.

Löhe, Wilhelm. *Gesammelte Werke.* Edited by K. Ghanzeret. 8 vols. Neuendettelsau: Freimund, 1951–66.

———. *Three Books about the Church.* Edited and translated by James I. Schaaf. Philadelphia: Fortress Press, 1969.

Lohse, Bernhard. *Martin Luther's Theology: Its Historical and Systematic Development.* Translated by R. A. Harrisville. Minneapolis: Fortress Press, 1999.

Loofs, Friedrich. "Der ariculus stantis et cadentis ecclesiae." *Theologische Studien und Kritiken* 90 (1917): 323–420.

Löscher, Valentin. *Timotheus verinus.* Wittenberg, 1718.

Lueking, Dean. *Mission in the Making.* St. Louis: Concordia, 1964.

Lund, Eric, ed. *Documents from the History of Lutheranism, 1517–1750.* Minneapolis: Fortress Press, 2001.

Lutheran Book of Worship. Minneapolis: Augsburg, 1978.

Lutheran Identity. Strasbourg: Institute for Ecumenical Research, 1977.

Lutherans and Catholics in Dialogue. Edited by P. Empie, T. A. Murphy, et al. 9 vols. Minneapolis: Augsburg Fortress, 1965–93.

Luther's Works. Edited by Jaroslav Pelikan and Helmut Lehmann. 55 vols. Philadelphia: Fortress Press; St. Louis: Concordia, 1955–1986.

Machiavelli, Niccolò. *The Prince.* In *Chief Works and Others.* Translated by A. H. Gilbert. 3 vols. Durham, N.C.: Duke University Press, 1965.

Mackinnon, James. *Luther and the Reformation.* 4 vols. London: Longmans, Green, 1925–30.

Mahling, Friedrich. *Die Innere Mission.* 2 vols. Gütersloh: Bertelsmann, 1937.

Maier, Paul C., ed. *Caspar Schwenckfeld on the Person and Work of Christ: A Study of Schwenckfeldian Theology at Its Core.* Assen: Van Gorcum, 1959.

Manschreck, Clyde Leonard. *Melanchthon: The Quiet Reformer.* New York: Abingdon, 1958.

———, trans. and ed. *Melanchthon on Christian Doctrine: Loci Communes, 1555.* A Library of Protestant Thought. New York: Oxford University Press, 1965.

Mansi, Giovanni D. *Sacrorum Conciliorum nova et amplissima.* 60 vols. Paris, 1899–1927.

Marburg Revisited: A Reexamination of Lutheran and Reformed Traditions. Edited by P. C. Empie and J. I. McCord. Minneapolis: Augsburg, 1966.

Martensen, Hans L. *Die christliche Dogmatik.* Leipzig, 1856.

———. *Die christliche Ethik.* 3 vols. Gotha, 1878.

———. *Christian Ethics.* 2 vols. Edinburgh, 1882.

Marty, Martin E. "The Church and Its Polity." In *Theology in the Life of the Church.* Edited by R. W. Bertram. Philadelphia: Fortress Press, 1966, 233–56.

Marx, Karl. *Capital, the Communist Manifesto, and Other Writings.* Edited by M. Eastman. New York: Modern Library, 1932.

Maser, Peter. *Die Kirchen in der DDR.* Deutsche Zeitbilder. Bonn: Bundeszentrale für Politische Bildung, 2000.

Mastrantonis, George. *Augsburg and Constantinople: The Correspondence between the Tübingen Theologians and Patriarch Jeremiah II of Constantinople and the Augsburg Confession.* The Archbishop Iakovos Library of Ecclesiastical and Historical Sources 7. Brookline, Mass.: Holy Cross Orthodox, 1982.

Maurer, Wilhelm. *Der junge Melanchthon zwischen Humanismus und Reformation.* 2 vols. Göttingen: Vandenhoeck & Ruprecht, 1967–69.

———. "Die Einheit der Theologie Luthers." In *Kirche und Geschichte: Gesammelte Aufsätze.* Vol. 1, *Luther und das evangelische Bekenntnis.* Edited by E.-W. Kohls and G. Müller. Göttingen: Vandenhoeck & Ruprecht, 1970. 11–21.

———. *Historical Commentary on the Augsburg Confession.* Translated by H. G. Anderson. Philadelphia: Fortress Press, 1986.

Mecenseffy, Grete. *Geschichte des Protestantismus in Österreich.* Graz: Böhlaus, 1956.

Mehlhausen, Joachim., ed. *Das Augsburger Interim von 1548: Nach den Reichstagsakten deutsch und lateinisch.* Texte zur Geschichte der evangelischen Theologie 3. Neukirchen-Vlyn: Neukirchener, 1970.

Meissen 1988: Relations between the Church of England, the Federation of the Evangelical Churches in the German Democratic Republic, and the Evangelical Church in Germany in the Federal Republic of Germany. London, 1988.

Mellinghoff, Gerhard, ed. *Lutherische Kirche Tanzania: Ein Handbuch.* Erlanger Taschenbücher 39. Erlangen: Ev.-Luth. Mission, 1976.

Mentzer, Balthasar. *Synopsis theologiae analytico ordine comprehensae.* 1610.

Meyer, Carl S., ed. *Readings in the History of the Lutheran Church–Missouri Synod.* St. Louis: Concordia, 1964.

Meyer, Harding, ed. *The Augsburg Confession in Ecumenical Perspective.* LWF Report 6–7. Geneva: Lutheran World Federation, 1980.

Migne, J. P., ed. *Patrologiae: Series Latina.* 221 vols. in 222. Paris, 1844–1904.

Mirbt, Carl, and Kurt Aland, eds. *Quellen zur Geschichte des Papsttums und des römischen Katholizismus.* Tübingen: Mohr (Siebeck), 1967.

Moody, Ernest A. *The Logic of William of Ockham.* London: Sheed & Ward, 1935.

Mortensen, Enok. *The Danish Lutheran Church in America: The History and Heritage of the American Evangelical Lutheran Church.* Studies in Church History, ser. 2, no. 25. Philadelphia: Board of Publication, Lutheran Church in America, 1967.

Moyo, Ambrose. "Whither Lutheranism? Lutheranism in Africa." *Word and World* 11 (1991): 257–64.

Mueller, David L. *An Introduction to the Theology of Albrecht Ritschl.* Philadelphia: Westminster, 1969.

Muhlenberg, Henry M. *The Journals of Henry Melchior Muhlenberg.* Edited by T. G. Tappert and J. W. Doberstein. 3 vols. Philadelphia: Lutheran Historical Society; Evansville, Ind.: Whipporwill, 1982.

Musteikis, Antanas. *The Reformation in Lithuania: Religious Fluctuations in the Sixteenth Century.* East European Monographs 246. Boulder: East European Monographs; New York: Columbia University Press, 1988.

Neill, Stephen. *A History of Christian Missions.* Vol. 6 of the *The Pelican History of the Church.* 2d ed., rev. by O. Chadwick. New York: Penguin, 1986.

Nelson, E. Clifford. *The Rise of World Lutheranism: An American Perspective.* Philadelphia: Fortress Press, 1982.

Nelson, E. Clifford, ed. (in collaboration with others). *The Lutherans in North America.* Rev. ed. Philadelphia: Fortress Press, 1980.

Nichol, Todd W. "Whither Lutheranism? A North American Perspective." *Word and World* 11, no. 3 (1991): 276–85.

Niebuhr, H. Richard. *The Kingdom of God in America.* New York: Harper, 1937.

———. *Christ and Culture.* New York: Harper, 1951.

———. *The Social Sources of Denominationalism.* New York: Meridian, 1957.

Nischan, Bodo. *Prince, People, and Confession: The Second Reformation in Brandenburg.* Philadelphia: University of Pennsylvania Press, 1994.

Nissen, Karsten. "Whither Lutheranism? Lutheran Churches of Western Europe." *Word and World* 11, no. 3 (1991): 249–56.

Noll, Mark A. *A History of Christianity in the United States and Canada.* Grand Rapids, Mich.: Eerdmans, 1992.

Nygren, Anders. *Agape and Eros.* Translated by P. S. Watson. Philadelphia: Westminster, 1953.

Ohl, Jeremiah Franklin. *The Inner Mission: A Handbook for Christian Workers.* Philadelphia: General Council Publication House, 1911.

Oosthuizen, Gerhardus C. *Theological Discussions and Confessional Developments in the Churches of Asia and Africa.* Franeker: Wever, 1958.

Owen, H. P. *Revelation and Existence: A Study in the Theology of Rudolf Bultmann.* Cardiff: University of Wales Press, 1957.

Oxford Dictionary of the Christian Church. Edited by E. A. Livingstone. 3d ed. Oxford: Oxford University Press, 1997.

Oxford Encyclopedia of the Reformation. Edited by H. J. Hillerbrand. 4 vols. New York: Oxford University Press, 1996.

Oyer, John S. *Lutheran Reformers against the Anabaptists: Luther, Melanchthon, and Menius, and the Anabaptists of Central Germany.* The Hague: Nijhoff, 1964.

Papal Documents on Mary. Edited by W. J. Doheny and J. P. Kelly. Milwaukee, Wisc.: Bruce, 1954.

Pesch, Otto Hermann. *The God Question in Thomas Aquinas and Martin Luther.* Translated by G. G. Krodel. Facet Historical Series 21. Philadelphia: Fortress Press, 1972.

———. *Das Zweite Vatikanische Konzil, 1962–1965: Vorgeschichte, Verlauf, Ergebnisse, Nachgeschichte.* Würzburg: Echter, 1993.

Peter, Carl J. "The Decree on Justification in the Council of Trent." In *Lutherans and Catholics in Dialogue.* Vol. 7, *Justification by Faith.* Edited by H. George Anderson, T. Austin Murphy, and Joseph A. Burgess. Minneapolis: Augsburg, 1985. 218–28.

Peters, Albrecht. "Systematische Besinnung zu einer Neuinterpretation der reformatorischen Rechtfertigungslehre." In *Rechtfertigung im neuzeitlichen Lebenszusammenhang: Studien zur Neuinterpretation der Rechtfertigungslehre.* Edited by W. Lohff and C. Walther. Gütersloh: Mohn, 1974. 107–25.

Peters, Ted. *God—The World's Future: Systematic Theology for a New Era.* 2d ed. Minneapolis: Fortress Press, 2000.

Pettegree, Andrew, ed. *The Early Reformation in Europe.* Cambridge: Cambridge University Press, 1992.

Pfnür, Vinzenz. *Die Einigung bei den Religionsgesprächen von Worms und Regensburg 1540/41: Eine Täuschung?* Gütersloh: Mohn, 1980.

Podczeck, Otto, ed. *A. H. Franckes Schrift über eine Reform des Erziehungs- und Bildungswesens als Ausgangspunkt einer geistlichen und sozialen Neuordnung der Evangelischen Kirche des 18. Jahrhunderts: Der grosse Aufsatz.* Sächsische Akademie der Wissenschaften. Berlin: Akademi, 1962.

Prenter, Regin. *Spiritus Creator.* Translated by J. M. Jensen. Philadelphia: Muhlenberg, 1953.

Preus, Robert D. *The Theology of Post-Reformation Lutheranism: A Study of Theological Prolegomena.* 2 vols. St. Louis: Concordia, 1970–72.

Proeve, E. H., and Proeve, H. F. W. *A Work of Love and Sacrifice: The Story of the Mission among the Dieri Tribe at Cooper's Creek.* Point Pas, Australia, 1952.

Raitt, Jill. "From Augsburg to Trent." In *Lutherans and Catholics in Dialogue.* Vol. 7, *Justification by Faith.* Edited by H. George Anderson, T. Austin Murphy, and Joseph A. Burgess. Minneapolis: Augsburg, 1985. 200–217.

Redeker, Martin. *Schleiermacher: Life and Thought.* Translated by J. Wallhausser. Philadelphia: Fortress Press, 1973.

Reed, Luther D. *The Lutheran Liturgy: A Study of the Common Liturgy of the Lutheran Church in America.* Rev. ed. Philadelphia: Muhlenberg, 1959.

Die Religion in Geschichte und Gegenwart. 7 vols. 3d ed. Tübingen: Mohr, 1957–1965.

Renkewitz, Heinz. *Hochmann von Hohenau (1670–1721): Quellenstudien zur Geschichte des Pietismus.* 2d ed. Witten, 1969. ET = *Hochmann von Hohenau (1670–1721).* Translated by W. G. Willoughby. Brethren Encyclopedia Monograph Series 4. Philadelphia: Brethren Encyclopedia, 1993.

Renouard, Yves. *The Avignon Papacy, 1305–1403.* Translated by D. Bethell. Hamden, Conn.: Archon, 1970.

Report of the Consultation of Lutheran/Orthodox Dialogues. Geneva: Lutheran World Federation, 1975.

Repp, Arthur C. *Luther's Catechism Comes to America: Theological Effects on the Issues of the Small Catechism Prepared in or for America prior to 1850.* ATLA Monograph Series 18. Metuchen, N.J.: Scarecrow; Philadelphia: American Theological Library Association, 1982.

Reu, J. M. *Thirty-five Years of Luther Research.* Chicago: Wartburg, 1917.

———. *The Augsburg Confession: A Collection of Sources with an Historical Introduction.* Chicago: Wartburg, 1930.

———. *Luther's German Bible: An Historical Presentation.* Columbus, Ohio: Lutheran Book Concern, 1934.

Reuter, Fritz, ed. *Der Reichstag zu Worms: Reichspolitik und Luthersache.* Worms: Stadtarchiv, 1971.

Riforgiato, Leonard R. *Missionary of Moderation: Henry Melchior Muhlenberg and the Lutheran Church in English America.* Lewisburg, Pa.: Bucknell University Press; London: Associated University Presses, 1980.

Ritschl, Albrecht. *The Christian Doctrine of Justification and Reconciliation.* New York, 1900.

———. *Die Geschichte des Pietismus.* 3 vols. 1880–86. Reprint, Bonn: Marcus, 1966.

Roberts, Michael. *The Early Vasas: A History of Sweden 1523–1611.* Cambridge: Cambridge University Press, 1968.

Rogge, Joachim. *Johann Agricolas Lutherverständnis unter besonderer Berücksichtigung des Antinomianismus.* Berlin, 1960.

Rogness, Michael. *Philip Melanchthon: Reformer without Honor.* Minneapolis: Augsburg, 1969.

Root, Michael. "The Concordat and the Northern European Poorvo Statement: Different Paths to the Same Goal." In *A Commentary on "Concordat of Agreement."* Edited by J. E. Griffiss and D. F. Martensen. Minneapolis: Augsburg; Cincinnati: Forward Movement, 1994.

Rouse, Ruth, and Stephen Charles Neill, eds. *A History of the Ecumenical Movement, 1517–1968.* 2 vols. 3d ed. Geneva: World Council of Churches, 1986.

Rupp, Gordon E., and Philip S. Watson, eds. "Diatribe or Discourse Concerning Free Choice." In *Luther and Erasmus: Free Will and Salvation.* Library of Christian Classics 17. Philadelphia: Westminster, 1969.

———. "Luther at the Castle Coburg, 1530." *Bulletin of the John Rylands University Library* 61 (1979): 182–205.

Ruse, Michael. *The Darwinian Revolution: Science Red in Tooth and Claw.* 2d ed. Chicago: University of Chicago Press, 1999.

Russell, William R. *Luther's Theological Testament: The Schmalkald Articles.* Minneapolis: Fortress Press, 1995.

Schartau, Henric. *Henric Schartau and the Order of Grace: Biography by Henrik Hägglund and Fifteen Sermons by Henric Schartau.* Translated by S. G. Hägglund. Rock Island, Ill.: Augustana Book Concern, 1928.

Scheel, Otto. *Martin Luther: Vom Katholizismus zur Reformation.* 2 vols. 3d ed. Tübingen, 1917–21.

Schlee, Ernst. *Der Streit des Daniel Hoffmann.* Marburg, 1862.

Schleiermacher, Friedrich. *The Christian Faith.* Translated by H. R. Mackintosh, J. S. Stewart, et al. Edinburgh: T. and T. Clark, 1928.

———. *On Religion: Speeches to Its Cultured Despisers.* Translated by J. Oman. The Library of Religion and Culture. New York: Harper, 1958.

Schlink, Edmund. *Theology of the Lutheran Confessions.* Translated by P. F. Koehneke and H. J. A. Bouman. Philadelphia: Muhlenberg, 1961.

Schmauk, Theodore E. "The Great War of Germany against Europe." *Lutheran Church Review* 33 (Oct. 1914): 704.

Schulze, Wilhelm A. "Luther und der Zins." *Luther* 42 (1971): 139–46.

Schweitzer, Albert. *The Quest of the Historical Jesus: The First Complete Edition.* Translated and edited by J. Bowden. Minneapolis: Fortress Press, 2001.

Schwiebert, Ernest G. *Luther and His Times.* St. Louis: Concordia, 1950.

Seebass, Friedrich. *Johann Christoph Blumhardt.* Hamburg, 1949.

Selge, Kurt-Victor. *Die Leipziger Disputation zwischen Luther und Eck.* ZKG 86 (1975): 26–40.

Sider, Ronald J., ed. *Karlstadt's Battle with Luther: Documents in a Liberal-Radical Debate.* Philadelphia: Fortress Press, 1978.

Smith, Adam. *An Inquiry into the Nature and Causes of the Wealth of Nations.* Great Books of the Western World 39. Chicago: Encyclopaedia Brittanica, 1955.

Smith, Ralph. *Luther, Ministry, and Ordination Rites in the Early Reformation Church.* Renaissance and Baroque Studies and Texts 15. New York: Lang, 1996.

Söderblom, Nathan. *The Living God.* Edinburgh: T. and T. Clark, 1933.

Spangenberg, August G. *Leben des Herrn Nikolaus Ludwig Grafen von Zinzendorf und Pottendorf.* 8 parts. 1772. Reprint, Hildesheim, N.Y.: Olms, 1971.

Spener, Philip J. *Theologische Bedenken.* 4 vols. and an addendum. 1700–1702, 1711.

———. *Pia Desideria oder Hertzliches Verlangen nach gottgefälliger Besserung der wahren Evangelischen Kirchen.* Edited by Kurt Aland. 1616. ET: *Pia Desideria.* Translated and edited by T. G. Tappert. Philadelphia: Fortress Press, 1964.

Spitz, Lewis W. *The Life of Dr. C. F. W. Walther.* St. Louis: Concordia, 1961.

Spitz, Lewis W., and Wenzel Lohff, eds. *Discord, Dialogue, and Concord: Studies in the Lutheran Reformation's Formula of Concord.* Philadelphia: Fortress Press, 1977.

Stace, W. T. *The Philosophy of Hegel: A Systematic Exposition.* New York: Dover, 1955.

Stacey, John. *John Wyclif and Reform*. Philadelphia: Westminster, 1964.

Stahl, Rainer. "Whither Lutheranism? An Eastern European Perspective." *Word and World* 11 (1991): 243–47.

Stange, Douglas C. *Radicalism for Humanity: A Study of Lutheran Abolitionism*. St. Louis: Concordia, 1970.

Stein, K. James. *Philip Jacob Spener: Pietist Patriarch*. Chicago: Covenant, 1986.

Steinmetz, David C. *Misericordia Dei: The Theology of Johannes von Staupitz in Its Late Medieval Setting*. Studies in Medieval and Reformation Thought 4. Leiden: Brill, 1968.

Stellhorn, A. C. *Schools of the Lutheran Church–Missouri Synod*. St. Louis: Concordia, 1963.

Stepping Stones to Further Jewish-Lutheran Relations: Key Lutheran Statements. Edited by H. H. Ditmanson. Minneapolis: Augsburg Fortress, 1990.

Stoeffler, F. Ernest. *The Rise of Evangelical Pietism*. Leiden: Brill, 1971.

———. *German Pietism during the Eighteenth Century*. Leiden: Brill, 1973.

Sträter, U. "Von Bedenken und Briefen." *Zeitschrift für Religions- und Zeitgeschichte* 40 (1988): 235–50.

Strauss, David F. *Leben Jesu*. 2 vols. Tübingen, 1835–36. ET = *The Life of Jesus, Critically Examined*. Translated by M. Evans. New York: Blanchard, 1855.

Strauss, Gerald. *Luther's House of Learning: Indoctrination of the Young in the German Reformation*. Baltimore, Md.: Johns Hopkins University Press, 1978.

Suelflow, August R. "Nietzsche and Schaff on American Lutheranism." *Concordia Historical Institute Quarterly* 23 (1951); 149–57.

Sundkler, Bengt. *Nathan Söderblom: His Life and Work*. Lund: Gleerup, 1968.

Supplementa Melanchthoniana: Werke Philipp Melanchthons, die im Corpus Reformatorum, vermisst werden. 5 vols. 1910. Reprint, Frankfurt: Minerva, 1968.

Sweet, William W. *Religion on the American Frontier, 1783–1840*. 4 vols. New York: Holt, 1931; Chicago: University of Chicago Press, 1939, 1946; New York: Cooper Square, 1964.

Swihart, Altman K. *Luther and the Lutheran Church, 1483–1960*. New York: Philosophical Library, 1960.

Tappert, Theodore G. "Henry Melchior Muhlenberg and the American Revolution." CH 11 (1942): 284–301.

———. *Lutheran Confessional Theology in America, 1840–1880*. A Library of Protestant Thought. New York: Oxford University Press, 1972.

Tentler, Thomas N. *Sin and Confession on the Eve of the Reformation*. Princeton, N.J.: Princeton University Press, 1977.

Terray, László G. *He Could Not Do Otherwise: Bishop Lajos Ordass, 1901–1978*. Translated by E. W. Gritsch. Grand Rapids, Mich.: Eerdmans, 1997.

Texte aus der VELKD (vereinigte evangelisch-lutherische Kirche Deutschlands). Hannover: Kirchenamt 17 (1981).

Theologische Realenzyklopädie. Edited by G. Krause and G. Müller. 31 vols. Berlin: de Gruyter, 1977–.

Theses Concerning Martin Luther, 1483–1983: The Luther Quincentenary in the German Democratic Republic. Berlin: Zeit im Bild, 1983.

Thompson, Albert Edward. *A Century of Jewish Missions.* Chicago: Revell, 1902.

Thomson, Harrison S. "Luther and Bohemia." *Archiv für Reformationsgeschichte* 44 (1953): 160–81.

Thulstrup, Niels. *Kierkegaard and the Church in Denmark.* Translated by F. H. Cryer. Copenhagen: Reitzel, 1984.

Tillich, Paul. *Systematic Theology.* 3 vols. Chicago: University of Chicago Press, 1951–57.

Tillmans, Walter C. *The World and Men around Luther.* Minneapolis: Augsburg, 1959.

Todd, John M. *Luther: A Life.* New York: Crossroad, 1982.

Tokuzen, Yoshikazu. "Whither Lutheranism? An Asian Perspective." *Word and World* 11 (1991): 265–68.

Tóth, William. "Highlights of the Hungarian Reformation." CH 9 (1940): 141–56.

Troeltsch, Ernst. *The Social Teaching of the Christian Churches.* Translated by O. Wyon. 2 vols. New York: Macmillan, 1931.

Turner, Frederick J. *The Frontier in American History.* New York: Holt, Rinehart and Winston, 1962.

Vajta, Vilmos. *Luther on Worship: An Interpretation.* Philadelphia: Muhlenberg, 1958.

———. *Die "diakonische Theologie" im Gesellschaftssystem Ungarns.* Frankfurt am Main: Lembeck, 1987.

Vajta, Vilmos, and Hans Weissgerber, eds. *The Church and the Confessions: The Role of the Confessions in the Life and Doctrine of the Lutheran Churches.* Philadelphia: Fortress Press, 1963.

Vatican Council II: More Postconciliar Documents. Edited by A. Flannery. Vatican Collection 2. Dublin: Dominican; Northport, N.Y.: Costello, 1982.

Wallmann, Johannes. *Der Theologiebegriff bei Johann Gerhard und Georg Calixt.* Tübingen: Mohr, 1961.

———. *Der Pietismus.* Edited by B. Moeller. Die Kirche und ihre Geschichte: Ein Handbuch. Göttingen: Vandenhoeck & Ruprecht, 1990.

Walther, C. F. W. *The Controversy Concerning Predestination.* Translated by A. Crull. St. Louis, 1881.

Watson, Philip J. *Let God Be God: An Interpretation of the Theology of Martin Luther.* Philadelphia: Fortress Press, 1966.

Weber, H. E. *Reformation, Orthodoxie und Rationalismus.* 2 vols. 1937–51. Reprint, Gütersloh, 1976.

Weinstein, Donald. *Savonarola and Florence: Prophecy and Patriotism in the Renaissance.* Princeton, N.J.: Princeton University Press, 1976.

Welch, Claude. *Protestant Thought in the Nineteenth Century.* 2 vols. New Haven, Conn.: Yale University Press, 1972–85.

Wenger, John C. "The Schleitheim Confession of Faith." *Mennonite Quarterly Review* 19 (1945): 243–53.

Wengert, Timothy J. *Law and Gospel: Philip Melanchthon's Debate with John Agricola of Eisleben over Poenitentia.* Texts and Studies in Reformation and Post-Reformation Thought. Carlisle, Cumbria, UK: Paternoster; Grand Rapids, Mich.: Baker, 1997.

Wentz, Abdel Ross. *Fliedner the Faithful.* Philadelphia: Board of Publication of the United Lutheran Church in America, 1936.

———. "Lutheran World Federation." In *The Encyclopedia of the Lutheran Church.* Edited by J. Bodensieck. 3 vols. Minneapolis: Augsburg, 1965. 2:1428–29.

———. *Pioneer in Christian Unity: Samuel Simon Schmucker.* Philadelphia: Fortress Press, 1967.

Wentz, Frederick K. *Lutherans in Concert.* Minneapolis: Augsburg, 1968.

The Westminster Dictionary of Church History. Edited by J. C. Brauer. Philadelphia: Westminster, 1971.

Wicks, Jared. "Abuses under Indictment at the Diet of Augsburg 1530." *Theological Studies* 41, 2 (1980): 253–301.

Williams, George H. *The Radical Reformation.* 3d ed. Sixteenth Century Essays and Studies 15. Kirksville, Mo.: Sixteenth Century Journal, 1992.

Witte, John, Jr. *Law and Protestantism: The Legal Teachings of the Lutheran Reformation.* Cambridge: Cambridge University Press, 2002.

Wittram, Reinhard, ed. *Baltische Kirchengeschichte: Beiträge zur Geschichte der Missionierung und der Reformation, der evangelisch-lutherischen Landeskirchen und des Volkskirchentums in den baltischen Landen.* Göttingen: Vandenhoeck & Ruprecht, 1956.

Wolf, Richard C. *Documents of Lutheran Unity in America.* Philadelphia: Fortress Press, 1966.

Zeeden, Ernst Walter. *The Legacy of Luther: Martin Luther and the Reformation in the Estimation of the German Lutherans from Luther's Death to the Beginning of the Age of Goethe.* Translated by R. M. Bethell. Westminster, Md.: Newman, 1954.

Zeitschrift für Kirchengeschichte. Stuttgart, 1877–.

Ziegenbalg, Bartholomy. *Genealogie der Malabrischen Götter.* Madras, 1867.

———. *Malabarisches Heidentum.* Edited by W. Caland. Amsterdam: Müller, 1926.

———. *Alte Briefe aus Indien.* Edited by A. Lehmann. Berlin: Evangelische Verlagsanstalt, 1957.

Zorn, H. M. *Bartholomaeus Ziegenbalg.* St. Louis: Concordia, 1933.

Index

Academy of Abo, 145
Accolti, Pietro, 26
Adiaphora, 90–91, 99, 137, 139
Africa, 207, 208, 245. *See also specific countries*
African Americans, 176, 190, 192
Agricola, John, 27, 86
Agricola, Michael, 54, 55
Aku, Andreas, 208
Albany, 173, 175
Albrecht of Brandenburg, Grandmaster Margrave, 56, 57
Albrecht II, Elector of Mainz, Archbishop of Magdeburg, 12, 16, 28, 32, 62
Aleander, Jerome, 28, 29
Alexander VI, Pope, 2, 3
Alexander, Solomon, 209
Alsace, 142
Althaus, Paul, 223
Altmann, Walter, 231
Alveld, Augustine, 21
Amana Society, 166
Ambrose, 250
Amsterdam, 169, 172, 176, 210
Anabaptists (Swiss Brethren), 44, 59, 67, 99, 112, 195, 212
Andreae, Jacob, 94, 95
Anglicans, 60, 69, 168, 169, 176, 184, 204, 207, 208, 209, 215, 218

Anna, Saint, 6, 83
Antinomians, 86–87
Anton, Paul, 149
Antonius, Friar, 53
Aquinas, Thomas, 4, 241
Apostolic succession, 153, 155, 242
Arason, Jon, 55
Argentina, 210, 248
Aristotle, 4, 8, 11, 13, 43, 95, 113, 114, 115, 123, 127
Arndt, John, 117, 119, 141–42, 147, 157
Arnold, Gottlieb, 163–64, 166
Arnzius, Bernard, 172
Aryans, 223
Asia, 205, 247. *See also specific countries and cities*
Aslaksson, Cort, 120, 126
Augsburg, 3, 90, 171
  Apology, 48
  Ban, 21, 26, 28, 40, 44, 60
  Barby Seminary, 157
  Confession (altered), 92, 191
  Confession (unaltered), xi, 45, 46–48, 49, 50, 52, 54, 55, 57, 58, 59, 60, 67, 71, 118, 146, 152, 154, 155, 165, 177, 184, 190, 238, 250
  Diet of, xi, 17, 45, 49
  Interim of, 66, 90
  Peace of, 67–68, 91, 92, 101, 109, 111, 112, 131, 132, 212, 222, 246, 254

August of Braunschweig, Duke, 132
August II, Elector of Saxony, 93, 94
August the Younger, Duke, 133
Augustana Synod, 190, 210, 218, 221
Augustine, 8, 11, 14, 16, 42, 71, 96, 112, 197, 250
Augustinian Hermits, 6, 7, 9, 11, 20
Aulén, Gustav, 231
Auler, John, 17
Aurifaber, John, 64
Australia, 181, 196, 206, 247
Austria, 56, 60, 112, 179, 190, 241, 245
Austrian Protestant Union, 241
Avignon papacy, 1, 2

Bach, Johann Sebastian, 117, 139, 179
Bad Boll, 186
Baltic, 56, 109, 145, 150, 156, 169, 243
Baltimore, Maryland, 174, 196, 241
Baltimore Declaration, 221
Ban, 21, 26, 28, 40, 44, 60
Baptism, 2, 21, 23, 24–25, 26, 37, 45, 47, 66, 71, 73–74, 137, 166, 182
Barby Seminary, 157
Barmen, 224

Declaration of, 224, 228
Rhenish Mission Society,
  204
Barnim of Pomerania, 19
Baroque era, 115, 153, 154,
  155
Barth, Karl, 228
Basel, 20, 42, 142, 186
  Mission Society of 204
Batak Church (Huria Kris-
  ten Batak Protestan), 236,
  247
  Confession, 236–38
Baur, Ferdinand Christian,
  200
Bavaria, 16, 180, 182
Bayle, Pierre, 151
Beck, Vilhelm, 188
Beissel, Conrad, 166
Belgium, 246
Bell, George, 218
Bellarmine, Robert, 85,
  121, 129
Bengel, John Albrecht, 159,
  160
Bergen, Norway, 53
Bergen Book, 95
Berggrav, Eivind, 225, 228,
  251
Berkenmeyer, William
  Christopher, 173
Berlin, 87, 146, 164, 200, 227
Berthelsdorf, 152
Bethel, 186
Bethlehem, Pennsylvania,
  155
Beza, Theodore, 93
Bible (Scripture), 4, 7, 10,
  12, 106, 121, 123, 148
  Authority of, 3, 15, 20, 23,
    24, 28, 29, 42, 59–60,
    128, 138, 195

Inspiration of, 8, 20, 53,
  64, 82–83, 120, 149,
  159–60, 170
Translation of, 32, 52, 54,
  59, 208
Bilfinger, George Bernhard,
  158
Bishops, 23, 26, 37, 40, 48,
  51, 52, 53, 105, 153, 176,
  194, 212, 246
Bismarck, Otto von, 179,
  184, 223
Bjork, Eric, 172
Blumhardt, John Christo-
  pher, 186
Bock, Hans, 30
Bodelschwingh, Frederick,
  186, 189
Bodelschwingh, Frederick,
  Jr., 187
Böhme, Anton Wilhelm,
  150, 167
Böhme, Jacob, 117, 146
Bohemia, 49, 58
Bohemian Confession, 58
Bohemian Brethren, 132
Bolivia, 248
Bonhoeffer, Dietrich, 222,
  225, 228
Book of Concord, 54,
  100–101, 109
Borgia, Caesare, 2
Borneo, 205, 247
Boerresen, Hans P., 205
Bossey, Switzerland, 243
Boxer Rebellion, 207
Braaten, Carl E., 232
Brahe, Tycho, 126
Brandenburg, 16, 89, 109,
  111, 146, 161
Braunschweig-Lüneburg,
  109

Brazil, 209, 238, 248
Breithaupt, Joachim J., 149
Brenz, John, 43, 90, 109
Brethren of the Common
  Life, 4
Bretke, Johan, 57
Brochmand, Jesper, 120
Brown, James A., 192
Brück, George, 46
Brüsewitz, Oskar, 226
Brunnquell, Ludwig, 157
Bucer, Martin, 43, 49
Budapest, 59, 235
Büchel, Anna, 166
Buenos Aires, 210
Buffalo, 195, 196
Bugenhagen, John, 36, 43,
  51, 53, 56
Bultmann, Rudolf, 229, 230
Buscher, Statius, 133

Cajetan, Thomas de Vio, 17,
  18, 26
Calixt, Frederick Ulrich, 134
Calixt, George, 131–33
Callenberg, John Henry,
  169
Calov, Abraham, 120, 126,
  127–28, 130, 134, 135
Calvin, John, 47, 85, 91,
  110, 175, 197
Campanius, John, 172
Campeggio, Lorenzo, Car-
  dinal, 59
Canada, 191, 193, 148, 248
Canstein, Freiherr Carl von,
  148, 248
Carey, William, 204
Carlstadt, Andreas Boden-
  stein, 18, 19, 20, 34, 37,
  41, 51
Cassander, Joris, 132

Catechism(s), 36, 40–41, 54, 57, 59, 71, 75–76, 112
Catharina of Gersdorf, Henriette, 151
Catherine of Bora, 38, 62, 63
Catherine of Siena, 2
Cave, William, 163
Cederquist, Karl, 208
Chalcedon, Council of, 60, 98
Charles V, Emperor, xi, 23, 27, 28, 29, 35, 45, 48, 49, 60, 61, 65, 67, 84, 171
Charles IX, King of Sweden, 53
Chemnitz, Martin, 94, 95, 118, 127
Chicago, Illinois, 194, 198
Chile, 210, 248
China, 169, 207, 297, 247
Christ, 2, 11, 20, 22, 43, 97, 98, 122, 128, 207, 219, 223
   Historical Jesus, 188, 201
   Mediator of salvation, 12, 13, 17, 165, 256
   Return of, 3, 34, 76, 79, 89, 97, 159, 160, 163, 165, 166
Christian II, King of Denmark, 51
Christian III, King of Denmark, 51, 52
Christian IV, King of Denmark, 54
Christian Socialists, 181, 187
Christianshaab, 170
Church, 1, 2, 3, 4, 7, 17, 20, 22, 26, 73, 78, 105, 154, 155
   Structure, 5, 23, 24, 40, 79, 109, 175, 184, 188, 202, 220

Marks, 11, 35, 60, 61
Parish, 37, 56–61, 160
Civil War, 192
Clausen, Claus L., 190
Cleen, Dietrich von, 30
Coburg Castle, 45
Cochläus, John, 30
Cologne, Germany, 20, 26
Colombia, 248
Columbus, Christopher, 171
Communism, 41, 179, 222, 226, 228
Concomitance, 24
Concordia Seminary, 194, 195, 249
Conferences
   Faith and Order, 220, 221
   Free, 192
   Life and Work, 220, 222, 243
   Synodical, 192, 193, 196
   World, 233
Confession, 2, 9, 40, 48
Confessing Church, 224, 228, 229
Confutation, 48
Congress of Vienna, 179, 190
Consensus of the first five centuries, 131
Constance, Council of, 2, 3, 20
Constantine I, Emperor, 5, 39, 250
Constantinople, 209
   Council of, 60
Controversies
   Genuflection, 182
   Syncretist, 134
   Synergist, 87–88
Copenhagen, 51, 111, 119, 120, 150
   Confession, 152

Copernicus, Nicholas, 15, 126
Costa Rica, 248
Councils, 17, 20, 26, 30, 49, 60, 116
Counter Reformation, 57, 60
Cranach, Lucas, 31, 33, 39, 69
Creeds, 4, 20, 36, 72–73, 92, 100
Crete, 134
Crüger, John, 117
Crypto-Calvinists, 80, 91, 93, 111, 197
Cuba, 210
Culture, 1, 5, 69, 176, 211, 257–56
Curitiba, Brazil, 238
Cytraeus, David, 94, 95
Czechoslovakia, 3, 56, 150, 165, 246

Dachau, Germany, 224
Dähne, George, 171
Danish Church Ordinance, 53, 55
Danish Lutheran Church, 51
Danish Mission Society, 205
Dannhauer, John, 119, 129
Danzig (Gdansk), Poland, 56, 58, 133
Dar es Salaam, 234, 239
Darwin, Charles, 179
Dass, Past (Petter), 112
David, Christian, 152, 170
Da Vinci, Leonardo, 4
Day, David A., 208
Day of the Church (Kirchentag), 185
Deaconesses, 185, 186
Decalogue, 22, 36, 71, 72

Delaware, 172
Dellwig an der Ruhr, 186
Denmark, 51, 52, 69, 109, 111, 120, 168, 180, 182, 202, 219, 242, 245
Descartes, René, 177
Dessau Military Alliance, 39
Devai, Matyas, 59
Dibelius, Otto, 227
Diets
 Augsburg, xi, 17, 45, 49
 Hungarian, 59
 Livonian, 57
 Nuremberg, 35
 Piotrikow, 58
 Regensburg, 133
 Speyer, 39, 41
 Västeras, 52
 Worms, 28, 29–30, 59, 68
Dilfeld, Conrad, 145
Dilthey, Wilhelm, 203
Dippel, John Conrad, 165
Disko Bay, Greenland, 170
Dober, Leonhard, 169
Dominicans, 16, 17, 20, 57
Dorner, Isaac A., 202
Dorsche, John, 119, 131
Dresden, 128, 146, 151, 163, 194, 206
 Colloquy, 93
 Consensus, 94
Dürer, Albrecht, 21
Düsseldorf, Germany, 152
Dutch Guyana, 171
Dutch Reformed, 172, 173, 176, 207

East Germany, 222, 226–28, 235, 246
Ebeling, Gerhard, 230
Eck, John, xi, 16, 18, 19, 20, 21, 26, 27, 48, 60

Eck, John von der, 29, 30, 31
Eckhart, John, 4
Ecuador, 248
Ecumenical dialogues, 239–44
 Anglican (Episcopal), 242–43
 Baptist, 243
 Catholic, 233, 240–41
 Conservative evangelical, 244
 Methodist, 243
 Orthodox, 243
 Reformed, 240, 241–42
Edinburgh, 215, 221, 222
Edward VII of England, 218
Egede, Hans, 170
Ehrenström, Nils, 222
Eielsen, Elling, 190
Einarsson, Gizur, 55
Eisenach, 6, 31, 89, 221
 World Conference, 233
Eisleben, Germany, 6, 64, 86
Elert, Werner, 231
Elizabeth I of England, 69
Eller, Elias, 166
El Salvador, 248
Elster Gate, 27
Emser, Jerome, 21
England, 3, 21, 66, 156, 160, 167, 179, 211, 245
Enlightenment, 150, 160, 161, 177, 180, 187, 199
Enthusiasm (Schwärmerei), 41, 63, 81, 112, 146, 158, 161, 195
Ephesus, Council of, 60
Ephrata, Pennsylvania, 166
Erasmus of Rotterdam, 4, 21, 32, 42, 51
Erastus (Thomas Lüber), 110

Erbermann, Vitus, 132
Erdmuthe, Dorothea of Reuss-Ebersdorf, 152
Erfurt, 6, 8, 20, 89, 146
Erik XIV, King of Sweden, 52
Eritrea, 208
Erlangen, 180, 204
 School, 181, 201, 202
Ernest, Duke of Sachsen Gotha, 146
Esbjorn, Lars P., 190
Eskimos. See Inuits.
Estonia, 56, 57
Ethiopia, 207, 242, 244
Eucharistic hospitality, 238

Fabritius, Jacob, 172
Fascism, 222
Faith, 11, 14, 20, 22, 113, 124, 151, 197, 211
Faith and Order Conference, 220, 221
Falckner, Justus, 172
Falk, John, 185
Federal Council of the Churches of Christ in America, 193
Feller, Joachim, 143
Ferdinand I, Emperor, 58, 59, 60, 66, 67
Ferdinand II, Emperor, 131
Fetis, Domenico, 151
Feuerbach, Ludwig, 201
Ficino, Marsilio, 4
Fifth Lateran Council, 5
Finke River Mission, 206
Finland, 51, 54, 109, 112, 180, 183, 245
Finnish Mission Society, 205
Firmian, Leopold Anthony von, Archbishop, 174

First Vatican Council, 83, 179
Fischer, John, 145
Flacius, Matthias, 87, 90, 94
Flierl, John, 206
Florida, 172
Formula of Concord, 95, 111, 118, 121, 164, 198
Fort Wayne, Indiana, 192
Fossum, Ludwig O., 209
Fourth Lateran Council, 4
Fox River Valley, 190
France, 21, 56, 66, 67, 160, 245. See also French Revolution
Francis I of France, 18
Francis of Sickingen, 36
Franciscans, 3
Francke, August Hermann, 146–48, 149–50, 158, 159, 160, 161, 171, 172
Francke, Gotthilf August, 150, 173, 174, 175
Franckean Synod, 190
Frankenhausen, battle of, 41
Frankfurt, 92, 145, 146
Frankfurt am Main, 142, 154, 165
Frankfurt an der Oder, 89
Franklin, Benjamin, 174
Fraternal Appeal of the General Synod, 192
Frederick I, King of Denmark, 51, 56
Frederick II, 111
Frederick III of the Palatinate, 92, 110
Frederick IV, 167, 168
Frederick William of Prussia, 135, 148, 154, 179, 180
Frederick III of Saxony, Elector, "the Wise," 9, 16,

17, 18, 22, 27, 28, 34, 37, 39, 127
Frederick V of Saxony, Elector, 111
Freedom, 11, 12, 25, 40, 69, 105, 118, 138
Freedom of the will, 40, 42, 84, 96
Free Masons, 192, 198
French Revolution, 179
Freylinghausen, John A., 149, 169
Fries, John F., 173
Fritzsche, Gotthard D., 206
Froben, John, 20, 21
Fuchs, Ernst, 230
Fugger Bank, 3
Funck, Jon, 90

Galesburg Rule, 192
Genähr, Ferdinand, 207
General Council, 192
General Synod, 189, 191, 194, 212
Geneva, 110, 141, 175, 220, 222
Genuflection controversy, 182
George, Duke of Saxony, 18, 30, 34
George Ernst of Henneberg, Count, 94
Georgia, 174, 192
Gerhard, John, 115, 118–19, 121, 122, 127, 131
Gerhardt, Paul, 117, 135
German Christians (Deutsche Christen), 223
Germantown, Pennsylvania, 162, 173
Germany, 2, 3, 4, 18, 23, 27, 38, 49, 56, 57, 59, 95, 109,

149, 157, 168, 183, 184, 190, 211, 222, 242, 245. See also specific towns and cities
Gettysburg College, 189
Gettysburg Seminary, 189
Gezelius, John, Jr., 145
Ghinucci, Jerome, Auditor-General Bishop, 16
Giessen, 119, 163
Gnesio-Lutherans, 80, 86, 87, 89, 92, 93, 94
Gobineau, Alphonse de, 179
God, 2, 3, 4, 6, 7, 9, 10, 22, 115, 116
Hidden, 13, 42, 62
Revealed, 13, 43, 62
See also Holy Spirit
Good works, 2, 14, 22–23, 26, 42, 47, 79, 88–89, 97
Gospel, 14, 35, 42, 43, 62, 102, 125, 167
Gossner, John, 204
Göttingen, Germany, 200
Gottskalksson, Oddur, 55
Government, 23, 34, 40, 47, 52, 53, 67, 111, 113, 143, 187, 188, 214, 225
Grace, 1, 12, 13, 15, 20, 26, 84
Graebner, August L., 206
Grau, Karl, 204
Greenland, 170
Great Church Order, 109
Greek Orthodox, 1, 19, 74, 80, 140, 207, 216, 219, 220, 257
Gregor, Christian, 155
Gregory IX, Pope, 5
Gregory XIII, Pope, 53
Grundtvig, Nikolaj F. S., 182
Grundtvigianism, 183

Guatemala, 248
Gustavus Adolfus II of
    Sweden, 177
Gustavus Vasa I of Sweden,
    52, 54
Gutenberg, Johann, 3
Gutmann, Bruno, 208
Gützlaff, Karl, 207
Guyana, 210, 248

Haderslev, Denmark, 51
Hadrian VI, Pope, 35
Hahn, Carl H., 208
Hahn, Michael, 160
Halle, 148, 151, 159, 165,
    167, 172, 202
Halle Foundation, 148,
    149, 166, 167, 171, 173
Halle Reports, 150, 174
Hamann, John George, 180
Hamburg, 55, 92, 146, 147,
    165, 173, 185
    Rough House, 180
Hanseatic Region, 53
Hapsburg, 60, 111, 112,
    150
Hardenberg, Albert, 93
Harless, Gottlieb, 181, 182,
    202
Harms, Klaus, 180
Harnack, Adolf von, 200,
    212
Hartwick, John Christo-
    pher, 173, 190
Hauge, Hans Nielsen, 183
Haugeans, 190, 207
Hazelius, Ernst L., 189
Hedinger, John Henry, 158
Hefner, Philip J., 232
Hegel, George W. F., 177,
    200, 201
Heidegger, Martin, 229

Heidelberg, 13, 110, 131,
    188, 200
    Catechism, 110
    Disputation, 13
Helie, Paul, 51
Hell, 2, 63, 98, 199
Helmstedt, 127, 131
Helsinki, 232
    Report, 233, 242
Helwig, Jacob, 145
Hemmingsen, Niels, 111
Henry of Braunschweig-
    Wolffenbüttel, 62
Henry VIII of England, 61
Henry II of France, 66
Herder, John G., 149, 187
Hermannstadt, 60
Hermann, Wilhelm, 154
Herrnhut, 121, 152, 154,
    155, 157, 160, 177
Herrnhut bonds, 154, 156
Hesse, 31, 66, 119
Heyer, John C. F., 205
Heyling, Peter, 207
Hindenburg, Paul von,
    223
Hirsch, Emanuel, 223
Hispanus, John, 26
History, 4, 38, 177–78, 200,
    230, 231
    Interpretation of, 163–64
Hitler, Adolf, 63, 222, 223,
    236, 257
Hobbes, Thomas, 110
Hoburg, Christian, 142
Hodkin, Henry, 211
Hoen, Cornelius, 43
Hoffmann, Daniel, 127
Hofgut, John, 173
Hofmann, John K. von, 201
Hohenau, Ernst Christoph
    Hochmann von, 165

Holbein, Hans, 69
Hollaz, David, 120–21, 140
Holy Spirit, 12, 37, 47,
    72–73, 87, 122, 145, 166,
    182
Honduras, 248
Hong Kong, 207, 247
Hope Valley Mission, 206
Huguenots, 172
Hülsemann, John, 119, 134
Humanism, 3, 4, 5, 6, 51,
    52, 53, 54, 58, 59, 110
Hume, David, 177
Hungarian Diet, 59
Hungary, 56, 59, 150, 228,
    235, 246
Hunnius, Aegidius, 118
Hus, Jan, 3, 20, 49
Hussites, 3, 58, 59, 152, 153
Hutten, Ulrich von, 21, 36
Hutter, Leonhart, 118
Hutterites, 67

Iceland, 51, 55, 192, 242
Ignatius of Loyola, 82
India, 150, 167, 168, 196,
    205, 247
Indonesia, 205, 236, 241,
    247
Indulgences, 5, 9, 12, 16,
    18, 20, 26, 32, 42
Infallibility, papal, 83, 179
Innocent III, Pope, 1, 56
Innocent VIII, Pope, 2
Innocent X, Pope, 112
Inqusition, 5
Inuits (Eskimos), 192
Iowa Synod, 215
Iran, 209
Irenaeus, 122
Ireland, 246
Israel, 11, 209, 247

Italy, 2, 3, 21, 50, 56, 60, 63, 222, 246
Ivan, Czar of Russia, 69

Jablonsky, Daniel Ernest, 153
Jäger, John Wolfgang, 158
Japan, 207, 247
Jenson, Robert W., 232
Jena, Germany, 88, 118, 119, 157
Jeremiah II, patriarch, 240
Jerusalem, 56, 185, 209
Jesuits, 53, 57, 207
Jews, 5, 62–63, 146, 150, 169, 192, 196, 223, 225
Joachim I, Elector of Brandenburg, 30, 66
Joachim II, 90
John XXIII, Pope, 2, 271
John, Elector of Saxony, 22, 41, 46, 49
John Frederick, 49, 62, 88, 111
John George of Brandenburg, Elector, 94
John George I of Saxony, Elector, 134
John III, King of Sweden, 53
Joint Declaration of Justification, 241
Joint Synod of Wisconsin, 193
Jonas, Justus, 19, 36, 39, 64
Jordan, 209, 247
Juengel, Eberhard, 232
Julius II, Pope, 2
Julius II of Braunschweig-Wolffenbüttel, 94
Junius, Franciscus, 131
Justification by Faith, 96, 102, 133, 140, 165, 232–33

according to Luther, 10–11, 14, 37, 49, 50, 72
according to Melanchthon, 46, 48, 61, 77–78
according to Roman Catholicism, 83–84, 90
Justinian I, Emperor, 44
Jutland, 52
Juusten, Paavali, 55

Kaldy, Zoltan, 235
Kalmar, Union of, 51
Kant, Immanuel, 149, 160, 177, 199
Karl Frederick, Duke, 158
Karl of Baden, 94
Käsemann, Ernst, 253–54
Kassel colloquy, 135
Kavel, August L. C., 206
Kenya, 208
Kepler, John, 126
Keyszer, Christian, 206
Kibira, Josiah, 244
Kierkegaard, Søren, 202–3, 204, 228
Kiel, Germany, 146, 180
Knoll, Michael Christian, 173
Knopcken, Andreas, 56–57
Knubel, Frederick H., 215
Kocherthal, Joshua, 172, 173
Königsberg, 56, 89, 120, 134, 149
Korea, 208, 247
Körner, Christopher, 95
Koster, Heinrich, 207
Krakow, 58
Krapf, John L., 207, 208
Krauth, Charles P., 192, 193
Kugler, Anna S., 205
Kurtz, Benjamin, 190, 191

Laestadius, Lars Levi, 183
Lambeth Quadrilateral, 242
Lapland, 182
Larsen, Lauritz, 195
Laski, Jan, 58
Latin America, 171, 181, 196, 209, 231, 248
Latomus, Jacobus, 33
Latvia, 56, 57
Lausanne, 220, 221
Law and gospel, 22, 33, 35, 86–87, 97, 103, 182, 219
Lebanon, 209
Leibniz, Gottfried W., 161
Leipzig, 16, 19, 87, 93, 119, 146, 182, 218
    Disputation, 18–20, 26, 63
    Interim, 67, 90
    Mission, 168, 196
Leo X, Pope, 11, 25, 26, 27, 28
Leuenberg Agreement, 241
Leyser, Polycarp, 118
Liberal arts, 6
Liberation theology, 231, 248
Liberia, 208
Lilje, Hans, 257
Lithuania, 56, 57, 58, 149
Livonian Diet of Wolmar, 57
Lock, Lars, 172
Locke, John, 128
Löhe, Wilhelm, 180, 184, 186, 194, 195, 204, 206
Lohmüller, John, 57
Lohse, Eduard, 230
Lombard, Peter, 8
London, 154, 174, 176
Lord's Supper (Eucharist), 40, 47, 53, 71, 74–75, 92–93, 97–98, 176, 180, 182

Celebration, 91, 117, 131, 138

Controversies, 42, 43–44, 98

Disputation, 18–20, 26, 63

Interpretations, 24–25, 42, 54, 63, 66, 92

"Real presence," 4, 43, 50, 91, 253

Löscher, Valentin, 128

Louvain, Belgium, 4, 17, 20, 26

Loy, Matthias, 197, 198

Ludwig VI of the Palatinate, 110

Ludwig Eberhard, Duke, 158

Lund, Sweden, 203, 234

Lundensian School, 231

Lüneburg, 162

Luther, Martin, xi, 1, 3, 4, 5, 6, 7, 9, 10, 16, 17, 19, 20, 21, 27, 28, 31, 36, 45, 48, 49, 52, 54, 56, 58, 59, 65, 85, 91, 96, 107, 112, 114, 115, 118, 122, 127, 130, 143, 145, 154, 164, 180, 193, 212, 223, 227, 229, 231, 240, 241, 257–60

Breakthrough, 10–11, 12

Diseases, 50, 64

Death, 64–65

Catherine of Bora (spouse), 38, 62, 63

Children of, 39, 62

Luther Rose (seal), 65, 258

Lutheran Church–Missouri Synod, 221, 234

Lutheran Confessions, xi, 15, 95, 106–7, 108, 114, 133, 134, 157, 162, 175, 177, 180, 181, 89, 191,

194, 195, 202, 221, 226, 254

Lutheran Free Church, 193

Lutheran-Jewish Dialogue, 244

Lutheran World Convention, 221

Lutheran World Federation, 221, 227, 233–36, 239, 255

Macarius, monk, 163

Macchiavelli, Niccolo, 1, 225

Madagascar, 208, 245

Magdeburg, archbishopric of, 8, 66

Magni, Petrus, 52

Magni, Valerian, 133

Magnus of Oesel, Duke, 69

Mainz, archbishopric of, 32

Major, George, 88–89

Malaysia, 247

Marburg, 119, 241

Articles, 119, 241, 252

Colloquy, 43–44

Marriage, 2, 35, 38–39, 152, 153, 165–66

Marsilius of Padua, 110

Martensen, Hans L., 202

Martin V, Pope, 2

Martini, Cornelius, 127

Marty, Martin E., 260

Martyrs, 9

Marx, Karl, 179, 186, 200

Mary, Mother of Jesus, 6, 8, 59, 82, 179

Maryland-Virginia Synod, 189

Mass, 7, 24, 37, 48, 52, 55, 83, 90

Mather, Cotton, 150

Maulbrunn Formula, 94, 241

Maurice of Saxony, 66, 67, 96

Maximilian I, Emperor, 16, 18

Maximilian II, Emperor, 58, 60

Mazzolini, Sylvester (Prierias), 16

Meissen Statement, 242

Melanchthon, Philip, 18, 19, 27, 31, 34, 36, 38, 39, 45, 48, 49, 50, 56, 60, 65, 76–77, 81–82, 92, 93, 113, 114, 239, 240

Melanchthon Lutherans, 191

Menius, Justus, 89

Mennonites, 67, 112, 165, 211

Mentzer, Balthasar, 119

Mercersburg Seminary, 191

Merit, 2, 11, 13, 17, 42, 80, 84

Metaphysics, 115, 119, 121

Methodism, 154, 174, 178, 184

Meyer, Robert T., 213

Michelfelder, Sylvester, 234

Middle East, 169, 209

Miltitz, Karl von, 17–18, 19, 25, 26

Milton, John, 117

Ministerium of Pennsylvania, 175, 177, 192

Ministry, 26, 37, 75, 137, 143

Common, 23, 26, 37, 68, 71, 104, 144, 161, 188

Ordained, 37, 40, 47, 103, 175, 182

Mission

Foreign, 167, 168–69, 170, 181, 187, 190, 196, 204–11, 259

Inner, 184–88, 189, 223
Missouri Synod, 192, 196, 199, 206, 209, 213, 214, 215
Mittelholzer, John R., 210
Mohacs, battle of, 59
Mohammed, prophet, 2, 69
Molinos, Michael, 147
Monasticism, 6, 8, 11, 33, 48, 53, 80
Moravia, 58
Moravian Brethren, 3, 58, 59, 121, 152, 153, 156, 169, 170, 175, 182, 208, 210, 272
Morrison, Robert, 207
Mosviolius, Martin, 57
Mühlberg, battle of, 66
Muhlenberg, Henry Melchior, 150, 173–74, 176, 177, 250
Muhlenberg, William, 191
Müller, Ludwig, 224
Münster, 44
Müntzer, Thomas, 34, 41, 78, 87
Musäus, John, 119
Musculus, Andreas, 39, 95
Muskego, Wisconsin, 190
Mussolini, Benito, 222
Mystical union (unio mystica), 116, 139
Mysticism, 4, 117, 141, 142, 152, 157, 161, 162, 165

Namibia, 235
Napoleon, 179
Nathin, John, 8
National Council of Churches, 193, 214
National Lutheran Council, 215

Naumann, Frederick, 187
Naumburg, 36, 92
Nazism, 222–23, 225
Neo-Lutherans, 182, 191
Nesib, Onesimus, 208
Netherlands (Holland, Low Countries), 4, 20, 110, 112, 151, 157, 172, 219, 246
Neuendettelsau, Germany, 180, 206
New Jerusalem, 168
New York, 172, 173, 196
New Zealand, 206, 247
Nicea, Council of, 19, 20, 39, 60
Niebuhr, Reinhold, 233
Niebuhr, H. Richard, 233
Niemöller, Martin, 224
Nietzsche, Friedrich, 179
Nightingale, Florence, 185
Nitschmann, Anna, 154
Nitschmann, David, 169
Nobel, Alfred, 221
Nominalism, 4, 11
Nommensen, Ludwig I., 205
North America, 3, 171–74, 181, 191–93, 205, 221, 233, 241, 248.
North Bremen Mission Society, 205, 207, 208
North Carolina, 192
Norway, 51, 53, 109, 180, 188, 190, 225, 242, 245, 257
Nova Scotia, 174, 190
Nuremberg, 8, 89
    Diet of, 35
    Truce of, 49
Nygren, Anders, 231, 257

Oberlin, John, 185
Obersalzberg, 223
Ockham, William, 4, 11
Oecolampadius, John, 43
Oertel, C. Richard, 209
Oetinger, Frederick Christopher, 159, 160
Ohio Synod, 192, 194
Ohio Joint Synod, 189, 198
Olav, Archbishop of Trondheim, 53
Old Lutherans, 180, 191
Oldwick, New Jersey, 173
Olson, Regina, 203
Ordass, Lajos, Bishop, 228, 235, 257
Order of Salvation, 116, 188, 211
Ordination, 2, 7
Osiander, Andreas, 89–90
Osiander II, Lukas, 157
Oslo, 53, 243
Ostrom, Albert, 210
Otten, Hermann, 249
Oxford Movement, 184

Pacific, 205
Palatinate, 88, 166
Palladius, Peter, 52
Pannenberg, Wolfhart, 230
Papacy, 2, 3, 5, 6, 17, 19, 20, 21, 23, 28, 30, 50, 60, 63, 91, 110, 146. See also Popes
Papua New Guinea, 206
Paraguay, 211, 248
Paris, 17, 20, 151, 217, 220
Passau Treaty, 67, 91
Passavant, William A., 188
Pastorius, Franz Daniel, 162
Paul III, Pope, 50, 60, 63, 65, 82

Payne, Daniel, 190
Peace, 217, 218, 221, 227
Peasant Rebellion, 1381,
    1525 3, 34, 41, 60
Pedersson, Geble, 53
Pelagius, 42, 197
Penance, 10, 12, 21, 26, 40,
    182, 183, 271
Penn, William, 162, 173
Pennsylvania, 162, 173, 174.
    See also Ministerium;
    Philadelphia
Perry County, Missouri,
    194
Peru, 210
Peter I, Czar of Russia, 243
Peters, Ted, 232
Petersen, Eleanor von Mer-
    lau, 146, 161
Petersen, John William, 146,
    161, 165
Petri, Laurentius, 52
Petri, Olavus, 52, 55
Peucer, Caspar, 93
Peutinger, Conrad, 30
Pezel, Christopher, 93
Pfeffinger, John, 88
Philadelphia, 152, 155, 175
Philadelphia Seminary, 192
Philip of Hesse, 43, 61–62,
    64
Philip II of Spain, 67
Philippines, 247
Philippists, 80, 86, 87, 89,
    92, 93, 94, 95, 197
Philosophy, 114, 115, 120,
    121, 127–28, 161, 180
Pieper, Francis A., 198
Pilgrimage, 9, 23
Pius IV, Pope, 84
Piotrikow, Diet of, 58
Pisa, 2

Pittsburgh, 185, 188
Pleissenburg Castle, 19
Plütschau, Henry, 167
Poland, 53, 56, 57, 58, 111,
    153
Pomerania, 19, 56, 109
Pontius Pilate, 9
Popes
    Alexander VI, 2, 3
    Gregory IX, 5
    Gregory XIII, 53
    Hadrian VI, 35
    Innocent III, 1, 56
    Innocent VIII, 2
    Innocent X, 112
    John XXIII, 2, 271
    Julius II, 2
    Leo X, 11, 25, 26, 27, 28
    Martin V, 2
    Paul III, 50, 60, 63, 65, 82
    Pius IV, 84
    Sylvester V, 19
Porvoo Common Statement,
    243
Poverty, 36, 185
Praetorius, Abdias, 89
Prague, 3, 58, 151
Prayer, 9, 21, 36, 54, 71, 73,
    141
Predestination (election),
    99, 193, 197
Prenter, Regin, 231
Pretenders, 173
Preus, J. A. O., 249
Preus, Robert, 249
Princeton Theological
    Seminary, 189
Protestantism, 1, 41, 84, 85,
    110, 164, 184, 215, 216,
    250, 255
Prussia, 59, 89, 109, 111,
    149, 171, 179, 180, 182,

    184, 185, 187, 190, 193,
    211, 212
Purgatory, 2, 12, 19, 26
Pullach Report, 242
Puerto Rico, 210

Quenstedt, John Andreas,
    118, 121, 124, 127
Quistorp, John, 119
Quistorp, John Jr., 119

Radical (Left Wing) Refor-
    mation, 45
Rakow Catechism, 130
Rationalism, 15, 82, 179,
    187, 194, 195, 199
Rautanen, Martin, 208
Reformation, 3, 5, 6, 12, 23,
    39, 53, 54, 161, 164, 179,
    189, 193, 212
Reformed, the, 3, 59, 69, 91,
    92, 111, 117, 131, 135,
    152, 166, 180, 197, 204
Regensburg
    Agreement of, 61
    Diet of, 133
Reichardt, Gertrude, 186
Reinhart, Martin, 51
Relics, 32
Rembrandt, 117
Renaissance, 3, 8, 117
Renatus, Christian, 153
Resen, Hans, 120
Resistance, 35, 44, 226
Reu, J. M., 215
Reuchlin, John, 4, 32
Rev, Hans, 53
Rhenish Mission, 206, 208
Richter, Christian, 148
Riga, 56, 57, 145
Ritschl, Albrecht, 200
Rock, John Frederick, 166

Roh, Jan, 59

Roman Catechism of Trent, 85, 111

Roman Catholicism, 1, 53, 55, 57, 58, 64, 68, 69, 70, 132, 134, 153, 185, 191, 193, 216, 219, 252

Romania, 56, 59, 246

Rome, 2, 8, 9, 12, 17, 19, 21, 26, 27, 44, 61, 90, 219, 250

Ronsdorf, Germany, 166

Roosevelt, Theodore, 250

Rosenbach, John George, 158

Rosenius, Carl Olof, 183, 193

Rosicrucians, 117

Rostock, Germany, 57, 119

Rothe, Richard, 188

Rudman, Andrew, 172

Ruotsalainen, Paavo, 183

Russia, 51, 69, 157, 179, 180, 190, 247

Sacraments, 2, 24–25, 37, 43, 78–79, 104

Saints, 7, 47, 79–80

Salvation, 17, 18, 72, 89, 114, 116, 125, 137, 151, 190, 201

Salzburg Exiles, 174

Sandusky Declaration, 221

Satan (Devil), 6, 15, 32, 36, 42, 63, 64, 153

Savannah, 154, 174

Savonarola, Jerome, 3

Saxony (electoral, ducal), 9, 17, 18, 39, 41, 59, 66, 92

Scandinavia, 51, 56, 58, 109, 145, 150, 169, 180, 184, 225, 240

Schaff, Philip, 191

Schartau, Henrik, 203

Schism, 5

Schleiermacher, Daniel, 166

Schleiermacher, Friedrich, 66, 199, 221, 228

Schmauk, Theodore E., 213

Schmidt, Frederick A., 197, 198

Schmidt, John, 119

Schmucker, Samuel S., 189, 190, 191, 192, 194, 255

Schneller, John L., 209

Schools, 37–38, 40, 54, 148, 187, 192–93, 196

Schultz, Albert, 149

Schulze, Jerome, Bishop, 16, 30

Schütz, John Jacob, 146, 161

Schurf, Jerome, 29, 30

Schwabach Articles, 44

Schwartz, Frederick, 169

Schwenckfeld, Caspar, 63, 99, 112

Second Vatican Council, 181, 238, 240

Sedition Act, 213

Seeberg, Reinhold, 212

Selassie, Haile, Emperor, 208

Selnecker, Nicholas, 94, 95, 122

Seminex faculty, 249

Sendomir, Polish Consensus of, 58, 131–32

Sigismund III Vasa, King of Sweden, 53, 58

Sigmund-Schultze, Frederick, 211

Siegel, August L., 210

Sihler, Wilhelm, 194

Silesia, 112, 151, 172, 181

Silesius, Angelicus, 117

Sin, 2, 7, 12, 13, 20, 26, 47, 79, 96

Singapore, 247

Skrefsrud, Lars O., 205

Skielderup, Jens, Bishop, 53

Skytte, Martin, 54

Slavery, 176, 190, 196, 210

Slovenia, 246

Smalcald
Articles, 50, 257
League, 49, 50, 61, 66
War, 61–62, 66

Smith, Adam, 179

Socialists, 179, 184, 187, 217

Socinians, 130

Söderblom, Nathan, Bishop, 217–18, 219, 221

Soft October Revolution, 227

Sommer, Peter N., 173

South Africa, 208, 231, 234, 235

South Korea, 247

Sozzini, Faustus, 130

Spain, 3, 156, 112

Spalatin, George, 16, 17, 27, 33, 36, 38

Spangenberg, August Gottlieb, 155, 157

Spener, Philip Jacob, 142–43, 148, 157, 161, 163

Speratus, Paul, 56, 59, 60

Speyer
Diet of, 39, 41
Protestation of, 41

Sprecher, Samuel, 191

Springfield, Illinois, 194, 206

Springfield, Ohio, 191

Staden, Hans, 209

Stahl, Frederick J., 188

St. Louis, Missouri, 193, 194

St. Thomas, Virgin Islands, 171, 210
Stalin, Joseph, 222
Staupitz, John von, 8, 9, 10, 13, 17
Stephan, Martin, 194
Stöcker, Adolf, 187
Stockholm, 51, 145, 165, 220, 221
Strasbourg, 49, 109, 118, 119, 142
  Ecumenical Institute, 238
Strauss, David F., 201
Strehlow, Karl, 206
Strehlow, Theodore, 206
Strigel, Viktorin, 88, 93
Stuttgart, 157, 158, 225
Sunday, Billy, 214
Suriname, 210
Svendsen, Niels, 112
Swabian Concord, 94
Swabian-Saxon Concord, 94
Sweden, 51, 52, 56, 57, 58, 109, 112, 160, 172, 180, 217, 219, 245
Swedenborg, Emanuel, 160
Swedish Mission Society, 205
Swenson, Gustav S., 210
Switzerland, 20, 112, 157, 165, 166, 219, 246
Sylvester V, Pope, 19
Sylvester, Janos, 59
Syncretist controversy, 134
Synergist controversy, 87–88
Synods, 175, 184, 190, 192
Syria, 209
Szalkai, Laszlo, Cardinal, 59
Sztarai, Michael, 59

Taiwan, 247

Tanzania, 187, 208, 215, 244
Tauler, John, 11, 145, 162
Tausen, Hans, 52
Tegetmeyer, Sylvester, 57
Temple, William, 219
Tetzel, John, 15–16
Teutonic Order of Knights, 56, 58, 59, 90
Theology, 11, 13–15, 42–43, 52, 66, 69, 107, 114, 121, 127–28, 130, 135, 149, 169, 187, 199, 228–33
Thirty Years War, 68, 110, 112, 117, 131, 132, 135, 139, 143, 146, 177
Thomas à Kempis, 4, 145
Thomasius, Gottfried, 201–2
Thomism, 4, 17
Thorlaksson, Gudbrandur, Bishop, 55
Thorn colloquium, 133
Thurzo, Alexius, 59
Tietjen, John H., 249
Tillich, Paul, 224, 231–32
Togoland, 208
Tokyo, 207
Torgau, 86, 95
  Book, 95
  Conclave, 45
  League of, 39, 49
Torkillus, Reorus, 172
Tradition, 5, 24, 34, 42, 71, 95, 128, 136, 250
Tranquebar, India, 167, 205
Transubstantiation, 4, 24–25
Transylvania, 59
Traub, Gottfried, 211–12
Trent, Council of, 63, 66, 82–84, 85, 86, 109, 116, 127, 128
Trier, archbishop of, 18, 29, 30

Troeltsch, Ernst, 201
Tübingen, 94, 109, 118, 152, 157, 158, 159, 199, 200–202, 240
Turkey, 209
Turks, 2, 5, 16, 40, 45, 49, 59, 62, 67
Turku, 54, 55, 112
Turner, Frederick J., 248
Two Realms (Kingdoms) Theory, 35, 106, 112–13, 201, 239, 245

Ulrich von Hutten, 21, 36
Ulrich of Württemberg, Duke, 94, 199
Union Churches (Lutheran-Reformed), 180, 181, 184, 193, 206, 211, 212
United States, 166, 171–78, 179, 181, 191–94, 221, 233, 248–50. *See also specific cities and states.*
United Synod South, 192
Uppsala, 52, 217, 219
Ursinus, Zacharias, 93
Uruguay, 211, 248

Vagabond preachers, 174
Västeras, Diet of, 52
Valentine, Milton, 193
Valparaiso, 210
Vehus, Chancellor of Baden, 30
Venezuela, 171, 210
Vergerio, Pietro, 49
Vienna, 2, 60, 179
Vilmar, August F. C., 180, 184
Visitations, 39–40

Wagner, Adolf, 187

Wagner, Richard, 179, 231

Waldenstrom, Paul P., 193

Walther, C. F. W., 193–94, 195, 196, 197, 198

Walther, Michael, 129

Warsaw Confederation, 58

Wartburg, Castle, 31

Washington, D.C., 215, 250

Washington Declaration, 221

Watchwords (*Losungen*), 156

Weidensee, Eberhard, 51

Weimar, 88, 185, 187

Wendt, John, 51

Wentz, Abdel R., 221

Wesley, Charles, 154

West Indies, 169, 170

West Virginia, 192

Westcott, Foss, Bishop, 215

Westphal, Joachim, 92, 94

Westphalia, Peace of, 111, 112

Wiborg, 55

Wichern, John, 185, 188, 189

Wigand, John, Bishop, 94

Willebrands, Cardinal, 240

William II of Prussia, Emperor, 211, 212

Winckler, John, 147

Wisconsin Synod, 195

Wittenberg, 8, 9, 10, 12, 13, 16, 17, 19, 22, 33, 35, 36, 39, 40, 50, 51, 52, 54, 57, 61, 89, 118, 120, 128, 151, 163, 185, 227

Concord, 50

Disturbances, 34

Nightingale of, 260

Opinion on bishops, 81

Wladislaus IV, King of Poland, 133

Wolf, John August, 173

Wolff, Christian, 161

Word of God, 30, 31, 34, 37, 47, 75, 102, 113, 122, 125, 136, 143, 144, 177, 194, 226

World War I, 202, 211, 215, 217

World War II, 222, 241

Worms, 29

Colloquy of, 92

Diet of, 28, 29–30, 59, 68

Edict of, 31, 35, 36, 39, 48, 49, 82

Worship, 35, 37, 38, 39, 40, 58, 71, 75, 117, 156, 173, 176, 181, 193, 213

Wren, Christopher, 117

Württemberg, 68, 92, 109, 158, 161, 166

Wycliffe, John, 3

Wynecken, Frederick, 194

Yugoslavia, 246

Zeeland, 52, 120, 202

Zinzendorf, Nicholas, 121, 151–54, 160, 165, 169, 170, 171

Ziegenbalg, Bartholomy, 167–68

Ziegenhagen, Frederick M., 174

Zurich, 44, 50, 110

Zwingli, Ulrich, 43, 47, 49, 59, 78, 92, 110, 191, 253

2003 ᛒ